Table of Contents

Mercury Retrograde 2021

	DATE	ET	PT			DATE	ET	PT
Mercury Retrograde	1/30	**10:52 am**	7:52 am	—	Mercury Direct	2/20	**7:52 pm**	4:52 pm
Mercury Retrograde	5/29	**6:34 pm**	3:34 pm	—	Mercury Direct	6/22	**6:00 pm**	3:00 pm
Mercury Retrograde	9/26		10:10 pm	—	Mercury Direct	10/18	**11:17 am**	8:17 am
Mercury Retrograde	9/27	**1:10 am**		—	Mercury Direct	10/18	**11:17 am**	8:17 am

Moon Void-of-Course 2021

Times are listed in Eastern Time in this table only. All other information in the *Pocket Planner* is listed in both Eastern time and Pacific time. Refer to "Time Zone Conversions" on page 8 for changing to other time zones. Note: All times are corrected for Daylight Saving Time.

Last Aspect		Moon Enters New Sign			Last Aspect		Moon Enters New Sign			Last Aspect		Moon Enters New Sign		
Date	Time	Date	Sign	Time	Date	Time	Date	Sign	Time	Date	Time	Date	Sign	Time
JANUARY					**FEBRUARY**					**MARCH**				
2	5:00 pm	2	♍	8:13 pm	1	6:10 am	1	♎	6:25 am	2	9:09 am	2	♏	3:38 pm
4	4:34 pm	5	♎	12:42 am	3	1:15 am	3	♏	9:15 am	4	11:10 am	4	♐	5:43 pm
7	12:55 am	7	♏	3:53 am	5	4:20 am	5	♐	12:16 pm	6	4:44 am	6	♑	9:20 pm
8	8:59 pm	9	♐	6:15 am	7	1:16 am	7	♑	3:52 pm	8	7:52 pm	9	♒	2:41 am
10	1:29 pm	11	♑	8:30 am	9	12:22 pm	9	♒	8:20 pm	10	10:32 pm	11	♓	9:44 am
13	2:22 am	13	♒	11:44 am	14	2:29 am	14	♈	10:54 am	13	11:38 am	13	♈	6:44 pm
14	4:28 am	15	♓	5:17 pm	16	7:17 pm	16	♉	10:12 pm	15	11:40 pm	16	♉	6:56 pm
17	10:44 pm	18	♈	2:07 am	19	2:28 am	19	♊	11:04 am	18	4:40 pm	18	♊	7:47 pm
20	3:29 am	20	♉	1:56 pm	21	1:39 pm	21	♋	10:53 pm	21	8:04 am	21	♋	8:18 am
22	4:28 pm	23	♊	2:43 am	23	11:54 pm	24	♌	7:23 am	23	11:26 am	23	♌	5:56 pm
25	2:17 am	25	♋	1:52 pm	26	6:32 am	26	♍	12:07 pm	25	9:27 am	25	♍	11:25 pm
27	12:55 pm	27	♌	9:54 pm	28	10:58 am	28	♎	2:17 pm	27	7:48 pm	28	♎	1:22 am
29	8:53 pm	30	♍	3:02 am						29	8:08 pm	30	♏	1:33 am
										31	8:29 pm	4/1	♐	1:59 am

Moon Void-of-Course 2021 (cont.)

APRIL

Last Aspect Date	Time	Moon Enters New Sign Date	Sign	Time
3/31	8:29 pm	1	♐	1:59 am
3	1:24 am	3	♑	4:13 am
5	3:05 am	5	♒	9:04 am
7	6:05 am	7	♓	4:30 pm
9	7:48 pm	10	♈	2:11 am
12	8:06 am	12	♉	1:44 pm
14	8:00 pm	15	♊	2:35 am
17	11:03 am	17	♋	3:25 pm
19	8:03 pm	19	♌	2:11 am
22	8:05 am	22	♍	9:08 am
26	6:50 am	24	♎	12:06 pm
26	8:40 am	26	♏	12:18 pm
28	8:31 am	28	♐	11:42 am
30	9:27 am	30	♑	12:16 pm

MAY

Last Aspect Date	Time	Moon Enters New Sign Date	Sign	Time
2	10:38 am	2	♒	3:31 pm
4	8:05 pm	4	♓	10:09 pm
7	3:36 am	7	♈	7:52 am
9	6:50 pm	9	♉	7:46 pm
12	8:23 am	12	♊	8:43 am
14	6:51 am	14	♋	9:30 pm
17	2:23 am	17	♌	8:44 am
19	3:13 pm	19	♍	4:59 pm
21	3:56 pm	21	♎	9:35 pm
23	5:36 pm	23	♏	11:00 pm
25	5:20 pm	25	♐	10:39 pm
27	1:35 pm	27	♑	10:23 pm
29	6:15 pm	30	♒	12:04 am

JUNE

Last Aspect Date	Time	Moon Enters New Sign Date	Sign	Time
1	2:14 am	1	♓	5:07 am
3	7:10 am	3	♈	1:59 pm
5	6:47 pm	6	♉	1:46 am
8	11:07 am	8	♊	2:47 pm
10	1:38 pm	11	♋	3:23 am
13	7:16 am	13	♌	2:22 pm
15	1:27 pm	15	♍	11:02 pm
17	11:54 pm	18	♎	4:54 am
20	6:52 pm	20	♏	7:58 am
22	2:43 am	22	♐	8:55 am
23	10:09 pm	24	♑	9:05 am
26	8:49 am	26	♒	10:09 am
27	3:08 pm	28	♓	1:51 pm
30	1:40 pm	30	♈	9:21 pm

JULY

Last Aspect Date	Time	Moon Enters New Sign Date	Sign	Time
3	12:15 am	3	♉	8:28 am
5	12:57 pm	5	♊	9:24 pm
8	12:20 am	8	♋	9:51 am
10	12:10 pm	10	♌	8:21 pm
12	8:29 am	13	♍	4:30 am
15	2:46 am	15	♎	10:32 am
17	7:03 am	17	♏	2:38 pm
19	12:30 pm	19	♐	5:08 pm
21	6:26 pm	21	♑	6:36 pm
23	12:34 pm	23	♒	8:12 pm
25	7:14 pm	25	♓	11:30 pm
27	9:13 pm	28	♈	5:58 am
30	3:38 pm	30	♉	4:08 pm

AUGUST

Last Aspect Date	Time	Moon Enters New Sign Date	Sign	Time
2	3:41 am	2	♊	4:46 am
4	3:38 pm	4	♋	5:17 pm
6	6:12 pm	7	♌	3:31 am
9	8:23 am	9	♍	10:56 am
11	7:22 am	11	♎	4:08 pm
13	4:39 pm	13	♏	8:01 pm
15	11:05 pm	15	♐	11:12 pm
17	9:43 pm	18	♑	1:58 am
19	7:59 pm	20	♒	4:49 am
22	8:02 am	22	♓	8:43 am
24	5:12 am	24	♈	2:57 pm
26	5:14 pm	27	♉	12:27 am
29	10:59 am	29	♊	12:42 pm
31	4:48 pm	9/1	♋	1:26 am

SEPTEMBER

Last Aspect Date	Time	Moon Enters New Sign Date	Sign	Time
8/31	4:48 pm	1	♋	1:26 am
3	1:37 am	3	♌	11:58 am
5	10:22 am	5	♍	7:06 pm
7	3:24 pm	7	♎	11:20 pm
10	12:48 am	10	♏	2:05 am
12	1:33 am	12	♐	4:34 am
14	6:57 am	14	♑	7:34 am
16	1:40 am	16	♒	11:23 am
18	5:14 am	18	♓	4:22 pm
20	7:55 pm	20	♈	11:13 pm
22	10:05 pm	23	♉	8:38 am
25	9:09 am	25	♊	8:36 pm
28	12:18 am	28	♋	9:34 am
30	10:49 am	30	♌	8:53 pm

OCTOBER

Last Aspect Date	Time	Moon Enters New Sign Date	Sign	Time
2	7:43 am	3	♍	4:48 am
5	4:46 am	5	♎	8:41 am
7	1:03 am	7	♏	10:22 am
9	2:05 am	9	♐	11:24 am
11	12:30 am	11	♑	1:15 pm
13	6:53 am	13	♒	4:47 pm
15	8:33 am	15	♓	10:22 pm
17	7:24 pm	18	♈	6:04 am
20	10:57 am	20	♉	3:59 pm
22	4:35 pm	23	♊	3:57 am
25	10:11 am	25	♋	5:00 pm
28	2:02 am	28	♌	5:07 am
30	3:05 am	30	♍	2:09 pm

NOVEMBER

Last Aspect Date	Time	Moon Enters New Sign Date	Sign	Time
1	1:00 pm	1	♎	7:11 pm
3	6:32 pm	3	♏	8:52 pm
5	12:10 pm	5	♐	8:52 pm
7	8:44 am	7	♑	8:03 pm
9	12:51 pm	9	♒	10:03 pm
11	2:52 pm	12	♓	2:54 am
14	12:40 am	14	♈	10:48 am
16	10:51 am	16	♉	9:18 pm
19	3:57 am	19	♊	9:33 am
21	10:52 am	21	♋	10:33 pm
24	12:46 am	24	♌	10:59 am
26	11:24 am	26	♍	9:12 pm
28	7:02 pm	29	♎	3:55 am
30	11:20 pm	12/1	♏	6:55 am

DECEMBER

Last Aspect Date	Time	Moon Enters New Sign Date	Sign	Time
11/30	11:20 pm	1	♏	6:55 am
3	12:22 am	3	♐	7:13 am
5	12:08 am	5	♑	6:31 am
6	11:42 pm	7	♒	6:49 am
9	5:00 am	9	♓	9:53 am
11	2:40 pm	11	♈	4:46 pm
13	9:52 pm	14	♉	3:11 am
16	11:08 am	16	♊	3:43 pm
19	1:02 am	19	♋	4:42 am
21	9:44 am	21	♌	4:54 pm
24	1:39 am	24	♍	3:24 am
26	3:39 am	26	♎	11:24 am
28	4:11 pm	28	♏	4:16 pm
30	12:10 pm	30	♐	6:08 pm

LLEWELLYN'S
2 · 0 · 2 · 1
ASTROLOGICAL
POCKET PLANNER

Daily Ephemeris & Aspectarian
2020-2022

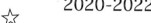

Cover design by Shannon McKuhen
Edited by Hanna Grimson

A special thanks to Phoebe Aina Allen for astrological proofreading.

Astrological calculations compiled and programmed by Rique Pottenger based on
the earlier work of Neil F. Michelsen. Reuse is prohibited.

Published by
LLEWELLYN WORLDWIDE LTD.
2143 Wooddale Drive
Woodbury, MN 55125-2989
www.llewellyn.com

Printed in the United States of America
Typography property of Llewellyn Worldwide Ltd.
Llewellyn is a registered trademark of Llewellyn Worldwide Ltd.

How to Use the *Pocket Planner*

by Leslie Nielsen

This handy guide contains information that can be most valuable to you as you plan your daily activities. As you read through the first few pages, you can start to get a feel for how well organized this guide is.

Read the Symbol Key on the next page, which is rather like astrological shorthand. The characteristics of the planets can give you direction in planning your strategies. Much like traffic signs that signal "go," "stop," or even "caution," you can determine for yourself the most propitious time to get things done.

You'll find tables that show the dates when Mercury is retrograde (℞) or direct (D). Because Mercury deals with the exchange of information, a retrograde Mercury makes miscommunication more noticeable.

There's also a section dedicated to the times when the Moon is void-of-course (V/C). These are generally poor times to conduct business because activities begun during these times usually end badly or fail to get started. If you make an appointment during a void-of-course, you might save yourself a lot of aggravation by confirming the time and date later. The Moon is only void-of-course for 7 percent of the time when business is usually conducted during a normal workday (that is, 8:00 am to 5:00 pm). Sometimes, by waiting a matter of minutes or a few hours until the Moon has left the void-of-course phase, you have a much better chance to make action move more smoothly. Moon voids can also be used successfully to do routine activities or inner work, such as dream therapy or personal contemplation.

You'll find Moon phases, as well as each of the Moon's entries into a new sign. Times are expressed in Eastern time (in bold type) and Pacific time (in regular type). The New Moon time is generally best for beginning new activities, as the Moon is increasing in light and can offer the element of growth to our endeavors. When the Moon is Full, its illumination is greatest and we can see the results of our efforts. When it moves from the Full stage back to the New stage, it can best be used to reflect on our projects. If necessary, we can make corrections at the New Moon.

The section of "Planetary Stations" on page 9 will give you the times when the planets are changing signs or direction, thereby affording us opportunities for new starts.

The ephemeris in the back of your *Pocket Planner* can be very helpful to you. As you start to work with the ephemeris, you may notice that not all planets seem to be comfortable in every sign. Think of the planets as actors and the signs as the costumes they wear. Sometimes, costumes just itch. If you find this to be so for a certain time period, you may choose to delay your plans for a time or be more creative with the energies at hand.

As you turn to the daily pages, you'll find information about the Moon's sign, phase, and the time it changes phase. You'll find icons indicating the best days to plant and fish. Also, you will find times and dates when the planets and asteroids change signs and go either retrograde or direct, major holidays, a three-month calendar, and room to record your appointments.

This guide is a powerful tool. Make the most of it!

Symbol Key

Planets:	☉ Sun	⚳ Ceres	♄ Saturn
	☽ Moon	⚴ Pallas	⚷ Chiron
	☿ Mercury	⚵ Juno	♅ Uranus
	♀ Venus	⚶ Vesta	♆ Neptune
	♂ Mars	♃ Jupiter	♇ Pluto

Signs:	♈ Aries	♌ Leo	♐ Sagittarius
	♉ Taurus	♍ Virgo	♑ Capricorn
	♊ Gemini	♎ Libra	♒ Aquarius
	♋ Cancer	♏ Scorpio	♓ Pisces

Aspects:	☌ Conjunction (0°)	⚺ Semisextile (30°)	⚹ Sextile (60°)
	□ Square (90°)	△ Trine (120°)	
	⚻ Quincunx (150°)	☍ Opposition (180°)	

| Motion: | ℞ Retrograde | D Direct |

Best Days for Planting: 🌱   Best Days for Fishing: 🐟

6

World Map of Time Zones

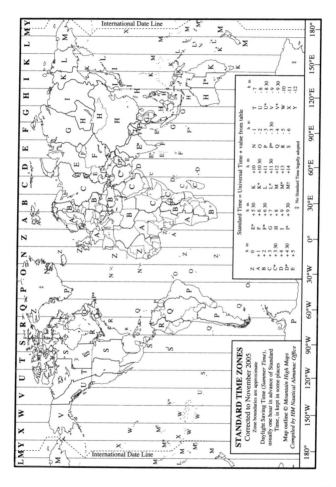

STANDARD TIME ZONES
Corrected to November 2005
Zone boundaries are approximate
Daylight Saving Time (*Summer Time*),
usually one hour in advance of Standard
Time, is kept in some places
Map outline © *Mountain High Maps*
Compiled by HM Nautical Almanac Office

Standard Time = Universal Time + value from table

	h m			h m
Z	0		N	− 1
A	+ 1		O	− 2
B	+ 2		P	− 3
C	+ 3		P*	− 3.30
C*	+ 3.30		Q	− 4
D	+ 4		R	− 5
D*	+ 4.30		S	− 6
E	+ 5		T	− 7
E*	+ 5.30		U	− 8
F	+ 6		U*	− 8.30
F*	+ 6.30		V	− 9
G	+ 7		V*	− 9.30
H	+ 8		W	− 10
I	+ 9		X	− 11
I*	+ 9.30		Y	− 12
K	+ 10			
K*	+ 10.30			
L	+ 11			
L*	+ 11.30			
M	+ 12			
M†	+ 14			

† No Standard Time legally adopted

International Date Line

Time Zone Conversions

World Time Zones
Compared to Eastern Standard Time

( )	From Map	(Y) Subtract 7 hours	(C*) Add 8.5 hours
(S)	CST/Subtract 1 hour	(A) Add 6 hours	(D*) Add 9.5 hours
(R)	EST	(B) Add 7 hours	(E*) Add 10.5 hours
(Q)	Add 1 hour	(C) Add 8 hours	(F*) Add 11.5 hours
(P)	Add 2 hours	(D) Add 9 hours	(I*) Add 14.5 hours
(O)	Add 3 hours	(E) Add 10 hours	(K*) Add 15.5 hours
(N)	Add 4 hours	(F) Add 11 hours	(L*) Add 16.5 hours
(Z)	Add 5 hours	(G) Add 12 hours	(M*) Add 18 hours
(T)	MST/Subtract 2 hours	(H) Add 13 hours	(P*) Add 2.5 hours
(U)	PST/Subtract 3 hours	(I) Add 14 hours	(U*) Subtract 3.5 hours
(V)	Subtract 4 hours	(K) Add 15 hours	(V*) Subtract 4.5 hours
(W)	Subtract 5 hours	(L) Add 16 hours	
(X)	Subtract 6 hours	(M) Add 17 hours	

World Map of Time Zones is supplied by HM Nautical Almanac Office © Center for the Central Laboratory of the Research Councils. Note: This is not an official map. Countries change their time zones as they wish.

Planetary Stations for 2021

	JAN	FEB	MAR	APR	MAY	JUN	JUL	AUG	SEP	OCT	NOV	DEC
☿		1/30–2/20				5/29–6/22				9/27–10/18		
♀												12/19–
♂												
♃								6/20–10/18				
♄							5/23–10/10					
♅	–1/14									8/19–1/18/22		
♆									6/25–12/1			
♇							4/27–10/6					
⚷										7/15–12/19		
⚳						4/12–8/2						
✶									7/14–11/8			
⚴											10/8–1/14/22	
⚸		1/19–4/20										

28 Monday

2nd ♊
☽ V/C   **10:01 pm**   7:01 pm

29 Tuesday

2nd ♊
☽ enters ♋   **5:28 am**   2:28 am
Full Moon   **10:28 pm**   7:28 pm

30 Wednesday

3rd ♋

31 Thursday

3rd ♋
☽ V/C   **8:45 am**   5:45 am
☽ enters ♌   **1:58 pm** 10:58 am

New Year's Eve

Eastern time in bold type
Pacific time in medium type

1 Friday
3rd ♌

New Year's Day • Kwanzaa ends

2 Saturday
3rd ♌
☽ v/c   **5:00 pm**   2:00 pm
☽ enters ♍   **8:13 pm**   5:13 pm

3 Sunday
3rd ♍

December 2020						
S	M	T	W	T	F	S
		1	2	3	4	5
6	7	8	9	10	11	12
13	14	15	16	17	18	19
20	21	22	23	24	25	26
27	28	29	31	31		

January 2021						
S	M	T	W	T	F	S
					1	2
3	4	5	6	7	8	9
10	11	12	13	14	15	16
17	18	19	20	21	22	23
24	25	26	27	28	29	30
31						

February 2021						
S	M	T	W	T	F	S
	1	2	3	4	5	6
7	8	9	10	11	12	13
14	15	16	17	18	19	20
21	22	23	24	25	26	27
28						

Eastern time in bold type
Pacific time in medium type

4 Monday

3rd ♍
| ☽ v/c | **4:34 pm** | 1:34 pm |
| ☽ enters ♎ | | 9:42 pm |

5 Tuesday

3rd ♍
☽ enters ♎ **12:42 am**

6 Wednesday

3rd ♎
4th Quarter	**4:37 am**	1:37 am
♂ enters ♉	**5:27 pm**	2:27 pm
☽ v/c		9:55 pm

7 Thursday

4th ♎
| ☽ v/c | **12:55 am** | |
| ☽ enters ♏ | **3:53 am** | 12:53 am |

Eastern time in bold type
Pacific time in medium type

8 Friday
4th ♏

☿ enters ≈	**7:00 am**	4:00 am
♀ enters ♑	**10:41 am**	7:41 am
☽ v/c	**8:59 pm**	5:59 pm

9 Saturday
4th ♏

| ☽ enters ♐ | **6:15 am** | 3:15 am |

10 Sunday
4th ♐

| ☽ v/c | **1:29 pm** | 10:29 am |

December 2020							January 2021							February 2021						
S	M	T	W	T	F	S	S	M	T	W	T	F	S	S	M	T	W	T	F	S
		1	2	3	4	5						1	2		1	2	3	4	5	6
6	7	8	9	10	11	12	3	4	5	6	7	8	9	7	8	9	10	11	12	13
13	14	15	16	17	18	19	10	11	12	13	14	15	16	14	15	16	17	18	19	20
20	21	22	23	24	25	26	17	18	19	20	21	22	23	21	22	23	24	25	26	27
27	28	29	30	31			24	25	26	27	28	29	30	28						
							31													

Eastern time in bold type
Pacific time in medium type

11 Monday

4th ♐
☽ enters ♑ **8:30 am** 5:30 am

12 Tuesday

4th ♑
New Moon   9:00 pm
☽ v/c   11:22 pm

13 Wednesday

4th ♑
New Moon **12:00 am**
☽ v/c   **2:22 am**
☽ enters ≈ **11:44 am** 8:44 am

14 Thursday

1st ≈
♅ D   **3:36 am** 12:36 am
☽ v/c   **4:28 am**   1:28 am

Eastern time in bold type
Pacific time in medium type

15 Friday
1st ≈
☽ enters ♓ **5:17 pm** 2:17 pm

16 Saturday
1st ♓

17 Sunday
1st ♓
☽ v/c **10:44 pm** 7:44 pm
☽ enters ♈   11:07 pm

December 2020						
S	M	T	W	T	F	S
		1	2	3	4	5
6	7	8	9	10	11	12
13	14	15	16	17	18	19
20	21	22	23	24	25	26
27	28	29	30	31		

January 2021						
S	M	T	W	T	F	S
					1	2
3	4	5	6	7	8	9
10	11	12	13	14	15	16
17	18	19	20	21	22	23
24	25	26	27	28	29	30
31						

February 2021						
S	M	T	W	T	F	S
	1	2	3	4	5	6
7	8	9	10	11	12	13
14	15	16	17	18	19	20
21	22	23	24	25	26	27
28						

18 Monday
1st ♓
☽ enters ♈ **2:07 am**

Martin Luther King Jr. Day

19 Tuesday
1st ♈
♅ ℞ **3:54 am** 12:54 am
☉ enters ≈ **3:40 pm** 12:40 pm

Sun enters Aquarius

20 Wednesday
1st ♈
☽ v/c **3:29 am** 12:29 am
☽ enters ♉ **1:56 pm** 10:56 am
2nd Quarter **4:02 pm** 1:02 pm

Inauguration Day

21 Thursday
2nd ♉

Eastern time in bold type
Pacific time in medium type

22 Friday
2nd ♉
☽ v/c	**4:28 pm**	1:28 pm
☽ enters ♊		11:43 pm

23 Saturday
2nd ♉
☽ enters ♊	**2:43 am**

24 Sunday
2nd ♊
☽ v/c	11:17 pm

December 2020						
S	M	T	W	T	F	S
		1	2	3	4	5
6	7	8	9	10	11	12
13	14	15	16	17	18	19
20	21	22	23	24	25	26
27	28	29	30	31		

January 2021						
S	M	T	W	T	F	S
					1	2
3	4	5	6	7	8	9
10	11	12	13	14	15	16
17	18	19	20	21	22	23
24	25	26	27	28	29	30
31						

February 2021						
S	M	T	W	T	F	S
	1	2	3	4	5	6
7	8	9	10	11	12	13
14	15	16	17	18	19	20
21	22	23	24	25	26	27
28						

25 Monday

2nd ♊
☽ v/c   **2:17 am**
☽ enters ♋   **1:52 pm** 10:52 am

26 Tuesday

2nd ♋

27 Wednesday

2nd ♋
☽ v/c   **12:55 pm** 9:55 am
☽ enters ♌   **9:54 pm** 6:54 pm

28 Thursday

2nd ♌
Full Moon   **2:16 pm** 11:16 am

29 Friday
3rd ♌
☽ v/c   **8:53 pm**   5:53 pm

30 Saturday
3rd ♌
☽ enters ♍   **3:02 am** 12:02 am
☿ ℞   **10:52 am**   7:52 am

Mercury retrograde until 2/20

31 Sunday
3rd ♍

December 2020						
S	M	T	W	T	F	S
		1	2	3	4	5
6	7	8	9	10	11	12
13	14	15	16	17	18	19
20	21	22	23	24	25	26
27	28	29	30	31		

January 2021						
S	M	T	W	T	F	S
					1	2
3	4	5	6	7	8	9
10	11	12	13	14	15	16
17	18	19	20	21	22	23
24	25	26	27	28	29	30
31						

February 2021						
S	M	T	W	T	F	S
	1	2	3	4	5	6
7	8	9	10	11	12	13
14	15	16	17	18	19	20
21	22	23	24	25	26	27
28						

1 Monday

3rd ♍
☽ v/c   **6:10 am**   3:10 am
☽ enters ♎   **6:25 am**   3:25 am
♀ enters ≈   **9:05 am**   6:05 am

2 Tuesday

3rd ♎
☽ v/c   10:15 pm

Imbolc • Groundhog Day

3 Wednesday

3rd ♎
☽ v/c   **1:15 am**
☽ enters ♏   **9:15 am**   6:15 am

4 Thursday

3rd ♏
4th Quarter   **12:37 pm**   9:37 am

5 Friday
4th ♏

☽ v/c	**4:20 am**	1:20 am
☽ enters ♐	**12:16 pm**	9:16 am

6 Saturday
4th ♐

☽ v/c   10:16 pm

7 Sunday
4th ♐

☽ v/c	**1:16 am**	
☽ enters ♑	**3:52 pm**	12:52 pm

January 2021						
S	M	T	W	T	F	S
					1	2
3	4	5	6	7	8	9
10	11	12	13	14	15	16
17	18	19	20	21	22	23
24	25	26	27	28	29	30
31						

February 2021						
S	M	T	W	T	F	S
	1	2	3	4	5	6
7	8	9	10	11	12	13
14	15	16	17	18	19	20
21	22	23	24	25	26	27
28						

March 2021						
S	M	T	W	T	F	S
	1	2	3	4	5	6
7	8	9	10	11	12	13
14	15	16	17	18	19	20
21	22	23	24	25	26	27
28	29	30	31			

8 Monday

4th ♑

9 Tuesday

4th ♑
☽ v/c   **12:22 pm** 9:22 am
☽ enters ♒   **8:20 pm** 5:20 pm

10 Wednesday

4th ♒

11 Thursday

4th ♒
☽ v/c   **2:06 pm** 11:06 am
New Moon   **2:06 pm** 11:06 am
☽ enters ♓   11:23 pm

Eastern time in bold type
Pacific time in medium type

12 Friday

1st ♒
☽ enters ♓   **2:23 am**

Lunar New Year (Ox)

13 Saturday

1st ♓
☽ v/c   11:29 pm

14 Sunday

1st ♓
☽ v/c   **2:29 am**
☽ enters ♈ **10:54 am** 7:54 am

Valentine's Day

January 2021								February 2021								March 2021						
S	M	T	W	T	F	S		S	M	T	W	T	F	S		S	M	T	W	T	F	S
					1	2			1	2	3	4	5	6			1	2	3	4	5	6
3	4	5	6	7	8	9		7	8	9	10	11	12	13		7	8	9	10	11	12	13
10	11	12	13	14	15	16		14	15	16	17	18	19	20		14	15	16	17	18	19	20
17	18	19	20	21	22	23		21	22	23	24	25	26	27		21	22	23	24	25	26	27
24	25	26	27	28	29	30		28								28	29	30	31			
31																						

Eastern time in bold type
Pacific time in medium type

15 Monday
1st ♈

Presidents' Day

16 Tuesday
1st ♈
☽ v/c   **7:17 pm**   4:17 pm
☽ enters ♉   **10:12 pm**   7:12 pm

Mardi Gras (Fat Tuesday)

17 Wednesday
1st ♉

Ash Wednesday

18 Thursday
1st ♉
☉ enters ♓   **5:44 am**   2:44 am
☽ v/c   11:28 pm

Sun enters Pisces

Eastern time in bold type
Pacific time in medium type

19 Friday

1st ♉
☽ v/c   **2:28 am**
☽ enters ♊   **11:04 am** 8:04 am
2nd Quarter **1:47 pm** 10:47 am

20 Saturday

2nd ♊
☿ D   **7:52 pm** 4:52 pm
♀ enters ♈   9:23 pm

21 Sunday
2nd ♊
♀ enters ♈ **12:23 am**
☽ v/c   **1:39 pm** 10:39 am
☽ enters ♋ **10:53 pm** 7:53 pm

January 2021						
S	M	T	W	T	F	S
					1	2
3	4	5	6	7	8	9
10	11	12	13	14	15	16
17	18	19	20	21	22	23
24	25	26	27	28	29	30
31						

February 2021						
S	M	T	W	T	F	S
	1	2	3	4	5	6
7	8	9	10	11	12	13
14	15	16	17	18	19	20
21	22	23	24	25	26	27
28						

March 2021						
S	M	T	W	T	F	S
	1	2	3	4	5	6
7	8	9	10	11	12	13
14	15	16	17	18	19	20
21	22	23	24	25	26	27
28	29	30	31			

Eastern time in bold type
Pacific time in medium type

22 Monday
2nd ⊙

23 Tuesday
2nd ⊙
☽ v/c   **11:54 pm**   8:54 pm

24 Wednesday
2nd ⊙
☽ enters ♌   **7:23 am**   4:23 am

25 Thursday
2nd ♌
♀ enters ♓   **8:11 am**   5:11 am

26 Friday
2nd ♌
☽ v/c **6:32 am** 3:32 am
☽ enters ♍ **12:07 pm** 9:07 am

Purim begins at sundown

27 Saturday
2nd ♍
Full Moon **3:17 am** 12:17 am

28 Sunday
3rd ♍
☽ v/c **10:58 am** 7:58 am
☽ enters ♎ **2:17 pm** 11:17 am

January 2021						
S	M	T	W	T	F	S
					1	2
3	4	5	6	7	8	9
10	11	12	13	14	15	16
17	18	19	20	21	22	23
24	25	26	27	28	29	30
31						

February 2021						
S	M	T	W	T	F	S
	1	2	3	4	5	6
7	8	9	10	11	12	13
14	15	16	17	18	19	20
21	22	23	24	25	26	27
28						

March 2021						
S	M	T	W	T	F	S
	1	2	3	4	5	6
7	8	9	10	11	12	13
14	15	16	17	18	19	20
21	22	23	24	25	26	27
28	29	30	31			

Eastern time in bold type
Pacific time in medium type

1 Monday

3rd ♎

2 Tuesday

3rd ♎
☽ v/c   **9:09 am** 6:09 am
☽ enters ♏ **3:38 pm** 12:38 pm

3 Wednesday

3rd ♏
♂ enters ♊ **10:30 pm** 7:30 pm

4 Thursday

3rd ♏
☽ v/c   **11:10 am** 8:10 am
☽ enters ♐ **5:43 pm** 2:43 pm

5 Friday
3rd ♐
4th Quarter **8:30 pm** 5:30 pm

6 Saturday
4th ♐
☽ v/c **4:44 am** 1:44 am
☽ enters ♑ **9:20 pm** 6:20 pm

7 Sunday
4th ♑
☿ enters ♓ **4:06 pm** 1:06 pm

February 2021						
S	M	T	W	T	F	S
	1	2	3	4	5	6
7	8	9	10	11	12	13
14	15	16	17	18	19	20
21	22	23	24	25	26	27
28						

March 2021						
S	M	T	W	T	F	S
	1	2	3	4	5	6
7	8	9	10	11	12	13
14	15	16	17	18	19	20
21	22	23	24	25	26	27
28	29	30	31			

April 2021						
S	M	T	W	T	F	S
				1	2	3
4	5	6	7	8	9	10
11	12	13	14	15	16	17
18	19	20	21	22	23	24
25	26	27	28	29	30	

Eastern time in bold type
Pacific time in medium type

8 Monday

4th ♑
☽ v/c   **7:52 pm** 4:52 pm
☽ enters ♒   11:41 pm

9 Tuesday

4th ♑
☽ enters ♒ **2:41 am**

10 Wednesday

4th ♒
☽ v/c   **10:32 pm** 7:32 pm

11 Thursday

4th ♒
☽ enters ♓ **9:44 am** 6:44 am

12 Friday
4th ♓

13 Saturday
4th ♓

New Moon	**5:21 am**	2:21 am
☽ v/c	**11:38 am**	8:38 am
☽ enters ♈	**6:44 pm**	3:44 pm

14 Sunday
1st ♈

Daylight Saving Time begins at 2 am

February 2021						
S	M	T	W	T	F	S
	1	2	3	4	5	6
7	8	9	10	11	12	13
14	15	16	17	18	19	20
21	22	23	24	25	26	27
28						

March 2021						
S	M	T	W	T	F	S
	1	2	3	4	5	6
7	8	9	10	11	12	13
14	15	16	17	18	19	20
21	22	23	24	25	26	27
28	29	30	31			

April 2021						
S	M	T	W	T	F	S
				1	2	3
4	5	6	7	8	9	10
11	12	13	14	15	16	17
18	19	20	21	22	23	24
25	26	27	28	29	30	

15 Monday

1st ♈
☿ enters ♓   **6:26 pm**   3:26 pm
☽ v/c   **11:40 pm**   8:40 pm

16 Tuesday

1st ♈
☽ enters ♉   **6:56 am**   3:56 am

17 Wednesday

1st ♉

 St. Patrick's Day

18 Thursday

1st ♉
☽ v/c   **4:40 pm**   1:40 pm
☽ enters ♊   **7:47 pm**   4:47 pm

Eastern time in bold type
Pacific time in medium type

19 Friday
1st ♊

20 Saturday
1st ♊
☉ enters ♈ **5:37 am** 2:37 am

Int'l Astrology Day
Sun enters Aries • Ostara • Spring Equinox • 5:37 am EDT/2:37 am PDT

21 Sunday
1st ♊
☽ v/c **8:04 am** 5:04 am
☽ enters ♋ **8:18 am** 5:18 am
♀ enters ♈ **10:16 am** 7:16 am
2nd Quarter **10:40 am** 7:40 am

February 2021						
S	M	T	W	T	F	S
	1	2	3	4	5	6
7	8	9	10	11	12	13
14	15	16	17	18	19	20
21	22	23	24	25	26	27
28						

March 2021						
S	M	T	W	T	F	S
	1	2	3	4	5	6
7	8	9	10	11	12	13
14	15	16	17	18	19	20
21	22	23	24	25	26	27
28	29	30	31			

April 2021						
S	M	T	W	T	F	S
				1	2	3
4	5	6	7	8	9	10
11	12	13	14	15	16	17
18	19	20	21	22	23	24
25	26	27	28	29	30	

Eastern time in bold type
Pacific time in medium type

22 Monday
2nd ♋

23 Tuesday
2nd ♋
☽ v/c   **11:26 am** 8:26 am
☽ enters ♌ **5:56 pm** 2:56 pm

24 Wednesday
2nd ♌

25 Thursday
2nd ♌
☽ v/c   **9:27 am** 6:27 am
☽ enters ♍ **11:25 pm** 8:25 pm

26 Friday
2nd ♍

27 Saturday
2nd ♍
☽ v/c   **7:48 pm**   4:48 pm
☽ enters ♎   10:22 pm

Passover begins at sundown

28 Sunday
2nd ♍
☽ enters ♎   **1:22 am**
Full Moon   **2:48 pm** 11:48 am

Palm Sunday

February 2021						
S	M	T	W	T	F	S
	1	2	3	4	5	6
7	8	9	10	11	12	13
14	15	16	17	18	19	20
21	22	23	24	25	26	27
28						

March 2021						
S	M	T	W	T	F	S
	1	2	3	4	5	6
7	8	9	10	11	12	13
14	15	16	17	18	19	20
21	22	23	24	25	26	27
28	29	30	31			

April 2021						
S	M	T	W	T	F	S
				1	2	3
4	5	6	7	8	9	10
11	12	13	14	15	16	17
18	19	20	21	22	23	24
25	26	27	28	29	30	

29 Monday

3rd ♎︎
☽ v/c   **8:08 pm**   5:08 pm
☽ enters ♏︎   10:33 pm

30 Tuesday

3rd ♎︎
☽ enters ♏︎   **1:33 am**

31 Wednesday

3rd ♏︎
☽ v/c   **8:29 pm**   5:29 pm
☽ enters ♐︎   10:59 pm

1 Thursday

3rd ♏︎
☽ enters ♐︎   **1:59 am**

April Fools' Day (All Fools' Day—Pagan)

2 Friday

3rd ✗
☽ v/c   10:24 pm

Good Friday

3 Saturday

3rd ✗
☽ v/c   **1:24 am**
☽ enters ♑   **4:13 am**   1:13 am
☿ enters ♈   **11:41 pm** 8:41 pm

Passover ends

4 Sunday

3rd ♑
4th Quarter   **6:02 am**   3:02 am

Easter

March 2021						
S	M	T	W	T	F	S
	1	2	3	4	5	6
7	8	9	10	11	12	13
14	15	16	17	18	19	20
21	22	23	24	25	26	27
28	29	30	31			

April 2021						
S	M	T	W	T	F	S
				1	2	3
4	5	6	7	8	9	10
11	12	13	14	15	16	17
18	19	20	21	22	23	24
25	26	27	28	29	30	

May 2021						
S	M	T	W	T	F	S
						1
2	3	4	5	6	7	8
9	10	11	12	13	14	15
16	17	18	19	20	21	22
23	24	25	26	27	28	29
30	31					

Eastern time in bold type
Pacific time in medium type

5 Monday

4th ♑
☽ v/c   **3:05 am** 12:05 am
☽ enters ♒   **9:04 am** 6:04 am

6 Tuesday

4th ♒

7 Wednesday

4th ♒
☽ v/c   **6:05 am** 3:05 am
☽ enters ♓   **4:30 pm** 1:30 pm

8 Thursday

4th ♓

9 Friday
4th ♓
☽ v/c **7:48 pm** 4:48 pm
☽ enters ♈ 11:11 pm

10 Saturday
4th ♓
☽ enters ♈ **2:11 am**

11 Sunday
4th ♈
New Moon **10:31 pm** 7:31 pm

		March 2021				
S	M	T	W	T	F	S
	1	2	3	4	5	6
7	8	9	10	11	12	13
14	15	16	17	18	19	20
21	22	23	24	25	26	27
28	29	30	31			

		April 2021				
S	M	T	W	T	F	S
				1	2	3
4	5	6	7	8	9	10
11	12	13	14	15	16	17
18	19	20	21	22	23	24
25	26	27	28	29	30	

		May 2021				
S	M	T	W	T	F	S
						1
2	3	4	5	6	7	8
9	10	11	12	13	14	15
16	17	18	19	20	21	22
23	24	25	26	27	28	29
30	31					

12 Monday

1st ♈

⚹ ℞	**6:13 am**	3:13 am
☽ v/c	**8:06 am**	5:06 am
☽ enters ♉	**1:44 pm**	10:44 am

Ramadan begins at sundown

13 Tuesday

1st ♉

14 Wednesday

1st ♉

♀ enters ♉	**2:22 pm**	11:22 am
☽ v/c	**8:00 pm**	5:00 pm
☽ enters ♊		11:35 pm

15 Thursday

1st ♉

| ☽ enters ♊ | **2:35 am** |

Eastern time in bold type
Pacific time in medium type

16 Friday
1st ♊

17 Saturday
1st ♊
☽ v/c   **11:03 am**   8:03 am
☽ enters ♋   **3:25 pm**   12:25 pm

18 Sunday
1st ♋

March 2021						
S	M	T	W	T	F	S
	1	2	3	4	5	6
7	8	9	10	11	12	13
14	15	16	17	18	19	20
21	22	23	24	25	26	27
28	29	30	31			

April 2021						
S	M	T	W	T	F	S
				1	2	3
4	5	6	7	8	9	10
11	12	13	14	15	16	17
18	19	20	21	22	23	24
25	26	27	28	29	30	

May 2021						
S	M	T	W	T	F	S
						1
2	3	4	5	6	7	8
9	10	11	12	13	14	15
16	17	18	19	20	21	22
23	24	25	26	27	28	29
30	31					

19 Monday

1st ♋
☿ enters ♉   **6:29 am** 3:29 am
☉ enters ♉   **4:33 pm** 1:33 pm
☽ v/c   **8:03 pm** 5:03 pm
☽ enters ♌   11:11 pm
2nd Quarter   11:59 pm

Sun enters Taurus

20 Tuesday

1st ♋
☽ enters ♌ **2:11 am**
2nd Quarter **2:59 am**
♅ D   **3:06 am** 12:06 am

21 Wednesday
2nd ♌

22 Thursday
2nd ♌
☽ v/c   **8:05 am** 5:05 am
☽ enters ♍ **9:08 am** 6:08 am

Earth Day

Eastern time in bold type
Pacific time in medium type

23 Friday
2nd ♍
♂ enters ♋ **7:49 am** 4:49 am

24 Saturday
2nd ♍
☽ v/c **6:50 am** 3:50 am
☽ enters ♎ **12:06 pm** 9:06 am

25 Sunday
2nd ♎

March 2021						
S	M	T	W	T	F	S
	1	2	3	4	5	6
7	8	9	10	11	12	13
14	15	16	17	18	19	20
21	22	23	24	25	26	27
28	29	30	31			

April 2021						
S	M	T	W	T	F	S
				1	2	3
4	5	6	7	8	9	10
11	12	13	14	15	16	17
18	19	20	21	22	23	24
25	26	27	28	29	30	

May 2021						
S	M	T	W	T	F	S
						1
2	3	4	5	6	7	8
9	10	11	12	13	14	15
16	17	18	19	20	21	22
23	24	25	26	27	28	29
30	31					

26 Monday

2nd ♎︎
☽ v/c	**8:40 am**	5:40 am
☽ enters ♏︎	**12:18 pm**	9:18 am
Full Moon	**11:32 pm**	8:32 pm

27 Tuesday

3rd ♏︎
| ♀ ℞ | **4:04 pm** | 1:04 pm |

28 Wednesday

3rd ♏︎
| ☽ v/c | **8:31 am** | 5:31 am |
| ☽ enters ♐︎ | **11:42 am** | 8:42 am |

29 Thursday

3rd ♐︎

30 Friday
3rd ♐
☽ v/c   **9:27 am**   6:27 am
☽ enters ♑ **12:16 pm**   9:16 am

Orthodox Good Friday

1 Saturday
3rd ♑

Beltane

2 Sunday
3rd ♑
☽ v/c   **10:38 am**   7:38 am
☽ enters ♒ **3:31 pm** 12:31 pm

Orthodox Easter

April 2021						
S	M	T	W	T	F	S
				1	2	3
4	5	6	7	8	9	10
11	12	13	14	15	16	17
18	19	20	21	22	23	24
25	26	27	28	29	30	

May 2021						
S	M	T	W	T	F	S
						1
2	3	4	5	6	7	8
9	10	11	12	13	14	15
16	17	18	19	20	21	22
23	24	25	26	27	28	29
30	31					

June 2021						
S	M	T	W	T	F	S
		1	2	3	4	5
6	7	8	9	10	11	12
13	14	15	16	17	18	19
20	21	22	23	24	25	26
27	28	29	30			

Eastern time in bold type
Pacific time in medium type

3 Monday

3rd ≈
4th Quarter **3:50 pm** 12:50 pm
☿ enters ♊ **10:49 pm** 7:49 pm

4 Tuesday

4th ≈
☽ v/c **8:05 pm** 5:05 pm
☽ enters ♓ **10:09 pm** 7:09 pm

5 Wednesday
4th ♓

Cinco de Mayo

6 Thursday
4th ♓

Eastern time in bold type
Pacific time in medium type

7 Friday

4th ♓
☽ v/c   **3:36 am** 12:36 am
☽ enters ♈   **7:52 am** 4:52 am

8 Saturday

4th ♈
♃ enters ♉   **4:54 am** 1:54 am
♀ enters ♊   **10:01 pm** 7:01 pm

9 Sunday

4th ♈
☽ v/c   **6:50 pm** 3:50 pm
☽ enters ♉   **7:46 pm** 4:46 pm

Mother's Day

April 2021						
S	M	T	W	T	F	S
				1	2	3
4	5	6	7	8	9	10
11	12	13	14	15	16	17
18	19	20	21	22	23	24
25	26	27	28	29	30	

May 2021						
S	M	T	W	T	F	S
						1
2	3	4	5	6	7	8
9	10	11	12	13	14	15
16	17	18	19	20	21	22
23	24	25	26	27	28	29
30	31					

June 2021						
S	M	T	W	T	F	S
		1	2	3	4	5
6	7	8	9	10	11	12
13	14	15	16	17	18	19
20	21	22	23	24	25	26
27	28	29	30			

Eastern time in bold type
Pacific time in medium type

10 Monday
4th ♉

11 Tuesday
4th ♉
New Moon   **3:00 pm** 12:00 pm

Ramadan ends

12 Wednesday
1st ♉
☽ v/c   **8:23 am** 5:23 am
☽ enters ♊   **8:43 am** 5:43 am

13 Thursday
1st ♊
♃ enters ♓   **6:36 pm** 3:36 pm

14 Friday
1st ♊
☽ v/c   **6:51 am** 3:51 am
☽ enters ♋ **9:30 pm** 6:30 pm

15 Saturday
1st ♋

16 Sunday
1st ♋
☽ v/c   11:23 pm

Shavuot begins at sundown

April 2021						
S	M	T	W	T	F	S
				1	2	3
4	5	6	7	8	9	10
11	12	13	14	15	16	17
18	19	20	21	22	23	24
25	26	27	28	29	30	

May 2021						
S	M	T	W	T	F	S
						1
2	3	4	5	6	7	8
9	10	11	12	13	14	15
16	17	18	19	20	21	22
23	24	25	26	27	28	29
30	31					

June 2021						
S	M	T	W	T	F	S
		1	2	3	4	5
6	7	8	9	10	11	12
13	14	15	16	17	18	19
20	21	22	23	24	25	26
27	28	29	30			

Eastern time in bold type
Pacific time in medium type

17 Monday

1st ♋
☽ v/c   **2:23 am**
☽ enters ♌   **8:44 am** 5:44 am

18 Tuesday

1st ♌

19 Wednesday

1st ♌
☽ v/c   **3:13 pm** 12:13 pm
2nd Quarter **3:13 pm** 12:13 pm
☽ enters ♍ **4:59 pm** 1:59 pm

20 Thursday

2nd ♍
☉ enters ♊ **3:37 pm** 12:37 pm

Sun enters Gemini

Eastern time in bold type
Pacific time in medium type

21 Friday
2nd ♍
| ☽ v/c | **3:56 pm** | 12:56 pm |
| ☽ enters ♎ | **9:35 pm** | 6:35 pm |

22 Saturday
2nd ♎

23 Sunday
2nd ♎
♄ R	**5:21 am**	2:21 am
☽ v/c	**5:36 pm**	2:36 pm
☽ enters ♏	**11:00 pm**	8:00 pm

April 2021	May 2021	June 2021
S M T W T F S	S M T W T F S	S M T W T F S
1 2 3	1	1 2 3 4 5
4 5 6 7 8 9 10	2 3 4 5 6 7 8	6 7 8 9 10 11 12
11 12 13 14 15 16 17	9 10 11 12 13 14 15	13 14 15 16 17 18 19
18 19 20 21 22 23 24	16 17 18 19 20 21 22	20 21 22 23 24 25 26
25 26 27 28 29 30	23 24 25 26 27 28 29	27 28 29 30
	30 31	

Eastern time in bold type
Pacific time in medium type

24 Monday
2nd ♏

25 Tuesday
2nd ♏
☽ v/c   **5:20 pm** 2:20 pm
☽ enters ♐ **10:39 pm** 7:39 pm

26 Wednesday
2nd ♐
Full Moon   **7:14 am** 4:14 am

Lunar Eclipse 5° ♐ 26'

27 Thursday
3rd ♐
☽ v/c   **1:35 pm** 10:35 am
☽ enters ♑ **10:23 pm** 7:23 pm

28 Friday

3rd ♑

29 Saturday

3rd ♑

☽ v/c	**6:15 pm**	3:15 pm
☿ ℞	**6:34 pm**	3:34 pm
☽ enters ♒		9:04 pm

Mercury retrograde until 6/22

30 Sunday

3rd ♑
☽ enters ♒ **12:04 am**

April 2021						
S	M	T	W	T	F	S
				1	2	3
4	5	6	7	8	9	10
11	12	13	14	15	16	17
18	19	20	21	22	23	24
25	26	27	28	29	30	

May 2021						
S	M	T	W	T	F	S
						1
2	3	4	5	6	7	8
9	10	11	12	13	14	15
16	17	18	19	20	21	22
23	24	25	26	27	28	29
30	31					

June 2021						
S	M	T	W	T	F	S
		1	2	3	4	5
6	7	8	9	10	11	12
13	14	15	16	17	18	19
20	21	22	23	24	25	26
27	28	29	30			

Eastern time in bold type
Pacific time in medium type

31 Monday
3rd ≈
☽ v/c   11:14 pm

Memorial Day

1 Tuesday
3rd ≈
☽ v/c   **2:14 am**
☽ enters ♓   **5:07 am**   2:07 am

2 Wednesday
3rd ♓
4th Quarter   **3:24 am**   12:24 am
♀ enters ♋   **9:19 am**   6:19 am

3 Thursday
4th ♓
☽ v/c   **7:10 am**   4:10 am
☽ enters ♈   **1:59 pm**   10:59 am

Eastern time in bold type
Pacific time in medium type

4 Friday
4th ♈

5 Saturday
4th ♈
☽ v/c   **6:47 pm** 3:47 pm
☽ enters ♉   10:46 pm

6 Sunday
4th ♈
☽ enters ♉   **1:46 am**

	May 2021					
S	M	T	W	T	F	S
						1
2	3	4	5	6	7	8
9	10	11	12	13	14	15
16	17	18	19	20	21	22
23	24	25	26	27	28	29
30	31					

	June 2021					
S	M	T	W	T	F	S
		1	2	3	4	5
6	7	8	9	10	11	12
13	14	15	16	17	18	19
20	21	22	23	24	25	26
27	28	29	30			

	July 2021					
S	M	T	W	T	F	S
				1	2	3
4	5	6	7	8	9	10
11	12	13	14	15	16	17
18	19	20	21	22	23	24
25	26	27	28	29	30	31

Eastern time in bold type
Pacific time in medium type

7 Monday
4th ♉

8 Tuesday
4th ♉
☽ v/c   **11:07 am** 8:07 am
☽ enters ♊   **2:47 pm** 11:47 am

9 Wednesday
4th ♊

10 Thursday
4th ♊
New Moon   **6:53 am** 3:53 am
☽ v/c   **1:38 pm** 10:38 am

Solar Eclipse 19° ♊ 47'

11 Friday
1st ♊
☽ enters ♋ **3:23 am** 12:23 am
♂ enters ♌ **9:34 am** 6:34 am

12 Saturday
1st ♋

13 Sunday
1st ♋
☽ v/c **7:16 am** 4:16 am
☽ enters ♌ **2:22 pm** 11:22 am

		May 2021				
S	M	T	W	T	F	S
						1
2	3	4	5	6	7	8
9	10	11	12	13	14	15
16	17	18	19	20	21	22
23	24	25	26	27	28	29
30	31					

		June 2021				
S	M	T	W	T	F	S
		1	2	3	4	5
6	7	8	9	10	11	12
13	14	15	16	17	18	19
20	21	22	23	24	25	26
27	28	29	30			

		July 2021				
S	M	T	W	T	F	S
				1	2	3
4	5	6	7	8	9	10
11	12	13	14	15	16	17
18	19	20	21	22	23	24
25	26	27	28	29	30	31

Eastern time in bold type
Pacific time in medium type

14 Monday
1st ♌

15 Tuesday
1st ♌
☽ v/c **1:27 pm** 10:27 am
☽ enters ♍ **11:02 pm** 8:02 pm

16 Wednesday
1st ♍

17 Thursday
1st ♍
☽ v/c **11:54 pm** 8:54 pm
2nd Quarter **11:54 pm** 8:54 pm

Eastern time in bold type
Pacific time in medium type

18 Friday

2nd ♍
)) enters ♎ **4:54 am** 1:54 am

19 Saturday

2nd ♎

20 Sunday

2nd ♎
)) v/c   **6:52 am** 3:52 am
)) enters ♏ **7:58 am** 4:58 am
♃ ℞   **11:06 am** 8:06 am
☉ enters ♋ **11:32 pm** 8:32 pm

Litha • Summer Solstice • Father's Day
Sun enters Cancer • 11:32 pm EDT/8:32 pm PDT

May 2021						
S	M	T	W	T	F	S
						1
2	3	4	5	6	7	8
9	10	11	12	13	14	15
16	17	18	19	20	21	22
23	24	25	26	27	28	29
30	31					

June 2021						
S	M	T	W	T	F	S
		1	2	3	4	5
6	7	8	9	10	11	12
13	14	15	16	17	18	19
20	21	22	23	24	25	26
27	28	29	30			

July 2021						
S	M	T	W	T	F	S
				1	2	3
4	5	6	7	8	9	10
11	12	13	14	15	16	17
18	19	20	21	22	23	24
25	26	27	28	29	30	31

Eastern time in bold type
Pacific time in medium type

21 Monday

2nd ♏
☽ v/c   11:43 pm

22 Tuesday

2nd ♏
☽ v/c   **2:43 am**
☽ enters ♐ **8:55 am** 5:55 am
☿ D   **6:00 pm** 3:00 pm

23 Wednesday

2nd ♐
☽ v/c   **10:09 pm** 7:09 pm

24 Thursday

2nd ♐
☽ enters ♑ **9:05 am** 6:05 am
Full Moon **2:40 pm** 11:40 am

Eastern time in bold type
Pacific time in medium type

25 Friday
3rd ♑
♆ R̥   **3:21 pm** 12:21 pm

26 Saturday
3rd ♑
☽ v/c   **8:49 am** 5:49 am
☽ enters ≈ **10:09 am** 7:09 am
♀ enters ♌   9:27 pm

27 Sunday
3rd ≈
♀ enters ♌ **12:27 am**
☽ v/c   **3:08 pm** 12:08 pm

	May 2021					
S	M	T	W	T	F	S
						1
2	3	4	5	6	7	8
9	10	11	12	13	14	15
16	17	18	19	20	21	22
23	24	25	26	27	28	29
30	31					

	June 2021					
S	M	T	W	T	F	S
		1	2	3	4	5
6	7	8	9	10	11	12
13	14	15	16	17	18	19
20	21	22	23	24	25	26
27	28	29	30			

	July 2021					
S	M	T	W	T	F	S
				1	2	3
4	5	6	7	8	9	10
11	12	13	14	15	16	17
18	19	20	21	22	23	24
25	26	27	28	29	30	31

Eastern time in bold type
Pacific time in medium type

28 Monday

3rd ≈
☽ enters ♓   **1:51 pm** 10:51 am

29 Tuesday

3rd ♓

30 Wednesday

3rd ♓
☽ v/c   **1:40 pm** 10:40 am
☽ enters ♈   **9:21 pm** 6:21 pm

1 Thursday

3rd ♈
4th Quarter **5:11 pm** 2:11 pm

2 Friday
4th ♈︎
☽ v/c   9:15 pm

3 Saturday
4th ♈︎

☽ v/c   **12:15 am**
☽ enters ♉︎   **8:28 am**   5:28 am

4 Sunday
4th ♉︎

Independence Day

June 2021						
S	M	T	W	T	F	S
		1	2	3	4	5
6	7	8	9	10	11	12
13	14	15	16	17	18	19
20	21	22	23	24	25	26
27	28	29	30			

July 2021						
S	M	T	W	T	F	S
				1	2	3
4	5	6	7	8	9	10
11	12	13	14	15	16	17
18	19	20	21	22	23	24
25	26	27	28	29	30	31

August 2021						
S	M	T	W	T	F	S
1	2	3	4	5	6	7
8	9	10	11	12	13	14
15	16	17	18	19	20	21
22	23	24	25	26	27	28
29	30	31				

Eastern time in bold type
Pacific time in medium type

5 Monday

4th ♉
☽ v/c   **12:57 pm**   9:57 am
☽ enters ♊   **9:24 pm**   6:24 pm

6 Tuesday

4th ♊

7 Wednesday

4th ♊
☽ v/c   9:20 pm

8 Thursday

4th ♊
☽ v/c   **12:20 am**
☽ enters ♋   **9:51 am**   6:51 am

9 Friday

4th ♋
New Moon   **9:17 pm**   6:17 pm

10 Saturday

1st ♋
☽ v/c   **12:10 pm**   9:10 am
☽ enters ♌   **8:21 pm**   5:21 pm

11 Sunday

1st ♌
☿ enters ♋   **4:35 pm**   1:35 pm

June 2021						
S	M	T	W	T	F	S
		1	2	3	4	5
6	7	8	9	10	11	12
13	14	15	16	17	18	19
20	21	22	23	24	25	26
27	28	29	30			

July 2021						
S	M	T	W	T	F	S
				1	2	3
4	5	6	7	8	9	10
11	12	13	14	15	16	17
18	19	20	21	22	23	24
25	26	27	28	29	30	31

August 2021						
S	M	T	W	T	F	S
1	2	3	4	5	6	7
8	9	10	11	12	13	14
15	16	17	18	19	20	21
22	23	24	25	26	27	28
29	30	31				

12 Monday
1st ♌
☽ v/c   **8:29 am** 5:29 am

13 Tuesday
1st ♌
☽ enters ♍ **4:30 am** 1:30 am

14 Wednesday
1st ♍
☿ R   **3:40 am** 12:40 am
☽ v/c   11:46 pm

15 Thursday
1st ♍
☽ v/c   **2:46 am**
☽ enters ♎ **10:32 am** 7:32 am
♀ R   **12:41 pm** 9:41 am

16 Friday
1st ♎

17 Saturday
1st ♎

2nd Quarter	**6:11 am**	3:11 am
☽ v/c	**7:03 am**	4:03 am
☽ enters ♏	**2:38 pm**	11:38 am

18 Sunday
2nd ♏

| ⚷ enters ♎ | 11:31 pm |

June 2021							July 2021							August 2021						
S	M	T	W	T	F	S	S	M	T	W	T	F	S	S	M	T	W	T	F	S
		1	2	3	4	5					1	2	3	1	2	3	4	5	6	7
6	7	8	9	10	11	12	4	5	6	7	8	9	10	8	9	10	11	12	13	14
13	14	15	16	17	18	19	11	12	13	14	15	16	17	15	16	17	18	19	20	21
20	21	22	23	24	25	26	18	19	20	21	22	23	24	22	23	24	25	26	27	28
27	28	29	30				25	26	27	28	29	30	31	29	30	31				

19 Monday

2nd ♏
♇ enters ♎ **2:31 am**
☽ v/c   **12:30 pm**   9:30 am
☽ enters ♐   **5:08 pm**   2:08 pm

20 Tuesday

2nd ♐

21 Wednesday

2nd ♐
☽ v/c   **6:26 pm**   3:26 pm
☽ enters ♑   **6:36 pm**   3:36 pm
♀ enters ♍   **8:37 pm**   5:37 pm

22 Thursday

2nd ♑
☉ enters ♌ **10:26 am**   7:26 am

Sun enters Leo

Eastern time in bold type
Pacific time in medium type

23 Friday

2nd ♑
D v/c | **12:34 pm** | 9:34 am
D enters ♒ | **8:12 pm** | 5:12 pm
Full Moon | **10:37 pm** | 7:37 pm

24 Saturday

3rd ♒

25 Sunday

3rd ♒
D v/c | **7:14 pm** | 4:14 pm
D enters ♓ | **11:30 pm** | 8:30 pm

	June 2021					
S	M	T	W	T	F	S
		1	2	3	4	5
6	7	8	9	10	11	12
13	14	15	16	17	18	19
20	21	22	23	24	25	26
27	28	29	30			

	July 2021					
S	M	T	W	T	F	S
				1	2	3
4	5	6	7	8	9	10
11	12	13	14	15	16	17
18	19	20	21	22	23	24
25	26	27	28	29	30	31

	August 2021					
S	M	T	W	T	F	S
1	2	3	4	5	6	7
8	9	10	11	12	13	14
15	16	17	18	19	20	21
22	23	24	25	26	27	28
29	30	31				

26 Monday
3rd ♓

27 Tuesday
3rd ♓
☿ enters ♌ **9:12 pm** 6:12 pm
☽ v/c **9:13 pm** 6:13 pm

28 Wednesday
3rd ♓
☽ enters ♈ **5:58 am** 2:58 am
♃ enters ♒ **8:43 am** 5:43 am

29 Thursday
3rd ♈
♂ enters ♍ **4:32 pm** 1:32 pm

Eastern time in bold type
Pacific time in medium type

30 Friday
3rd ♈
☽ v/c **3:38 pm** 12:38 pm
☽ enters ♉ **4:08 pm** 1:08 pm

31 Saturday
3rd ♉
♀ enters ♊ **4:13 am** 1:13 am
4th Quarter **9:16 am** 6:16 am

1 Sunday
4th ♉

Lammas

July 2021						
S	M	T	W	T	F	S
				1	2	3
4	5	6	7	8	9	10
11	12	13	14	15	16	17
18	19	20	21	22	23	24
25	26	27	28	29	30	31

August 2021						
S	M	T	W	T	F	S
1	2	3	4	5	6	7
8	9	10	11	12	13	14
15	16	17	18	19	20	21
22	23	24	25	26	27	28
29	30	31				

September 2021						
S	M	T	W	T	F	S
			1	2	3	4
5	6	7	8	9	10	11
12	13	14	15	16	17	18
19	20	21	22	23	24	25
26	27	28	29	30		

2 Monday

4th ♉
☽ v/c	**3:41 am**	12:41 am
☽ enters ♊	**4:46 am**	1:46 am
☿ D	**7:43 pm**	4:43 pm

3 Tuesday

4th ♊

4 Wednesday

4th ♊
| ☽ v/c | **3:38 pm** | 12:38 pm |
| ☽ enters ♋ | **5:17 pm** | 2:17 pm |

5 Thursday

4th ♋

6 Friday
4th ♋
☽ v/c   **6:12 pm** 3:12 pm

7 Saturday
4th ♋
☽ enters ♌   **3:31 am** 12:31 am

8 Sunday
4th ♌
New Moon   **9:50 am** 6:50 am

Islamic New Year begins at sundown

July 2021						
S	M	T	W	T	F	S
				1	2	3
4	5	6	7	8	9	10
11	12	13	14	15	16	17
18	19	20	21	22	23	24
25	26	27	28	29	30	31

August 2021						
S	M	T	W	T	F	S
1	2	3	4	5	6	7
8	9	10	11	12	13	14
15	16	17	18	19	20	21
22	23	24	25	26	27	28
29	30	31				

September 2021						
S	M	T	W	T	F	S
			1	2	3	4
5	6	7	8	9	10	11
12	13	14	15	16	17	18
19	20	21	22	23	2	25
26	27	28	29	30		

Eastern time in bold type
Pacific time in medium type

9 Monday

1st ♌
☽ v/c   **8:23 am**   5:23 am
☽ enters ♍ **10:56 am** 7:56 am

10 Tuesday

1st ♍

11 Wednesday

1st ♍
☽ v/c   **7:22 am**   4:22 am
☽ enters ♎ **4:08 pm** 1:08 pm
☿ enters ♍ **5:57 pm** 2:57 pm

12 Thursday

1st ♎

13 Friday

1st ♎︎
☽ v/c   **4:39 pm**   1:39 pm
☽ enters ♏︎   **8:01 pm**   5:01 pm

14 Saturday

1st ♏︎

15 Sunday

1st ♏︎
2nd Quarter **11:20 am** 8:20 am
☽ v/c   **11:05 pm** 8:05 pm
☽ enters ♐︎ **11:12 pm** 8:12 pm
♀ enters ♎︎   9:27 pm

		July 2021				
S	M	T	W	T	F	S
				1	2	3
4	5	6	7	8	9	10
11	12	13	14	15	16	17
18	19	20	21	22	23	24
25	26	27	28	29	30	31

		August 2021				
S	M	T	W	T	F	S
1	2	3	4	5	6	7
8	9	10	11	12	13	14
15	16	17	18	19	20	21
22	23	24	25	26	27	28
29	30	31				

		September 2021				
S	M	T	W	T	F	S
			1	2	3	4
5	6	7	8	9	10	11
12	13	14	15	16	17	18
19	20	21	22	23	24	25
26	27	28	29	30		

Eastern time in bold type
Pacific time in medium type

16 Monday

2nd ♐
♀ enters ♎ **12:27 am**

17 Tuesday

2nd ♐
☽ v/c **9:43 pm** 6:43 pm
☽ enters ♑ 10:58 pm

18 Wednesday

2nd ♐
☽ enters ♑ **1:58 am**

19 Thursday

2nd ♑
☽ v/c **7:59 pm** 4:59 pm
♅ R **9:40 pm** 6:40 pm

20 Friday
2nd ♑
☽ enters ♒   **4:49 am**   1:49 am

21 Saturday
2nd ♒

22 Sunday
2nd ♒
☽ v/c   **8:02 am**   5:02 am
Full Moon   **8:02 am**   5:02 am
☽ enters ♓   **8:43 am**   5:43 am
☉ enters ♍   **5:35 pm**   2:35 pm

Sun enters Virgo

July 2021						
S	M	T	W	T	F	S
				1	2	3
4	5	6	7	8	9	10
11	12	13	14	15	16	17
18	19	20	21	22	23	24
25	26	27	28	29	30	31

August 2021						
S	M	T	W	T	F	S
1	2	3	4	5	6	7
8	9	10	11	12	13	14
15	16	17	18	19	20	21
22	23	24	25	26	27	28
29	30	31				

September 2021						
S	M	T	W	T	F	S
			1	2	3	4
5	6	7	8	9	10	11
12	13	14	15	16	17	18
19	20	21	22	23	24	25
26	27	28	29	30		

23 Monday
3rd ♓

24 Tuesday
3rd ♓
☽ v/c   **5:12 am**   2:12 am
☽ enters ♈   **2:57 pm**   11:57 am

25 Wednesday
3rd ♈

26 Thursday
3rd ♈
☽ v/c   **5:14 pm**   2:14 pm
☽ enters ♉   9:27 pm

27 Friday
3rd ♈
☽ enters ♉ **12:27 am**

28 Saturday
3rd ♉

29 Sunday
3rd ♉
☽ v/c   **10:59 am**   7:59 am
☽ enters ♊   **12:42 pm**   9:42 am
☿ enters ♎   10:10 pm

July 2021						
S	M	T	W	T	F	S
				1	2	3
4	5	6	7	8	9	10
11	12	13	14	15	16	17
18	19	20	21	22	23	24
25	26	27	28	29	30	31

August 2021						
S	M	T	W	T	F	S
1	2	3	4	5	6	7
8	9	10	11	12	13	14
15	16	17	18	19	20	21
22	23	24	25	26	27	28
29	30	31				

September 2021						
S	M	T	W	T	F	S
			1	2	3	4
5	6	7	8	9	10	11
12	13	14	15	16	17	18
19	20	21	22	23	24	25
26	27	28	29	30		

Eastern time in bold type
Pacific time in medium type

30 Monday

3rd ♊
☿ enters ♎ **1:10 am**
4th Quarter **3:13 am** 12:13 am

31 Tuesday

4th ♊
☽ v/c **4:48 pm** 1:48 pm
☽ enters ♋ 10:26 pm

1 Wednesday

4th ♊
☽ enters ♋ **1:26 am**

2 Thursday

4th ♋
☽ v/c 10:37 pm

3 Friday

4th ♋
☽ v/c   **1:37 am**
☽ enters ♌ **11:58 am** 8:58 am

4 Saturday

4th ♌

5 Sunday

4th ♌
☽ v/c   **10:22 am** 7:22 am
☽ enters ♍ **7:06 pm** 4:06 pm

August 2021						
S	M	T	W	T	F	S
1	2	3	4	5	6	7
8	9	10	11	12	13	14
15	16	17	18	19	20	21
22	23	24	25	26	27	28
29	30	31				

September 2021						
S	M	T	W	T	F	S
			1	2	3	4
5	6	7	8	9	10	11
12	13	14	15	16	17	18
19	20	21	22	23	24	25
26	27	28	29	30		

October 2021						
S	M	T	W	T	F	S
					1	2
3	4	5	6	7	8	9
10	11	12	13	14	15	16
17	18	19	20	21	22	23
24	25	26	27	28	29	30
31						

Eastern time in bold type
Pacific time in medium type

6 Monday

4th ♍
New Moon   **8:52 pm**   5:52 pm

Labor Day • Rosh Hashanah begins at sundown

7 Tuesday

1st ♍
☽ v/c   **3:24 pm** 12:24 pm
☽ enters ♎ **11:20 pm** 8:20 pm

8 Wednesday

1st ♎

9 Thursday

1st ♎
☽ v/c   9:48 pm
☽ enters ♏   11:05 pm

Eastern time in bold type
Pacific time in medium type

10 Friday

1st ♎︎
☽ v/c   **12:48 am**
☽ enters ♏︎ **2:05 am**
♀ enters ♏︎ **4:39 pm**   1:39 pm

11 Saturday

1st ♏︎
☽ v/c   10:33 pm

12 Sunday

1st ♏︎
☽ v/c   **1:33 am**
☽ enters ♐︎ **4:34 am**   1:34 am

August 2021						
S	M	T	W	T	F	S
1	2	3	4	5	6	7
8	9	10	11	12	13	14
15	16	17	18	19	20	21
22	23	24	25	26	27	28
29	30	31				

September 2021						
S	M	T	W	T	F	S
			1	2	3	4
5	6	7	8	9	10	11
12	13	14	15	16	17	18
19	20	21	22	23	24	25
26	27	28	29	30		

October 2021						
S	M	T	W	T	F	S
					1	2
3	4	5	6	7	8	9
10	11	12	13	14	15	16
17	18	19	20	21	22	23
24	25	26	27	28	29	30
31						

Eastern time in bold type
Pacific time in medium type

13 Monday

1st ♐
2nd Quarter **4:39 pm** 1:39 pm

14 Tuesday

2nd ♐
☽ v/c **6:57 am** 3:57 am
☽ enters ♑ **7:34 am** 4:34 am
♂ enters ♎ **8:14 pm** 5:14 pm

15 Wednesday

2nd ♑
☽ v/c 10:40 pm

Yom Kippur begins at sundown

16 Thursday

2nd ♑
☽ v/c **1:40 am**
☽ enters ♒ **11:23 am** 8:23 am

Eastern time in bold type
Pacific time in medium type

17 Friday
2nd ≈

18 Saturday
2nd ≈
☽ v/c   **5:14 am**   2:14 am
☽ enters ♓   **4:22 pm**   1:22 pm

19 Sunday
2nd ♓

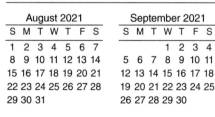

August 2021						
S	M	T	W	T	F	S
1	2	3	4	5	6	7
8	9	10	11	12	13	14
15	16	17	18	19	20	21
22	23	24	25	26	27	28
29	30	31				

September 2021						
S	M	T	W	T	F	S
			1	2	3	4
5	6	7	8	9	10	11
12	13	14	15	16	17	18
19	20	21	22	23	24	25
26	27	28	29	30		

October 2021						
S	M	T	W	T	F	S
					1	2
3	4	5	6	7	8	9
10	11	12	13	14	15	16
17	18	19	20	21	22	23
24	25	26	27	28	29	30
31						

20 Monday

2nd ♓

♆ enters ♏ **12:57 pm** 9:57 am
☽ v/c **7:55 pm** 4:55 pm
Full Moon **7:55 pm** 4:55 pm
☽ enters ♈ **11:13 pm** 8:13 pm

Sukkot begins at sundown

21 Tuesday

3rd ♈

UN International Day of Peace

22 Wednesday

3rd ♈
☉ enters ♎ **3:21 pm** 12:21 pm
☽ v/c **10:05 pm** 7:05 pm

Sun enters Libra • Mabon • Fall Equinox •3:21 pm EDT/12:21 pm PDT

23 Thursday

3rd ♈
☽ enters ♉ **8:38 am** 5:38 am

Eastern time in bold type
Pacific time in medium type

24 Friday
3rd ♉

25 Saturday
3rd ♉
☽ v/c   **9:09 am**   6:09 am
☽ enters ♊   **8:36 pm**   5:36 pm

26 Sunday
3rd ♊
☿ ℞   10:10 pm

Mercury retrograde until 10/18

August 2021						
S	M	T	W	T	F	S
1	2	3	4	5	6	7
8	9	10	11	12	13	14
15	16	17	18	19	20	21
22	23	24	25	26	27	28
29	30	31				

September 2021						
S	M	T	W	T	F	S
			1	2	3	4
5	6	7	8	9	10	11
12	13	14	15	16	17	18
19	20	21	22	23	24	25
26	27	28	29	30		

October 2021						
S	M	T	W	T	F	S
					1	2
3	4	5	6	7	8	9
10	11	12	13	14	15	16
17	18	19	20	21	22	23
24	25	26	27	28	29	30
31						

Eastern time in bold type
Pacific time in medium type

27 Monday

3rd ♊
☿ Rₓ   **1:10 am**
☽ v/c   9:18 pm

Sukkot ends
Mercury retrograde until 10/18

28 Tuesday

3rd ♊
☽ v/c   **12:18 am**
☽ enters ♋   **9:34 am**   6:34 am
4th Quarter   **9:57 pm**   6:57 pm

29 Wednesday

4th ♋

30 Thursday

4th ♋
☽ v/c   **10:49 am**   7:49 am
☽ enters ♌   **8:53 pm**   5:53 pm

Eastern time in bold type
Pacific time in medium type

1 Friday
4th ♌

2 Saturday
4th ♌
☽ v/c   **7:43 pm**   4:43 pm

3 Sunday
4th ♌
☽ enters ♍   **4:38 am**   1:38 am

September 2021	October 2021	November 2021
S M T W T F S	S M T W T F S	S M T W T F S
1 2 3 4	1 2	1 2 3 4 5 6
5 6 7 8 9 10 11	3 4 5 6 7 8 9	7 8 9 10 11 12 13
12 13 14 15 16 17 18	10 11 12 13 14 15 16	14 15 16 17 18 19 20
19 20 21 22 23 24 25	17 18 19 20 21 22 23	21 22 23 24 25 26 27
26 27 28 29 30	24 25 26 27 28 29 30	28 29 30
	31	

Eastern time in bold type
Pacific time in medium type

4 Monday
4th ♍

5 Tuesday
4th ♍
☽ v/c   **4:46 am**   1:46 am
☽ enters ♎ **8:41 am**   5:41 am

6 Wednesday
4th ♎
New Moon **7:05 am**   4:05 am
☿ D   **2:29 pm** 11:29 am
☽ v/c   10:03 pm

7 Thursday
1st ♎
☽ v/c   **1:03 am**
♀ enters ♐ **7:21 am**   4:21 am
☽ enters ♏ **10:22 am**   7:22 am

8 Friday
1st ♏
♀ ℞   **9:31 pm** 6:31 pm
☽ v/c   11:05 pm

9 Saturday
1st ♏
☽ v/c   **2:05 am**
☽ enters ♐ **11:24 am** 8:24 am

10 Sunday
1st ♐
♄ D   **10:17 pm** 7:17 pm
☽ v/c   9:30 pm

September 2021						
S	M	T	W	T	F	S
			1	2	3	4
5	6	7	8	9	10	11
12	13	14	15	16	17	18
19	20	21	22	23	24	25
26	27	28	29	30		

October 2021						
S	M	T	W	T	F	S
					1	2
3	4	5	6	7	8	9
10	11	12	13	14	15	16
17	18	19	20	21	22	23
24	25	26	27	28	29	30
31						

November 2021						
S	M	T	W	T	F	S
	1	2	3	4	5	6
7	8	9	10	11	12	13
14	15	16	17	18	19	20
21	22	23	24	25	26	27
28	29	30				

11 Monday

1st ♐

☽ v/c   **12:30 am**

☽ enters ♑   **1:15 pm** 10:15 am

Columbus Day • Indigenous Peoples' Day

12 Tuesday

1st ♑

2nd Quarter **11:25 pm** 8:25 pm

13 Wednesday

2nd ♑

☽ v/c   **6:53 am** 3:53 am

☽ enters ♒   **4:47 pm** 1:47 pm

14 Thursday

2nd ♒

Eastern time in bold type
Pacific time in medium type

15 Friday

2nd ≈
☽ v/c   **8:33 am**   5:33 am
☽ enters ♓   **10:22 pm**   7:22 pm

16 Saturday

2nd ♓

17 Sunday

2nd ♓
☽ v/c   **7:24 pm**   4:24 pm
♃ D   10:30 pm

		September 2021				
S	M	T	W	T	F	S
			1	2	3	4
5	6	7	8	9	10	11
12	13	14	15	16	17	18
19	20	21	22	23	24	25
26	27	28	29	30		

		October 2021				
S	M	T	W	T	F	S
					1	2
3	4	5	6	7	8	9
10	11	12	13	14	15	16
17	18	19	20	21	22	23
24	25	26	27	28	29	30
31						

		November 2021				
S	M	T	W	T	F	S
	1	2	3	4	5	6
7	8	9	10	11	12	13
14	15	16	17	18	19	20
21	22	23	24	25	26	27
28	29	30				

Eastern time in bold type
Pacific time in medium type

18 Monday

2nd ♓
♃ D	**1:30 am**	
☽ enters ♈	**6:04 am**	3:04 am
☿ D	**11:17 am**	8:17 am

19 Tuesday

2nd ♈

20 Wednesday

2nd ♈
☽ v/c	**10:57 am**	7:57 am
Full Moon	**10:57 am**	7:57 am
☽ enters ♉	**3:59 pm**	12:59 pm

21 Thursday

3rd ♉

Eastern time in bold type
Pacific time in medium type

22 Friday

3rd ♉
☽ v/c   **4:35 pm**   1:35 pm
☉ enters ♏   9:51 pm

Sun enters Scorpio (PDT)

23 Saturday

3rd ♉
☉ enters ♏ **12:51 am**
☽ enters ♊   **3:57 am** 12:57 am

Sun enters Scorpio (EDT)

24 Sunday

3rd ♊

September 2021						
S	M	T	W	T	F	S
			1	2	3	4
5	6	7	8	9	10	11
12	13	14	15	16	17	18
19	20	21	22	23	24	25
26	27	28	29	30		

October 2021						
S	M	T	W	T	F	S
					1	2
3	4	5	6	7	8	9
10	11	12	13	14	15	16
17	18	19	20	21	22	23
24	25	26	27	28	29	30
31						

November 2021						
S	M	T	W	T	F	S
	1	2	3	4	5	6
7	8	9	10	11	12	13
14	15	16	17	18	19	20
21	22	23	24	25	26	27
28	29	30				

Eastern time in bold type
Pacific time in medium type

25 Monday

3rd ♊
☽ v/c   **10:11 am** 7:11 am
☽ enters ♋ **5:00 pm** 2:00 pm

26 Tuesday

3rd ♋

27 Wednesday

3rd ♋
☽ v/c   11:02 pm

28 Thursday

3rd ♋
☽ v/c   **2:02 am**
☽ enters ♌ **5:07 am** 2:07 am
4th Quarter **4:05 pm** 1:05 pm

Eastern time in bold type
Pacific time in medium type

29 Friday
4th ♌

30 Saturday
4th ♌
☽ v/c   **3:05 am** 12:05 am
♂ enters ♏ **10:21 am** 7:21 am
☽ enters ♍ **2:09 pm** 11:09 am

31 Sunday
4th ♍

Halloween • Samhain

September 2021						
S	M	T	W	T	F	S
			1	2	3	4
5	6	7	8	9	10	11
12	13	14	15	16	17	18
19	20	21	22	23	24	25
26	27	28	29	30		

October 2021						
S	M	T	W	T	F	S
					1	2
3	4	5	6	7	8	9
10	11	12	13	14	15	16
17	18	19	20	21	22	23
24	25	26	27	28	29	30
31						

November 2021						
S	M	T	W	T	F	S
	1	2	3	4	5	6
7	8	9	10	11	12	13
14	15	16	17	18	19	20
21	22	23	24	25	26	27
28	29	30				

Eastern time in bold type
Pacific time in medium type

1 Monday

4th ♍

☽ v/c   **1:00 pm** 10:00 am
☽ enters ♎   **7:11 pm**   4:11 pm

All Saints' Day

2 Tuesday

4th ♎

Election Day (general)

3 Wednesday

4th ♎

☽ v/c   **6:32 pm** 3:32 pm
☽ enters ♏   **8:52 pm** 5:52 pm

4 Thursday

4th ♏

New Moon   **5:15 pm** 2:15 pm

Eastern time in bold type
Pacific time in medium type

5 Friday

1st ♏
♀ enters ♑	**6:44 am**	3:44 am
☽ v/c	**12:10 pm**	9:10 am
☿ enters ♏	**6:35 pm**	3:35 pm
☽ enters ♐	**8:52 pm**	5:52 pm

6 Saturday

1st ♐

7 Sunday

1st ♐
| ☽ v/c | **8:44 am** | 5:44 am |
| ☽ enters ♑ | **8:03 pm** | 5:03 pm |

Daylight Saving Time ends at 2 am

October 2021
S M T W T F S
1 2
3 4 5 6 7 8 9
10 11 12 13 14 15 16
17 18 19 20 21 22 23
24 25 26 27 28 29 30
31

November 2021
S M T W T F S
1 2 3 4 5 6
7 8 9 10 11 12 13
14 15 16 17 18 19 20
21 22 23 24 25 26 27
28 29 30

December 2021
S M T W T F S
1 2 3 4
5 6 7 8 9 10 11
12 13 14 15 16 17 18
19 20 21 22 23 24 25
26 27 28 29 30 31

8 Monday

1st ♈︎
♀ D   **4:23 am** 1:23 am

9 Tuesday

1st ♈︎
☽ v/c   **12:51 pm** 9:51 am
☽ enters ♒︎ **10:03 pm** 7:03 pm

10 Wednesday

1st ♒︎

11 Thursday

1st ♒︎
2nd Quarter **7:46 am** 4:46 am
☽ v/c   **2:52 pm** 11:52 am
☽ enters ♓︎   11:54 pm

Veterans Day

12 Friday
2nd ≈
☽ enters ♓ **2:54 am**

13 Saturday
2nd ♓
☽ v/c   9:40 pm

14 Sunday
2nd ♓
☽ v/c   **12:40 am**
☽ enters ♈ **10:48 am** 7:48 am
⚵ enters ♑ **3:23 pm** 12:23 pm

October 2021						
S	M	T	W	T	F	S
					1	2
3	4	5	6	7	8	9
10	11	12	13	14	15	16
17	18	19	20	21	22	23
24	25	26	27	28	29	30
31						

November 2021						
S	M	T	W	T	F	S
	1	2	3	4	5	6
7	8	9	10	11	12	13
14	15	16	17	18	19	20
21	22	23	24	25	26	27
28	29	30				

December 2021						
S	M	T	W	T	F	S
			1	2	3	4
5	6	7	8	9	10	11
12	13	14	15	16	17	18
19	20	21	22	23	24	25
26	27	28	29	30	31	

Eastern time in bold type
Pacific time in medium type

15 Monday
2nd ♈

16 Tuesday
2nd ♈
⚵ enters ♐ **9:07 am** 6:07 am
☽ v/c **10:51 am** 7:51 am
☽ enters ♉ **9:18 pm** 6:18 pm

17 Wednesday
2nd ♉

18 Thursday
2nd ♉

Eastern time in bold type
Pacific time in medium type

19 Friday

2nd ♉
☽ v/c	**3:57 am**	12:57 am
Full Moon	**3:57 am**	12:57 am
☽ enters ♊	**9:33 am**	6:33 am

Lunar Eclipse 27° ♉ 14'

20 Saturday

3rd ♊

21 Sunday

3rd ♊
☽ v/c	**10:52 am**	7:52 am
☉ enters ♐	**9:34 pm**	6:34 pm
☽ enters ♋	**10:33 pm**	7:33 pm

Sun enters Sagittarius

October 2021						
S	M	T	W	T	F	S
					1	2
3	4	5	6	7	8	9
10	11	12	13	14	15	16
17	18	19	20	21	22	23
24	25	26	27	28	29	30
31						

November 2021						
S	M	T	W	T	F	S
	1	2	3	4	5	6
7	8	9	10	11	12	13
14	15	16	17	18	19	20
21	22	23	24	25	26	27
28	29	30				

December 2021						
S	M	T	W	T	F	S
			1	2	3	4
5	6	7	8	9	10	11
12	13	14	15	16	17	18
19	20	21	22	23	24	25
26	27	28	29	30	31	

Eastern time in bold type
Pacific time in medium type

22 Monday
3rd ♋

23 Tuesday
3rd ♋
☽ v/c   9:46 pm

24 Wednesday
3rd ♋
☽ v/c   **12:46 am**
☿ enters ♐   **10:36 am**   7:36 am
☽ enters ♌   **10:59 am**   7:59 am

25 Thursday
3rd ♌

Thanksgiving Day

Eastern time in bold type
Pacific time in medium type

26 Friday

3rd ♌
☽ v/c   **11:24 am**   8:24 am
☽ enters ♍   **9:12 pm**   6:12 pm

27 Saturday

3rd ♍
4th Quarter   **7:28 am**   4:28 am

28 Sunday

4th ♍
☽ v/c   **7:02 pm**   4:02 pm

Hanukkah begins at sundown

October 2021						
S	M	T	W	T	F	S
					1	2
3	4	5	6	7	8	9
10	11	12	13	14	15	16
17	18	19	20	21	22	23
24	25	26	27	28	29	30
31						

November 2021						
S	M	T	W	T	F	S
	1	2	3	4	5	6
7	8	9	10	11	12	13
14	15	16	17	18	19	20
21	22	23	24	25	26	27
28	29	30				

December 2021						
S	M	T	W	T	F	S
			1	2	3	4
5	6	7	8	9	10	11
12	13	14	15	16	17	18
19	20	21	22	23	24	25
26	27	28	29	30	31	

Eastern time in bold type
Pacific time in medium type

29 Monday

4th ♍
☽ enters ♎ **3:55 am** 12:55 am

30 Tuesday

4th ♎
☽ v/c **11:20 pm** 8:20 pm

1 Wednesday

4th ♎
☽ enters ♏ **6:55 am** 3:55 am
♆ D **8:22 am** 5:22 am

2 Thursday

4th ♏
☽ v/c 9:22 pm

3 Friday
4th ♏
☽ v/c   **12:22 am**
☽ enters ♐   **7:13 am**   4:13 am
New Moon   11:43 pm

4 Saturday
4th ♐
New Moon   **2:43 am**
☽ v/c   9:08 pm

Solar Eclipse 12° ♐ 22'

5 Sunday
1st ♐
☽ v/c   **12:08 am**
☽ enters ♑ **6:31 am** 3:31 am

November 2021						
S	M	T	W	T	F	S
	1	2	3	4	5	6
7	8	9	10	11	12	13
14	15	16	17	18	19	20
21	22	23	24	25	26	27
28	29	30				

December 2021						
S	M	T	W	T	F	S
			1	2	3	4
5	6	7	8	9	10	11
12	13	14	15	16	17	18
19	20	21	22	23	24	25
26	27	28	29	30	31	

January 2022						
S	M	T	W	T	F	S
						1
2	3	4	5	6	7	8
9	10	11	12	13	14	15
16	17	18	19	20	21	22
23	24	25	26	27	28	29
30	31					

6 Monday

1st ♑

☽ v/c   **11:42 pm**   8:42 pm

Hanukkah ends

7 Tuesday

1st ♑

☽ enters ♒   **6:49 am**   3:49 am

8 Wednesday

1st ♒

9 Thursday

1st ♒

☽ v/c   **5:00 am**   2:00 am

☽ enters ♓   **9:53 am**   6:53 am

10 Friday
1st ♓
2nd Quarter **8:36 pm** 5:36 pm

11 Saturday
2nd ♓
☽ v/c **2:40 pm** 11:40 am
☽ enters ♈ **4:46 pm** 1:46 pm

12 Sunday
2nd ♈

November 2021						
S	M	T	W	T	F	S
	1	2	3	4	5	6
7	8	9	10	11	12	13
14	15	16	17	18	19	20
21	22	23	24	25	26	27
28	29	30				

December 2021						
S	M	T	W	T	F	S
			1	2	3	4
5	6	7	8	9	10	11
12	13	14	15	16	17	18
19	20	21	22	23	24	25
26	27	28	29	30	31	

January 2022						
S	M	T	W	T	F	S
						1
2	3	4	5	6	7	8
9	10	11	12	13	14	15
16	17	18	19	20	21	22
23	24	25	26	27	28	29
30	31					

13 Monday

2nd ♈
♂ enters ♐ **4:53 am** 1:53 am
☿ enters ♑ **12:52 pm** 9:52 am
☽ v/c **9:52 pm** 6:52 pm

14 Tuesday

2nd ♈
☽ enters ♉ **3:11 am** 12:11 am

15 Wednesday

2nd ♉

16 Thursday

2nd ♉
☽ v/c **11:08 am** 8:08 am
☽ enters ♊ **3:43 pm** 12:43 pm

Eastern time in bold type
Pacific time in medium type

17 Friday
2nd ♊

18 Saturday
2nd ♊
Full Moon **11:36 pm** 8:36 pm
☽ v/c 10:02 pm

19 Sunday
3rd ♊
☽ v/c **1:02 am**
☽ enters ♋ **4:42 am** 1:42 am
♀ ℞ **5:36 am** 2:36 am
⚷ D **11:33 am** 8:33 am

Venus retrograde until 1/29/22

November 2021						
S	M	T	W	T	F	S
	1	2	3	4	5	6
7	8	9	10	11	12	13
14	15	16	17	18	19	20
21	22	23	24	25	26	27
28	29	30				

December 2021						
S	M	T	W	T	F	S
			1	2	3	4
5	6	7	8	9	10	11
12	13	14	15	16	17	18
19	20	21	22	23	24	25
26	27	28	29	30	31	

January 2022						
S	M	T	W	T	F	S
						1
2	3	4	5	6	7	8
9	10	11	12	13	14	15
16	17	18	19	20	21	22
23	24	25	26	27	28	29
30	31					

20 Monday
3rd ⊗

21 Tuesday
3rd ⊗

☿ enters ♉	**5:38 am**	2:38 am
☽ v/c	**9:44 am**	6:44 am
☉ enters ♑	**10:59 am**	7:59 am
☽ enters ♌	**4:54 pm**	1:54 pm

Sun enters Capricorn • Yule • Winter Solstice • 10:59 am EDT/7:59 am PDT

22 Wednesday
3rd ♌

23 Thursday
3rd ♌

☽ v/c   10:39 pm

24 Friday

3rd ♌
☽ v/c   **1:39 am**
☽ enters ♍   **3:24 am** 12:24 am

Christmas Eve

25 Saturday

3rd ♍

Christmas Day

26 Sunday

3rd ♍
☽ v/c   **3:39 am** 12:39 am
☽ enters ♎   **11:24 am** 8:24 am
4th Quarter **9:24 pm** 6:24 pm

Kwanzaa begins

November 2021						
S	M	T	W	T	F	S
	1	2	3	4	5	6
7	8	9	10	11	12	13
14	15	16	17	18	19	20
21	22	23	24	25	26	27
28	29	30				

December 2021						
S	M	T	W	T	F	S
			1	2	3	4
5	6	7	8	9	10	11
12	13	14	15	16	17	18
19	20	21	22	23	24	25
26	27	28	29	30	31	

January 2022						
S	M	T	W	T	F	S
						1
2	3	4	5	6	7	8
9	10	11	12	13	14	15
16	17	18	19	20	21	22
23	24	25	26	27	28	29
30	31					

Eastern time in bold type
Pacific time in medium type

27 Monday
4th ♎

28 Tuesday
4th ♎
☽ v/c   **4:11 pm**   1:11 pm
☽ enters ♏ **4:16 pm**   1:16 pm
♃ enters ♓ **11:09 pm** 8:09 pm

29 Wednesday
4th ♏

30 Thursday
4th ♏
☽ v/c   **12:10 pm** 9:10 am
☽ enters ♐ **6:08 pm** 3:08 pm

31 Friday
4th ♐

New Year's Eve

1 Saturday
4th ♐
☽ v/c	**3:16 am**	12:16 am
☽ enters ♑	**6:02 pm**	3:02 pm
☿ enters ♒		11:10 pm

Kwanzaa ends • New Year's Day

2 Sunday
4th ♑
| ☿ enters ♒ | **2:10 am** | |
| New Moon | **1:33 pm** | 10:33 am |

November 2021						
S	M	T	W	T	F	S
	1	2	3	4	5	6
7	8	9	10	11	12	13
14	15	16	17	18	19	20
21	22	23	24	25	26	27
28	29	30				

December 2021						
S	M	T	W	T	F	S
			1	2	3	4
5	6	7	8	9	10	11
12	13	14	15	16	17	18
19	20	21	22	23	24	25
26	27	28	29	30	31	

January 2022						
S	M	T	W	T	F	S
						1
2	3	4	5	6	7	8
9	10	11	12	13	14	15
16	17	18	19	20	21	22
23	24	25	26	27	28	29
30	31					

Eastern time in bold type
Pacific time in medium type

The Year 2021

January

S	M	T	W	T	F	S
					1	2
3	4	5	6	7	8	9
10	11	12	13	14	15	16
17	18	19	20	21	22	23
24	25	26	27	28	29	30
31						

February

S	M	T	W	T	F	S
	1	2	3	4	5	6
7	8	9	10	11	12	13
14	15	16	17	18	19	20
21	22	23	24	25	26	27
28						

March

S	M	T	W	T	F	S
	1	2	3	4	5	6
7	8	9	10	11	12	13
14	15	16	17	18	19	20
21	22	23	24	25	26	27
28	29	30	31			

April

S	M	T	W	T	F	S
				1	2	3
4	5	6	7	8	9	10
11	12	13	14	15	16	17
18	19	20	21	22	23	24
25	26	27	28	29	30	

May

S	M	T	W	T	F	S
						1
2	3	4	5	6	7	8
9	10	11	12	13	14	15
16	17	18	19	20	21	22
23	24	25	26	27	28	29
30	31					

June

S	M	T	W	T	F	S
		1	2	3	4	5
6	7	8	9	10	11	12
13	14	15	16	17	18	19
20	21	22	23	24	25	26
27	28	29	30			

July

S	M	T	W	T	F	S
				1	2	3
4	5	6	7	8	9	10
11	12	13	14	15	16	17
18	19	20	21	22	23	24
25	26	27	28	29	30	31

August

S	M	T	W	T	F	S
1	2	3	4	5	6	7
8	9	10	11	12	13	14
15	16	17	18	19	20	21
22	23	24	25	26	27	28
29	30	31				

September

S	M	T	W	T	F	S
			1	2	3	4
5	6	7	8	9	10	11
12	13	14	15	16	17	18
19	20	21	22	23	24	25
26	27	28	29	30		

October

S	M	T	W	T	F	S
					1	2
3	4	5	6	7	8	9
10	11	12	13	14	15	16
17	18	19	20	21	22	23
24	25	26	27	28	29	30
31						

November

S	M	T	W	T	F	S
	1	2	3	4	5	6
7	8	9	10	11	12	13
14	15	16	17	18	19	20
21	22	23	24	25	26	27
28	29	30				

December

S	M	T	W	T	F	S
			1	2	3	4
5	6	7	8	9	10	11
12	13	14	15	16	17	18
19	20	21	22	23	24	25
26	27	28	29	30	31	

The Year 2022

January
S	M	T	W	T	F	S
						1
2	3	4	5	6	7	8
9	10	11	12	13	14	15
16	17	18	19	20	21	22
23	24	25	26	27	28	29
30	31					

February
S	M	T	W	T	F	S
		1	2	3	4	5
6	7	8	9	10	11	12
13	14	15	16	17	18	19
20	21	22	23	24	25	26
27	28					

March
S	M	T	W	T	F	S
		1	2	3	4	5
6	7	8	9	10	11	12
13	14	15	16	17	18	19
20	21	22	23	24	25	26
27	28	29	30	31		

April
S	M	T	W	T	F	S
					1	2
3	4	5	6	7	8	9
10	11	12	13	14	15	16
17	18	19	20	21	22	23
24	25	26	27	28	29	30

May
S	M	T	W	T	F	S
1	2	3	4	5	6	7
8	9	10	11	12	13	14
15	16	17	18	19	20	21
22	23	24	25	26	27	28
29	30	31				

June
S	M	T	W	T	F	S
			1	2	3	4
5	6	7	8	9	10	11
12	13	14	15	16	17	18
19	20	21	22	23	24	25
26	27	28	29	30		

July
S	M	T	W	T	F	S
					1	2
3	4	5	6	7	8	9
10	11	12	13	14	15	16
17	18	19	20	21	22	23
24	25	26	27	28	29	30
31						

August
S	M	T	W	T	F	S
	1	2	3	4	5	6
7	8	9	10	11	12	13
14	15	16	17	18	19	20
21	22	23	24	25	26	27
28	29	30	31			

September
S	M	T	W	T	F	S
				1	2	3
4	5	6	7	8	9	10
11	12	13	14	15	16	17
18	19	20	21	22	23	24
25	26	27	28	29	30	

October
S	M	T	W	T	F	S
						1
2	3	4	5	6	7	8
9	10	11	12	13	14	15
16	17	18	19	20	21	22
23	24	25	26	27	28	29
30	31					

November
S	M	T	W	T	F	S
		1	2	3	4	5
6	7	8	9	10	11	12
13	14	15	16	17	18	19
20	21	22	23	24	25	26
27	28	29	30			

December
S	M	T	W	T	F	S
				1	2	3
4	5	6	7	8	9	10
11	12	13	14	15	16	17
18	19	20	21	22	23	24
25	26	27	28	29	30	31

JANUARY 2020

☽ Last Aspect day	ET / hr:mn / PT	asp	☽ Ingress sign day	ET / hr:mn / PT
1	**9:14 pm** 6:14 pm	△♂	♈ 1	**11:00 pm** 8:00 pm
3	**8:18 pm** 5:18 pm	□♇	♉ 4	**11:15 am** 8:15 am
6	**7:08 am** 4:08 am	△♇	♊ 6	**9:11 pm** 6:11 pm
8	**5:16 pm** 2:16 pm	△♀	♋ 9	**3:43 am** 12:43 am
10	**6:58 pm** 3:58 pm	☍♇	♌ 11	**7:16 am** 4:16 am
13	**8:42 am** 5:42 am	☍♀	♍ 13	**9:06 am** 6:06 am
15	**7:12 am** 4:12 am	△☿	♎ 15	**10:43 am** 7:43 am
17	**7:58 am** 4:58 am	□☉	♏ 17	**1:20 pm** 10:20 am
19	**4:22 pm** 1:22 pm	⚹☉	♐ 19	**5:41 pm** 2:41 pm
20	**11:46 pm** 8:46 pm	□♆	♑ 21	9:00 pm
20	**11:46 pm** 8:46 pm	□♆	♑ 22	**12:00 am**
23	**9:08 pm** 6:08 pm	☌♄	♒ 24	**8:20 am** 5:20 am
25	**2:06 pm** 11:06 am	☌☿	♓ 26	**6:44 pm** 3:44 pm
28	**8:08 pm** 5:08 pm	⚹♄	♈ 29	**6:51 am** 3:51 am
31	**10:10 am** 7:10 am	⚹☿	♉ 31	**7:28 pm** 4:28 pm

☽ Phases & Eclipses phase	day	ET / hr:mn / PT
2nd Quarter	2	**11:45 pm** 8:45 pm
Full Moon	10	**2:21 pm** 11:21 am
☋	10	20° ♋ 00'
4th Quarter	17	**7:58 am** 4:58 am
New Moon	24	**4:42 pm** 1:42 pm

Planet Ingress	day	ET / hr:mn / PT
♂ ♐	3	**4:37 am** 1:37 am
♀ ♓	13	**1:39 pm** 10:39 am
☿ ♒	16	**1:31 pm** 10:31 am
♀ ♑	18	**5:33 am** 2:33 am
☉ ♒	20	**9:55 am** 6:55 am
⚳ ♒	31	**3:01 am** 12:01 am

Planetary Motion	day	ET / hr:mn / PT
♅ D	10	**8:49 pm** 5:49 pm

1 WEDNESDAY
- ☽ ⚹ ♄ **5:43 am** 2:43 am
- ☽ ⚹ ♇ **7:39 am** 4:39 am
- ☽ △ ♂ **9:14 pm** 6:14 pm

2 THURSDAY
- ☽ ⚺ ♅ **4:26 am** 1:26 am
- ♀ ⚺ ♆ **7:56 am** 4:56 am
- ☿ ☌ ♃ **11:42 am** 8:42 am
- ☽ □ ♃ **1:19 pm** 10:19 am
- ☽ □ ☿ **1:32 pm** 10:32 am
- ☽ □ ☉ **11:45 pm** 8:45 pm

3 FRIDAY
- ☽ ⚺ ♆ **7:56 am** 4:56 am
- ☽ ⚹ ♀ **10:38 am** 7:38 am
- ☽ □ ♄ **6:50 pm** 3:50 pm
- ☽ □ ♇ **8:18 pm** 5:18 pm

4 SATURDAY
- ☽ ⚻ ♂ **1:03 pm** 10:03 am
- ☽ ☌ ♅ **4:31 pm** 1:31 pm
- ☽ △ ♃ 11:20 pm

5 SUNDAY
- ☽ △ ♃ **2:20 am**
- ☽ △ ☿ **10:18 am** 7:18 am
- ☽ △ ☉ **4:37 pm** 1:37 pm
- ☽ ⚹ ♆ **7:15 pm** 4:15 pm

6 MONDAY
- ☽ □ ♀ **4:08 am** 1:08 am
- ☽ △ ♄ **6:07 am** 3:07 am
- ☽ △ ♇ **7:08 am** 4:08 am
- ☉ ⚹ ♆ 10:21 pm
- ☽ ☍ ♂ 11:05 pm
- ☽ ⚺ ♅ 11:09 pm
- ♀ ⚺ ♄ 11:39 pm

7 TUESDAY
- ☉ ⚹ ♆ **1:21 am**
- ☽ ☍ ♂ **2:05 am**
- ☽ ⚺ ♅ **2:09 am**
- ♀ ⚺ ♄ **2:39 am**
- ♂ ⚻ ♅ **3:13 am** 12:13 am
- ♀ ⚺ ♇ **11:53 am** 8:53 am
- ☽ ⚻ ♃ **12:28 pm** 9:28 am
- ☽ ⚻ ☿ 11:49 pm

8 WEDNESDAY
- ☽ ⚻ ☿ **2:49 am**
- ☽ □ ♆ **3:27 am** 12:27 am
- ☽ ⚻ ☉ **5:35 am** 2:35 am
- ☿ ⚹ ♆ **8:03 am** 5:03 am
- ☽ ⚻ ♄ **2:04 pm** 11:04 am
- ☽ ⚻ ♇ **2:40 pm** 11:40 am
- ☽ △ ♀ **5:16 pm** 2:16 pm

9 THURSDAY
- ☽ ⚹ ♅ **8:23 am** 5:23 am
- ☽ ⚻ ♂ **11:09 am** 8:09 am
- ☽ ☍ ♃ **7:00 pm** 4:00 pm

10 FRIDAY
- ☽ △ ♆ **8:19 am** 5:19 am
- ☉ ☌ ☿ **10:19 am** 7:19 am
- ☽ ☍ ☉ **2:21 pm** 11:21 am
- ☽ ☍ ☿ **2:33 pm** 11:33 am
- ☽ ☍ ♄ **6:43 pm** 3:43 pm
- ☽ ☍ ♇ **6:58 pm** 3:58 pm
- ☽ ⚻ ♀ 11:12 pm

11 SATURDAY
- ☽ ⚻ ♀ **2:12 am**
- ☽ □ ♅ **11:43 am** 8:43 am
- ☽ △ ♂ **4:54 pm** 1:54 pm
- ☽ ⚻ ♃ **10:43 pm** 7:43 pm

12 SUNDAY
- ☿ ☌ ♄ **4:51 am** 1:51 am
- ☿ ☌ ♇ **5:14 am** 2:14 am
- ☽ ⚻ ♆ **10:50 am** 7:50 am
- ♄ ☌ ♇ **11:59 am** 8:59 am
- ☽ ⚻ ☉ **8:23 pm** 5:23 pm
- ☽ ⚻ ♇ **9:12 pm** 6:12 pm
- ☽ ⚻ ♄ **9:15 pm** 6:15 pm
- ☽ ⚻ ☿ **11:13 pm** 8:13 pm

13 MONDAY
- ☉ ☌ ♇ **8:21 am** 5:21 am
- ☽ ☍ ♀ **8:42 am** 5:42 am
- ☉ ☌ ♄ **10:15 am** 7:15 am
- ☽ △ ♅ **1:29 pm** 10:29 am
- ☽ □ ♂ **9:00 pm** 6:00 pm
- ☽ △ ♃ 10:07 pm

14 TUESDAY
- ☽ △ ♃ **1:07 am**
- ☽ ☍ ♆ **12:27 pm** 9:27 am
- ☽ △ ♇ **10:51 pm** 7:51 pm
- ☽ △ ♄ **11:12 pm** 8:12 pm
- ☽ △ ☉ 10:41 pm

15 WEDNESDAY
- ☽ △ ☉ **1:41 am**
- ☽ △ ☿ **7:12 am** 4:12 am
- ☽ ⚻ ♀ **2:52 pm** 11:52 am
- ☽ ⚻ ♅ **3:09 pm** 12:09 pm
- ♀ ⚹ ♅ **6:18 pm** 3:18 pm
- ☽ ⚹ ♂ 10:14 pm

16 THURSDAY
- ☽ ⚹ ♂ **1:14 am**
- ☽ □ ♃ **3:45 am** 12:45 am
- ☽ ⚻ ♆ **2:36 pm** 11:36 am
- ☽ □ ♇ 10:16 pm
- ☽ □ ♄ 10:56 pm

17 FRIDAY
- ☽ □ ♇ **1:16 am**
- ☽ □ ♄ **1:56 am**
- ☽ □ ☉ **7:58 am** 4:58 am
- ☽ □ ☿ **4:36 pm** 1:36 pm
- ☽ ☍ ♅ **5:55 pm** 2:55 pm
- ☽ △ ♀ **10:26 pm** 7:26 pm

18 SATURDAY
- ☿ □ ♅ **3:32 am** 12:32 am
- ☽ ⚺ ♂ **6:56 am** 3:56 am
- ☽ ⚹ ♃ **7:45 am** 4:45 am
- ☽ △ ♆ **6:13 pm** 3:13 pm

19 SUNDAY
- ☽ ⚹ ♇ **5:18 am** 2:18 am
- ☽ ⚹ ♄ **6:19 am** 3:19 am
- ♂ ⚺ ♃ **7:46 am** 4:46 am
- ☽ ⚹ ☉ **4:22 pm** 1:22 pm
- ☽ ⚻ ♅ **10:28 pm** 7:28 pm

20 MONDAY
- ☽ ⚹ ☿ **4:40 am** 1:40 am
- ☽ □ ♀ **8:20 am** 5:20 am
- ☽ ⚺ ♃ **1:42 pm** 10:42 am
- ☽ ☌ ♂ **2:47 pm** 11:47 am
- ☽ □ ♆ **11:46 pm** 8:46 pm

21 TUESDAY
- ☽ ⚺ ♇ **11:17 am** 8:17 am
- ☽ ⚺ ♄ **12:41 pm** 9:41 am

22 WEDNESDAY
- ☽ ⚺ ☉ **3:14 am** 12:14 am
- ☽ △ ♅ **5:00 am** 2:00 am
- ☽ ⚺ ☿ **7:47 pm** 4:47 pm
- ☽ ⚹ ♀ **8:52 pm** 5:52 pm
- ☽ ☌ ♃ **9:45 pm** 6:45 pm
- ☽ ⚺ ♂ 9:58 pm
- ☉ □ ♅ 10:54 pm

23 THURSDAY
- ☽ ⚺ ♂ **12:58 am**
- ☉ □ ♅ **1:54 am**
- ☽ ⚹ ♆ **7:20 am** 4:20 am
- ♀ ⚹ ♃ **8:07 am** 5:07 am
- ☿ ⚺ ♃ **12:17 pm** 9:17 am
- ☽ ☌ ♇ **7:18 pm** 4:18 pm
- ☿ ⚺ ♀ **8:07 pm** 5:07 pm
- ☽ ☌ ♄ **9:08 pm** 6:08 pm

24 FRIDAY
- ☽ □ ♅ **1:34 pm** 10:34 am
- ☽ ☌ ☉ **4:42 pm** 1:42 pm

25 SATURDAY
- ☽ ⚺ ♃ **7:56 am** 4:56 am
- ☿ ⚹ ♂ **8:09 am** 5:09 am
- ☽ ⚺ ♀ **12:08 pm** 9:08 am
- ☽ ⚹ ♂ **1:34 pm** 10:34 am
- ☽ ☌ ☿ **2:06 pm** 11:06 am
- ☽ ⚺ ♆ **4:58 pm** 1:58 pm

26 SUNDAY
- ☽ ⚺ ♇ **5:23 am** 2:23 am
- ☽ ⚺ ♄ **7:42 am** 4:42 am
- ☿ ⚺ ♆ **10:50 am** 7:50 am
- ♀ □ ♂ **8:37 pm** 5:37 pm
- ☽ ⚹ ♅ 9:12 pm

27 MONDAY
- ☽ ⚹ ♅ **12:12 am**
- ☽ ⚺ ☉ **8:47 am** 5:47 am
- ♀ ☌ ♆ **3:00 pm** 12:00 pm
- ☽ ⚹ ♃ **8:13 pm** 5:13 pm

28 TUESDAY
- ☽ □ ♂ **4:30 am** 1:30 am
- ☽ ☌ ♆ **4:34 am** 1:34 am
- ♂ □ ♆ **5:34 am** 2:34 am
- ☽ ☌ ♀ **6:02 am** 3:02 am
- ☽ ⚺ ☿ **11:27 am** 8:27 am
- ☽ ⚹ ♇ **5:21 pm** 2:21 pm
- ☽ ⚹ ♄ **8:08 pm** 5:08 pm

29 WEDNESDAY
- ☽ ⚺ ♅ **12:31 pm** 9:31 am
- ☽ ⚹ ☉ 11:50 pm

30 THURSDAY
- ☽ ⚹ ☉ **2:50 am**
- ☿ ⚺ ♇ **5:26 am** 2:26 am
- ☽ □ ♃ **9:54 am** 6:54 am
- ☽ ⚺ ♆ **5:21 pm** 2:21 pm
- ☽ △ ♂ **8:49 pm** 5:49 pm
- ☽ ⚺ ♀ 10:26 pm

31 FRIDAY
- ☽ ⚺ ♀ **1:26 am**
- ☿ ⚺ ♄ **4:26 am** 1:26 am
- ☽ □ ♇ **6:11 am** 3:11 am
- ☽ □ ♄ **9:24 am** 6:24 am
- ☽ ⚹ ☿ **10:10 am** 7:10 am
- ☽ ☌ ♅ 10:10 pm

Eastern time in bold type
Pacific time in medium type

JANUARY 2020

DATE	SID.TIME	SUN	MOON	NODE	MERCURY	VENUS	MARS	JUPITER	SATURN	URANUS	NEPTUNE	PLUTO	CERES	PALLAS	JUNO	VESTA	CHIRON
1 W	6 40 28	10♑00 34	16♋08	8♋28R	4♑23	14≈25	28♏23	6♑40	21♑24	2♉42R	16♓16	22♑23	17♐54	22♓52	17≏22	12≈08	1♈36
2 Th	6 44 25	11 01 44	28 01	8 23	5 58	15 38	29 03	6 54	21 31	2 41	16 17	22 25	18 18	23 17	17 34	12 08	1 37
3 F	6 48 21	12 02 54	9♍53	8 23D	7 33	16 52	29 44	7 08	21 38	2 41	16 18	22 27	18 42	23 41	17 46	12 09	1 38
4 Sa	6 52 18	13 04 04	21 50	8 23	9 08	18 05	0♐24	7 22	21 45	2 41	16 19	22 29	19 06	24 06	17 58	12 11	1 39
5 Su	6 56 14	14 05 13	3♎55	8 23	10 44	19 18	1 05	7 35	21 52	2 40	16 21	22 31	19 30	24 31	18 09	12 13	1 40
6 M	7 0 11	15 06 22	16 14	8 24	12 20	20 32	1 45	7 49	21 59	2 40	16 22	22 33	19 54	24 56	18 21	12 16	1 42
7 T	7 4 7	16 07 31	28 50	8 24	13 56	21 45	2 25	8 03	22 06	2 39	16 23	22 35	20 18	25 21	18 32	12 20	1 43
8 W	7 8 4	17 08 39	11♏47	8 25	15 33	22 58	3 06	8 17	22 13	2 39	16 25	22 37	20 42	25 45	18 42	12 23	1 44
9 Th	7 12 1	18 09 48	25 05	8 26	17 10	24 11	3 46	8 31	22 20	2 39	16 26	22 39	21 06	26 10	18 53	12 27	1 46
10 F	7 15 57	19 10 56	8♐44	8 26R	18 47	25 24	4 27	8 44	22 27	2 39	16 27	22 41	21 30	26 35	19 03	12 32	1 47
11 Sa	7 19 54	20 12 03	22 44	8 26	20 25	26 37	5 08	8 58	22 34	2 39D	16 29	22 43	21 54	26 59	19 13	12 37	1 49
12 Su	7 23 50	21 13 11	7♑00	8 25	22 04	27 50	5 48	9 12	22 42	2 39	16 30	22 45	22 18	27 24	19 22	12 42	1 50
13 M	7 27 47	22 14 18	21 27	8 23	23 43	29 03	6 29	9 25	22 49	2 39	16 32	22 47	22 42	27 48	19 32	12 47	1 52
14 T	7 31 43	23 15 25	6♒00	8 21	25 22	0♓16	7 09	9 39	22 56	2 39	16 33	22 49	23 06	28 12	19 41	12 53	1 54
15 W	7 35 40	24 16 31	20 32	8 19	27 02	1 29	7 50	9 53	23 03	2 39	16 35	22 51	23 30	28 37	19 50	13 00	1 55
16 Th	7 39 36	25 17 38	4♓58	8 18	28 42	2 42	8 31	10 06	23 10	2 40	16 36	22 53	23 54	29 01	19 58	13 06	1 57
17 F	7 43 33	26 18 44	19 14	8 17D	0≈23	3 54	9 11	10 20	23 17	2 40	16 38	22 55	24 18	29 25	20 06	13 14	1 59
18 Sa	7 47 30	27 19 51	3♈18	8 17	2 04	5 07	9 52	10 34	23 24	2 40	16 40	22 57	24 42	29 49	20 14	13 21	2 01
19 Su	7 51 26	28 20 57	17 08	8 18	3 46	6 20	10 33	10 47	23 31	2 41	16 41	22 59	25 06	0♈13	20 21	13 29	2 03
20 M	7 55 23	29 22 03	0♉44	8 19	5 28	7 32	11 13	11 01	23 38	2 41	16 43	23 01	25 30	0 38	20 26	13 37	2 05
21 T	7 59 19	0≈23 08	14 07	8 21	7 10	8 44	11 54	11 14	23 45	2 42	16 45	23 03	25 54	1 01	20 35	13 45	2 07
22 W	8 3 16	1 24 13	27 17	8 22R	8 53	9 57	12 35	11 28	23 53	2 42	16 46	23 05	26 18	1 25	20 42	13 54	2 09
23 Th	8 7 12	2 25 18	10♊14	8 22	10 36	11 09	13 16	11 41	24 00	2 43	16 48	23 07	26 41	1 49	20 48	14 04	2 11
24 F	8 11 9	3 26 22	23 00	8 21	12 20	12 21	13 57	11 54	24 07	2 43	16 50	23 09	27 05	2 13	20 54	14 13	2 13
25 Sa	8 15 6	4 27 26	5♋33	8 19	14 03	13 33	14 37	12 08	24 14	2 44	16 52	23 11	27 29	2 37	20 59	14 23	2 15
26 Su	8 19 2	5 28 28	17 56	8 16	15 46	14 45	15 18	12 21	24 21	2 45	16 53	23 13	27 53	3 00	21 04	14 33	2 17
27 M	8 22 59	6 29 30	0♌08	8 11	17 30	15 57	15 59	12 34	24 28	2 46	16 55	23 15	28 17	3 24	21 09	14 44	2 19
28 T	8 26 55	7 30 30	12 12	8 05	19 13	17 09	16 40	12 48	24 35	2 46	16 57	23 17	28 41	3 47	21 14	14 54	2 22
29 W	8 30 52	8 31 30	24 08	8 00	20 56	18 20	17 21	13 01	24 42	2 47	16 59	23 19	29 04	4 11	21 18	15 06	2 24
30 Th	8 34 48	9 32 28	6♍00	7 55	22 38	19 32	18 02	13 14	24 49	2 48	17 01	23 21	29 28	4 34	21 22	15 17	2 26
31 F	8 38 45	10 33 26	17 52	7 51	24 19	20 44	18 43	13 27	24 56	2 49	17 03	23 23	29 52	4 57	21 25	15 29	2 29

EPHEMERIS CALCULATED FOR 12 MIDNIGHT GREENWICH MEAN TIME. ALL OTHER DATA AND FACING ASPECTARIAN PAGE IN **EASTERN TIME (BOLD)** AND PACIFIC TIME (REGULAR).

FEBRUARY 2020

☽ Last Aspect day	ET / hr:mn / PT	asp	☽ Ingress sign day	ET / hr:mn / PT
3	**6:28 am** 3:28 am	□ ☿	♊ 3	**6:29 am** 3:29 am
5	**9:20 am** 6:20 am	□ ♀	♋ 5	**2:03 pm** 11:03 am
7	**10:43 am** 7:43 am	☍ ♄	♌ 7	**5:45 pm** 2:45 pm
9	**11:08 am** 8:08 am	△ ♂	♍ 9	**6:39 pm** 3:39 pm
11	**1:26 pm** 10:26 am	□ ♂	♎ 11	**6:37 pm** 3:37 pm
13	**4:40 pm** 1:40 pm	⚹ ♂	♏ 13	**7:37 pm** 4:37 pm
15	**5:20 pm** 2:20 pm	⚹ ♄	♐ 15	**11:07 pm** 8:07 pm
18	**4:03 am** 1:03 am	⚹ ☉	♑ 18	**5:37 am** 2:37 am
20	**9:18 am** 6:18 am	☌ ♄	♒ 20	**2:42 pm** 11:42 am
21	**11:08 pm** 8:08 pm	⚹ ♀	♓ 22	10:37 pm

☽ Last Aspect day	ET / hr:mn / PT	asp	☽ Ingress sign day	ET / hr:mn / PT
21	**11:08 pm** 8:08 pm	⚹ ♀	♓ 23	**1:37 am**
25	**9:12 am** 6:12 am	⚹ ♄	♈ 25	**1:47 pm** 10:47 am
27	**10:25 pm** 7:25 pm	□ ♄	♉ 27	11:30 pm
27	**10:25 pm** 7:25 pm	□ ♄	♉ 28	**2:30 am**

☽ Phases & Eclipses phase	day	ET / hr:mn / PT
2nd Quarter	1	**8:42 pm** 5:42 pm
Full Moon	8	11:33 pm
Full Moon	9	**2:33 am**
4th Quarter	15	**5:17 pm** 2:17 pm
New Moon	23	**10:32 am** 7:32 am

Planet Ingress	day	ET / hr:mn / PT
☿ ♓	3	**6:37 am** 3:37 am
♀ ♈	7	**3:02 pm** 12:02 pm
♂ ♑	16	**6:33 am** 3:33 am
☉ ♓	18	**11:57 pm** 8:57 pm

Planetary Motion	day	ET / hr:mn / PT
⚵ ℞	8	**12:59 pm** 9:59 am
☿ ℞	16	**7:54 pm** 4:54 pm

1 SATURDAY
☽ ☌ ♅ **1:10 am**
☽ □ ☉ **8:42 pm** 5:42 pm
☽ △ ♃ **11:12 pm** 8:12 pm
♀ ⚹ ♇ 11:07 pm

2 SUNDAY
♀ ⚹ ♇ **2:07 am**
☽ ⚹ ♆ **5:30 am** 2:30 am
☽ ⚻ ♂ **12:14 pm** 9:14 am
☽ △ ♇ **5:54 pm** 2:54 pm
☽ ⚹ ♀ **7:32 pm** 4:32 pm
☽ △ ♄ **9:24 pm** 6:24 pm

3 MONDAY
☽ □ ☿ **6:28 am** 3:28 am
☉ ⚺ ♃ **10:00 am** 7:00 am
☽ ⚺ ♅ **12:01 pm** 9:01 am
♀ ⚹ ♄ **5:01 pm** 2:01 pm

4 TUESDAY
☽ ⚻ ♃ **9:45 am** 6:45 am
☽ △ ☉ **11:20 am** 8:20 am
☽ □ ♆ **2:50 pm** 11:50 am
☽ ☍ ♂ 9:07 pm
☽ ⚻ ♇ 11:27 pm

5 WEDNESDAY
☽ ☍ ♂ **12:07 am**
☽ ⚻ ♇ **2:27 am**
☿ ⚹ ♅ **4:43 am** 1:43 am
☽ ⚻ ♄ **6:04 am** 3:04 am
☽ □ ♀ **9:20 am** 6:20 am
☽ ⚹ ♅ **7:17 pm** 4:17 pm
☽ △ ☿ **9:00 pm** 6:00 pm

6 THURSDAY
☉ ⚺ ♆ **9:39 am** 6:39 am
☽ ☍ ♃ **4:14 pm** 1:14 pm
☽ △ ♆ **8:15 pm** 5:15 pm
☽ ⚻ ☉ **9:03 pm** 6:03 pm
♂ ⚺ ♇ **11:03 pm** 8:03 pm

7 FRIDAY
☽ ☍ ♇ **7:02 am** 4:02 am
☽ ⚻ ♂ **7:26 am** 4:26 am
☽ ☍ ♄ **10:43 am** 7:43 am
☽ △ ♀ **5:59 pm** 2:59 pm
☽ □ ♅ **10:43 pm** 7:43 pm

8 SATURDAY
☽ ⚻ ☿ **5:26 am** 2:26 am
☽ ⚻ ♃ **7:04 pm** 4:04 pm
☽ ⚻ ♆ **10:15 pm** 7:15 pm
☽ ☍ ☉ 11:33 pm

9 SUNDAY
☽ ☍ ☉ **2:33 am**
☽ ⚻ ♇ **8:30 am** 5:30 am
☽ △ ♂ **11:08 am** 8:08 am
☽ ⚻ ♄ **12:17 pm** 9:17 am
☽ ⚻ ♀ **11:02 pm** 8:02 pm
☽ △ ♅ **11:31 pm** 8:31 pm

10 MONDAY
♀ ⚺ ♅ **5:23 am** 2:23 am
☽ ☍ ☿ **9:51 am** 6:51 am
♂ ⚺ ♄ **4:30 pm** 1:30 pm

☽ △ ♃ **7:55 pm** 4:55 pm
☽ ☍ ♆ **10:29 pm** 7:29 pm

11 TUESDAY
☽ ⚻ ☉ **6:05 am** 3:05 am
☽ △ ♇ **8:36 am** 5:36 am
☽ △ ♄ **12:37 pm** 9:37 am
☽ □ ♂ **1:26 pm** 10:26 am
☽ ⚻ ♅ **11:36 pm** 8:36 pm

12 WEDNESDAY
☽ ☍ ♀ **3:06 am** 12:06 am
☽ ⚻ ☿ **12:55 pm** 9:55 am
☉ ⚺ ♇ **8:25 pm** 5:25 pm
☽ □ ♃ **8:54 pm** 5:54 pm
☽ ⚻ ♆ **10:57 pm** 7:57 pm

13 THURSDAY
☽ □ ♇ **9:20 am** 6:20 am
☽ △ ☉ **10:17 am** 7:17 am
☽ □ ♄ **1:46 pm** 10:46 am
☽ ⚹ ♂ **4:40 pm** 1:40 pm
☽ ☍ ♅ 9:54 pm

14 FRIDAY
☽ ☍ ♅ **12:54 am**
☽ ⚻ ♀ **8:52 am** 5:52 am
☽ △ ☿ **4:43 pm** 1:43 pm
☽ ⚹ ♃ **11:52 pm** 8:52 pm
☽ △ ♆ 10:25 pm

15 SATURDAY
☽ △ ♆ **1:25 am**
☽ ⚹ ♇ **12:21 pm** 9:21 am
☽ □ ☉ **5:17 pm** 2:17 pm

☽ ⚹ ♄ **5:20 pm** 2:20 pm
☉ ⚺ ♄ **5:57 pm** 2:57 pm
☽ ⚺ ♂ **10:43 pm** 7:43 pm

16 SUNDAY
☽ ⚻ ♅ **4:49 am** 1:49 am
☽ △ ♀ **6:06 pm** 3:06 pm
☽ □ ☿ **10:10 pm** 7:10 pm

17 MONDAY
☽ ⚺ ♃ **5:52 am** 2:52 am
☽ □ ♆ **6:49 am** 3:49 am
☽ ⚺ ♇ **6:22 pm** 3:22 pm
☽ ⚺ ♄ **11:58 pm** 8:58 pm

18 TUESDAY
☽ ⚹ ☉ **4:03 am** 1:03 am
☽ ☌ ♂ **8:16 am** 5:16 am
☽ △ ♅ **11:45 am** 8:45 am
☿ ⚺ ♀ **12:02 pm** 9:02 am

19 WEDNESDAY
☽ ⚹ ☿ **4:56 am** 1:56 am
☽ □ ♀ **7:08 am** 4:08 am
☽ ☌ ♃ **2:50 pm** 11:50 am
☽ ⚹ ♆ **3:05 pm** 12:05 pm

20 THURSDAY
☽ ☌ ♇ **3:07 am** 12:07 am
☽ ☌ ♄ **9:18 am** 6:18 am
♃ ⚹ ♆ **10:56 am** 7:56 am
☽ ⚺ ☉ **6:08 pm** 3:08 pm
☽ ⚺ ♂ **8:50 pm** 5:50 pm
☽ □ ♅ **9:13 pm** 6:13 pm

21 FRIDAY
♂ △ ♅ **4:10 am** 1:10 am
☽ ⚺ ☿ **12:15 pm** 9:15 am
☽ ⚹ ♀ **11:08 pm** 8:08 pm
☽ ⚺ ♆ 10:31 pm
☽ ⚺ ♃ 11:02 pm

22 SATURDAY
☽ ⚺ ♆ **1:31 am**
☽ ⚺ ♃ **2:02 am**
☉ ⚹ ♅ **9:13 am** 6:13 am
☽ ⚺ ♇ **1:51 pm** 10:51 am
☽ ⚺ ♄ **8:36 pm** 5:36 pm
♀ ⚺ ♆ 10:27 pm

23 SUNDAY
♀ ⚺ ♆ **1:27 am**
☽ ⚹ ♅ **8:29 am** 5:29 am
☽ ☌ ☉ **10:32 am** 7:32 am
☽ ⚹ ♂ **11:30 am** 8:30 am
♀ □ ♃ **11:59 am** 8:59 am
☽ ☌ ☿ **7:39 pm** 4:39 pm

24 MONDAY
☽ ☌ ♆ **1:26 pm** 10:26 am
☽ ⚹ ♃ **2:45 pm** 11:45 am
☽ ⚺ ♀ **5:05 pm** 2:05 pm
☉ ⚹ ♂ **9:06 pm** 6:06 pm
☽ ⚹ ♇ 10:57 pm

25 TUESDAY
☽ ⚹ ♇ **1:57 am**
☽ ⚹ ♄ **9:12 am** 6:12 am
☉ ☌ ☿ **8:45 pm** 5:45 pm

☽ ⚺ ♅ **8:56 pm** 5:56 pm
☿ ⚹ ♂ 9:59 pm

26 WEDNESDAY
☿ ⚹ ♂ **12:59 am**
☽ ⚺ ☿ **3:11 am** 12:11 am
☽ □ ♂ **3:32 am** 12:32 am
☽ ⚺ ☉ **4:26 am** 1:26 am
☽ ⚺ ♆ 11:14 pm

27 THURSDAY
☽ ⚺ ♆ **2:14 am**
☽ □ ♃ **4:22 am** 1:22 am
☽ ☌ ♀ **12:05 pm** 9:05 am
☽ □ ♇ **2:47 pm** 11:47 am
☽ □ ♄ **10:25 pm** 7:25 pm

28 FRIDAY
☽ ☌ ♅ **9:50 am** 6:50 am
☽ ⚹ ☿ **10:51 am** 7:51 am
♀ □ ♇ **5:08 pm** 2:08 pm
☽ △ ♂ **7:56 pm** 4:56 pm
☿ ⚹ ♅ **10:13 pm** 7:13 pm
☽ ⚹ ☉ **10:40 pm** 7:40 pm

29 SATURDAY
☽ ⚹ ♆ **2:50 pm** 11:50 am
☽ △ ♃ **5:41 pm** 2:41 pm

Eastern time in bold type
Pacific time in medium type

FEBRUARY 2020

DATE	SID.TIME	SUN	MOON	NODE	MERCURY	VENUS	MARS	JUPITER	SATURN	URANUS	NEPTUNE	PLUTO	CERES	PALLAS	JUNO	VESTA	CHIRON
1 Sa	8 42 41	11♒34 22	29♓46	7♋49R	25♒59	21♓55	19♐24	13♑40	25♑03	2♉50	17♓05	23♑25	0♒16	5♐20	21♎28	15♐41	2♈31
2 Su	8 46 38	12 35 17	11♉48	7 48	27 37	23 06	20 05	13 53	25 10	2 51	17 07	23 27	0 40	5 43	21 31	15 53	2 34
3 M	8 50 34	13 36 10	24 03	7 48	29 14	24 17	20 46	14 06	25 16	2 53	17 09	23 29	1 03	6 06	21 33	16 05	2 36
4 T	8 54 31	14 37 02	6♊35	7 50	0♓48	25 29	21 27	14 19	25 23	2 54	17 11	23 31	1 27	6 29	21 35	16 18	2 39
5 W	8 58 28	15 37 53	19 28	7 51	2 20	26 40	22 08	14 32	25 30	2 55	17 13	23 33	1 50	6 52	21 37	16 31	2 42
6 Th	9 2 24	16 38 43	2♋47	7 53R	3 48	27 50	22 49	14 45	25 37	2 56	17 15	23 34	2 14	7 15	21 38	16 45	2 44
7 F	9 6 21	17 39 31	16 33	7 52	5 11	29 01	23 30	14 58	25 44	2 58	17 17	23 36	2 38	7 37	21 39	16 58	2 47
8 Sa	9 10 17	18 40 18	0♌45	7 50	6 31	0♈12	24 11	15 10	25 50	2 59	17 19	23 38	3 01	8 00	21 39R	17 12	2 50
9 Su	9 14 14	19 41 03	15 21	7 46	7 44	1 22	24 52	15 23	25 57	3 01	17 21	23 40	3 25	8 22	21 39	17 26	2 52
10 M	9 18 10	20 41 47	0♍13	7 40	8 52	2 32	25 33	15 35	26 04	3 02	17 23	23 42	3 48	8 44	21 39	17 41	2 55
11 T	9 22 7	21 42 30	15♍14	7 34	9 53	3 43	26 14	15 48	26 11	3 04	17 25	23 44	4 12	9 07	21 38	17 56	2 58
12 W	9 26 4	22 43 11	0♎14	7 27	10 46	4 53	26 55	16 00	26 17	3 05	17 27	23 46	4 35	9 29	21 37	18 10	3 01
13 Th	9 30 0	23 43 52	15 04	7 20	11 30	6 03	27 36	16 13	26 24	3 07	17 29	23 47	4 59	9 51	21 36	18 25	3 04
14 F	9 33 57	24 44 31	29 38	7 16	12 06	7 12	28 18	16 25	26 30	3 08	17 31	23 49	5 22	10 13	21 34	18 41	3 07
15 Sa	9 37 53	25 45 09	13♏50	7 13D	12 32	8 22	28 59	16 37	26 37	3 10	17 33	23 51	5 45	10 35	21 32	18 56	3 10
16 Su	9 41 50	26 45 46	27 40	7 12	12 48	9 31	29 40	16 50	26 43	3 12	17 36	23 53	6 08	10 56	21 29	19 12	3 12
17 M	9 45 46	27 46 22	11♐08	7 13	12 53R	10 40	0♑21	17 02	26 50	3 14	17 38	23 54	6 32	11 18	21 26	19 28	3 15
18 T	9 49 43	28 46 57	24 17	7 14	12 49	11 50	1 03	17 14	26 56	3 16	17 40	23 56	6 55	11 39	21 23	19 44	3 18
19 W	9 53 39	29 47 31	7♑09	7 16R	12 33	12 59	1 44	17 26	27 03	3 18	17 42	23 58	7 18	12 01	21 19	20 01	3 22
20 Th	9 57 36	0♓48 03	19 47	7 14	12 08	14 08	2 25	17 38	27 09	3 20	17 44	24 00	7 41	12 22	21 15	20 17	3 25
21 F	10 1 33	1 48 34	2♒13	7 11	11 34	15 16	3 07	17 50	27 15	3 22	17 46	24 01	8 04	12 43	21 11	20 34	3 28
22 Sa	10 5 29	2 49 03	14 30	7 05	10 51	16 25	3 48	18 01	27 22	3 24	17 49	24 03	8 27	13 04	21 06	20 51	3 31
23 Su	10 9 26	3 49 31	26 40	6 57	10 01	17 33	4 29	18 13	27 28	3 26	17 51	24 05	8 50	13 25	21 00	21 08	3 34
24 M	10 13 22	4 49 57	8♓43	6 46	9 04	18 41	5 11	18 25	27 34	3 28	17 53	24 06	9 13	13 46	20 55	21 26	3 37
25 T	10 17 19	5 50 22	20 41	6 34	8 04	19 49	5 52	18 36	27 40	3 30	17 55	24 08	9 36	14 07	20 49	21 43	3 40
26 W	10 21 15	6 50 44	2♈26	6 22	7 00	20 57	6 33	18 48	27 46	3 32	17 58	24 09	9 59	14 27	20 42	22 01	3 44
27 Th	10 25 12	7 51 05	14 26	6 11	5 55	22 05	7 15	18 59	27 52	3 34	18 00	24 11	10 22	14 48	20 35	22 19	3 47
28 F	10 29 8	8 51 24	26 17	6 01	4 50	23 12	7 56	19 10	27 58	3 37	18 02	24 12	10 45	15 08	20 28	22 37	3 50
29 Sa	10 33 5	9 51 42	8♉11	5 54	3 48	24 19	8 38	19 22	28 04	3 39	18 04	24 14	11 08	15 28	20 21	22 56	3 53

EPHEMERIS CALCULATED FOR 12 MIDNIGHT GREENWICH MEAN TIME. ALL OTHER DATA AND FACING ASPECTARIAN PAGE IN **EASTERN TIME (BOLD)** AND PACIFIC TIME (REGULAR).

MARCH 2020

Eastern time in bold type
Pacific time in medium type

MARCH 2020

DATE	SID.TIME	SUN	MOON	NODE	MERCURY	VENUS	MARS	JUPITER	SATURN	URANUS	NEPTUNE	PLUTO	CERES	PALLAS	JUNO	VESTA	CHIRON
1 Su	10 37 1	10♓51 57	20♊12	5♋49R	2♓48R	25♈26	9♐19	19♑33	28♑10	3♉41	18♓07	24♑16	11♒30	15♐48	20♎13R	23♑14	3♈57
2 M	10 40 58	11 52 10	2♋23	5 47D	1 53	26 33	10 01	19 44	28 16	3 44	18 09	24 17	11 53	16 06	20 05	23 33	4 00
3 T	10 44 55	12 52 21	14 49	5 47	1 03	27 39	10 42	19 55	28 21	3 46	18 11	24 18	12 15	16 28	19 56	23 52	4 03
4 W	10 48 51	13 52 30	27 36	5 47R	0 18	28 45	11 23	20 05	28 27	3 49	18 13	24 20	12 38	16 47	19 47	24 11	4 07
5 Th	10 52 48	14 52 37	10♋48	5 47	29♒41	29 51	12 05	20 16	28 33	3 51	18 16	24 21	13 00	17 07	19 38	24 30	4 10
6 F	10 56 44	15 52 42	24 28	5 46	29 09	0♉57	12 46	20 27	28 38	3 54	18 18	24 23	13 23	17 26	19 29	24 49	4 13
7 Sa	11 0 41	16 52 45	8♌39	5 42	28 45	2 03	13 28	20 37	28 44	3 56	18 20	24 24	13 45	17 45	19 19	25 09	4 17
8 Su	11 4 37	17 52 45	23 17	5 36	28 28	3 08	14 09	20 48	28 49	3 59	18 23	24 25	14 07	18 04	19 09	25 28	4 20
9 M	11 8 34	18 52 44	8♍19	5 27	28 17	4 13	14 51	20 58	28 55	4 02	18 25	24 27	14 30	18 23	18 58	25 48	4 24
10 T	11 12 30	19 52 40	23 35	5 16	28 13D	5 17	15 33	21 08	29 00	4 04	18 27	24 28	14 52	18 42	18 47	26 08	4 27
11 W	11 16 27	20 52 35	8♎54	5 05	28 15	6 22	16 14	21 18	29 06	4 07	18 29	24 29	15 14	19 00	18 36	26 28	4 31
12 Th	11 20 24	21 52 28	24 05	4 55	28 23	7 26	16 56	21 28	29 11	4 10	18 32	24 31	15 36	19 19	18 25	26 48	4 34
13 F	11 24 20	22 52 19	8♏58	4 47	28 37	8 30	17 37	21 38	29 16	4 12	18 34	24 32	15 58	19 37	18 14	27 08	4 37
14 Sa	11 28 17	23 52 08	23 26	4 42	28 56	9 33	18 19	21 48	29 21	4 15	18 36	24 33	16 20	19 55	18 02	27 29	4 41
15 Su	11 32 13	24 51 56	7♐26	4 39	29 21	10 36	19 01	21 58	29 26	4 18	18 38	24 34	16 42	20 13	17 50	27 49	4 44
16 M	11 36 10	25 51 42	20 59	4 38D	29 50	11 39	19 42	22 07	29 31	4 21	18 41	24 35	17 03	20 31	17 37	28 10	4 48
17 T	11 40 6	26 51 27	4♑06	4 38	0♓23	12 42	20 24	22 17	29 36	4 24	18 43	24 37	17 25	20 48	17 25	28 31	4 51
18 W	11 44 3	27 51 09	16 52	4 36	1 01	13 44	21 05	22 26	29 41	4 27	18 45	24 38	17 47	21 06	17 12	28 52	4 55
19 Th	11 47 59	28 50 50	29 21	4 34	1 43	14 46	21 47	22 35	29 45	4 30	18 47	24 39	18 08	21 23	16 59	29 13	4 58
20 F	11 51 56	29 50 29	11♒37	4 31	2 29	15 47	22 29	22 45	29 50	4 32	18 50	24 40	18 30	21 40	16 46	29 34	5 02
21 Sa	11 55 53	0♈50 07	23 43	4 24	3 18	16 48	23 10	22 54	29 55	4 35	18 52	24 41	18 51	21 57	16 33	29 55	5 06
22 Su	11 59 49	1 49 42	5♓43	4 14	4 10	17 49	23 52	23 02	29 59	4 38	18 54	24 42	19 12	22 13	16 19	0♒17	5 09
23 M	12 3 46	2 49 16	17 38	4 06	5 05	18 49	24 34	23 11	0≈04	4 42	18 56	24 43	19 34	22 30	16 06	0 38	5 13
24 T	12 7 42	3 48 47	29 31	3 46	6 03	19 49	25 16	23 20	0 08	4 45	18 59	24 44	19 55	22 46	15 52	1 00	5 16
25 W	12 11 39	4 48 17	11♈23	3 32	7 04	20 48	25 57	23 28	0 12	4 48	19 01	24 45	20 16	23 02	15 38	1 22	5 20
26 Th	12 15 35	5 47 44	23 15	3 17	8 08	21 47	26 39	23 37	0 17	4 51	19 03	24 46	20 37	23 18	15 24	1 44	5 23
27 F	12 19 32	6 47 09	5♉09	3 05	9 14	22 46	27 21	23 45	0 21	4 54	19 05	24 47	20 58	23 34	15 10	2 06	5 27
28 Sa	12 23 28	7 46 33	17 07	2 49	10 22	23 44	28 02	23 53	0 25	4 57	19 07	24 47	21 19	23 49	14 56	2 28	5 30
29 Su	12 27 25	8 45 54	29 10	2 49	11 33	24 41	28 44	24 01	0 29	5 00	19 10	24 48	21 39	24 04	14 41	2 50	5 34
30 M	12 31 21	9 45 12	11♊23	2 45	12 46	25 38	29 26	24 09	0 33	5 03	19 12	24 49	22 00	24 19	14 27	3 12	5 37
31 T	12 35 18	10 44 23	23 49	2 44D	14 00	26 35	0♑07	24 16	0 37	5 07	19 14	24 50	22 21	24 34	14 13	3 34	5 41

EPHEMERIS CALCULATED FOR 12 MIDNIGHT GREENWICH MEAN TIME. ALL OTHER DATA AND FACING ASPECTARIAN PAGE IN **EASTERN TIME (BOLD)** AND PACIFIC TIME (REGULAR).

APRIL 2020

☽ Last Aspect day	ET / hr:mn / PT	asp	☽ Ingress sign	day	ET / hr:mn / PT
2	**12:49 pm** 9:49 am	✶ ♀	♌	2	**2:26 pm** 11:26 am
3	**3:29 pm** 12:29 pm	△ ⊙	♍	4	**5:18 pm** 2:18 pm
6	**9:29 am** 6:29 am	△ ♃	♎	6	**5:16 pm** 2:16 pm
8	**8:50 am** 5:50 am	☐ ♃	♏	8	**4:17 pm** 1:17 pm
10	**3:35 pm** 12:35 pm	△ ☿	♐	10	**4:35 pm** 1:35 pm
12	**7:46 am** 4:46 am	△ ⊙	♑	12	**8:05 pm** 5:05 pm
14	**7:47 pm** 4:47 pm	☌ ♃	♒	15	**3:37 am** 12:37 am
17	**10:34 am** 7:34 am	✶ ⊙	♓	17	**2:29 pm** 11:29 am
19	**7:31 pm** 4:31 pm	✶ ♃	♈	20	**3:00 am** 12:00 am
22	**8:32 am** 5:32 am	☐ ♃	♉	22	**3:36 pm** 12:36 pm

☽ Last Aspect day	ET / hr:mn / PT	asp	☽ Ingress sign	day	ET / hr:mn / PT
24	**8:43 pm** 5:43 pm	△ ♃	♊	25	**3:20 am** 12:20 am
27	**1:00 pm** 10:00 am	✶ ☿	♋	27	**1:28 pm** 10:28 am
29	**3:29 pm** 12:29 pm	☍ ♃	♌	29	**9:06 pm** 6:06 pm

☽ Phases & Eclipses phase	day	ET / hr:mn / PT
2nd Quarter	1	**6:21 am** 3:21 am
Full Moon	7	**10:35 pm** 7:35 pm
4th Quarter	14	**6:56 pm** 3:56 pm
New Moon	22	**10:26 pm** 7:26 pm
2nd Quarter	30	**4:38 pm** 1:38 pm

Planet Ingress		day	ET / hr:mn / PT
♀	♊	3	**1:11 pm** 10:11 am
☿	♈	10	9:48 pm
☿	♈	11	**12:48 am**
⊙	♉	19	**10:45 am** 7:45 am
⚳	♓	23	**4:20 pm** 1:20 pm
☿	♉	27	**3:53 pm** 12:53 pm
⚴	♒	29	**8:29 pm** 5:29 pm

Planetary Motion		day	ET / hr:mn / PT
♇	℞	25	**2:54 pm** 11:54 am

1 WEDNESDAY
☽ ☐ ⊙ **6:21 am** 3:21 am
☽ △ ☿ **1:51 pm** 10:51 am
☽ △ ♆ **7:23 pm** 4:23 pm

2 THURSDAY
☽ ☍ ♃ **4:49 am** 1:49 am
☽ ☍ ♇ **5:20 am** 2:20 am
☽ ✶ ♀ **12:49 pm** 9:49 am
☽ ☍ ♄ **3:49 pm** 12:49 pm
☽ ☍ ♂ **6:13 pm** 3:13 pm
☽ ☐ ♅ **11:40 pm** 8:40 pm

3 FRIDAY
☽ △ ⊙ **3:29 pm** 12:29 pm
☿ ☌ ♆ **9:15 pm** 6:15 pm
☽ ⚻ ♆ **11:42 pm** 8:42 pm
☽ ⚻ ☿ **11:58 pm** 8:58 pm

4 SATURDAY
☽ ⚻ ♃ **8:46 am** 5:46 am
☽ ⚻ ♇ **8:52 am** 5:52 am
♀ △ ♄ **1:09 pm** 10:09 am
☽ ⚻ ♄ **6:48 pm** 3:48 pm
☽ ☐ ♀ **7:08 pm** 4:08 pm
♃ ☌ ♇ **10:45 pm** 7:45 pm
☽ ⚻ ♂ **11:20 pm** 8:20 pm
☽ △ ♅ 11:06 pm

5 SUNDAY
☽ △ ♅ **2:06 am**
☽ ⚻ ⊙ **8:12 pm** 5:12 pm
☽ ☍ ♆ 9:38 pm

Eastern time in bold type
Pacific time in medium type

6 MONDAY
☽ ☍ ♆ **12:38 am**
☽ ☍ ☿ **5:49 am** 2:49 am
☽ △ ♇ **9:15 am** 6:15 am
☽ △ ♃ **9:29 am** 6:29 am
☽ △ ♄ **6:52 pm** 3:52 pm
☽ △ ♀ **9:56 pm** 6:56 pm
☽ △ ♂ 10:20 pm
☽ ⚻ ♅ 10:54 pm

7 TUESDAY
☽ △ ♂ **1:20 am**
☽ ⚻ ♅ **1:54 am**
♂ ☐ ♅ **2:50 pm** 11:50 am
☿ ✶ ♇ **5:28 pm** 2:28 pm
☿ ✶ ♃ **10:20 pm** 7:20 pm
☽ ☍ ⊙ **10:35 pm** 7:35 pm
☽ ⚻ ♆ **11:49 pm** 8:49 pm

8 WEDNESDAY
☽ ☐ ♇ **8:17 am** 5:17 am
☽ ☐ ♃ **8:50 am** 5:50 am
☽ ⚻ ☿ **9:54 am** 6:54 am
☽ ☐ ♄ **6:03 pm** 3:03 pm
⊙ ⚺ ♆ **6:34 pm** 3:34 pm
☽ ⚻ ♀ **11:46 pm** 8:46 pm
☽ ☍ ♅ 10:09 pm
☽ ☐ ♂ 11:41 pm

9 THURSDAY
☽ ☍ ♅ **1:09 am**
☽ ☐ ♂ **2:41 am**

☽ △ ♆ **11:32 pm** 8:32 pm
☽ ⚻ ⊙ 10:32 pm
♀ ⚺ ♅ 11:40 pm

10 FRIDAY
☽ ⚻ ⊙ **1:32 am**
♀ ⚺ ♅ **2:40 am**
☽ ✶ ♇ **8:15 am** 5:15 am
☽ ✶ ♃ **9:08 am** 6:08 am
☽ △ ☿ **3:35 pm** 12:35 pm
☽ ✶ ♄ **6:37 pm** 3:37 pm
☽ ⚻ ♅ 11:08 pm

11 SATURDAY
☽ ⚻ ♅ **2:08 am**
☽ ☍ ♀ **3:28 am** 12:28 am
☽ ✶ ♂ **6:03 am** 3:03 am
☿ ✶ ♄ **7:58 pm** 4:58 pm
☽ ☐ ♆ 10:53 pm

12 SUNDAY
☽ ☐ ♆ **1:53 am**
☽ △ ⊙ **7:46 am** 4:46 am
☽ ⚺ ♇ **11:09 am** 8:09 am
☽ ⚺ ♃ **12:26 pm** 9:26 am
☽ ⚺ ♄ **10:27 pm** 7:27 pm
☽ ☐ ☿ 11:00 pm

13 MONDAY
☽ ☐ ☿ **2:00 am**
☽ △ ♅ **6:36 am** 3:36 am
☽ ⚻ ♀ **11:10 am** 8:10 am
☽ ⚺ ♂ **1:33 pm** 10:33 am

14 TUESDAY
⊙ ☐ ♇ **7:07 am** 4:07 am
☽ ✶ ♆ **8:10 am** 5:10 am
☿ ⚺ ♅ **4:06 pm** 1:06 pm
☽ ☌ ♇ **6:02 pm** 3:02 pm
☽ ☐ ⊙ **6:56 pm** 3:56 pm
☽ ☌ ♃ **7:47 pm** 4:47 pm

15 WEDNESDAY
☽ ☌ ♄ **6:21 am** 3:21 am
⊙ ☐ ♃ **6:59 am** 3:59 am
☽ ☐ ♅ **3:09 pm** 12:09 pm
☽ ✶ ☿ **6:41 pm** 3:41 pm
☽ △ ♀ **11:29 pm** 8:29 pm
☽ ☌ ♂ 10:42 pm

16 THURSDAY
☽ ☌ ♂ **1:42 am**
☽ ⚺ ♆ **6:13 pm** 3:13 pm

17 FRIDAY
☽ ⚺ ♇ **4:28 am** 1:28 am
☽ ⚺ ♃ **6:43 am** 3:43 am
☽ ✶ ⊙ **10:34 am** 7:34 am
☽ ⚺ ♄ **5:32 pm** 2:32 pm
☿ ✶ ♀ 10:36 pm
☽ ✶ ♅ 11:47 pm

18 SATURDAY
☿ ✶ ♀ **1:36 am**
☽ ✶ ♅ **2:47 am**
☽ ☐ ♀ **2:57 pm** 11:57 am
☽ ⚺ ☿ **4:22 pm** 1:22 pm
☽ ⚺ ♂ **5:07 pm** 2:07 pm
☿ ✶ ♂ **11:55 pm** 8:55 pm

19 SUNDAY
☽ ☌ ♆ **6:32 am** 3:32 am
☽ ✶ ♇ **4:51 pm** 1:51 pm
☽ ✶ ♃ **7:31 pm** 4:31 pm

20 MONDAY
☽ ⚺ ⊙ **4:28 am** 1:28 am
☽ ✶ ♄ **6:16 am** 3:16 am
☽ ⚺ ♅ **3:43 pm** 12:43 pm

21 TUESDAY
⊙ ☐ ♄ **3:00 am** 12:00 am
☽ ✶ ♀ **7:17 am** 4:17 am
☽ ✶ ♂ **9:35 am** 6:35 am
☽ ☌ ☿ **4:06 pm** 1:06 pm
☽ ⚺ ♆ **7:23 pm** 4:23 pm

22 WEDNESDAY
☽ ☐ ♇ **5:31 am** 2:31 am
☽ ☐ ♃ **8:32 am** 5:32 am
☿ ⚺ ♆ **1:11 pm** 10:11 am
☽ ☐ ♄ **6:59 pm** 3:59 pm
☽ ☌ ⊙ **10:26 pm** 7:26 pm

23 THURSDAY
☽ ☌ ♅ **4:29 am** 1:29 am
☽ ⚺ ♀ **10:50 pm** 7:50 pm
☽ ☐ ♂ 10:30 pm

24 FRIDAY
☽ ☐ ♂ **1:30 am**
☽ ✶ ♆ **7:38 am** 4:38 am
☽ ⚺ ☿ **3:30 pm** 12:30 pm
☽ △ ♇ **5:27 pm** 2:27 pm
☽ △ ♃ **8:43 pm** 5:43 pm

25 SATURDAY
☿ ☐ ♇ **3:36 am** 12:36 am
☽ △ ♄ **6:47 am** 3:47 am
☽ ⚺ ⊙ **3:10 pm** 12:10 pm
☽ ⚺ ♅ **4:13 pm** 1:13 pm
☿ ☐ ♃ 9:31 pm

26 SUNDAY
☿ ☐ ♃ **12:31 am**
⊙ ☌ ♅ **5:01 am** 2:01 am
☽ ☌ ♀ **12:39 pm** 9:39 am
☽ △ ♂ **3:55 pm** 12:55 pm
☽ ☐ ♆ **6:31 pm** 3:31 pm

27 MONDAY
☽ ⚻ ♇ **3:54 am** 12:54 am
☽ ⚻ ♃ **7:20 am** 4:20 am
☽ ✶ ☿ **1:00 pm** 10:00 am
☽ ⚻ ♄ **4:54 pm** 1:54 pm
☽ ✶ ♅ 11:08 pm

28 TUESDAY
☽ ✶ ♅ **2:08 am**
☽ ✶ ⊙ **5:38 am** 2:38 am
☿ ☐ ♄ **1:28 pm** 10:28 am
♂ ⚺ ♆ **4:48 pm** 1:48 pm
☽ ⚺ ♀ **11:45 pm** 8:45 pm

29 WEDNESDAY
☽ △ ♆ **3:12 am** 12:12 am
☽ ⚻ ♂ **3:46 am** 12:46 am
☽ ☍ ♇ **12:01 pm** 9:01 am
☽ ☍ ♃ **3:29 pm** 12:29 pm
☽ ☍ ♄ 9:27 pm

30 THURSDAY
☽ ☍ ♄ **12:27 am**
☽ ☐ ☿ **6:46 am** 3:46 am
☽ ☐ ♅ **9:21 am** 6:21 am
☽ ☐ ⊙ **4:38 pm** 1:38 pm
☿ ☌ ♅ **11:41 pm** 8:41 pm

APRIL 2020

DATE	SID.TIME	SUN	MOON	NODE	MERCURY	VENUS	MARS	JUPITER	SATURN	URANUS	NEPTUNE	PLUTO	CERES	PALLAS	JUNO	VESTA	CHIRON
1 W	12 39 15	11♈43 43	6♋33	2♋44R	15♈17	27♓31	0≈49	24♑24	0≈40	5♉10	19♓16	24♑51	22≈41	24♑49	13♎59R	3♊57	5♈44
2 Th	12 43 11	12 42 55	19 39	2 44	16 36	28 26	1 31	24 31	0 44	5 13	19 18	24 52	23 01	25 03	13 44	4 19	5 48
3 F	12 47 8	13 42 05	3♌11	2 42	17 56	29 21	2 13	24 38	0 48	5 16	19 20	24 52	23 22	25 17	13 30	4 42	5 51
4 Sa	12 51 4	14 41 12	17 10	2 39	19 18	0♈15	2 54	24 46	0 51	5 20	19 23	24 53	23 42	25 31	13 16	5 05	5 55
5 Su	12 55 1	15 40 17	1♍39	2 33	20 42	1 09	3 36	24 52	0 55	5 23	19 25	24 53	24 02	25 45	13 01	5 28	5 58
6 M	12 58 57	16 39 19	16 32	2 25	22 08	2 02	4 18	24 59	0 58	5 26	19 27	24 54	24 22	25 58	12 47	5 50	6 02
7 T	13 2 54	17 38 19	1♎44	2 15	23 35	2 54	4 59	25 06	1 01	5 29	19 29	24 54	24 42	26 12	12 33	6 13	6 05
8 W	13 6 50	18 37 18	17 05	2 04	25 04	3 46	5 41	25 12	1 04	5 33	19 31	24 55	25 02	26 24	12 19	6 36	6 09
9 Th	13 10 47	19 36 14	2♏21	1 54	26 35	4 37	6 23	25 19	1 08	5 36	19 33	24 55	25 21	26 37	12 05	7 00	6 12
10 F	13 14 44	20 35 08	17 24	1 46	28 07	5 27	7 04	25 25	1 11	5 40	19 35	24 56	25 41	26 50	11 51	7 23	6 16
11 Sa	13 18 40	21 34 00	2✕03	1 41	29 41	6 16	7 46	25 31	1 13	5 43	19 37	24 56	26 00	27 02	11 37	7 46	6 19
12 Su	13 22 37	22 32 51	16 15	1 38	1♈16	7 05	8 28	25 37	1 16	5 46	19 39	24 57	26 20	27 14	11 24	8 09	6 23
13 M	13 26 33	23 31 40	29 57	1 37R	2 53	7 52	9 10	25 43	1 18	5 50	19 41	24 57	26 39	27 25	11 10	8 33	6 26
14 T	13 30 30	24 30 27	13♑11	1 37R	4 32	8 39	9 51	25 48	1 22	5 53	19 43	24 58	26 58	27 37	10 57	8 56	6 29
15 W	13 34 26	25 29 13	26 00	1 38	6 12	9 25	10 33	25 54	1 24	5 56	19 45	24 58	27 17	27 48	10 44	9 20	6 33
16 Th	13 38 23	26 27 56	8≈27	1 37	7 54	10 10	11 15	25 59	1 27	6 00	19 47	24 58	27 35	27 59	10 31	9 44	6 36
17 F	13 42 19	27 26 39	20 43	1 34	9 37	10 54	11 56	26 04	1 29	6 03	19 49	24 58	27 55	28 10	10 18	10 07	6 39
18 Sa	13 46 16	28 25 19	2♓45	1 29	11 22	11 37	12 38	26 09	1 31	6 07	19 50	24 59	28 13	28 20	10 06	10 31	6 43
19 Su	13 50 13	29 23 57	14 41	1 21	13 09	12 19	13 20	26 14	1 34	6 10	19 52	24 59	28 32	28 30	9 53	10 55	6 46
20 M	13 54 9	0♉22 34	26 32	1 12	14 57	13 00	14 01	26 18	1 36	6 14	19 54	24 59	28 50	28 40	9 41	11 19	6 49
21 T	13 58 6	1 21 09	8♈24	1 01	16 47	13 40	14 43	26 23	1 38	6 17	19 56	24 59	29 09	28 49	9 29	11 43	6 53
22 W	14 2 2	2 19 42	20 16	0 49	18 38	14 19	15 25	26 27	1 40	6 20	19 58	24 59	29 27	28 58	9 18	12 07	6 56
23 Th	14 5 59	3 18 13	2♉11	0 38	20 31	14 56	16 06	26 31	1 41	6 24	20 00	24 59	29 45	29 07	9 06	12 31	6 59
24 F	14 9 55	4 16 43	14 11	0 29	22 26	15 33	16 48	26 35	1 43	6 27	20 01	24 59	0♓03	29 15	8 55	12 55	7 02
25 Sa	14 13 52	5 15 11	26 17	0 21	24 22	16 08	17 29	26 39	1 45	6 31	20 03	25 00R	0 20	29 24	8 44	13 20	7 06
26 Su	14 17 48	6 13 36	8Ⅱ30	0 16	26 20	16 41	18 11	26 42	1 46	6 34	20 05	25 00	0 38	29 32	8 34	13 44	7 09
27 M	14 21 45	7 12 00	20 52	0 14D	28 20	17 13	18 52	26 45	1 48	6 38	20 07	25 00	0 56	29 39	8 24	14 08	7 12
28 T	14 25 42	8 10 22	3♋27	0 14	0♉21	17 44	19 34	26 49	1 49	6 41	20 08	24 59	1 13	29 46	8 14	14 33	7 15
29 W	14 29 38	9 08 41	16 16	0 14	2 23	18 13	20 15	26 52	1 50	6 45	20 10	24 59	1 30	29 53	8 04	14 57	7 18
30 Th	14 33 35	10 06 59	29 23	0 16R	4 27	18 41	20 57	26 54	1 51	6 48	20 12	24 59	1 47	0≈00	7 55	15 22	7 21

EPHEMERIS CALCULATED FOR 12 MIDNIGHT GREENWICH MEAN TIME. ALL OTHER DATA AND FACING ASPECTARIAN PAGE IN **EASTERN TIME (BOLD)** AND PACIFIC TIME (REGULAR).

MAY 2020

☽ Last Aspect day	ET / hr:mn / PT		asp	☽ Ingress sign	day	ET / hr:mn / PT	
1	**12:04 pm**	9:04 am	☍♂	♍	1		10:35 pm
1	**12:04 pm**	9:04 am	☍♂	♍	2	**1:35 am**	
3	**10:25 pm**	7:25 pm	△♃	♎	4	**3:09 am**	12:09 am
5	**10:31 pm**	7:31 pm	□♃	♏	6	**3:05 am**	12:05 am
7	**10:39 pm**	7:39 pm	⚹♃	♐	8	**3:15 am**	12:15 am
9		11:11 pm	⚹♂	♑	10	**5:39 am**	2:39 am
10	**2:11 am**		⚹♂	♑	10	**5:39 am**	2:39 am
12	**6:30 am**	3:30 am	☌♃	♒	12	**11:39 am**	8:39 am
14	**10:03 am**	7:03 am	□☉	♓	14	**9:24 pm**	6:24 pm
17	**3:59 am**	12:59 am	⚹♃	♈	17	**9:36 am**	6:36 am

☽ Last Aspect day	ET / hr:mn / PT		asp	☽ Ingress sign	day	ET / hr:mn / PT	
19	**4:33 pm**	1:33 pm	□♃	♉	19	**10:10 pm**	7:10 pm
22	**4:01 am**	1:01 am	△♃	♊	22	**9:36 am**	6:36 am
24	**7:09 am**	4:09 am	☌☿	♋	24	**7:09 pm**	4:09 pm
26	**9:06 pm**	6:06 pm	☍♃	♌	26		11:33 pm
26	**9:06 pm**	6:06 pm	☍♃	♌	27	**2:33 am**	
28	**9:30 am**	6:30 am	⚹♀	♍	29	**7:40 am**	4:40 am
31	**5:17 am**	2:17 am	△♃	♎	31	**10:38 am**	7:38 am

☽ Phases & Eclipses phase	day	ET / hr:mn / PT	
Full Moon	7	**6:45 am**	3:45 am
4th Quarter	14	**10:03 am**	7:03 am
New Moon	22	**1:39 pm**	10:39 am
2nd Quarter	29	**11:30 pm**	8:30 pm

Planet Ingress	day	ET / hr:mn / PT	
☿ ♊	11	**5:58 pm**	2:58 pm
♂ ♓	12		9:17 pm
♂ ♓	13	**12:17 am**	
☉ ♊	20	**9:49 am**	6:49 am
☿ ♋	28	**2:09 pm**	11:09 am

Planetary Motion	day	ET / hr:mn / PT	
♄ ℞	10		9:09 pm
♄ ℞	11	**12:09 am**	
♀ ℞	12		11:45 pm
♀ ℞	13	**2:45 am**	
♃ ℞	14	**10:32 am**	7:32 am
♇ ℞	17	**4:29 am**	1:29 am
⚵ D	26	**10:51 pm**	7:51 pm

1 FRIDAY
☽ ⚹ ♀ **7:16 am** 4:16 am
☽ ⚻ ♆ **8:51 am** 5:51 am
☽ ☍ ♂ **12:04 pm** 9:04 am
☽ ⚻ ♇ **5:02 pm** 2:02 pm
☽ ⚻ ♃ **8:28 pm** 5:28 pm

2 SATURDAY
☽ ⚻ ♄ **4:48 am** 1:48 am
☽ △ ♅ **1:19 pm** 10:19 am
☽ △ ☿ **7:38 pm** 4:38 pm
☽ △ ☉ **11:40 pm** 8:40 pm

3 SUNDAY
☽ □ ♀ **11:06 am** 8:06 am
☽ ☍ ♆ **11:22 am** 8:22 am
☽ ⚻ ♂ **4:47 pm** 1:47 pm
☽ △ ♇ **7:01 pm** 4:01 pm
☽ △ ♃ **10:25 pm** 7:25 pm
♀ □ ♆ **11:52 pm** 8:52 pm

4 MONDAY
☽ △ ♄ **6:15 am** 3:15 am
☽ ⚻ ♅ **2:32 pm** 11:32 am
☉ ☌ ☿ **5:41 pm** 2:41 pm

5 TUESDAY
☽ ⚻ ☉ **3:39 am** 12:39 am
☽ ⚻ ☿ **4:34 am** 1:34 am
☽ ⚻ ♆ **11:43 am** 8:43 am
☽ △ ♀ **12:23 pm** 9:23 am
♂ ⚺ ♇ **4:11 pm** 1:11 pm
☽ □ ♇ **7:05 pm** 4:05 pm
☽ △ ♂ **7:13 pm** 4:13 pm
☽ □ ♃ **10:31 pm** 7:31 pm

6 WEDNESDAY
☽ □ ♄ **6:10 am** 3:10 am
☽ ☍ ♅ **2:31 pm** 11:31 am

7 THURSDAY
☿ ⚹ ♆ **6:42 am** 3:42 am
☽ ☍ ☉ **6:45 am** 3:45 am
☽ △ ♆ **11:40 am** 8:40 am
☽ ☍ ☿ **12:30 pm** 9:30 am
☽ ⚻ ♀ **1:04 pm** 10:04 am
☿ ⚺ ♀ **4:39 pm** 1:39 pm
☽ ⚹ ♇ **7:03 pm** 4:03 pm
☽ □ ♂ **9:33 pm** 6:33 pm
☽ ⚹ ♃ **10:39 pm** 7:39 pm

8 FRIDAY
☽ ⚹ ♄ **6:27 am** 3:27 am
☽ ⚻ ♅ **3:15 pm** 12:15 pm
♂ ⚺ ♃ **9:53 pm** 6:53 pm

9 SATURDAY
☿ △ ♇ **9:17 am** 6:17 am
☽ ⚻ ☉ **11:35 am** 8:35 am
☽ □ ♆ **1:14 pm** 10:14 am
☽ ☍ ♀ **3:13 pm** 12:13 pm
☽ ⚺ ♇ **8:55 pm** 5:55 pm
☽ ⚻ ☿ **11:03 pm** 8:03 pm
☽ ⚺ ♃ 9:49 pm
☽ ⚹ ♂ 11:11 pm

10 SUNDAY
☽ ⚺ ♃ **12:49 am**
☽ ⚹ ♂ **2:11 am**
☽ ⚺ ♄ **9:03 am** 6:03 am
☿ △ ♃ **10:36 am** 7:36 am
☉ ⚹ ♆ **12:16 pm** 9:16 am
☽ △ ♅ **6:38 pm** 3:38 pm

11 MONDAY
☿ □ ♂ **3:33 am** 12:33 am
☽ ⚹ ♆ **6:05 pm** 3:05 pm
☽ △ ☉ **8:24 pm** 5:24 pm
☽ ⚻ ♀ **8:30 pm** 5:30 pm
☉ ⚺ ♀ **9:57 pm** 6:57 pm
☽ ☌ ♇ 11:14 pm

12 TUESDAY
☽ ☌ ♇ **2:14 am**
☽ ☌ ♃ **6:30 am** 3:30 am
☽ ⚺ ♂ **10:56 am** 7:56 am
☽ △ ☿ **3:07 pm** 12:07 pm
☽ ☌ ♄ **3:18 pm** 12:18 pm
☿ △ ♄ **4:14 pm** 1:14 pm
☽ □ ♅ 10:52 pm

13 WEDNESDAY
☽ □ ♅ **1:52 am**
☽ ⚺ ♆ 11:50 pm

14 THURSDAY
☽ ⚺ ♆ **2:50 am**
☽ △ ♀ **5:20 am** 2:20 am
☽ □ ☉ **10:03 am** 7:03 am
☽ ⚺ ♇ **11:23 am** 8:23 am
☽ ⚺ ♃ **3:58 pm** 12:58 pm
☽ ☌ ♂ 9:06 pm
☽ ⚺ ♄ 10:15 pm
☉ △ ♇ 11:49 pm

15 FRIDAY
☽ ☌ ♂ **12:06 am**
☽ ⚺ ♄ **1:15 am**
☉ △ ♇ **2:49 am**
☿ ⚺ ♅ **11:17 am** 8:17 am
☽ ⚹ ♅ **12:41 pm** 9:41 am
☽ □ ☿ **12:57 pm** 9:57 am
♂ ⚺ ♄ **8:25 pm** 5:25 pm

16 SATURDAY
☽ ☌ ♆ **2:34 pm** 11:34 am
☽ □ ♀ **4:35 pm** 1:35 pm
☽ ⚹ ♇ **11:15 pm** 8:15 pm

17 SUNDAY
☽ ⚹ ☉ **3:13 am** 12:13 am
☽ ⚹ ♃ **3:59 am** 12:59 am
☉ △ ♃ **12:40 pm** 9:40 am
☽ ⚹ ♄ **1:29 pm** 10:29 am
☽ ⚺ ♂ **4:01 pm** 1:01 pm
☽ ⚺ ♅ 10:27 pm

18 MONDAY
☽ ⚺ ♅ **1:27 am**
☽ ⚹ ☿ **1:17 pm** 10:17 am

19 TUESDAY
☽ ⚺ ♆ **3:20 am** 12:20 am
☽ ⚹ ♀ **4:17 am** 1:17 am
☽ □ ♇ **11:51 am** 8:51 am
☽ □ ♃ **4:33 pm** 1:33 pm
☽ ⚺ ☉ **9:09 pm** 6:09 pm
☽ □ ♄ 10:58 pm

20 WEDNESDAY
☽ □ ♄ **1:58 am**
☽ ⚹ ♂ **8:10 am** 5:10 am
☽ ☌ ♅ **2:07 pm** 11:07 am
♀ □ ♆ **7:03 pm** 4:03 pm

21 THURSDAY
☽ ⚺ ☿ **12:01 pm** 9:01 am
☽ ⚺ ♀ **2:46 pm** 11:46 am
☽ ⚹ ♆ **3:19 pm** 12:19 pm
☽ △ ♇ **11:29 pm** 8:29 pm

22 FRIDAY
☽ △ ♃ **4:01 am** 1:01 am
☿ ☌ ♀ **4:41 am** 1:41 am
☉ △ ♄ **8:02 am** 5:02 am
☿ □ ♆ **11:43 am** 8:43 am
☽ △ ♄ **1:12 pm** 10:12 am
☽ ☌ ☉ **1:39 pm** 10:39 am
☽ □ ♂ **10:43 pm** 7:43 pm
☽ ⚺ ♅ 10:20 pm

23 SATURDAY
☽ ⚺ ♅ **1:20 am**
☽ ☌ ♀ **11:15 pm** 8:15 pm
☽ □ ♆ 10:34 pm

24 SUNDAY
☽ □ ♆ **1:34 am**
☽ ☌ ☿ **7:09 am** 4:09 am
☽ ⚻ ♇ **9:19 am** 6:19 am
☽ ⚻ ♃ **1:38 pm** 10:38 am
☽ ⚻ ♄ **10:32 pm** 7:32 pm
☿ ⚻ ♇ 9:26 pm
♂ ⚹ ♅ 11:48 pm

25 MONDAY
☿ ⚻ ♇ **12:26 am**
♂ ⚹ ♅ **2:48 am**
☽ ⚺ ☉ **3:43 am** 12:43 am
☽ ⚹ ♅ **10:34 am** 7:34 am
☽ △ ♂ **10:58 am** 7:58 am

26 TUESDAY
☽ ⚺ ♀ **5:31 am** 2:31 am
☽ △ ♆ **9:43 am** 6:43 am
☿ ⚻ ♃ **11:35 am** 8:35 am
☽ ☍ ♇ **5:03 pm** 2:03 pm
☽ ☍ ♃ **9:06 pm** 6:06 pm
☽ ⚺ ☿ **10:19 pm** 7:19 pm

27 WEDNESDAY
☽ ☍ ♄ **5:42 am** 2:42 am
☽ ⚹ ☉ **3:02 pm** 12:02 pm
☽ □ ♅ **5:34 pm** 2:34 pm
☽ ⚻ ♂ **8:36 pm** 5:36 pm

28 THURSDAY
☽ ⚹ ♀ **9:30 am** 6:30 am
☽ ⚻ ♆ **3:36 pm** 12:36 pm
☽ ⚻ ♇ **10:31 pm** 7:31 pm
☽ ⚻ ♃ 11:17 pm

29 FRIDAY
☽ ⚻ ♃ **2:17 am**
☉ ⚺ ♅ **4:13 am** 1:13 am
☽ ⚹ ☿ **9:32 am** 6:32 am
☽ ⚻ ♄ **10:35 am** 7:35 am
☿ ⚻ ♄ **8:25 pm** 5:25 pm
☽ △ ♅ **10:15 pm** 7:15 pm
☽ □ ☉ **11:30 pm** 8:30 pm

30 SATURDAY
☽ ☍ ♂ **3:34 am** 12:34 am
☽ □ ♀ **11:18 am** 8:18 am
☽ ☍ ♆ **7:14 pm** 4:14 pm
☽ △ ♇ 10:46 pm

31 SUNDAY
☽ △ ♇ **1:46 am**
☽ △ ♃ **5:17 am** 2:17 am
☽ △ ♄ **1:20 pm** 10:20 am
☽ □ ☿ **5:16 pm** 2:16 pm
☽ ⚻ ♅ 9:52 pm

Eastern time in bold type
Pacific time in medium type

MAY 2020

DATE	SID.TIME	SUN	MOON	NODE	MERCURY	VENUS	MARS	JUPITER	SATURN	URANUS	NEPTUNE	PLUTO	CERES	PALLAS	JUNO	VESTA	CHIRON
1 F	14 37 31	11♉05 14	12♋52	06♑16R	8♊33	19♈07	21♑38	26♑57	1♒52	6♉52	20♓13	24♑59R	2♌04	0♒06	7♌45R	15♓46	7♈24
2 Sa	14 41 28	12 03 28	26 43	0 15	8 39	19 31	21 38	26 59	1 53	6 55	20 15	24 59	2 21	0 12	7 37	16 11	7 28
3 Su	14 45 24	13 01 39	10♌58	0 12	10 47	19 54	23 01	27 02	1 54	6 58	20 16	24 59	2 37	0 18	7 28	16 35	7 31
4 M	14 49 21	13 59 48	25 35	0 07	12 55	20 15	23 42	27 04	1 55	7 02	20 18	24 59	2 54	0 23	7 20	17 00	7 34
5 T	14 53 17	14 57 56	10♍29	0 01	15 05	20 34	24 23	27 06	1 56	7 05	20 19	24 58	3 10	0 28	7 12	17 25	7 36
6 W	14 57 14	15 56 01	25 33	29♑55	17 15	20 51	25 05	27 07	1 56	7 09	20 21	24 58	3 26	0 32	7 05	17 50	7 39
7 Th	15 01 11	16 54 05	10♎37	29 48	19 25	21 06	25 46	27 09	1 57	7 12	20 22	24 58	3 42	0 36	6 58	18 14	7 42
8 F	15 05 7	17 52 07	25 33	29 43	21 35	21 19	26 27	27 10	1 57	7 16	20 23	24 57	3 58	0 40	6 51	18 39	7 45
9 Sa	15 09 4	18 50 07	10♏10	29 40	23 45	21 29	27 08	27 11	1 57	7 19	20 25	24 57	4 14	0 43	6 45	19 04	7 48
10 Su	15 13 0	19 48 06	24 24	29 39D	25 55	21 38	27 49	27 12	1 57	7 22	20 26	24 57	4 29	0 47	6 39	19 29	7 51
11 M	15 16 57	20 46 04	8♐12	29 39	28 03	21 44	28 31	27 13	1 57R	7 26	20 28	24 56	4 44	0 49	6 33	19 54	7 54
12 T	15 20 53	21 44 00	21 32	29 40	0♊11	21 48	29 12	27 14	1 57	7 29	20 29	24 56	4 59	0 51	6 28	20 19	7 56
13 W	15 24 50	22 41 55	4♑27	29 41	2 17	21 50R	29 53	27 14	1 57	7 32	20 30	24 55	5 14	0 53	6 23	20 44	7 59
14 Th	15 28 46	23 39 49	17 01	29 43R	4 22	21 50	0♒34	27 14R	1 57	7 36	20 32	24 55	5 29	0 55	6 18	21 10	8 02
15 F	15 32 43	24 37 41	29 17	29 43	6 24	21 47	1 15	27 14	1 57	7 39	20 33	24 54	5 44	0 56	6 14	21 35	8 05
16 Sa	15 36 40	25 35 32	11♒21	29 41	8 25	21 42	1 56	27 14	1 56	7 42	20 34	24 54	5 58	0 57	6 10	22 00	8 07
17 Su	15 40 36	26 33 22	23 17	29 39	10 23	21 34	2 36	27 14	1 56	7 46	20 35	24 53	6 12	0 57R	6 06	22 25	8 10
18 M	15 44 33	27 31 11	5♓08	29 35	12 19	21 24	3 17	27 13	1 55	7 49	20 37	24 53	6 26	0 57	6 03	22 51	8 12
19 T	15 48 29	28 28 58	17 00	29 30	14 12	21 11	3 58	27 13	1 54	7 52	20 38	24 52	6 40	0 57	6 00	23 16	8 15
20 W	15 52 26	29 26 44	28 55	29 24	16 02	20 56	4 39	27 12	1 54	7 56	20 39	24 51	6 54	0 56	5 57	23 41	8 17
21 Th	15 56 22	0♊55	10♈55	29 19	17 50	20 39	5 19	27 11	1 53	7 59	20 40	24 51	7 07	0 54	5 55	24 07	8 20
22 F	16 0 19	1 22 13	23 04	29 15	19 35	20 19	6 00	27 09	1 52	8 02	20 41	24 50	7 20	0 53	5 53	24 32	8 22
23 Sa	16 4 15	2 19 56	5♉21	29 12	21 16	19 58	6 40	27 08	1 51	8 05	20 42	24 49	7 33	0 51	5 51	24 58	8 25
24 Su	16 8 12	3 17 37	17 48	29 10D	22 55	19 34	7 21	27 06	1 49	8 09	20 43	24 48	7 46	0 48	5 50	25 23	8 27
25 M	16 12 9	4 15 17	0♊27	29 09	24 30	19 07	8 01	27 04	1 48	8 12	20 44	24 48	7 59	0 45	5 49	25 49	8 29
26 T	16 16 5	5 12 56	13 18	29 10	26 02	18 39	8 42	27 02	1 47	8 15	20 45	24 47	8 11	0 42	5 49	26 14	8 31
27 W	16 20 2	6 10 33	26 23	29 11	27 31	18 09	9 22	27 00	1 45	8 18	20 46	24 46	8 23	0 38	5 48D	26 40	8 34
28 Th	16 23 58	7 08 09	9♊43	29 13	28 57	17 38	10 02	26 57	1 44	8 21	20 46	24 45	8 35	0 34	5 48	27 05	8 36
29 F	16 27 55	8 05 44	23 18	29 13	0♋20	17 07	10 42	26 55	1 42	8 24	20 47	24 44	8 47	0 29	5 49	27 31	8 38
30 Sa	16 31 51	9 03 17	7♋09	29 14R	1 39	16 35	11 22	26 52	1 40	8 27	20 48	24 43	8 58	0 24	5 50	27 57	8 40
31 Su	16 35 48	10 00 48	21 16	29 14	2 55	15 55	12 02	26 49	1 39	8 31	20 49	24 42	9 09	0 19	5 51	28 22	8 42

EPHEMERIS CALCULATED FOR 12 MIDNIGHT GREENWICH MEAN TIME. ALL OTHER DATA AND FACING ASPECTARIAN PAGE IN **EASTERN TIME (BOLD)** AND PACIFIC TIME (REGULAR).

JUNE 2020

☽ Last Aspect day	ET / hr:mn / PT		asp	☽ Ingress sign	day	ET / hr:mn / PT	
2	**6:40 am**	3:40 am	□♃	♏	2	**12:06 pm**	9:06 am
4	**7:36 am**	4:36 am	⚹♃	♐	4	**1:17 pm**	10:17 am
5		9:10 pm	□♆	♑	6	**3:44 pm**	12:44 pm
6	**12:10 am**		□♆	♑	6	**3:44 pm**	12:44 pm
8	**2:06 pm**	11:06 am	☌♃	♒	8	**8:54 pm**	5:54 pm
10	**10:35 am**	7:35 am	△☉	♓	11	**5:32 am**	2:32 am
13	**8:45 am**	5:45 am	⚹♃	♈	13	**5:03 pm**	2:03 pm
15	**8:49 pm**	5:49 pm	□♃	♉	16	**5:35 am**	2:35 am
18	**8:02 am**	5:02 am	△♃	♊	18	**5:00 pm**	2:00 pm
20	**5:48 pm**	2:48 pm	□♂	♋	20		11:02 pm
20	**5:48 pm**	2:48 pm	□♂	♋	21	**2:02 am**	
23	**3:20 am**	12:20 am	△♂	♌	23	**8:33 am**	5:33 am
23		10:34 pm	□♅	♍	25	**1:05 pm**	10:05 am
24	**1:34 am**		□♅	♍	25	**1:05 pm**	10:05 am
27	**4:02 pm**	1:02 pm	☍♂	♎	27	**4:16 pm**	1:16 pm
29	**9:02 am**	6:02 am	□♃	♏	29	**6:48 pm**	3:48 pm

☽ Phases & Eclipses phase	day	ET / hr:mn / PT	
Full Moon	5	**3:12 pm**	12:12 pm
●	5	15° ♐ 34'	
4th Quarter	12		11:24 pm
4th Quarter	13	**2:24 am**	
New Moon	20		11:41 pm
New Moon	21	**2:41 am**	
●	20/21	0° ♋ 21'	
2nd Quarter	28	**4:16 am**	1:16 am

Planet Ingress		day	ET / hr:mn / PT	
⚴	♑	2	**8:55 pm**	5:55 pm
⚶	♋	3	**2:55 pm**	11:55 am
☉	♋	20	**5:44 pm**	2:44 pm
♂	♈	27	**9:45 pm**	6:45 pm

Planetary Motion		day	ET / hr:mn / PT	
☿	℞	17		9:59 pm
☿	℞	18	**12:59 am**	
♆	℞	22		9:32 pm
♆	℞	23	**12:32 am**	
♀	D	24		11:48 pm
♀	D	25	**2:48 am**	

1 MONDAY
☽ ⚻ ♅ **12:52 am**
☽ △ ☉ **5:28 am** 2:28 am
☽ ⚻ ♂ **8:15 am** 5:15 am
☽ △ ♀ **11:20 am** 8:20 am
☽ ⚻ ♆ **9:05 pm** 6:05 pm

2 TUESDAY
☽ □ ♇ **3:22 am** 12:22 am
☽ □ ♃ **6:40 am** 3:40 am
☽ □ ♄ **2:38 pm** 11:38 am
♀ □ ♂ **8:41 pm** 5:41 pm
☽ △ ☿ **10:41 pm** 7:41 pm
☽ ☍ ♅ 11:17 pm

3 WEDNESDAY
☽ ☍ ♅ **2:17 am**
☽ ⚻ ☉ **10:05 am** 7:05 am
☽ ⚻ ♀ **10:28 am** 7:28 am
☽ △ ♂ **11:44 am** 8:44 am
☉ ☌ ♀ **1:44 pm** 10:44 am
☽ △ ♆ **10:14 pm** 7:14 pm

4 THURSDAY
☽ ⚹ ♇ **4:27 am** 1:27 am
☽ ⚹ ♃ **7:36 am** 4:36 am
☽ ⚹ ♄ **3:43 pm** 12:43 pm

5 FRIDAY
☽ ⚻ ☿ **3:38 am** 12:38 am
☽ ⚻ ♅ **3:50 am** 12:50 am
☿ ⚹ ♅ **7:05 am** 4:05 am
☽ ☍ ♀ **9:57 am** 6:57 am
☽ ☍ ☉ **3:12 pm** 12:12 pm
☽ □ ♂ **3:44 pm** 12:44 pm
☽ □ ♆ 9:10 pm

6 SATURDAY
☽ □ ♆ **12:10 am**
☽ ⚺ ♇ **6:30 am** 3:30 am
☽ ⚺ ♃ **9:36 am** 6:36 am
☉ □ ♂ **3:11 pm** 12:11 pm
☽ ⚺ ♄ **6:08 pm** 3:08 pm

7 SUNDAY
☽ △ ♅ **7:08 am** 4:08 am
☽ ☍ ☿ **10:06 am** 7:06 am
☽ ⚻ ♀ **11:11 am** 8:11 am
☿ ⚺ ♀ **9:29 pm** 6:29 pm
☽ ⚹ ♂ **10:07 pm** 7:07 pm
☽ ⚻ ☉ **10:51 pm** 7:51 pm

8 MONDAY
☽ ⚹ ♆ **4:25 am** 1:25 am
☽ ☌ ♇ **11:01 am** 8:01 am
☽ ☌ ♃ **2:06 pm** 11:06 am
☽ ☌ ♄ **11:17 pm** 8:17 pm

9 TUESDAY
☽ □ ♅ **1:30 pm** 10:30 am
☽ △ ♀ **3:15 pm** 12:15 pm
☽ ⚻ ☿ **7:33 pm** 4:33 pm

10 WEDNESDAY
☽ ⚺ ♂ **8:15 am** 5:15 am
☽ △ ☉ **10:35 am** 7:35 am
☽ ⚺ ♆ **12:01 pm** 9:01 am
☽ ⚺ ♇ **6:56 pm** 3:56 pm
☽ ⚺ ♃ **9:56 pm** 6:56 pm

11 THURSDAY
☉ □ ♆ **5:37 am** 2:37 am
♀ ⚺ ♅ **5:50 am** 2:50 am
☽ ⚺ ♄ **7:51 am** 4:51 am
☽ □ ♀ **10:35 pm** 7:35 pm
☽ ⚹ ♅ **11:20 pm** 8:20 pm

12 FRIDAY
☽ △ ☿ **8:07 am** 5:07 am
☽ ☌ ♂ **10:13 pm** 7:13 pm
☽ ☌ ♆ **10:51 pm** 7:51 pm
☽ □ ☉ 11:24 pm

13 SATURDAY
☽ □ ☉ **2:24 am**
☽ ⚹ ♇ **5:56 am** 2:56 am
☽ ⚹ ♃ **8:45 am** 5:45 am
♂ ☌ ♆ **10:13 am** 7:13 am
☽ ⚹ ♄ **7:12 pm** 4:12 pm

14 SUNDAY
☽ ⚹ ♀ **8:24 am** 5:24 am
☽ ⚺ ♅ **11:38 am** 8:38 am
☉ ⚻ ♇ **9:58 pm** 6:58 pm
☽ □ ☿ **10:07 pm** 7:07 pm

15 MONDAY
☽ ⚺ ♆ **11:21 am** 8:21 am
☽ ⚺ ♂ **2:08 pm** 11:08 am
☽ □ ♇ **6:22 pm** 3:22 pm
☽ ⚹ ☉ **8:11 pm** 5:11 pm
☽ □ ♃ **8:49 pm** 5:49 pm

16 TUESDAY
☉ ⚻ ♃ **3:33 am** 12:33 am
☽ □ ♄ **7:29 am** 4:29 am
☽ ⚺ ♀ **7:01 pm** 4:01 pm
☽ ☌ ♅ 9:15 pm

17 WEDNESDAY
☽ ☌ ♅ **12:15 am**
☽ ⚹ ☿ **11:03 am** 8:03 am
☽ ⚹ ♆ **11:18 pm** 8:18 pm

18 THURSDAY
☽ ⚹ ♂ **5:16 am** 2:16 am
☽ △ ♇ **6:01 am** 3:01 am
☽ △ ♃ **8:02 am** 5:02 am
☽ ⚺ ☉ **12:54 pm** 9:54 am
☽ △ ♄ **6:34 pm** 3:34 pm
♂ ⚹ ♇ **7:08 pm** 4:08 pm

19 FRIDAY
☽ ☌ ♀ **4:40 am** 1:40 am
☽ ⚺ ♅ **11:12 am** 8:12 am
☽ ⚺ ☿ **9:09 pm** 6:09 pm

20 SATURDAY
♂ ⚹ ♃ **3:56 am** 12:56 am
☽ □ ♆ **9:07 am** 6:07 am
☽ ⚻ ♇ **3:26 pm** 12:26 pm
☽ ⚻ ♃ **5:01 pm** 2:01 pm
☽ □ ♂ **5:48 pm** 2:48 pm
☽ ☌ ☉ 11:41 pm

21 SUNDAY
☽ ☌ ☉ **2:41 am**
☽ ⚻ ♄ **3:17 am** 12:17 am
☉ ⚻ ♄ **10:14 am** 7:14 am
☽ ⚺ ♀ **12:22 pm** 9:22 am
☽ ⚹ ♅ **7:35 pm** 4:35 pm

22 MONDAY
☽ ☌ ☿ **4:01 am** 1:01 am
☽ △ ♆ **4:22 pm** 1:22 pm
☽ ☍ ♇ **10:19 pm** 7:19 pm
☽ ☍ ♃ **11:29 pm** 8:29 pm

23 TUESDAY
☽ △ ♂ **3:20 am** 12:20 am
☽ ☍ ♄ **9:31 am** 6:31 am
☽ ⚺ ☉ **1:20 pm** 10:20 am
☽ ⚹ ♀ **6:05 pm** 3:05 pm
☽ □ ♅ 10:34 pm

24 WEDNESDAY
☽ □ ♅ **1:34 am**
☽ ⚺ ☿ **8:09 am** 5:09 am
☽ ⚻ ♆ **9:25 pm** 6:25 pm

25 THURSDAY
☽ ⚻ ♇ **3:05 am** 12:05 am
☽ ⚻ ♃ **3:53 am** 12:53 am
☽ ⚻ ♂ **10:29 am** 7:29 am
☽ ⚻ ♄ **1:47 pm** 10:47 am
☽ ⚹ ☉ **9:33 pm** 6:33 pm
☽ □ ♀ **10:17 pm** 7:17 pm

26 FRIDAY
☽ △ ♅ **5:44 am** 2:44 am
☉ ⚺ ♀ **8:41 am** 5:41 am
☽ ⚹ ☿ **10:18 am** 7:18 am
☽ ☍ ♆ 9:56 pm

27 SATURDAY
☽ ☍ ♆ **12:56 am**
☽ △ ♇ **6:24 am** 3:24 am
☽ △ ♃ **6:51 am** 3:51 am
☽ ☍ ♂ **4:02 pm** 1:02 pm
☽ △ ♄ **4:44 pm** 1:44 pm
☽ △ ♀ 10:34 pm

28 SUNDAY
☽ △ ♀ **1:34 am**
☽ □ ☉ **4:16 am** 1:16 am
♂ ⚹ ♄ **6:59 am** 3:59 am
☽ ⚻ ♅ **8:47 am** 5:47 am
☽ □ ☿ **11:14 am** 8:14 am

29 MONDAY
☽ ⚻ ♆ **3:35 am** 12:35 am
☽ □ ♇ **8:55 am** 5:55 am
☽ □ ♃ **9:02 am** 6:02 am
☽ □ ♄ **7:01 pm** 4:01 pm
☽ ⚻ ♂ **8:47 pm** 5:47 pm
♃ ☌ ♇ 10:46 pm

30 TUESDAY
♃ ☌ ♇ **1:46 am**
☽ ⚻ ♀ **4:34 am** 1:34 am
☽ △ ☉ **10:20 am** 7:20 am
☽ ☍ ♅ **11:21 am** 8:21 am
☽ △ ☿ **11:39 am** 8:39 am
☿ ⚹ ♅ **6:12 pm** 3:12 pm
☉ ☌ ☿ **10:53 pm** 7:53 pm
☉ ⚹ ♅ 11:07 pm

Eastern time in bold type
Pacific time in medium type

JUNE 2020

DATE	SID. TIME	SUN	MOON	NODE	MERCURY	VENUS	MARS	JUPITER	SATURN	URANUS	NEPTUNE	PLUTO	CERES	PALLAS	JUNO	VESTA	CHIRON
1 M	16 39 44	10♊58 18	5♎38	29♊13R	4♋07	15♊18R	12♓42	26♑46R	1♒37R	8♉34	20♓50	24♑42R	9♓20	0≈13R	5≈52	28♊48	8♈44
2 T	16 43 41	11 55 47	20 11	29 11	5 16	14 41	13 22	26 43	1 35	8 37	20 50	24 41	9 31	0 07	5 54	29 14	8 46
3 W	16 47 38	12 53 14	4♏50	29 09	6 21	14 04	14 01	26 40	1 33	8 40	20 51	24 40	9 42	0 00	5 56	29 40	8 48
4 Th	16 51 34	13 50 41	19 30	29 07	7 23	13 26	14 41	26 35	1 30	8 43	20 52	24 39	9 52	29♑53	5 59	0♋05	8 50
5 F	16 55 31	14 48 06	4✕04	29 06	8 21	12 48	15 20	26 32	1 28	8 46	20 52	24 38	10 02	29 46	6 01	0 31	8 52
6 Sa	16 59 27	15 45 31	18 25	29 05D	9 16	12 11	16 00	26 28	1 26	8 48	20 53	24 37	10 12	29 38	6 04	0 57	8 54
7 Su	17 3 24	16 42 54	2✗28	29 05	10 06	11 34	16 39	26 23	1 23	8 51	20 53	24 36	10 21	29 30	6 08	1 23	8 55
8 M	17 7 20	17 40 17	16 11	29 06	10 53	10 58	17 19	26 19	1 21	8 54	20 54	24 34	10 30	29 21	6 11	1 49	8 57
9 T	17 11 17	18 37 39	29 30	29 06	11 35	10 23	17 58	26 15	1 18	8 57	20 54	24 33	10 39	29 12	6 15	2 15	8 59
10 W	17 15 13	19 35 00	12≈28	29 07	12 14	9 49	18 37	26 10	1 16	9 00	20 55	24 32	10 48	29 02	6 19	2 41	9 00
11 Th	17 19 10	20 32 21	25 05	29 08	12 48	9 17	19 16	26 05	1 13	9 03	20 55	24 31	10 56	28 53	6 24	3 07	9 02
12 F	17 23 7	21 29 41	7✕24	29 08	13 19	8 46	19 55	26 00	1 10	9 05	20 56	24 30	11 05	28 42	6 28	3 33	9 03
13 Sa	17 27 3	22 27 01	19 30	29 09R	13 44	8 17	20 33	25 55	1 07	9 08	20 56	24 29	11 13	28 32	6 33	3 59	9 05
14 Su	17 31 0	23 24 20	1♈28	29 09	14 06	7 50	21 12	25 50	1 04	9 11	20 56	24 28	11 20	28 21	6 39	4 25	9 06
15 M	17 34 56	24 21 39	13 21	29 08	14 22	7 25	21 50	25 44	1 01	9 14	20 57	24 26	11 27	28 10	6 44	4 51	9 08
16 T	17 38 53	25 18 58	25 14	29 08	14 35	7 02	22 29	25 39	0 58	9 16	20 57	24 25	11 34	27 58	6 50	5 17	9 09
17 W	17 42 49	26 16 16	7♉01	29 07	14 43	6 41	23 07	25 33	0 55	9 19	20 57	24 24	11 41	27 46	6 56	5 43	9 10
18 Th	17 46 46	27 13 34	19 17	29 07	14 46R	6 23	23 45	25 27	0 52	9 21	20 57	24 23	11 48	27 34	7 03	6 09	9 12
19 F	17 50 42	28 10 51	1♊33	29 07	14 44	6 07	24 23	25 21	0 48	9 24	20 57	24 22	11 54	27 23	7 10	6 35	9 13
20 Sa	17 54 39	29 08 09	14 02	29 07	14 39	5 53	25 01	25 15	0 45	9 26	20 56	24 20	12 00	27 08	7 16	7 01	9 14
21 Su	17 58 36	0♋05 25	26 46	29 07R	14 29	5 42	25 38	25 09	0 41	9 29	20 56	24 19	12 05	26 55	7 24	7 27	9 15
22 M	18 2 32	1 02 42	9♋45	29 07	14 14	5 33	26 16	25 03	0 38	9 31	20 56	24 18	12 10	26 41	7 31	7 53	9 16
23 T	18 6 29	1 59 58	22 59	29 07	13 56	5 26	26 53	24 56	0 34	9 34	20 56R	24 16	12 15	26 27	7 39	8 20	9 17
24 W	18 10 25	2 57 13	6♌27	29 06	13 34	5 22	27 30	24 50	0 31	9 36	20 56	24 15	12 20	26 13	7 47	8 46	9 18
25 Th	18 14 22	3 54 28	20 08	29 06	13 08	5 20D	28 07	24 43	0 27	9 39	20 56	24 14	12 24	25 59	7 55	9 12	9 19
26 F	18 18 18	4 51 42	4♍01	29 05	12 40	5 21	28 44	24 36	0 23	9 41	20 57	24 12	12 28	25 44	8 03	9 38	9 20
27 Sa	18 22 15	5 48 56	18 03	29 05	12 09	5 24	29 21	24 29	0 20	9 43	20 57	24 11	12 32	25 29	8 12	10 04	9 20
28 Su	18 26 12	6 46 09	2♎12	29 05D	11 36	5 29	29 57	24 22	0 16	9 45	20 57	24 10	12 35	25 14	8 21	10 31	9 21
29 M	18 30 8	7 43 22	16 26	29 05	11 01	5 36	0♈34	24 15	0 12	9 48	20 57	24 08	12 38	24 58	8 30	10 57	9 22
30 T	18 34 5	8 40 34	0♏43	29 05	10 25	5 45	1 10	24 08	0 08	9 50	20 57	24 07	12 41	24 43	8 39	11 23	9 23

EPHEMERIS CALCULATED FOR 12 MIDNIGHT GREENWICH MEAN TIME. ALL OTHER DATA AND FACING ASPECTARIAN PAGE IN **EASTERN TIME (BOLD)** AND PACIFIC TIME (REGULAR).

JULY 2020

☽ Last Aspect day	ET / hr:mn / PT	asp	☽ Ingress sign	day	ET / hr:mn / PT
1	**9:20 pm** 6:20 pm	⚹ ♄	♐	1	**9:21 pm** 6:21 pm
3	**9:06 am** 6:06 am	□ ♆	♑	3	9:48 pm
3	**9:06 am** 6:06 am	□ ♆	♑	4	**12:48 am**
6	**5:35 am** 2:35 am	☌ ♄	♒	6	**6:08 am** 3:08 am
6	9:37 pm	□ ♅	♓	8	**2:13 pm** 11:13 am
7	**12:37 am**	□ ♅	♓	8	**2:13 pm** 11:13 am
10	**11:49 pm** 8:49 pm	⚹ ♄	♈	10	10:06 pm
10	**11:49 pm** 8:49 pm	⚹ ♄	♈	11	**1:06 am**
13	**11:54 am** 8:54 am	□ ♄	♉	13	**1:34 pm** 10:34 am
15	**11:21 pm** 8:21 pm	△ ♄	♊	15	10:19 pm

☽ Last Aspect day	ET / hr:mn / PT	asp	☽ Ingress sign	day	ET / hr:mn / PT
15	**11:21 pm** 8:21 pm	△ ♄	♊	16	**1:19 am**
17	**5:14 pm** 2:14 pm	□ ♆	♋	18	**10:24 am** 7:24 am
20	**1:55 pm** 10:55 am	☍ ♄	♌	20	**4:16 pm** 1:16 pm
21	**8:27 pm** 5:27 pm	⚹ ♀	♍	22	**7:40 pm** 4:40 pm
24	**7:08 pm** 4:08 pm	△ ♄	♎	24	**9:54 pm** 6:54 pm
26	**9:09 pm** 6:09 pm	□ ♄	♏	26	9:12 pm
26	**9:09 pm** 6:09 pm	□ ♄	♏	27	**12:12 am**
28	9:01 pm	⚹ ♄	♐	29	**3:25 am** 12:25 am
29	**12:01 am**	⚹ ♄	♐	29	**3:25 am** 12:25 am
30	**8:08 pm** 5:08 pm	☍ ♀	♑	31	**7:58 am** 4:58 am

☽ Phases & Eclipses phase	day	ET / hr:mn / PT
Full Moon	4	9:44 pm
Full Moon	5	**12:44 am**
☊	4/5	13° ♑ 38'
4th Quarter	12	**7:29 pm** 4:29 pm
New Moon	20	**1:33 pm** 10:33 am
2nd Quarter	27	**8:33 am** 5:33 am

Planet Ingress	day	ET / hr:mn / PT
♄ ♑	1	**7:39 pm** 4:39 pm
☉ ♌	22	**4:37 am** 1:37 am

Planetary Motion	day	ET / hr:mn / PT
⚳ ℞	6	9:01 pm
⚳ ℞	7	**12:01 am**
⚷ ℞	11	**5:09 pm** 2:09 pm

1 WEDNESDAY
☉ ⚹ ♅ **2:07 am**
☽ △ ♆ **6:02 am** 3:02 am
☽ ⚹ ♃ **11:06 am** 8:06 am
☽ ⚹ ♇ **11:20 am** 8:20 am
☽ ⚹ ♄ **9:20 pm** 6:20 pm
☽ △ ♂ 10:35 pm

2 THURSDAY
☽ △ ♂ **1:35 am**
☽ ☍ ♀ **8:02 am** 5:02 am
☽ ⚻ ☿ **12:20 pm** 9:20 am
☽ ⚻ ♅ **2:13 pm** 11:13 am
☽ ⚻ ☉ **4:45 pm** 1:45 pm

3 FRIDAY
☽ □ ♆ **9:06 am** 6:06 am
☽ ⚺ ♃ **1:51 pm** 10:51 am
☽ ⚺ ♇ **2:26 pm** 11:26 am
☽ ⚺ ♄ 9:32 pm

4 SATURDAY
☽ ⚺ ♄ **12:32 am**
☽ □ ♂ **7:28 am** 4:28 am
☽ ⚻ ♀ **12:55 pm** 9:55 am
☽ ☍ ☿ **2:13 pm** 11:13 am
☽ △ ♅ **6:19 pm** 3:19 pm
☽ ☍ ☉ 9:44 pm

5 SUNDAY
☽ ☍ ☉ **12:44 am**
☿ ⚺ ♀ **10:45 am** 7:45 am
☽ ⚹ ♆ **1:44 pm** 10:44 am
☽ ☌ ♃ **6:13 pm** 3:13 pm
☽ ☌ ♇ **7:14 pm** 4:14 pm

6 MONDAY
☽ ☌ ♄ **5:35 am** 2:35 am
☽ ⚹ ♂ **3:37 pm** 12:37 pm
☽ ⚻ ☿ **6:20 pm** 3:20 pm
☽ △ ♀ **8:22 pm** 5:22 pm
☽ □ ♅ 9:37 pm

7 TUESDAY
☽ □ ♅ **12:37 am**
☽ ⚻ ☉ **11:37 am** 8:37 am
☽ ⚺ ♆ **8:53 pm** 5:53 pm
☽ ⚺ ♃ 10:05 pm
☽ ⚺ ♇ 11:36 pm

8 WEDNESDAY
☽ ⚺ ♃ **1:05 am**
☽ ⚺ ♇ **2:36 am**
☿ □ ♂ **6:42 am** 3:42 am
☽ ⚺ ♄ **1:19 pm** 10:19 am
☽ △ ☿ 10:35 pm
☽ ⚺ ♂ 11:56 pm

9 THURSDAY
☽ △ ☿ **1:35 am**
☽ ⚺ ♂ **2:56 am**
☽ □ ♀ **7:15 am** 4:15 am
☽ ⚹ ♅ **9:50 am** 6:50 am
☽ △ ☉ 11:09 pm

10 FRIDAY
☽ △ ☉ **2:09 am**
☽ ☌ ♆ **6:57 am** 3:57 am
☽ ⚹ ♃ **10:47 am** 7:47 am
☽ ⚹ ♇ **12:52 pm** 9:52 am
☽ ⚹ ♄ **11:49 pm** 8:49 pm

11 SATURDAY
☽ □ ☿ **12:09 pm** 9:09 am
☽ ☌ ♂ **5:16 pm** 2:16 pm
☽ ⚹ ♀ **9:21 pm** 6:21 pm
☽ ⚺ ♅ **9:36 pm** 6:36 pm

12 SUNDAY
♀ ⚺ ♅ **3:12 am** 12:12 am
☉ △ ♆ **2:43 pm** 11:43 am
☽ ⚺ ♆ **7:06 pm** 4:06 pm
☽ □ ☉ **7:29 pm** 4:29 pm
☽ □ ♃ **10:25 pm** 7:25 pm
☽ □ ♇ 10:03 pm

13 MONDAY
☽ □ ♇ **1:03 am**
☽ □ ♄ **11:54 am** 8:54 am
☽ ⚹ ☿ 9:56 pm

14 TUESDAY
☽ ⚹ ☿ **12:56 am**
☉ ☍ ♃ **3:58 am** 12:58 am
☽ ⚺ ♂ **8:43 am** 5:43 am
☽ ☌ ♅ **10:14 am** 7:14 am
☽ ⚺ ♀ **12:47 pm** 9:47 am

15 WEDNESDAY
☽ ⚹ ♆ **7:16 am** 4:16 am
☽ △ ♃ **9:56 am** 6:56 am
☽ ⚹ ☉ **12:50 pm** 9:50 am
☽ △ ♇ **1:01 pm** 10:01 am
☉ ☍ ♇ **3:13 pm** 12:13 pm
♂ ⚺ ♅ **7:55 pm** 4:55 pm
☽ △ ♄ **11:21 pm** 8:21 pm

16 THURSDAY
☽ ⚺ ☿ **1:40 pm** 10:40 am
☽ ⚺ ♅ **9:21 pm** 6:21 pm
☽ ⚹ ♂ **10:26 pm** 7:26 pm
☽ ☌ ♀ 11:40 pm

17 FRIDAY
☽ ☌ ♀ **2:40 am**
☽ □ ♆ **5:14 pm** 2:14 pm
☽ ⚻ ♃ **7:15 pm** 4:15 pm
☽ ⚻ ♇ **10:39 pm** 7:39 pm

18 SATURDAY
☽ ⚺ ☉ **3:13 am** 12:13 am
☽ ⚻ ♄ **8:13 am** 5:13 am
☽ ☌ ☿ 9:19 pm

19 SUNDAY
☽ ☌ ☿ **12:19 am**
☽ ⚹ ♅ **5:24 am** 2:24 am
☽ □ ♂ **8:38 am** 5:38 am
☽ ⚺ ♀ **1:12 pm** 10:12 am
☽ △ ♆ 9:01 pm
☽ ☍ ♃ 10:27 pm

20 MONDAY
☽ △ ♆ **12:01 am**
☽ ☍ ♃ **1:27 am**
☽ ☍ ♇ **5:04 am** 2:04 am
☽ ☌ ☉ **1:33 pm** 10:33 am
☽ ☍ ♄ **1:55 pm** 10:55 am
☉ ☍ ♄ **6:28 pm** 3:28 pm

21 TUESDAY
☽ ⚺ ☿ **8:22 am** 5:22 am
☽ □ ♅ **10:22 am** 7:22 am
☽ △ ♂ **3:23 pm** 12:23 pm
☽ ⚹ ♀ **8:27 pm** 5:27 pm

22 WEDNESDAY
☽ ⚻ ♆ **3:59 am** 12:59 am
☽ ⚻ ♃ **4:57 am** 1:57 am
☽ ⚻ ♇ **8:48 am** 5:48 am
☿ ⚹ ♅ **4:25 pm** 1:25 pm
☽ ⚻ ♄ **5:08 pm** 2:08 pm
☽ ⚺ ☉ **8:45 pm** 5:45 pm

23 THURSDAY
☽ △ ♅ **1:16 pm** 10:16 am
☽ ⚹ ☿ **2:47 pm** 11:47 am
☽ ⚻ ♂ **7:55 pm** 4:55 pm
☽ □ ♀ 10:46 pm

24 FRIDAY
☽ □ ♀ **1:46 am**
☽ ☍ ♆ **6:23 am** 3:23 am
☽ △ ♃ **6:57 am** 3:57 am
☽ △ ♇ **11:05 am** 8:05 am
☽ △ ♄ **7:08 pm** 4:08 pm
☽ ⚹ ☉ 11:33 pm

25 SATURDAY
☽ ⚹ ☉ **2:33 am**
☽ ⚻ ♅ **3:28 pm** 12:28 pm
☽ □ ☿ **9:11 pm** 6:11 pm
☽ ☍ ♂ **11:50 pm** 8:50 pm

26 SUNDAY
☽ △ ♀ **6:45 am** 3:45 am
☽ ⚻ ♆ **8:29 am** 5:29 am
☽ □ ♃ **8:41 am** 5:41 am
☽ □ ♇ **1:12 pm** 10:12 am
☽ □ ♄ **9:09 pm** 6:09 pm

27 MONDAY
☽ □ ☉ **8:33 am** 5:33 am
♃ ⚹ ♆ **12:07 pm** 9:07 am
♀ ⚻ ♃ **1:36 pm** 10:36 am
♀ □ ♆ **1:48 pm** 10:48 am
☿ □ ♂ **5:46 pm** 2:46 pm
☽ ☍ ♅ **6:04 pm** 3:04 pm

28 TUESDAY
☽ ⚻ ♂ **4:18 am** 1:18 am
☽ △ ☿ **5:04 am** 2:04 am
☽ ⚹ ♃ **11:08 am** 8:08 am
☽ △ ♆ **11:18 am** 8:18 am
☽ ⚻ ♀ **12:38 pm** 9:38 am
☽ ⚹ ♇ **4:05 pm** 1:05 pm
☽ ⚹ ♄ 9:01 pm

29 WEDNESDAY
☽ ⚹ ♄ **12:01 am**
☽ △ ☉ **3:47 pm** 12:47 pm
☽ ⚻ ♅ **9:47 pm** 6:47 pm

30 THURSDAY
☽ △ ♂ **10:02 am** 7:02 am
☿ ☍ ♃ **10:17 am** 7:17 am
☿ △ ♆ **2:45 pm** 11:45 am
☽ ⚺ ♃ **2:47 pm** 11:47 am
☽ □ ♆ **3:20 pm** 12:20 pm
☽ ⚻ ☿ **3:25 pm** 12:25 pm
☽ ☍ ♀ **8:08 pm** 5:08 pm
☽ ⚺ ♇ **8:14 pm** 5:14 pm
♀ ⚻ ♇ **9:51 pm** 6:51 pm

31 FRIDAY
☽ ⚺ ♄ **4:12 am** 1:12 am
☽ ⚻ ☉ 9:46 pm
☽ △ ♅ 11:56 pm

Eastern time in bold type
Pacific time in medium type

JULY 2020

DATE	SID.TIME	SUN	MOON	NODE	MERCURY	VENUS	MARS	JUPITER	SATURN	URANUS	NEPTUNE	PLUTO	CERES	PALLAS	JUNO	VESTA	CHIRON
1 W	18 38 1	9♋37 46	14♏59	29♊06	9♋49R	5♊56	1♈46	24♑01R	0≈04R	9♉52	20♓57R	24♑05R	12♓43	24♐27R	8♎49	11♋49	9♈23
2 Th	18 41 58	10 34 57	29 12	29 07	9 13	6 10	2 21	23 54	0 00	9 54	20 56	24 04	12 45	24 11	8 59	12 16	9 24
3 F	18 45 54	11 32 08	13♐18	29 05	8 38	6 25	2 57	23 46	29♑56	9 56	20 56	24 03	12 46	23 55	9 09	12 42	9 24
4 Sa	18 49 51	12 29 19	27 14	29 08R	8 04	6 43	3 32	23 39	29 52	9 58	20 56	24 01	12 48	23 39	9 19	13 08	9 25
5 Su	18 53 47	13 26 30	10♑57	29 08	7 33	7 02	4 08	23 32	29 48	10 00	20 55	24 00	12 49	23 23	9 29	13 34	9 25
6 M	18 57 44	14 23 41	24 24	29 07	7 04	7 23	4 42	23 24	29 43	10 02	20 55	23 58	12 49	23 07	9 40	14 01	9 25
7 T	19 1 41	15 20 52	7≈34	29 05	6 38	7 46	5 17	23 17	29 39	10 04	20 55	23 57	12 49R	22 50	9 51	14 27	9 26
8 W	19 5 37	16 18 03	20 26	29 03	6 16	8 10	5 52	23 09	29 35	10 06	20 54	23 56	12 49	22 34	10 02	14 53	9 26
9 Th	19 9 34	17 15 15	3♓01	29 00	5 57	8 36	6 26	23 01	29 31	10 07	20 54	23 54	12 49	22 17	10 13	15 20	9 26
10 F	19 13 30	18 12 26	16 20	28 58	5 43	9 04	7 00	22 54	29 27	10 09	20 54	23 53	12 48	22 01	10 24	15 46	9 26
11 Sa	19 17 27	19 09 38	27 27	28 55	5 34	9 33	7 34	22 46	29 22	10 11	20 53	23 51	12 47	21 44	10 36	16 12	9 26R
12 Su	19 21 23	20 06 51	9♈25	28 54	5 30D	10 03	8 07	22 38	29 18	10 12	20 52	23 50	12 45	21 27	10 48	16 38	9 26
13 M	19 25 20	21 04 03	21 18	28 54D	5 31	10 35	8 41	22 31	29 13	10 14	20 51	23 48	12 43	21 11	11 00	17 05	9 26
14 T	19 29 16	22 01 17	3♉12	28 54	5 37	11 09	9 14	22 23	29 09	10 16	20 51	23 47	12 41	20 54	11 12	17 31	9 26
15 W	19 33 13	22 58 31	15 10	28 55	5 48	11 43	9 46	22 15	29 05	10 17	20 50	23 45	12 38	20 38	11 24	17 57	9 26
16 Th	19 37 10	23 55 46	27 17	28 57	6 05	12 19	10 19	22 07	29 00	10 19	20 49	23 44	12 36	20 21	11 36	18 24	9 26
17 F	19 41 6	24 53 01	9♊38	28 58	6 27	12 56	10 51	22 00	28 56	10 20	20 49	23 43	12 34	20 05	11 49	18 50	9 26
18 Sa	19 45 3	25 50 17	22 16	28 59R	6 55	13 35	11 23	21 52	28 51	10 22	20 48	23 41	12 32	19 49	12 02	19 17	9 25
19 Su	19 48 59	26 47 33	5♋13	29 00	7 28	14 14	11 54	21 44	28 47	10 23	20 47	23 40	12 24	19 32	12 15	19 43	9 25
20 M	19 52 56	27 44 50	18 31	28 58	8 07	14 54	12 26	21 37	28 43	10 24	20 46	23 38	12 20	19 16	12 28	20 09	9 25
21 T	19 56 52	28 42 08	2♌08	28 56	8 52	15 36	12 57	21 29	28 38	10 25	20 45	23 37	12 15	19 00	12 41	20 36	9 24
22 W	20 0 49	29 39 26	16 03	28 52	9 41	16 18	13 27	21 21	28 34	10 27	20 45	23 35	12 10	18 45	12 55	21 02	9 24
23 Th	20 4 45	0♌36 44	0♍12	28 47	10 36	17 02	13 57	21 14	28 29	10 28	20 44	23 34	12 05	18 29	13 08	21 28	9 23
24 F	20 8 42	1 34 03	14 30	28 43	11 36	17 46	14 27	21 06	28 25	10 29	20 43	23 32	11 59	18 14	13 22	21 55	9 23
25 Sa	20 12 39	2 31 22	28 52	28 38	12 42	18 31	14 57	20 59	28 20	10 30	20 42	23 31	11 53	17 58	13 36	22 21	9 22
26 Su	20 16 35	3 28 42	13♎13	28 35	13 52	19 17	15 26	20 51	28 16	10 31	20 41	23 30	11 46	17 43	13 50	22 47	9 21
27 M	20 20 32	4 26 02	27 31	28 34D	15 08	20 04	15 55	20 44	28 12	10 32	20 40	23 28	11 39	17 29	14 04	23 14	9 20
28 T	20 24 28	5 23 22	11♏50	28 34	16 28	20 51	16 23	20 37	28 07	10 33	20 39	23 27	11 32	17 14	14 19	23 40	9 20
29 W	20 28 25	6 20 43	25 42	28 35	17 53	21 40	16 51	20 30	28 03	10 34	20 38	23 25	11 25	17 00	14 33	24 06	9 20
30 Th	20 32 21	7 18 05	9♐34	28 36	19 25	22 29	17 18	20 23	27 58	10 35	20 37	23 24	11 17	16 46	14 48	24 33	9 18
31 F	20 36 18	8 15 26	23 15	28 37R	20 57	23 19	17 46	20 15	27 54	10 36	20 36	23 23	11 09	16 33	15 03	24 59	9 17

EPHEMERIS CALCULATED FOR 12 MIDNIGHT GREENWICH MEAN TIME. ALL OTHER DATA AND FACING ASPECTARIAN PAGE IN **EASTERN TIME (BOLD)** AND PACIFIC TIME (REGULAR).

AUGUST 2020

Last Aspect / Ingress

D Last Aspect			D Ingress		
day	ET / hr:mn / PT		asp	sign	day ET / hr:mn / PT
2	9:59 am 6:59 am	⊙ △ ♄	≈ 2	2:11 pm 11:11 am
4	5:45 pm 2:45 pm	⊙ □ ♃	⅋ 4	10:28 pm 7:28 pm
6	8:53 am 5:53 am	⊙ ∆ ♀	♈ 7	9:05 am 6:05 am
9	3:50 pm12:50 pm	⊙ ♂	♉ 9	9:28 pm 6:28 pm
12	2:55 am12:55 am	☽ ∆	♊ 12	9:46 am 6:46 am
14	7:19 am 4:19 am	☽ ♂	♋ 14	7:35 pm 4:35 pm
16	7:59 pm 4:59 pm	☽ ♂	♌ 16	
18	10:38 pm		17	1:38 pm
19	1:38 am		♍ 19	4:20 am 1:20 am

D Ingress		
sign day	ET / hr:mn / PT	
≏ 21	5:16 am 2:16 am	
♏ 23	6:16 am 3:16 am	
♐ 25	6:16 am 3:16 am	
♑ 27	8:49 am 5:49 am	
♒ 29	8:37 pm 5:37 pm	
♓ 9/1	5:34 am 2:34 am	

Planet Ingress

planet	sign	day	ET / hr:mn / PT
☿	♌	4	11:32 pm 8:32 pm
♀	♋	7	11:21 am 8:21 am
☿	♍	19	7:17 am 4:17 am
⊙	♍	22	9:30 pm 6:30 pm

Planetary Motion

planet		day	ET / hr:mn / PT
♆	R	15	10:25 pm 7:25 pm

Phases & Eclipses

phase	day	ET / hr:mn / PT
Full Moon	3	11:59 am 8:59 am
4th Quarter	11	11:45 am 8:45 am
New Moon	18	10:42 am 7:42 am
2nd Quarter	25	1:58 pm 10:58 am

Eastern time in **bold type**
Pacific time in medium type

---

1 SATURDAY
☽ ∆ ♀ **12:46 pm** 9:46 am
...

2 SUNDAY

3 MONDAY

4 TUESDAY

5 WEDNESDAY

6 THURSDAY

7 FRIDAY

8 SATURDAY

9 SUNDAY

10 MONDAY

11 TUESDAY

12 WEDNESDAY

13 THURSDAY

14 FRIDAY

15 SATURDAY

16 SUNDAY

17 MONDAY

18 TUESDAY

19 WEDNESDAY

20 THURSDAY

21 FRIDAY

22 SATURDAY

23 SUNDAY

24 MONDAY

25 TUESDAY

26 WEDNESDAY

27 THURSDAY

28 FRIDAY

29 SATURDAY

30 SUNDAY

31 MONDAY

AUGUST 2020

DATE	SID.TIME	SUN	MOON	NODE	MERCURY	VENUS	MARS	JUPITER	SATURN	URANUS	NEPTUNE	PLUTO	CERES	PALLAS	JUNO	VESTA	CHIRON
1 Sa	20 40 14	9♌12 49	6♑45	28♊37R	22♋35	24♊08	18♈13	20♑08R	27♑50R	10♉36	20♓34R	23♑21R	11♒00R	16♓19R	15♎18	25♋25	9♈16R
2 Su	20 44 11	10 10 12	20 03	28 35	24 17	25 00	18 39	20 02	27 46	10 37	20 33	23 20	10 52	16 06	15 33	25 51	9 15
3 M	20 48 8	11 07 36	3♒09	28 26	26 02	25 52	19 05	19 55	27 41	10 38	20 32	23 18	10 42	15 53	15 48	26 18	9 14
4 T	20 52 4	12 05 01	16 03	28 26	27 51	26 44	19 31	19 48	27 37	10 38	20 31	23 17	10 33	15 40	16 03	26 44	9 13
5 W	20 56 1	13 02 27	28 43	28 18	29 43	27 37	19 56	19 42	27 33	10 39	20 30	23 16	10 23	15 28	16 19	27 10	9 11
6 Th	20 59 57	13 59 54	11♓10	28 10	1♌38	28 31	20 21	19 35	27 29	10 39	20 29	23 14	10 14	15 16	16 34	27 37	9 10
7 F	21 3 54	14 57 22	23 24	28 02	3 35	29 25	20 45	19 29	27 25	10 40	20 27	23 13	10 03	15 05	16 50	28 03	9 10
8 Sa	21 7 50	15 54 51	5♈28	27 55	5 34	0♋20	21 08	19 23	27 20	10 40	20 26	23 12	9 53	14 53	17 05	28 29	9 08
9 Su	21 11 47	16 52 21	17 25	27 49	7 34	1 15	21 31	19 17	27 16	10 40	20 25	23 10	9 42	14 43	17 21	28 55	9 06
10 M	21 15 43	17 49 52	29 17	27 45	9 37	2 11	21 54	19 11	27 12	10 41	20 23	23 09	9 31	14 32	17 37	29 21	9 05
11 T	21 19 40	18 47 25	11♉08	27 43D	11 40	3 07	22 16	19 05	27 08	10 41	20 22	23 08	9 20	14 22	17 53	29 48	9 03
12 W	21 23 37	19 45 00	23 09	27 44	13 43	4 04	22 38	18 59	27 04	10 41	20 21	23 07	9 09	14 12	18 10	0♌14	9 02
13 Th	21 27 33	20 42 36	5♊11	27 45R	15 45	5 01	22 59	18 54	27 01	10 41	20 19	23 05	8 57	14 03	18 26	0 40	9 00
14 F	21 31 30	21 40 13	17 32	27 45	17 48	5 58	23 19	18 48	26 57	10 41	20 18	23 04	8 45	13 54	18 42	1 06	8 59
15 Sa	21 35 26	22 37 52	0♋13	27 44	19 50	6 56	23 39	18 43	26 53	10 42R	20 17	23 03	8 33	13 45	18 59	1 32	8 57
16 Su	21 39 23	23 35 32	13♋17	27 40	21 52	7 55	23 58	18 38	26 49	10 42	20 15	23 02	8 21	13 37	19 16	1 59	8 55
17 M	21 43 19	24 33 14	26 46	27 27	23 53	8 54	24 17	18 33	26 46	10 41	20 14	23 01	8 09	13 29	19 32	2 25	8 54
18 T	21 47 16	25 30 57	10♌41	27 18	25 54	9 53	24 35	18 28	26 42	10 41	20 12	22 59	7 56	13 21	19 49	2 51	8 52
19 W	21 51 12	26 28 42	24 58	27 09	27 54	10 53	24 53	18 23	26 38	10 41	20 11	22 58	7 44	13 14	20 06	3 17	8 50
20 Th	21 55 9	27 26 28	9♍32	27 00	29 53	11 53	25 09	18 19	26 35	10 41	20 09	22 57	7 31	13 07	20 23	3 43	8 48
21 F	21 59 6	28 24 15	24 17	26 54	1♍47	12 53	25 25	18 14	26 31	10 40	20 08	22 56	7 18	13 01	20 40	4 09	8 46
22 Sa	22 3 2	29 22 03	9♎05	26 50	3 47	13 54	25 40	18 10	26 28	10 40	20 06	22 55	7 05	12 55	20 58	4 35	8 44
23 Su	22 6 59	0♍19 53	23 46	26 48D	5 42	14 55	25 55	18 06	26 25	10 40	20 05	22 54	6 52	12 50	21 15	5 01	8 42
24 M	22 10 55	1 17 44	8♏16	26 47	7 35	15 56	26 09	18 02	26 22	10 40	20 03	22 53	6 38	12 44	21 32	5 27	8 40
25 T	22 14 52	2 15 36	22 31	26 48R	9 28	16 58	26 22	17 59	26 18	10 39	20 02	22 52	6 25	12 40	21 50	5 53	8 38
26 W	22 18 48	3 13 29	6♐28	26 46	11 19	18 00	26 35	17 55	26 15	10 39	20 00	22 51	6 12	12 35	22 07	6 19	8 36
27 Th	22 22 45	4 11 24	20 11	26 45	13 09	19 02	26 47	17 52	26 12	10 38	19 59	22 50	5 59	12 31	22 25	6 45	8 34
28 F	22 26 41	5 09 19	3♑33	26 44	14 58	20 04	26 58	17 49	26 09	10 38	19 57	22 49	5 45	12 28	22 43	7 11	8 32
29 Sa	22 30 38	6 07 17	16 43	26 43	16 45	21 07	27 08	17 46	26 06	10 37	19 55	22 48	5 32	12 24	23 01	7 37	8 30
30 Su	22 34 35	7 05 15	29 40	26 42	18 31	22 10	27 17	17 43	26 04	10 36	19 54	22 47	5 19	12 22	23 19	8 03	8 28
31 M	22 38 31	8 03 15	12♒26	26 42	20 15	23 14	27 26	17 41	26 01	10 36	19 52	22 46	5 05	12 19	23 37	8 29	8 26

EPHEMERIS CALCULATED FOR 12 MIDNIGHT GREENWICH MEAN TIME. ALL OTHER DATA AND FACING ASPECTARIAN PAGE IN **EASTERN TIME (BOLD)** AND PACIFIC TIME (REGULAR).

SEPTEMBER 2020

☽ Last Aspect day	ET / hr:mn / PT	asp	☽ Ingress sign	day	ET / hr:mn / PT
1	**12:56 am**	✶♂	♓	1	**5:34 am** 2:34 am
3	**10:34 am** 7:34 am	△♀	♈	3	**4:22 pm** 1:22 pm
5	9:45 pm	☌♂	♉	6	**4:43 am** 1:43 am
6	**12:45 am**	☌♂	♉	6	**4:43 am** 1:43 am
8	**8:47 am** 5:47 am	△♄	♊	8	**5:28 pm** 2:28 pm
10	9:48 pm	✶♂	♋	11	**4:23 am** 1:23 am
11	**12:48 am**	✶♂	♋	11	**4:23 am** 1:23 am
13	**8:05 am** 5:05 am	□♂	♌	13	**11:32 am** 8:32 am
15	**11:09 am** 8:09 am	△♂	♍	15	**2:37 pm** 11:37 am
17	**7:42 am** 4:42 am	△♄	♎	17	**2:56 pm** 11:56 am
19	**10:29 am** 7:29 am	☍♂	♏	19	**2:33 pm** 11:33 am
21	**2:13 pm** 11:13 am	✶☉	♐	21	**3:32 pm** 12:32 pm
23	**1:31 pm** 10:31 am	△♂	♑	23	**7:16 pm** 4:16 pm
25	**11:36 pm** 8:36 pm	□☿	♒	25	11:08 pm
25	**11:36 pm** 8:36 pm	□☿	♒	26	**2:08 am**
28	**3:18 am** 12:18 am	✶♂	♓	28	**11:34 am** 8:34 am
30	**1:30 pm** 10:30 am	✶♄	♈	30	**10:47 pm** 7:47 pm

☽ Phases & Eclipses phase	day	ET / hr:mn / PT
Full Moon	1	10:22 pm
Full Moon	2	**1:22 am**
4th Quarter	10	**5:26 am** 2:26 am
New Moon	17	**7:00 am** 4:00 am
2nd Quarter	23	**9:55 pm** 6:55 pm

Planet Ingress		day	ET / hr:mn / PT
☿	♎	5	**3:46 pm** 12:46 pm
♀	♌	6	**3:22 am** 12:22 am
⚵	♏	20	**7:19 am** 4:19 am
☉	♎	22	**9:31 am** 6:31 am
⚳	♒	27	**3:08 am** 12:08 am
☿	♏	27	**3:41 am** 12:41 am

Planetary Motion		day	ET / hr:mn / PT
♀	D	5	**9:06 pm** 6:06 pm
♂	℞	9	**6:22 pm** 3:22 pm
♃	D	12	**8:41 pm** 5:41 pm
♄	D	28	10:11 pm
♄	D	29	**1:11 am**

1 TUESDAY
☽ ✶ ♂ **12:56 am**
☿ △ ♇ **6:42 am** 3:42 am
☽ ☍ ☉ 10:22 pm
☽ ✶ ♅ 11:04 pm

2 WEDNESDAY
☽ ☍ ☉ **1:22 am**
☽ ✶ ♅ **2:04 am**
♀ ☍ ♄ **8:18 am** 5:18 am
☉ △ ♅ **10:09 am** 7:09 am
☽ ✶ ♃ **3:48 pm** 12:48 pm
☽ ☌ ♆ **8:09 pm** 5:09 pm
☽ ✶ ♇ 10:55 pm

3 THURSDAY
☽ ✶ ♇ **1:55 am**
☿ △ ♄ **3:23 am** 12:23 am
☽ ✶ ♄ **8:10 am** 5:10 am
☽ ☍ ☿ **8:56 am** 5:56 am
☽ △ ♀ **10:34 am** 7:34 am
☽ ⚺ ♂ **12:07 pm** 9:07 am

4 FRIDAY
♀ □ ♂ **5:12 am** 2:12 am
☿ ⚻ ♂ **9:15 am** 6:15 am
☽ ⚺ ♅ **1:24 pm** 10:24 am
☿ ✶ ♀ **4:32 pm** 1:32 pm
☽ ⚻ ☉ **6:00 pm** 3:00 pm

5 SATURDAY
☽ □ ♃ **3:26 am** 12:26 am
☽ ⚺ ♆ **7:55 am** 4:55 am
☽ □ ♇ **1:54 pm** 10:54 am
☽ □ ♄ **8:09 pm** 5:09 pm
☽ ☌ ♂ 9:45 pm

6 SUNDAY
☽ ☌ ♂ **12:45 am**
☽ □ ♀ **4:52 am** 1:52 am
☽ ⚻ ☿ **6:46 am** 3:46 am
☽ ☌ ♅ 11:00 pm

7 MONDAY
☽ ☌ ♅ **2:00 am**
☽ △ ☉ **12:09 pm** 9:09 am
☽ △ ♃ **4:08 pm** 1:08 pm
☽ ✶ ♆ **8:35 pm** 5:35 pm
☽ △ ♇ 11:39 pm

8 TUESDAY
☽ △ ♇ **2:39 am**
☽ △ ♄ **8:47 am** 5:47 am
☽ ⚺ ♂ **1:42 pm** 10:42 am
☽ ✶ ♀ **11:41 pm** 8:41 pm

9 WEDNESDAY
☽ △ ☿ **4:38 am** 1:38 am
☉ △ ♃ **12:04 pm** 9:04 am
☽ ⚺ ♅ **2:17 pm** 11:17 am

10 THURSDAY
☽ ⚻ ♃ **4:02 am** 1:02 am
☽ □ ☉ **5:26 am** 2:26 am
☽ □ ♆ **8:16 am** 5:16 am
☽ ⚻ ♇ **2:11 pm** 11:11 am
☽ ⚻ ♄ **7:57 pm** 4:57 pm
☽ ✶ ♂ 9:48 pm

11 FRIDAY
☽ ✶ ♂ **12:48 am**
☽ ⚺ ♀ **3:51 pm** 12:51 pm
☉ ☍ ♆ **4:26 pm** 1:26 pm
☽ □ ☿ **10:49 pm** 7:49 pm
☽ ✶ ♅ **11:57 pm** 8:57 pm

12 SATURDAY
☿ ⚻ ♅ **8:35 am** 5:35 am
☽ ☍ ♃ **12:54 pm** 9:54 am
☽ △ ♆ **4:45 pm** 1:45 pm
☽ ✶ ☉ **6:44 pm** 3:44 pm
☽ ☍ ♇ **10:19 pm** 7:19 pm

13 SUNDAY
☽ ☍ ♄ **3:37 am** 12:37 am
☽ □ ♂ **8:05 am** 5:05 am
☽ ☌ ♀ 11:53 pm

14 MONDAY
☽ ☌ ♀ **2:53 am**
☽ □ ♅ **5:33 am** 2:33 am
☽ ✶ ☿ **10:53 am** 7:53 am
☽ ⚻ ♃ **5:38 pm** 2:38 pm
☉ △ ♇ **7:09 pm** 4:09 pm
☽ ⚻ ♆ **9:05 pm** 6:05 pm
☽ ⚻ ♇ 11:18 pm
☽ ⚺ ☉ 11:50 pm

15 TUESDAY
☽ ⚻ ♇ **2:18 am**
☽ ⚺ ☉ **2:50 am**
☽ ⚻ ♄ **7:10 am** 4:10 am
☽ △ ♂ **11:09 am** 8:09 am
♀ □ ♅ **11:29 am** 8:29 am

16 WEDNESDAY
☽ △ ♅ **7:24 am** 4:24 am
☽ ⚺ ♀ **9:04 am** 6:04 am
☽ ⚺ ☿ **5:43 pm** 2:43 pm
☽ △ ♃ **6:54 pm** 3:54 pm
☽ ☍ ♆ **10:03 pm** 7:03 pm

17 THURSDAY
☽ △ ♇ **3:06 am** 12:06 am
☿ □ ♃ **6:34 am** 3:34 am
☽ ☌ ☉ **7:00 am** 4:00 am
☽ △ ♄ **7:42 am** 4:42 am
☽ ⚻ ♂ **11:17 am** 8:17 am
☉ △ ♄ **5:36 pm** 2:36 pm

18 FRIDAY
☽ ⚻ ♅ **7:09 am** 4:09 am
☽ ✶ ♀ **12:41 pm** 9:41 am
☿ ⚻ ♆ **4:05 pm** 1:05 pm
☽ □ ♃ **6:36 pm** 3:36 pm
☽ ⚻ ♆ **9:35 pm** 6:35 pm
☽ ☌ ☿ **10:08 pm** 7:08 pm
☽ □ ♇ 11:39 pm

19 SATURDAY
☽ □ ♇ **2:39 am**
☽ □ ♄ **7:14 am** 4:14 am
☽ ⚺ ☉ **9:53 am** 6:53 am
☽ ☍ ♂ **10:29 am** 7:29 am
☉ ⚻ ♂ **5:55 pm** 2:55 pm

20 SUNDAY
☽ ☍ ♅ **6:56 am** 3:56 am
☽ □ ♀ **4:42 pm** 1:42 pm
☽ ✶ ♃ **6:51 pm** 3:51 pm
☽ △ ♆ **9:47 pm** 6:47 pm
☿ □ ♇ 10:21 pm

21 MONDAY
☿ □ ♇ **1:21 am**
☽ ✶ ♇ **3:07 am** 12:07 am
☽ ⚺ ☿ **3:17 am** 12:17 am
☽ ✶ ♄ **7:50 am** 4:50 am
☽ ⚻ ♂ **10:45 am** 7:45 am
☽ ✶ ☉ **2:13 pm** 11:13 am
♀ ⚻ ♃ **9:12 pm** 6:12 pm

22 TUESDAY
☽ ⚻ ♅ **8:38 am** 5:38 am
☽ ⚺ ♃ **9:27 pm** 6:27 pm
☽ △ ♀ **11:34 pm** 8:34 pm
☽ □ ♆ 9:20 pm

23 WEDNESDAY
☽ □ ♆ **12:20 am**
☽ ⚺ ♇ **6:04 am** 3:04 am
☿ □ ♄ **6:38 am** 3:38 am
♀ ⚻ ♆ **8:45 am** 5:45 am
☽ ⚺ ♄ **11:04 am** 8:04 am
☽ ✶ ☿ **11:31 am** 8:31 am
☽ △ ♂ **1:31 pm** 10:31 am
☽ □ ☉ **9:55 pm** 6:55 pm

24 THURSDAY
☿ ☍ ♂ **6:53 am** 3:53 am
☽ △ ♅ **1:20 pm** 10:20 am

25 FRIDAY
☽ ☌ ♃ **3:11 am** 12:11 am
☽ ✶ ♆ **6:00 am** 3:00 am
☽ ⚻ ♀ **10:29 am** 7:29 am
☽ ☌ ♇ **12:09 pm** 9:09 am
☽ ☌ ♄ **5:26 pm** 2:26 pm
☽ □ ♂ **7:12 pm** 4:12 pm
☽ □ ☿ **11:36 pm** 8:36 pm

26 SATURDAY
♀ ⚻ ♇ **5:22 am** 2:22 am
☽ △ ☉ **9:30 am** 6:30 am
☽ □ ♅ **9:01 pm** 6:01 pm

27 SUNDAY
☽ ⚺ ♃ **11:51 am** 8:51 am
☽ ⚺ ♆ **2:29 pm** 11:29 am
☽ ⚺ ♇ **9:00 pm** 6:00 pm
☽ ☍ ♀ 10:04 pm
☽ ⚺ ♄ 11:30 pm

28 MONDAY
☽ ☍ ♀ **1:04 am**
☽ ⚺ ♄ **2:30 am**
☽ ✶ ♂ **3:18 am** 12:18 am
☽ △ ☿ **2:44 pm** 11:44 am
♀ ⚻ ♄ **4:23 pm** 1:23 pm
♀ △ ♂ **9:01 pm** 6:01 pm
☽ ⚻ ☉ 9:14 pm

29 TUESDAY
☽ ⚻ ☉ **12:14 am**
☽ ✶ ♅ **6:58 am** 3:58 am
♂ □ ♄ **5:50 pm** 2:50 pm
☽ ✶ ♃ **10:40 pm** 7:40 pm
☽ ☌ ♆ 10:00 pm

30 WEDNESDAY
☽ ☌ ♆ **1:00 am**
☽ ✶ ♇ **7:50 am** 4:50 am
☽ ⚺ ♂ **1:04 pm** 10:04 am
☽ ✶ ♄ **1:30 pm** 10:30 am
☽ ⚻ ♀ **6:17 pm** 3:17 pm

Eastern time in bold type
Pacific time in medium type

SEPTEMBER 2020

DATE	SID.TIME	SUN	MOON	NODE	MERCURY	VENUS	MARS	JUPITER	SATURN	URANUS	NEPTUNE	PLUTO	CERES	PALLAS	JUNO	VESTA	CHIRON
1 T	22 42 28	9♍01 16	25≈02	26Ⅱ26℞	21♍59	24♋18	27♈34	17♑38℞	25♑56℞	10♉35℞	19♓51℞	22♑46℞	4♓52℞	12♑17℞	23≈55	8♋54	8♈23℞
2 W	22 46 24	9 59 19	7♓47	26 14	23 41	25 22	27 41	17 36	25 56	10 34	19 49	22 44	4 39	12 15	24 13	9 20	8 21
3 Th	22 50 21	10 57 23	19 43	26 01	25 22	26 26	27 48	17 34	25 53	10 33	19 47	22 43	4 26	12 14	24 31	9 46	8 19
4 F	22 54 17	11 55 29	1♈50	25 48	27 01	27 30	27 53	17 32	25 51	10 32	19 46	22 42	4 13	12 13	24 49	10 12	8 16
5 Sa	22 58 14	12 53 37	13 49	25 36	28 40	28 35	27 58	17 31	25 49	10 31	19 44	22 41	4 00	12 13	25 08	10 37	8 14
6 Su	23 2 10	13 51 47	25 42	25 26	0♎17	29 40	28 02	17 29	25 46	10 30	19 42	22 41	3 47	12 12D	25 26	11 03	8 12
7 M	23 6 7	14 49 58	7♉32	25 18	1 53	0♌45	28 05	17 28	25 44	10 29	19 41	22 40	3 34	12 13	25 45	11 29	8 09
8 T	23 10 4	15 48 12	19 22	25 13	3 28	1 51	28 07	17 27	25 42	10 28	19 39	22 39	3 21	12 13	26 03	11 54	8 07
9 W	23 14 0	16 46 28	1Ⅱ16	25 10	5 02	2 56	28 08℞	17 26	25 40	10 27	19 39	22 38	3 09	12 14	26 22	12 20	8 04
10 Th	23 17 57	17 44 45	13 20	25 10	6 34	4 02	28 09	17 25	25 38	10 26	19 37	22 38	2 57	12 15	26 41	12 45	8 02
11 F	23 21 53	18 43 05	25 38	25 10	8 06	5 08	28 08	17 25	25 36	10 25	19 34	22 37	2 44	12 17	26 59	13 11	7 59
12 Sa	23 25 50	19 41 27	8♋16	25 09	9 36	6 15	28 07	17 24	25 35	10 23	19 33	22 36	2 32	12 19	27 18	13 36	7 57
13 Su	23 29 46	20 39 51	21 19	25 07	11 05	7 21	28 04	17 24D	25 33	10 22	19 31	22 36	2 21	12 21	27 37	14 02	7 54
14 M	23 33 43	21 38 18	4♌49	25 03	12 33	8 28	28 01	17 24	25 32	10 21	19 29	22 35	2 09	12 24	27 56	14 27	7 52
15 T	23 37 39	22 36 46	18 49	24 56	14 00	9 35	27 57	17 25	25 30	10 19	19 28	22 35	1 58	12 27	28 15	14 53	7 49
16 W	23 41 36	23 35 16	3♍17	24 47	15 25	10 42	27 52	17 25	25 29	10 18	19 26	22 34	1 47	12 30	28 34	15 18	7 47
17 Th	23 45 33	24 33 48	18 07	24 36	16 49	11 50	27 46	17 26	25 28	10 16	19 24	22 34	1 36	12 34	28 53	15 43	7 44
18 F	23 49 29	25 32 22	3♎12	24 25	18 13	12 57	27 40	17 27	25 26	10 15	19 23	22 33	1 25	12 37	29 12	16 08	7 41
19 Sa	23 53 26	26 30 58	18 21	24 14	19 34	14 05	27 32	17 28	25 25	10 13	19 21	22 33	1 15	12 42	29 32	16 34	7 39
20 Su	23 57 22	27 29 36	3♏24	24 06	20 55	15 13	27 24	17 29	25 24	10 12	19 21	22 32	1 05	12 46	29 51	16 59	7 36
21 M	0 1 19	28 28 16	18 12	24 00	22 14	16 21	27 15	17 31	25 24	10 10	19 18	22 32	0 55	12 51	0♓10	17 24	7 33
22 T	0 5 15	29 26 57	2♐47	23 57	23 32	17 29	27 05	17 32	25 23	10 10	19 16	22 32	0 45	12 56	0 30	17 49	7 31
23 W	0 9 12	0♎25 40	16 44	23 56D	24 49	18 37	26 54	17 34	25 22	10 07	19 14	22 31	0 36	13 02	0 49	18 14	7 28
24 Th	0 13 8	1 24 25	0♑25	23 55℞	26 03	19 46	26 42	17 36	25 22	10 05	19 13	22 31	0 27	13 08	1 09	18 39	7 25
25 F	0 17 5	2 23 11	13 43	23 55	27 17	20 54	26 30	17 38	25 21	10 03	19 11	22 31	0 19	13 14	1 28	19 04	7 23
26 Sa	0 21 1	3 21 59	26 43	23 53	28 28	22 03	26 17	17 41	25 21	10 01	19 10	22 30	0 10	13 20	1 48	19 29	7 20
27 Su	0 24 58	4 20 49	9≈27	23 49	29 38	23 12	26 03	17 43	25 20	10 00	19 08	22 30	0 02	13 27	2 07	19 54	7 17
28 M	0 28 55	5 19 41	21 59	23 42	0♏46	24 21	25 49	17 46	25 20	9 58	19 06	22 30	29≈55	13 34	2 27	20 18	7 15
29 T	0 32 51	6 18 34	4♓19	23 32	1 52	25 31	25 34	17 49	25 20D	9 56	19 05	22 30	29 47	13 41	2 47	20 43	7 12
30 W	0 36 48	7 17 29	16 31	23 22	2 56	26 40	25 19	17 52	25 20	9 54	19 03	22 30	29 40	13 49	3 06	21 08	7 09

EPHEMERIS CALCULATED FOR 12 MIDNIGHT GREENWICH MEAN TIME. ALL OTHER DATA AND FACING ASPECTARIAN PAGE IN **EASTERN TIME (BOLD)** AND PACIFIC TIME (REGULAR).

OCTOBER 2020

☽ Last Aspect day	ET / hr:mn / PT	asp	☽ Ingress sign	day	ET / hr:mn / PT
2	10:47 pm	□ ♄	♉	3	**11:12 am** 8:12 am
3	**1:47 am**	□ ♄	♉	3	**11:12 am** 8:12 am
5	**2:41 pm** 11:41 am	△ ♄	♊	5	9:03 pm
5	**2:41 pm** 11:41 am	△ ♄	♊	6	**12:03 am**
7	**9:57 pm** 6:57 pm	⚹ ♂	♋	8	**11:45 am** 8:45 am
10	**12:04 pm** 9:04 am	☍ ♄	♌	10	**8:24 pm** 5:24 pm
12	**10:29 am** 7:29 am	△ ♂	♍	12	9:56 pm
12	**10:29 am** 7:29 am	△ ♂	♍	13	**12:56 am**
14	**6:47 pm** 3:47 pm	△ ♄	♎	14	10:54 pm
14	**6:47 pm** 3:47 pm	△ ♄	♎	15	**1:54 am**
16	**6:11 pm** 3:11 pm	□ ♄	♏	16	10:05 pm

☽ Last Aspect day	ET / hr:mn / PT	asp	☽ Ingress sign	day	ET / hr:mn / PT
16	**6:11 pm** 3:11 pm	□ ♄	♏	17	**1:05 am**
18	**5:43 pm** 2:43 pm	⚹ ♄	♐	18	9:43 pm
18	**5:43 pm** 2:43 pm	⚹ ♄	♐	19	**12:43 am**
20	**11:38 pm** 8:38 pm	⚹ ☉	♑	20	11:44 pm
20	**11:38 pm** 8:38 pm	⚹ ☉	♑	21	**2:44 am**
22	9:35 pm	☌ ♄	♒	23	**8:17 am** 5:17 am
23	**12:35 am**	☌ ♄	♒	23	**8:17 am** 5:17 am
24	**5:54 pm** 2:54 pm	⚹ ♂	♓	25	**5:18 pm** 2:18 pm
27	**8:46 pm** 5:46 pm	⚹ ♄	♈	28	**4:45 am** 1:45 am
30	**12:12 pm** 9:12 am	☍ ☿	♉	30	**5:19 pm** 2:19 pm

☽ Phases & Eclipses phase	day	ET / hr:mn / PT
Full Moon	1	**5:05 pm** 2:05 pm
4th Quarter	9	**8:40 pm** 5:40 pm
New Moon	16	**3:31 pm** 12:31 pm
2nd Quarter	23	**9:23 am** 6:23 am
Full Moon	31	**10:49 am** 7:49 am

Planet Ingress		day	ET / hr:mn / PT
♀	♍	2	**4:48 pm** 1:48 pm
⚶	♍	22	**3:38 am** 12:38 am
☉	♏	22	**7:00 pm** 4:00 pm
☿	♎	27	**9:33 pm** 6:33 pm
♀	♎	27	**9:41 pm** 6:41 pm

Planetary Motion		day	ET / hr:mn / PT
♇	D	4	**9:32 am** 6:32 am
☿	℞	13	**9:05 pm** 6:05 pm
⚳	D	18	**12:59 pm** 9:59 pm

1 THURSDAY
☽ ⚻ ☿ **7:39 am** 4:39 am
☽ ☍ ☉ **5:05 pm** 2:05 pm
☽ ⚺ ♅ **6:29 pm** 3:29 pm

2 FRIDAY
☉ ⚻ ♅ **9:31 am** 6:31 am
☽ □ ♃ **10:58 am** 7:58 am
☽ ⚺ ♆ **12:55 pm** 9:55 am
☽ □ ♇ **8:00 pm** 5:00 pm
☽ ☌ ♂ **11:57 pm** 8:57 pm
☽ □ ♄ 10:47 pm

3 SATURDAY
☽ □ ♄ **1:47 am**
☽ △ ♀ **1:13 pm** 10:13 am
☽ ☍ ☿ 10:17 pm

4 SUNDAY
☽ ☍ ☿ **1:17 am**
☽ ☌ ♅ **6:59 am** 3:59 am
☽ ⚻ ☉ **11:15 am** 8:15 am
☽ △ ♃ 9:07 pm
☽ ⚹ ♆ 10:37 pm

5 MONDAY
☽ △ ♃ **12:07 am**
☽ ⚹ ♆ **1:37 am**
☽ △ ♇ **8:50 am** 5:50 am
☽ ⚺ ♂ **11:19 am** 8:19 am
☽ △ ♄ **2:41 pm** 11:41 am

6 TUESDAY
☽ □ ♀ **8:41 am** 5:41 am
☽ ⚻ ☿ **6:11 pm** 3:11 pm
☽ ⚺ ♅ **7:29 pm** 4:29 pm

7 WEDNESDAY
☽ △ ☉ **5:18 am** 2:18 am
☽ ⚻ ♃ **12:53 pm** 9:53 am
☽ □ ♆ **1:51 pm** 10:51 am
☿ ☍ ♅ **4:55 pm** 1:55 pm
☽ ⚻ ♇ **9:01 pm** 6:01 pm
☽ ⚹ ♂ **9:57 pm** 6:57 pm
☽ ⚻ ♄ 11:46 pm

8 THURSDAY
☽ ⚻ ♄ **2:46 am**
☽ ⚹ ♀ 11:16 pm

9 FRIDAY
☽ ⚹ ♀ **2:16 am**
☽ ⚹ ♅ **6:14 am** 3:14 am
☽ △ ☿ **8:03 am** 5:03 am
♂ □ ♇ **9:09 am** 6:09 am
☽ □ ☉ **8:40 pm** 5:40 pm
☽ ☍ ♃ **11:17 pm** 8:17 pm
☽ △ ♆ **11:44 pm** 8:44 pm

10 SATURDAY
☽ □ ♂ **6:05 am** 3:05 am
☽ ☍ ♇ **6:36 am** 3:36 am
☽ ☍ ♄ **12:04 pm** 9:04 am
♀ △ ♅ **7:08 pm** 4:08 pm

11 SUNDAY
☉ □ ♃ **9:34 am** 6:34 am
☉ ⚻ ♆ **11:31 am** 8:31 am
☽ □ ♅ **1:27 pm** 10:27 am
☽ ⚺ ♀ **3:16 pm** 12:16 pm
☽ □ ☿ **4:50 pm** 1:50 pm

12 MONDAY
♃ ⚹ ♆ **3:06 am** 12:06 am
☽ ⚻ ♆ **5:43 am** 2:43 am
☽ ⚻ ♃ **5:44 am** 2:44 am
☽ ⚹ ☉ **7:09 am** 4:09 am
☽ △ ♂ **10:29 am** 7:29 am
☽ ⚻ ♇ **12:11 pm** 9:11 am
☿ ⚹ ♀ **12:39 pm** 9:39 am
☽ ⚻ ♄ **5:18 pm** 2:18 pm

13 TUESDAY
☽ △ ♅ **4:35 pm** 1:35 pm
☉ ☍ ♂ **7:26 pm** 4:26 pm
☽ ⚹ ☿ **8:19 pm** 5:19 pm
☽ ☌ ♀ **10:55 pm** 7:55 pm

14 WEDNESDAY
☽ ☍ ♆ **7:47 am** 4:47 am
☽ △ ♃ **8:12 am** 5:12 am
☽ ⚻ ♂ **11:16 am** 8:16 am
☽ ⚺ ☉ **12:46 pm** 9:46 am
☽ △ ♇ **1:55 pm** 10:55 am
☽ △ ♄ **6:47 pm** 3:47 pm

15 THURSDAY
☉ □ ♇ **6:15 am** 3:15 am
☽ ⚻ ♅ **4:39 pm** 1:39 pm

☽ ⚺ ☿ **7:57 pm** 4:57 pm
☽ ⚺ ♀ 11:53 pm

16 FRIDAY
☽ ⚺ ♀ **2:53 am**
☽ ⚻ ♆ **7:20 am** 4:20 am
☽ □ ♃ **8:06 am** 5:06 am
☽ ☍ ♂ **9:49 am** 6:49 am
☽ □ ♇ **1:22 pm** 10:22 am
☽ ☌ ☉ **3:31 pm** 12:31 pm
☽ □ ♄ **6:11 pm** 3:11 pm

17 SATURDAY
☽ ☍ ♅ **3:37 pm** 12:37 pm
☽ ☌ ☿ **5:52 pm** 2:52 pm

18 SUNDAY
☽ ⚹ ♀ **6:05 am** 3:05 am
☽ △ ♆ **6:28 am** 3:28 am
☽ ⚹ ♃ **7:39 am** 4:39 am
☽ ⚻ ♂ **8:08 am** 5:08 am
☉ □ ♄ **9:58 am** 6:58 am
♀ ☍ ♆ **10:49 am** 7:49 am
☽ ⚹ ♇ **12:43 pm** 9:43 am
☽ ⚹ ♄ **5:43 pm** 2:43 pm
☽ ⚺ ☉ **6:15 pm** 3:15 pm
♂ □ ♃ 10:38 pm

19 MONDAY
♂ □ ♃ **1:38 am**
♀ ⚻ ♂ **3:03 am** 12:03 am
♀ △ ♃ **3:35 am** 12:35 am
☽ ⚻ ♅ **3:40 pm** 12:40 pm
☽ ⚺ ☿ **4:02 pm** 1:02 pm
☿ ☍ ♅ **10:53 pm** 7:53 pm

20 TUESDAY
☽ □ ♆ **7:19 am** 4:19 am
☽ △ ♂ **8:08 am** 5:08 am
☽ ⚺ ♃ **9:01 am** 6:01 am
☽ □ ♀ **11:28 am** 8:28 am
☽ ⚺ ♇ **2:00 pm** 11:00 am
☽ ⚺ ♄ **7:24 pm** 4:24 pm
☽ ⚹ ☉ **11:38 pm** 8:38 pm

21 WEDNESDAY
☽ ⚹ ☿ **3:49 pm** 12:49 pm
♀ △ ♇ **5:42 pm** 2:42 pm
☽ △ ♅ **6:33 pm** 3:33 pm

22 THURSDAY
♂ ⚺ ♆ **5:10 am** 2:10 am
☽ □ ♂ **11:16 am** 8:16 am
☽ ⚹ ♆ **11:23 am** 8:23 am
☽ ☌ ♃ **1:44 pm** 10:44 am
☽ ☌ ♇ **6:40 pm** 3:40 pm
☽ △ ♀ **9:09 pm** 6:09 pm
☽ ☌ ♄ 9:35 pm

23 FRIDAY
☽ ☌ ♄ **12:35 am**
☽ □ ☉ **9:23 am** 6:23 am
☽ □ ☿ **5:49 pm** 2:49 pm
☽ □ ♅ 10:02 pm

24 SATURDAY
☽ □ ♅ **1:02 am**
♀ △ ♄ **11:41 am** 8:41 am
☽ ⚹ ♂ **5:54 pm** 2:54 pm
☽ ⚺ ♆ **7:05 pm** 4:05 pm

☽ ⚺ ♃ **10:13 pm** 7:13 pm
☽ ⚺ ♇ 11:57 pm

25 SUNDAY
☽ ⚺ ♇ **2:57 am**
☽ ⚺ ♄ **9:21 am** 6:21 am
☽ ⚻ ♀ **11:37 am** 8:37 am
☉ ☌ ☿ **2:23 pm** 11:23 am
☽ △ ☿ **9:59 pm** 6:59 pm
☽ △ ☉ **11:31 pm** 8:31 pm

26 MONDAY
☽ ⚹ ♅ **10:44 am** 7:44 am

27 TUESDAY
☽ ⚺ ♂ **3:23 am** 12:23 am
☽ ☌ ♆ **5:40 am** 2:40 am
☽ ⚹ ♃ **9:38 am** 6:38 am
☽ ⚹ ♇ **1:58 pm** 10:58 am
☽ ⚹ ♄ **8:46 pm** 5:46 pm
☿ ⚺ ♀ **9:37 pm** 6:37 pm

28 WEDNESDAY
☽ ⚻ ☿ **4:08 am** 1:08 am
☽ ☍ ♀ **5:32 am** 2:32 am
☽ ⚻ ☉ **4:34 pm** 1:34 pm
☽ ⚺ ♅ **10:25 pm** 7:25 pm

29 THURSDAY
☽ ☌ ♂ **2:33 pm** 11:33 am
☽ ⚺ ♆ **5:51 pm** 2:51 pm
☽ □ ♃ **10:39 pm** 7:39 pm
☽ □ ♇ 11:26 pm

30 FRIDAY
☽ □ ♇ **2:26 am**
☽ □ ♄ **9:30 am** 6:30 am
☽ ☍ ☿ **12:12 pm** 9:12 am
☽ ⚻ ♀ 10:02 pm

31 SATURDAY
☽ ⚻ ♀ **1:02 am**
☽ ☍ ☉ **10:49 am** 7:49 am
☽ ☌ ♅ **10:55 am** 7:55 am
☉ ☍ ♅ **11:53 am** 8:53 am
☽ ⚺ ♂ 11:22 pm

Eastern time in bold type
Pacific time in medium type

OCTOBER 2020

DATE	SID.TIME	SUN	MOON	NODE	MERCURY	VENUS	MARS	JUPITER	SATURN	URANUS	NEPTUNE	PLUTO	CERES	PALLAS	JUNO	VESTA	CHIRON
1 Th	0 40 44	8♎16 26	28♒36	23♊07Rx	3♏57	27♌50	25♈09Rx	17♑55	25♑20	9♉52Rx	19♓02Rx	22♑29Rx	29♒34Rx	13♓57	3♏26	21♌32	7♈06Rx
2 F	0 44 41	9 15 25	10♓35	22 53	4 56	28 59	24 46	17 59	25 21	9 50	19 00	22 29	29 27	14 05	3 46	21 57	7 04
3 Sa	0 48 37	10 14 26	22 29	22 41	5 52	0♍09	24 29	18 03	25 21	9 48	18 59	22 29	29 22	14 13	4 06	22 21	7 01
4 Su	0 52 34	11 13 29	4♈20	22 30	6 45	1 19	24 12	18 06	25 21	9 46	18 57	22 29D	29 16	14 21	4 26	22 46	6 58
5 M	0 56 30	12 12 34	16 09	22 17	7 35	2 29	23 54	18 11	25 22	9 44	18 56	22 29	29 11	14 30	4 46	23 10	6 56
6 T	1 00 27	13 11 42	28 00	22 11	8 21	3 40	23 36	18 15	25 23	9 41	18 54	22 29	29 06	14 39	5 06	23 34	6 53
7 W	1 04 24	14 10 52	9♉55	22 13	9 04	4 50	23 18	18 19	25 23	9 39	18 53	22 29	29 01	14 49	5 26	23 58	6 50
8 Th	1 08 20	15 10 04	21 58	22 13D	9 42	6 01	22 59	18 24	25 24	9 37	18 51	22 29	28 57	14 58	5 46	24 23	6 48
9 F	1 12 17	16 09 18	4♊15	22 13	10 16	7 11	22 40	18 28	25 25	9 35	18 50	22 29	28 54	15 08	6 06	24 47	6 45
10 Sa	1 16 13	17 08 35	16 45	22 14Rx	10 45	8 22	22 21	18 33	25 26	9 33	18 49	22 30	28 50	15 18	6 26	25 11	6 42
11 Su	1 20 10	18 07 54	29 47	22 13	11 08	9 33	22 02	18 39	25 27	9 31	18 47	22 30	28 47	15 28	6 46	25 35	6 40
12 M	1 24 06	19 07 16	13♋11	22 11	11 25	10 44	21 43	18 44	25 28	9 28	18 46	22 30	28 44	15 39	7 06	25 59	6 37
13 T	1 28 03	20 06 39	27 05	22 06	11 36	11 55	21 23	18 49	25 30	9 26	18 44	22 30	28 42	15 50	7 26	26 22	6 34
14 W	1 31 59	21 06 05	10♌28	21 59	11♏40Rx	13 07	21 04	18 55	25 31	9 24	18 43	22 31	28 40	16 02	7 46	26 46	6 32
15 Th	1 35 56	22 05 33	26 18	21 50	11 37	14 18	20 45	19 01	25 33	9 21	18 42	22 31	28 39	16 12	8 07	27 10	6 29
16 F	1 39 53	23 05 03	11♍27	21 41	11 23	15 30	20 26	19 07	25 35	9 19	18 40	22 31	28 37	16 23	8 27	27 33	6 27
17 Sa	1 43 49	24 04 36	26 45	21 32	11 06	16 41	20 08	19 13	25 36	9 17	18 39	22 31	28 37	16 35	8 47	27 57	6 24
18 Su	1 47 46	25 04 10	12♎01	21 25	10 38	17 53	19 49	19 19	25 38	9 14	18 38	22 32	28 36D	16 46	9 07	28 20	6 21
19 M	1 51 42	26 03 47	27 05	21 20	10 01	19 05	19 31	19 25	25 40	9 12	18 37	22 32	28 36	16 58	9 28	28 43	6 19
20 T	1 55 39	27 03 25	11♏48	21 18D	9 15	20 17	19 13	19 32	25 42	9 10	18 35	22 33	28 36	17 10	9 48	29 07	6 16
21 W	1 59 35	28 03 05	26 05	21 18	8 22	21 29	18 56	19 39	25 44	9 07	18 34	22 33	28 37	17 23	10 08	29 30	6 14
22 Th	2 03 32	29 02 47	9♐55	21 19	7 21	22 41	18 39	19 45	25 46	9 05	18 33	22 33	28 38	17 35	10 29	29 53	6 11
23 F	2 07 28	0♏02 31	23 18	21 20Rx	6 13	23 53	18 23	19 53	25 48	9 02	18 32	22 34	28 39	17 48	10 49	0♍16	6 09
24 Sa	2 11 25	1 02 16	6♑18	21 20	5 01	25 05	18 07	20 00	25 51	9 00	18 31	22 35	28 41	18 01	11 10	0 38	6 07
25 Su	2 15 22	2 02 03	18 59	21 18	3 46	26 17	17 51	20 07	25 53	8 57	18 30	22 35	28 43	18 14	11 30	1 01	6 04
26 M	2 19 18	3 01 51	1♒23	21 14	2 30	27 30	17 36	20 15	25 55	8 55	18 29	22 36	28 46	18 28	11 50	1 24	6 02
27 T	2 23 15	4 01 41	13 35	21 09	1 15	28 42	17 22	20 22	25 58	8 53	18 28	22 37	28 49	18 41	12 11	1 46	6 00
28 W	2 27 11	5 01 33	25 38	21 01	0 04	29 55	17 09	20 30	26 01	8 50	18 27	22 38	28 52	18 55	12 31	2 09	5 57
29 Th	2 31 08	6 01 27	7♓35	20 52	28♎59	1♎08	16 56	20 38	26 04	8 48	18 26	22 39	28 55	19 09	12 52	2 31	5 55
30 F	2 35 04	7 01 22	19 28	20 44	28 02	2 20	16 44	20 46	26 07	8 45	18 25	22 40	28 59	19 23	13 12	2 53	5 53
31 Sa	2 39 01	8 01 20	1♈20	20 35	27 14	3 33	16 33	20 54	26 10	8 43	18 24	22 40	29 03	19 37	13 33	3 15	5 51

EPHEMERIS CALCULATED FOR 12 MIDNIGHT GREENWICH MEAN TIME. ALL OTHER DATA AND FACING ASPECTARIAN PAGE IN **EASTERN TIME (BOLD)** AND PACIFIC TIME (REGULAR).

NOVEMBER 2020

☽ Last Aspect day	ET / hr:mn	PT	asp	☽ Ingress sign	day	ET / hr:mn	PT
1	9:29 pm	6:29 pm	△♄	♊	2	5:00 am	2:00 am
4	8:49 am	5:49 am	△☿	♋	4	4:45 pm	1:45 pm
6	8:27 pm	5:27 pm	□☿	♌	6		11:18 pm
6	8:27 pm	5:27 pm	□☿	♌	7	2:18 am	
9	6:05 am	3:05 am	✶☿	♍	9	8:30 am	5:30 am
11	5:58 am	2:58 am	△♄	♎	11	11:09 am	8:09 am
13	6:32 am	3:32 am	□♄	♏	13	11:19 am	8:19 am
15	6:13 am	3:13 am	✶♄	♐	15	10:47 am	7:47 am
16		11:55 pm	✶♀	♑	17	11:35 am	8:35 am
17	2:55 am		✶♀	♑	17	11:35 am	8:35 am
19	11:30 am	8:30 am	✶☉	♒	19	3:25 pm	12:25 pm
20	7:49 pm	4:49 pm	✶♂	♓	21	11:06 pm	8:06 pm
24	5:44 am	2:44 am	✶♄	♈	24	10:05 am	7:05 am
26	6:46 pm	3:46 pm	□♄	♉	26	10:43 pm	7:43 pm
29	7:48 am	4:48 am	△♄	♊	29	11:16 am	8:16 am
30	11:22 pm	8:22 pm	□♆	♋	12/1	10:33 pm	7:33 pm

☽ Phases & Eclipses phase	day	ET / hr:mn	PT
4th Quarter	8	8:46 am	5:46 am
New Moon	14		9:07 pm
New Moon	15	12:07 am	
2nd Quarter	21	11:45 pm	8:45 pm
Full Moon	30	4:30 am	1:30 am
☊	30	8° ♊ 38'	

Planet Ingress		day	ET / hr:mn	PT
⚳	♓	9	9:48 am	6:48 am
☿	♏	10	4:55 pm	1:55 pm
♀	♏	21	8:22 am	5:22 am
☉	♐	21	3:40 pm	12:40 pm

Planetary Motion		day	ET / hr:mn	PT
☿	D	3	12:50 pm	9:50 am
♂	D	13	7:36 pm	4:36 pm
♆	D	28	7:36 pm	4:36 pm

1 SUNDAY
☽ ⚺ ♂ **1:22 am**
☽ ✶ ♆ **5:31 am** 2:31 am
☽ △ ♃ **11:07 am** 8:07 am
☿ □ ♄ **2:06 pm** 11:06 am
☽ △ ♇ **2:14 pm** 11:14 am
☽ ⚻ ☿ **9:15 pm** 6:15 pm
☽ △ ♄ **9:29 pm** 6:29 pm

2 MONDAY
☽ △ ♀ **7:31 pm** 4:31 pm
☽ ⚺ ♅ **10:14 pm** 7:14 pm

3 TUESDAY
☽ ⚻ ☉ **3:52 am** 12:52 am
☽ ✶ ♂ **12:57 pm** 9:57 am
☽ □ ♆ **5:43 pm** 2:43 pm
♀ ⚻ ♅ **9:22 pm** 6:22 pm
☽ ⚻ ♃ 9:00 pm
☽ ⚻ ♇ 11:24 pm

4 WEDNESDAY
☽ ⚻ ♃ **12:00 am**
☽ ⚻ ♇ **2:24 am**
☽ △ ☿ **8:49 am** 5:49 am
☽ ⚻ ♄ **9:43 am** 6:43 am

5 THURSDAY
☽ ✶ ♅ **9:19 am** 6:19 am
☽ □ ♀ **1:22 pm** 10:22 am
☽ △ ☉ **8:07 pm** 5:07 pm
☽ □ ♂ **11:08 pm** 8:08 pm

6 FRIDAY
☿ □ ♄ **4:12 am** 1:12 am
☽ △ ♆ **4:13 am** 1:13 am
☽ ☍ ♃ **11:01 am** 8:01 am
☽ ☍ ♇ **12:41 pm** 9:41 am
☽ ☍ ♄ **7:52 pm** 4:52 pm
☽ □ ☿ **8:27 pm** 5:27 pm

7 SATURDAY
☉ ⚻ ♂ **6:41 am** 3:41 am
☽ □ ♅ **5:49 pm** 2:49 pm

8 SUNDAY
☽ ✶ ♀ **3:36 am** 12:36 am
☽ △ ♂ **6:39 am** 3:39 am
☽ □ ☉ **8:46 am** 5:46 am
☽ ⚻ ♆ **11:46 am** 8:46 am
☽ ⚻ ♃ **6:49 pm** 3:49 pm
☽ ⚻ ♇ **7:49 pm** 4:49 pm
☽ ⚻ ♄ 11:44 pm

9 MONDAY
☽ ⚻ ♄ **2:44 am**
☽ ✶ ☿ **6:05 am** 3:05 am
♀ ☍ ♂ **11:08 am** 8:08 am
☽ △ ♅ **10:50 pm** 7:50 pm
☉ △ ♆ 9:11 pm

10 TUESDAY
☉ △ ♆ **12:11 am**
☽ ⚻ ♂ **10:45 am** 7:45 am
☽ ⚺ ♀ **1:04 pm** 10:04 am
☽ ☍ ♆ **3:42 pm** 12:42 pm

☽ ✶ ☉ **4:53 pm** 1:53 pm
☽ △ ♃ **10:55 pm** 7:55 pm
☽ △ ♇ **11:20 pm** 8:20 pm

11 WEDNESDAY
☽ △ ♄ **5:58 am** 2:58 am
☽ ⚺ ☿ **12:35 pm** 9:35 am
♀ ⚻ ♆ **7:31 pm** 4:31 pm
☽ ⚻ ♅ 9:31 pm

12 THURSDAY
☽ ⚻ ♅ **12:31 am**
☽ ☍ ♂ **11:50 am** 8:50 am
☽ ⚻ ♆ **4:37 pm** 1:37 pm
♃ ☌ ♇ **4:39 pm** 1:39 pm
☽ ☌ ♀ **6:31 pm** 3:31 pm
☽ ⚺ ☉ **9:17 pm** 6:17 pm
☽ □ ♇ 9:00 pm
☽ □ ♃ 9:05 pm

13 FRIDAY
☽ □ ♇ **12:00 am**
☽ □ ♃ **12:05 am**
☽ □ ♄ **6:32 am** 3:32 am
☽ ☌ ☿ **4:44 pm** 1:44 pm
☽ ☍ ♅ 9:10 pm

14 SATURDAY
☽ ☍ ♅ **12:10 am**
☽ ⚻ ♂ **11:23 am** 8:23 am
☉ ✶ ♇ **2:48 pm** 11:48 am
☽ △ ♆ **4:05 pm** 1:05 pm
☽ ⚺ ♀ **10:11 pm** 7:11 pm
☉ ✶ ♃ **10:57 pm** 7:57 pm
☽ ✶ ♇ **11:31 pm** 8:31 pm

☽ ✶ ♃ 9:03 pm
☽ ☌ ☉ 9:07 pm

15 SUNDAY
☽ ✶ ♃ **12:03 am**
☽ ☌ ☉ **12:07 am**
☽ ✶ ♄ **6:13 am** 3:13 am
♀ □ ♇ **2:43 pm** 11:43 am
☽ ⚺ ☿ **8:48 pm** 5:48 pm
☽ ⚻ ♅ **11:40 pm** 8:40 pm
♀ □ ♃ 9:33 pm

16 MONDAY
♀ □ ♃ **12:33 am**
☽ △ ♂ **11:21 am** 8:21 am
☽ □ ♆ **4:07 pm** 1:07 pm
☽ ⚺ ♇ **11:53 pm** 8:53 pm
☽ ⚺ ♃ 9:58 pm
☽ ✶ ♀ 11:55 pm

17 TUESDAY
☽ ⚺ ♃ **12:58 am**
☽ ✶ ♀ **2:55 am**
☿ ☍ ♅ **3:07 am** 12:07 am
☽ ⚺ ☉ **4:03 am** 1:03 am
☽ ⚺ ♄ **7:03 am** 4:03 am
☽ △ ♅ 10:00 pm

18 WEDNESDAY
☽ △ ♅ **1:00 am**
☽ ✶ ☿ **3:32 am** 12:32 am
☽ □ ♂ **1:42 pm** 10:42 am
☽ ✶ ♆ **6:34 pm** 3:34 pm
☉ ✶ ♄ 11:18 pm
☽ ☌ ♇ 11:58 pm

19 THURSDAY
☉ ✶ ♄ **2:18 am**
☽ ☌ ♇ **2:58 am**
☽ ☌ ♃ **4:43 am** 1:43 am
♀ □ ♄ **6:29 am** 3:29 am
☽ ☌ ♄ **10:51 am** 7:51 am
☽ □ ♀ **11:16 am** 8:16 am
☽ ✶ ☉ **11:30 am** 8:30 am
☉ ⚺ ♀ **11:45 pm** 8:45 pm

20 FRIDAY
☽ □ ♅ **5:41 am** 2:41 am
☽ □ ☿ **3:15 pm** 12:15 pm
☽ ✶ ♂ **7:49 pm** 4:49 pm
☽ ⚺ ♆ 9:42 pm

21 SATURDAY
☽ ⚺ ♆ **12:42 am**
☽ ⚺ ♇ **9:51 am** 6:51 am
☽ ⚺ ♃ **12:25 pm** 9:25 am
☽ ⚺ ♄ **6:34 pm** 3:34 pm
☽ □ ☉ **11:45 pm** 8:45 pm
☽ △ ♀ 9:43 pm

22 SUNDAY
☽ △ ♀ **12:43 am**
☿ ⚻ ♂ **9:00 am** 6:00 am
☽ ✶ ♅ **2:11 pm** 11:11 am

23 MONDAY
☽ ⚺ ♂ **5:52 am** 2:52 am
☽ △ ☿ **8:37 am** 5:37 am
☽ ☌ ♆ **10:31 am** 7:31 am
☽ ✶ ♇ **8:18 pm** 5:18 pm

☿ △ ♆ **11:40 pm** 8:40 pm
☽ ✶ ♃ **11:47 pm** 8:47 pm

24 TUESDAY
☽ ✶ ♄ **5:44 am** 2:44 am
☽ △ ☉ **4:13 pm** 1:13 pm
☽ ⚻ ♀ **6:36 pm** 3:36 pm
☽ ⚺ ♅ 10:35 pm

25 WEDNESDAY
☽ ⚺ ♅ **1:35 am**
☽ ☌ ♂ **6:39 pm** 3:39 pm
☽ ⚺ ♆ **10:43 pm** 7:43 pm

26 THURSDAY
☽ ⚻ ☿ **5:46 am** 2:46 am
☽ □ ♇ **8:50 am** 5:50 am
☽ □ ♃ **1:15 pm** 10:15 am
☽ □ ♄ **6:46 pm** 3:46 pm

27 FRIDAY
☿ ✶ ♇ **5:38 am** 2:38 am
☽ ⚻ ☉ **10:35 am** 7:35 am
♀ ☍ ♅ **12:11 pm** 9:11 am
☽ ☌ ♅ **2:10 pm** 11:10 am
☽ ☍ ♀ **2:25 pm** 11:25 am

28 SATURDAY
☽ ⚺ ♂ **8:17 am** 5:17 am
☽ ✶ ♆ **11:29 am** 8:29 am
☽ △ ♇ **9:40 pm** 6:40 pm
☿ ✶ ♃ **9:51 pm** 6:51 pm
☽ △ ♃ 11:53 pm

29 SUNDAY
☽ △ ♃ **2:53 am**
☉ ⚻ ♅ **3:20 am** 12:20 am
☽ ☍ ☿ **3:33 am** 12:33 am
☽ △ ♄ **7:48 am** 4:48 am
☽ ⚺ ♅ 11:19 pm

30 MONDAY
☽ ⚺ ♅ **2:19 am**
☽ ☍ ☉ **4:30 am** 1:30 am
☽ ⚻ ♀ **9:38 am** 6:38 am
☿ ✶ ♄ **2:01 pm** 11:01 am
☽ ✶ ♂ **9:13 pm** 6:13 pm
☽ □ ♆ **11:22 pm** 8:22 pm

Eastern time in bold type
Pacific time in medium type

NOVEMBER 2020

DATE	SID.TIME	SUN	MOON	NODE	MERCURY	VENUS	MARS	JUPITER	SATURN	URANUS	NEPTUNE	PLUTO	CERES	PALLAS	JUNO	VESTA	CHIRON
1 Su	2 42 57	9♏01 19	13♓10	20♊29R,	26♎37R,	4♎46	16♈28R,	21♑03	26♑13	8♉40R,	18♓23R,	22♑40	29♒08	19♒51	13♏53	3♍37	5♈48R,
2 M	2 46 54	10 01 20	25 03	20 23	26 11	5 59	16 12	21 11	26 16	8 38	18 22	22 41	29 13	20 05	14 14	3 59	5 46
3 T	2 50 50	11 01 23	6♈58	20 21	25 57 D	7 12	16 03	21 20	26 20	8 35	18 21	22 42	29 18	20 20	14 34	4 21	5 44
4 W	2 54 47	12 01 28	18 59	20 19 D	25 54	8 25	15 54	21 28	26 23	8 33	18 20	22 43	29 23	20 35	14 55	4 42	5 42
5 Th	2 58 44	13 01 35	1♉09	20 20	26 03	9 39	15 47	21 37	26 26	8 30	18 19	22 44	29 29	20 50	15 15	5 04	5 40
6 F	3 2 40	14 01 44	13 30	20 21	26 21	10 52	15 40	21 46	26 30	8 28	18 18	22 45	29 35	21 05	15 36	5 25	5 38
7 Sa	3 6 37	15 01 56	26 06	20 23	26 50	12 05	15 34	21 55	26 34	8 25	18 18	22 46	29 42	21 20	15 56	5 47	5 36
8 Su	3 10 33	16 02 09	9♊02	20 24R,	27 28	13 19	15 29	22 05	26 37	8 23	18 17	22 47	29 48	21 35	16 17	6 08	5 34
9 M	3 14 30	17 02 24	22 20	20 24	28 13	14 32	15 24	22 14	26 41	8 21	18 17	22 48	29 55	21 51	16 37	6 29	5 32
10 T	3 18 26	18 02 41	6♋04	20 23	29 06	15 46	15 21	22 24	26 45	8 18	18 16	22 49	0♓03	22 06	16 58	6 50	5 31
11 W	3 22 23	19 03 01	20 14	20 20	0♏05	16 59	15 18	22 33	26 49	8 16	18 16	22 50	0 11	22 22	17 18	7 10	5 29
12 Th	3 26 20	20 03 22	4♌48	20 17	1 10	18 13	15 16	22 43	26 53	8 13	18 15	22 51	0 19	22 38	17 39	7 31	5 27
13 F	3 30 16	21 03 45	19 44	20 12	2 19	19 27	15 14	22 53	26 57	8 11	18 15	22 52	0 27	22 54	17 59	7 51	5 25
14 Sa	3 34 13	22 04 10	4♍52	20 08	3 33	20 41	15 14 D	23 03	27 01	8 08	18 14	22 53	0 35	23 10	18 20	8 11	5 24
15 Su	3 38 9	23 04 37	20 04	20 05	4 50	21 55	15 14	23 13	27 06	8 06	18 13	22 54	0 44	23 26	18 40	8 32	5 22
16 M	3 42 6	24 05 05	5♎09	20 05	6 10	23 08	15 16	23 23	27 10	8 04	18 13	22 55	0 53	23 43	19 01	8 51	5 20
17 T	3 46 2	25 05 35	19 58	20 02 D	7 32	24 22	15 18	23 33	27 15	8 01	18 12	22 57	1 03	23 59	19 21	9 11	5 19
18 W	3 49 59	26 06 07	4♏26	20 03	8 57	25 36	15 21	23 44	27 19	7 59	18 12	22 58	1 13	24 16	19 42	9 31	5 17
19 Th	3 53 55	27 06 40	18 26	20 04	10 23	26 50	15 24	23 54	27 24	7 57	18 11	22 59	1 24	24 33	20 02	9 50	5 16
20 F	3 57 52	28 07 14	2♐00	20 05	11 51	28 05	15 28	24 05	27 28	7 55	18 11	23 00	1 33	24 49	20 23	10 10	5 15
21 Sa	4 1 49	29 07 49	15 07	20 07	13 20	29 19	15 33	24 16	27 33	7 52	18 11	23 02	1 43	25 06	20 43	10 29	5 13
22 Su	4 5 45	0♐08 26	27 52	20 07R,	14 50	0♏33	15 39	24 27	27 38	7 50	18 11	23 03	1 54	25 23	21 04	10 48	5 12
23 M	4 9 42	1 09 03	10♑17	20 07	16 21	1 47	15 46	24 38	27 43	7 48	18 10	23 04	2 05	25 41	21 24	11 06	5 11
24 T	4 13 38	2 09 42	22 27	20 06	17 52	3 01	15 53	24 49	27 48	7 46	18 10	23 06	2 16	25 58	21 45	11 25	5 10
25 W	4 17 35	3 10 22	4♒27	20 04	19 24	4 16	16 01	25 00	27 53	7 43	18 10	23 07	2 28	26 15	22 05	11 43	5 08
26 Th	4 21 31	4 11 03	16 20	20 02	20 57	5 30	16 10	25 11	27 58	7 41	18 10	23 09	2 40	26 33	22 25	12 01	5 07
27 F	4 25 28	5 11 45	28 10	19 59	22 30	6 44	16 19	25 23	28 03	7 39	18 10	23 10	2 52	26 50	22 46	12 19	5 06
28 Sa	4 29 24	6 12 28	10♓00	19 57	24 03	7 59	16 29	25 34	28 08	7 37	18 10 D	23 12	3 04	27 08	23 06	12 37	5 05
29 Su	4 33 21	7 13 13	21 54	19 55	25 36	9 13	16 40	25 45	28 14	7 35	18 10	23 13	3 16	27 26	23 26	12 55	5 04
30 M	4 37 18	8 13 59	3♈52	19 54	27 09	10 28	16 51	25 57	28 19	7 33	18 10	23 15	3 29	27 43	23 46	13 12	5 03

EPHEMERIS CALCULATED FOR 12 MIDNIGHT GREENWICH MEAN TIME. ALL OTHER DATA AND FACING ASPECTARIAN PAGE IN **EASTERN TIME (BOLD)** AND PACIFIC TIME (REGULAR).

DECEMBER 2020

☽ Last Aspect day	ET / hr:mn / PT		asp	☽ Ingress sign	day	ET / hr:mn / PT	
11/30	**11:22 pm**	8:22 pm	□♆	♋	1	**10:33 pm**	7:33 pm
4	**5:29 am**	2:29 am	☍♄	♌	4	**7:53 am**	4:53 am
5	**5:28 pm**	2:28 pm	△♂	♍	6	**2:46 pm**	11:46 am
8	**5:35 pm**	2:35 pm	△♄	♎	8	**7:01 pm**	4:01 pm
10	**7:56 pm**	4:56 pm	□♄	♏	10	**8:59 pm**	5:59 pm
12	**8:58 pm**	5:58 pm	⚹♄	♐	12	**9:39 pm**	6:39 pm
14	**11:17 am**	8:17 am	☌☉	♑	14	**10:35 pm**	7:35 pm
16		9:34 pm	☌♃	♒	16		10:27 pm
17	**12:34 am**		☌♃	♒	17	**1:27 am**	
19	**3:45 am**	12:45 am	⚹☉	♓	19	**7:39 am**	4:39 am
21	**5:25 am**	2:25 am	⚹♇	♈	21	**5:32 pm**	2:32 pm
23	**5:51 pm**	2:51 pm	☌♂	♉	24	**5:55 am**	2:55 am
26	**6:32 am**	3:32 am	△♇	♊	26	**6:33 pm**	3:33 pm
28	**10:01 pm**	7:01 pm	⚹♂	♋	29	**5:28 am**	2:28 am
31	**8:45 am**	5:45 am	□♂	♌	31	**1:58 pm**	10:58 am

☽ Phases & Eclipses phase	day	ET / hr:mn / PT	
4th Quarter	7	**7:37 pm**	4:37 pm
New Moon	14	**11:17 am**	8:17 am
●	14	23° ♐ 08'	
2nd Quarter	21	**6:41 pm**	3:41 pm
Full Moon	29	**10:28 pm**	7:28 pm

Planet Ingress	day	ET / hr:mn / PT	
☿ ♐	1	**2:51 pm**	11:51 am
♀ ♒	7	**7:14 am**	4:14 am
♀ ♐	15	**11:21 am**	8:21 am
♄ ♒	16		9:04 pm
♄ ♒	17	**12:04am**	
⚵ ♐	18	**12:25 pm**	9:25 am
♃ ♒	19	**8:07 am**	5:07 am
☿ ♑	20	**6:07 pm**	3:07 pm
☉ ♑	21	**5:02 am**	2:02 am

Planetary Motion	day	ET / hr:mn / PT	
⚷ D	15	**5:17 pm**	2:17 pm

1 TUESDAY
☽ ⚻ ♇ **9:26 am** 6:26 am
☽ ⚻ ♃ **3:22 pm** 12:22 pm
☽ ⚻ ♄ **7:38 pm** 4:38 pm
☽ ⚻ ☿ **11:40 pm** 8:40 pm

2 WEDNESDAY
☽ ⚹ ♅ **1:00 pm** 10:00 am
☽ ⚻ ☉ **8:28 pm** 5:28 pm
☽ △ ♀ 11:43 pm

3 THURSDAY
☽ △ ♀ **2:43 am**
☽ □ ♂ **8:28 am** 5:28 am
☽ △ ♆ **9:32 am** 6:32 am
☽ ☍ ♇ **7:22 pm** 4:22 pm
☽ ☍ ♃ 10:52 pm

4 FRIDAY
☽ ☍ ♃ **1:52 am**
☽ ☍ ♄ **5:29 am** 2:29 am
☽ △ ☿ **4:52 pm** 1:52 pm
☽ □ ♅ **9:38 pm** 6:38 pm

5 SATURDAY
☽ △ ☉ **9:41 am** 6:41 am
♂ ⚺ ♆ **4:44 pm** 1:44 pm
☽ □ ♀ **4:47 pm** 1:47 pm
☽ ⚻ ♆ **5:27 pm** 2:27 pm
☽ △ ♂ **5:28 pm** 2:28 pm
♀ △ ♆ **11:53 pm** 8:53 pm
♀ ⚻ ♂ 10:41 pm
☽ ⚻ ♇ 11:56 pm

Eastern time in bold type
Pacific time in medium type

6 SUNDAY
♀ ⚻ ♂ **1:41 am**
☽ ⚻ ♇ **2:56 am**
☿ ⚻ ♅ **7:43 am** 4:43 am
☽ ⚻ ♃ **9:53 am** 6:53 am
☽ ⚻ ♄ **12:53 pm** 9:53 am

7 MONDAY
☽ △ ♅ **3:45 am** 12:45 am
☽ □ ☿ **6:24 am** 3:24 am
☽ □ ☉ **7:37 pm** 4:37 pm
☽ ☍ ♆ **10:45 pm** 7:45 pm
☽ ⚻ ♂ **11:47 pm** 8:47 pm

8 TUESDAY
☽ ⚹ ♀ **3:21 am** 12:21 am
☽ △ ♇ **7:52 am** 4:52 am
☽ △ ♃ **3:09 pm** 12:09 pm
☽ △ ♄ **5:35 pm** 2:35 pm

9 WEDNESDAY
☽ ⚻ ♅ **7:17 am** 4:17 am
☉ □ ♆ **2:41 pm** 11:41 am
☽ ⚹ ☿ **4:13 pm** 1:13 pm
☽ ⚻ ♆ 10:33 pm
☽ ⚹ ☉ 11:22 pm

10 THURSDAY
☽ ⚻ ♆ **1:33 am**
☽ ⚹ ☉ **2:22 am**
☽ ☍ ♂ **3:31 am** 12:31 am
♀ ⚹ ♇ **6:52 am** 3:52 am
☽ □ ♇ **10:21 am** 7:21 am
☽ ⚺ ♀ **10:40 am** 7:40 am
☽ □ ♃ **5:58 pm** 2:58 pm

☽ □ ♄ **7:56 pm** 4:56 pm
☉ △ ♂ 10:01 pm

11 FRIDAY
☉ △ ♂ **1:01 am**
☽ ☍ ♅ **8:43 am** 5:43 am
☽ ⚺ ☿ **11:18 pm** 8:18 pm
☽ △ ♆ 11:35 pm

12 SATURDAY
☽ △ ♆ **2:35 am**
☽ ⚻ ♂ **5:30 am** 2:30 am
☽ ⚺ ☉ **6:58 am** 3:58 am
☽ ⚹ ♇ **11:17 am** 8:17 am
☽ ☌ ♀ **3:59 pm** 12:59 pm
☽ ⚹ ♃ **7:23 pm** 4:23 pm
☽ ⚹ ♄ **8:58 pm** 5:58 pm

13 SUNDAY
☿ □ ♆ **6:38 am** 3:38 am
☽ ⚻ ♅ **9:13 am** 6:13 am

14 MONDAY
☽ □ ♆ **3:15 am** 12:15 am
☽ ☌ ☿ **5:42 am** 2:42 am
☽ △ ♂ **7:14 am** 4:14 am
☽ ☌ ☉ **11:17 am** 8:17 am
☽ ⚺ ♇ **12:07 pm** 9:07 am
♀ ⚹ ♃ **3:58 pm** 12:58 pm
☽ ⚺ ♃ **8:59 pm** 5:59 pm
☽ ⚺ ♀ **9:23 pm** 6:23 pm
☽ ⚺ ♄ **10:13 pm** 7:13 pm
☿ △ ♂ **11:24 pm** 8:24 pm
☉ ⚺ ♇ **11:39 pm** 8:39 pm

15 TUESDAY
♀ ⚹ ♄ **8:00 am** 5:00 am
☽ △ ♅ **10:22 am** 7:22 am

16 WEDNESDAY
☽ ⚹ ♆ **5:12 am** 2:12 am
☽ □ ♂ **10:32 am** 7:32 am
☽ ⚺ ☿ **2:03 pm** 11:03 am
☽ ☌ ♇ **2:33 pm** 11:33 am
☽ ⚺ ☉ **5:32 pm** 2:32 pm
☿ ⚺ ♇ **6:35 pm** 3:35 pm
☽ ☌ ♃ 9:34 pm
☽ ☌ ♄ 10:28 pm

17 THURSDAY
☽ ☌ ♃ **12:34 am**
☽ ☌ ♄ **1:28 am**
☽ ⚹ ♀ **5:16 am** 2:16 am
☽ □ ♅ **1:50 pm** 10:50 am

18 FRIDAY
☽ ⚺ ♆ **10:01 am** 7:01 am
☽ ⚹ ♂ **5:08 pm** 2:08 pm
☽ ⚺ ♇ **8:06 pm** 5:06 pm
☽ ⚹ ☿ 11:49 pm

19 SATURDAY
☽ ⚹ ☿ **2:49 am**
☽ ⚹ ☉ **3:45 am** 12:45 am
☽ ⚺ ♃ **7:38 am** 4:38 am
☽ ⚺ ♄ **8:07 am** 5:07 am
☽ □ ♀ **5:40 pm** 2:40 pm
☽ ⚹ ♅ **8:50 pm** 5:50 pm
☉ ☌ ☿ **10:26 pm** 7:26 pm

20 SUNDAY
☽ ☌ ♆ **6:34 pm** 3:34 pm
☿ ⚺ ♃ **11:34 pm** 8:34 pm
☿ ⚺ ♄ 9:37 pm
♀ ⚻ ♅ 10:12 pm

21 MONDAY
☿ ⚺ ♄ **12:37 am**
♀ ⚻ ♅ **1:12 am**
☽ ⚺ ♂ **3:52 am** 12:52 am
☽ ⚹ ♇ **5:25 am** 2:25 am
♃ ☌ ♄ **1:21 pm** 10:21 am
☉ ⚺ ♄ **4:52 pm** 1:52 pm
☉ ⚺ ♃ **5:22 pm** 2:22 pm
☽ ⚹ ♄ **6:33 pm** 3:33 pm
☽ ⚹ ♃ **6:36 pm** 3:36 pm
☽ □ ☉ **6:41 pm** 3:41 pm
☽ □ ☿ **9:04 pm** 6:04 pm

22 TUESDAY
☽ ⚺ ♅ **7:22 am** 4:22 am
☽ △ ♀ **10:56 am** 7:56 am

23 WEDNESDAY
☽ ⚺ ♆ **6:17 am** 3:17 am
♂ □ ♇ **9:53 am** 6:53 am
☽ □ ♇ **5:37 pm** 2:37 pm
☽ ☌ ♂ **5:51 pm** 2:51 pm

24 THURSDAY
☽ □ ♄ **7:31 am** 4:31 am
☽ □ ♃ **8:10 am** 5:10 am
☽ △ ☉ **12:48 pm** 9:48 am
☽ △ ☿ **6:57 pm** 3:57 pm

☽ ☌ ♅ **7:56 pm** 4:56 pm
☿ △ ♅ 11:05 pm

25 FRIDAY
☿ △ ♅ **2:05 am**
☽ ⚻ ♀ **6:49 am** 3:49 am
☽ ⚹ ♆ **7:10 pm** 4:10 pm

26 SATURDAY
☽ △ ♇ **6:32 am** 3:32 am
☽ ⚺ ♂ **8:42 am** 5:42 am
☽ △ ♄ **8:41 pm** 5:41 pm
☽ △ ♃ **9:54 pm** 6:54 pm

27 SUNDAY
☽ ⚻ ☉ **6:53 am** 3:53 am
☽ ⚺ ♅ **8:13 am** 5:13 am
☽ ⚻ ☿ **4:33 pm** 1:33 pm
☉ △ ♅ **10:25 pm** 7:25 pm
☽ ☍ ♀ 10:47 pm

28 MONDAY
☽ ☍ ♀ **1:47 am**
☽ □ ♆ **6:59 am** 3:59 am
☽ ⚻ ♇ **6:03 pm** 3:03 pm
☽ ⚹ ♂ **10:01 pm** 7:01 pm

29 TUESDAY
☽ ⚻ ♄ **8:04 am** 5:04 am
☽ ⚻ ♃ **9:47 am** 6:47 am
☽ ⚹ ♅ **6:32 pm** 3:32 pm
☽ ☍ ☉ **10:28 pm** 7:28 pm

30 WEDNESDAY
♀ □ ♆ **5:19 am** 2:19 am
☽ ☍ ☿ **11:04 am** 8:04 am

☽ △ ♆ **4:31 pm** 1:31 pm
☽ ⚻ ♀ **5:42 pm** 2:42 pm

31 THURSDAY
☽ ☍ ♇ **3:10 am** 12:10 am
☽ □ ♂ **8:45 am** 5:45 am
☽ ☍ ♄ **4:56 pm** 1:56 pm
☽ ☍ ♃ **7:05 pm** 4:05 pm
☽ □ ♅ 11:26 pm

DECEMBER 2020

DATE	SID.TIME	SUN	MOON	NODE	MERCURY	VENUS	MARS	JUPITER	SATURN	URANUS	NEPTUNE	PLUTO	CERES	PALLAS	JUNO	VESTA	CHIRON
1 T	4 41 14	9♐14 46	15Ⅱ57	19Ⅱ53D	28♏43	11♏42	17♈03	26♑09	28♑24	7♉31R	18♓10	23♑16	3♓42	28♐19	24♏07	13♍29	5♈06R
2 W	4 45 11	10 15 34	28 11	19 53	0♐16	12 57	17 16	26 21	28 30	7 29	18 10	23 18	3 55	28 19	24 27	13 46	5 02
3 Th	4 49 7	11 16 24	10♋34	19 54	1 50	14 11	17 29	26 32	28 35	7 27	18 10	23 19	4 09	28 37	24 47	14 03	5 01
4 F	4 53 4	12 17 14	23 09	19 55	3 23	15 26	17 43	26 44	28 41	7 25	18 10	23 21	4 22	28 56	25 07	14 19	5 01
5 Sa	4 57 0	13 18 06	5♌58	19 55	4 57	16 41	17 57	26 56	28 47	7 23	18 10	23 22	4 36	29 14	25 27	14 35	5 00
6 Su	5 0 57	14 19 00	19 02	19 56	6 31	17 55	18 12	27 09	28 52	7 21	18 11	23 24	4 50	29 32	25 47	14 51	4 59
7 M	5 4 53	15 19 54	2♍22	19 56	8 05	19 10	18 27	27 21	28 58	7 20	18 11	23 25	5 04	29 51	26 07	15 07	4 59
8 T	5 8 50	16 20 50	16 01	19 56R	9 38	20 25	18 43	27 33	29 04	7 18	18 11	23 27	5 19	0♑09	26 27	15 23	4 58
9 W	5 12 47	17 21 47	29 59	19 56	11 12	21 40	19 00	27 45	29 10	7 16	18 11	23 29	5 34	0 28	26 47	15 38	4 58
10 Th	5 16 43	18 22 45	14♎15	19 56	12 46	22 55	19 17	27 58	29 16	7 14	18 12	23 31	5 48	0 46	27 07	15 53	4 58
11 F	5 20 40	19 23 45	28 48	19 56D	14 20	24 09	19 35	28 10	29 22	7 13	18 12	23 32	6 03	1 05	27 27	16 08	4 57
12 Sa	5 24 36	20 24 46	13♏32	19 55	15 54	25 24	19 53	28 23	29 28	7 11	18 13	23 34	6 19	1 24	27 47	16 22	4 57
13 Su	5 28 33	21 25 47	28 22	19 55	17 28	26 39	20 11	28 36	29 34	7 10	18 13	23 36	6 34	1 43	28 07	16 37	4 57
14 M	5 32 29	22 26 50	13♐10	19 56R	19 02	27 54	20 30	28 48	29 40	7 08	18 14	23 38	6 50	2 01	28 27	16 51	4 57
15 T	5 36 26	23 27 54	27 50	19 56	20 36	29 09	20 50	29 01	29 46	7 07	18 14	23 39	7 06	2 20	28 47	17 04	4 57
16 W	5 40 22	24 28 58	12♑14	19 56	22 10	0♐24	21 10	29 14	29 52	7 05	18 15	23 41	7 22	2 39	29 06	17 18	4 56
17 Th	5 44 19	25 30 03	26 17	19 56	23 45	1 39	21 30	29 27	29 59	7 04	18 15	23 43	7 38	2 59	29 26	17 31	4 56
18 F	5 48 16	26 31 08	9≈57	19 55	25 19	2 54	21 51	29 40	0≈05	7 02	18 16	23 45	7 54	3 18	29 46	17 44	4 57
19 Sa	5 52 12	27 32 14	23 11	19 54	26 54	4 09	22 12	29 53	0 11	7 01	18 17	23 47	8 11	3 37	0♐05	17 56	4 57
20 Su	5 56 9	28 33 20	6♓02	19 53	28 29	5 24	22 34	0≈06	0 18	7 00	18 17	23 48	8 27	3 56	0 25	18 08	4 57
21 M	6 0 5	29 34 26	18 31	19 52D	0♑03	6 39	22 56	0 19	0 24	6 58	18 18	23 50	8 44	4 16	0 44	18 20	4 57
22 T	6 4 2	0♑35 33	0♈44	19 52	1 39	7 54	23 18	0 32	0 31	6 57	18 19	23 52	9 01	4 35	1 04	18 32	4 57
23 W	6 7 58	1 36 40	12 44	19 52	3 14	9 09	23 41	0 46	0 37	6 56	18 20	23 54	9 18	4 54	1 23	18 43	4 58
24 Th	6 11 55	2 37 46	24 37	19 54	4 50	10 24	24 04	0 59	0 44	6 55	18 21	23 56	9 36	5 14	1 43	18 54	4 58
25 F	6 15 51	3 38 53	6♉26	19 55	6 25	11 39	24 28	1 12	0 50	6 54	18 21	23 58	9 53	5 33	2 02	19 04	4 59
26 Sa	6 19 48	4 40 01	18 17	19 56	8 01	12 54	24 51	1 26	0 57	6 53	18 22	24 00	10 11	5 53	2 21	19 15	4 59
27 Su	6 23 45	5 41 08	0Ⅱ14	19 57	9 38	14 09	25 16	1 39	1 04	6 52	18 23	24 02	10 29	6 12	2 40	19 24	5 00
28 M	6 27 41	6 42 16	12 19	19 58R	11 14	15 24	25 40	1 53	1 10	6 51	18 24	24 03	10 46	6 32	2 59	19 34	5 00
29 T	6 31 38	7 43 23	24 35	19 58	12 51	16 39	26 05	2 06	1 17	6 50	18 25	24 05	11 05	6 52	3 18	19 43	5 01
30 W	6 35 34	8 44 31	7♋04	19 57	14 28	17 54	26 30	2 20	1 24	6 49	18 26	24 07	11 23	7 12	3 37	19 52	5 02
31 Th	6 39 31	9 45 39	19 47	19 56	16 05	19 10	26 56	2 33	1 31	6 49	18 27	24 09	11 41	7 31	3 56	20 00	5 03

EPHEMERIS CALCULATED FOR 12 MIDNIGHT GREENWICH MEAN TIME. ALL OTHER DATA AND FACING ASPECTARIAN PAGE IN **EASTERN TIME (BOLD)** AND PACIFIC TIME (REGULAR).

JANUARY 2021

D Last Aspect / D Ingress

day	ET / hr:mn / PT	asp	sign day	ET / hr:mn / PT
5:00 pm 2:00 pm	♐ 2	8:13 in 5:13 pm
4 4:34 am 1:34 am			4:34 am 1:34 am
4 4:34 am 1:34 am			9:55 am
6			
12:55 am			11:17 am
8 8:59 pm 5:59 pm			3:15 am
10 1:29 pm10:29 am			11:22 pm
12			
13 2:22 am			
14 4:26 am 1:26 am			2:17 pm

D Ingress

day	sign ET / hr:mn / PT	asp
2:26 am	☿	4:37 am 1:37
6:18 am 3:18 am		5:32 am
10:55 am 7:55 am		3:23 am
11:39 am 8:39 am		9:21 pm
		9:55 pm

D Last Aspect / D Ingress

day	ET / hr:mn / PT	asp	sign day	ET / hr:mn / PT
17 10:44 am 7:44 am		♈ 17	11:07 am
17 10:44 am 7:44 am		♉ 18	2:07 pm 9:00 pm
20 3:29 am1:29 am		♊ 20	1:56 pm 10:56 am
22 4:28 pm 1:28 pm		♋ 22	11:43 am
22 4:28 pm 1:28 pm		♌ 24	2:43 am
24		♍ 25	1:52 pm 10:52 am
25 2:17 am		♎ 25	1:52 pm 10:52 am
26 13 11:44 am 8:44 am		♏ 27	9:54 am 6:54 am
29 8:53 pm 5:53 pm		♐ 30	3:02 am 12:02 am

D Phases & Eclipses

phase	day	ET / hr:mn / PT
4th Quarter	6	4:37 am 1:37 am
New Moon	12	
New Moon	13 12:00 am	
2nd Quarter	20	4:02 pm 1:02 pm
Full Moon	28	2:16 pm 11:16 am

Planet Ingress

	day	ET / hr:mn / PT
♂ ♈	6	5:27 am 2:27 am
♀ ♑	8	7:00 am 4:00 am
♀ ≈	8	10:41 am 7:41 am
☉ ≈	19	3:40 pm 12:40 pm

Planetary Motion

	day	ET / hr:mn / PT
♄ D	14	3:36 pm 12:36 pm
⚴ R₂	19	3:54 am 12:54 am
♀ R₂	30	10:52 am 7:52 am

---

1 FRIDAY
2:26 am	1:37
6:18 am 3:18 am	
10:55 am 7:55 am	
11:39 am 8:39 am	

2 SATURDAY
2:02 am	
6:24 am 3:24 am	
9:57 am 6:57 am	
5:00 pm 2:00 pm	
11:32 am 8:32 am	
	11:05 pm

3 SUNDAY
2:05 am	
8:12 am 5:12 am	
8:44 am 5:44 am	
9:19 am 6:19 am	

4 MONDAY
4:50 am 1:50 am	
2:11 pm11:11 am	
2:52 pm11:52 am	
4:34 am 1:34 am	
7:58 am 4:58 am	
11:19 am 8:19 am	

5 TUESDAY
4:22 am 1:22 am	
2:17 am 4:17 am	
12:19 pm 9:19 am	

6 WEDNESDAY
4:37 am	1:37
8:32 am	5:32 am
6:23 pm	3:23 pm

7 THURSDAY
12:21 am	
12:55 am	
4:14 am 1:14 am	
7:54 am 4:54 am	
11:11 am 8:11 am	
	3:16 pm12:16 pm
7:04 pm 4:04 pm	

8 FRIDAY
11:11 am 8:11 am	
11:14 am 8:14 am	
11:53 am 8:53 am	
8:59 am 5:59 am	
9:44 pm 6:44 pm	

9 SATURDAY
8:07 am 5:07 am	
8:17 am 5:17 am	
9:15 am 6:15 am	
10:38 am 7:38 am	
10:53 am 7:53 am	
2:18 pm11:18 am	
5:30 pm 2:30 pm	
10:17 pm 7:17 pm	

10 SUNDAY
1:29 pm10:29 am	
♀ ♄	3:39 pm12:39 pm
☿	5:12 pm 2:12 pm
11:17 pm 8:17 pm	

11 MONDAY
12:16 am	9:16
12:19 am	9:19 am
1:20 am10:20 am	
3:14 pm12:14 pm	
5:28 pm 2:28 pm	
6:02 pm 3:02 pm	
7:51 pm 4:51 pm	

12 TUESDAY
10:00 am 7:00 am	
4:17 pm 1:17 pm	
9:40 pm 6:40 pm	
	9:00 pm
	11:22 pm

13 WEDNESDAY
12:00 am	
2:22 am	
6:02 am 3:02 am	
5:11 pm 2:11 pm	
5:30 pm 2:30 pm	
9:22 pm 6:22 pm	
11:26 pm 8:26 pm	
11:54 pm 8:54 pm	

14 THURSDAY
4:26 am 1:26 am	
9:19 am 6:19 am	
☿ ♄	8:55 pm 5:55 pm

15 FRIDAY
7:33 am 4:33 am	
9:21 am 6:21 am	
11:33 am 8:33 am	

16 SATURDAY
1:29 am	
5:03 am 2:03 am	
5:43 am 2:43 am	
12:02 pm 9:02 am	
6:33 pm 3:33 pm	

17 SUNDAY
4:35 am 1:35 am	
3:55 am 12:55 am	
5:50 am 2:50 am	
10:44 am 7:44 am	

18 MONDAY
9:20 am 6:20 am	
1:16 pm10:16 am	
3:20 pm12:20 pm	
3:45 pm12:45 pm	

19 TUESDAY
4:43 am 1:43 am	
12:54 am 9:54 am	
3:34 pm12:34 pm	

20 WEDNESDAY
3:29 am12:29 am	
1:04 pm10:04 am	
3:38 pm12:38 pm	
10:00 pm 7:00 pm	

21 THURSDAY
3:37 am12:37 am	
4:08 am 1:08 am	
5:15 am 2:15 am	
	9:28 pm

22 FRIDAY
12:28 am	
8:59 am 5:59 am	
4:28 pm 1:28 pm	

23 SATURDAY
4:27 am 1:27 am	
	1:28 pm
	11:49 pm

24 SUNDAY
4:36 am 1:36 am	
7:26 am 4:26 am	
	11:17 pm

25 MONDAY
2:17 am	
4:12 am 1:12 am	
10:38 am 7:38 am	
	11:23 pm
	11:49 pm

26 TUESDAY
2:23 am	
2:49 am	3:32 am
6:32 am 3:32 am	
7:48 am 4:48 am	
8:17 am 5:17 am	
9:35 am 6:35 am	
	10:57 am

27 WEDNESDAY
1:57 am	
10:37 am 7:37 am	
12:55 pm 9:55 am	
2:09 pm11:09 am	

28 THURSDAY
6:41 am 3:41 am	
10:11 am 7:11 am	
11:18 am 8:18 am	
2:16 pm11:16 am	
4:27 pm 2:32 pm	
8:40 pm 5:40 pm	

29 FRIDAY
8:10 am 5:10 am	
12:19 pm 9:19 am	

30 SATURDAY
11:54 am 8:54 am	
2:52 pm11:52 am	
8:01 pm 5:01 pm	
10:51 pm 7:51 pm	
11:57 pm 8:57 pm	

31 SUNDAY
12:09 pm 9:09 am	
10:17 pm 7:17 pm	
	9:05 pm

Eastern time in bold type
Pacific time in medium type

JANUARY 2021

DATE	SID.TIME	SUN	MOON	NODE	MERCURY	VENUS	MARS	JUPITER	SATURN	URANUS	NEPTUNE	PLUTO	CERES	PALLAS	JUNO	VESTA	CHIRON
1 F	6 43 27	10♑46 47	2♌44	19♊50R	17♑43	20♐25	27♈21	2≈47	1≈37	6♉48R	18♓28	24♑11	12♓00	7≈51	4♐15	20♍09	5♈04
2 Sa	6 47 24	11 47 56	15 55	19 49	19 21	21 40	27 48	3 01	1 44	6 47	18 30	24 13	12 18	8 11	4 34	20 16	5 04
3 Su	6 51 21	12 49 04	29 19	19 46	20 59	22 55	28 14	3 14	1 51	6 47	18 31	24 15	12 37	8 31	4 52	20 24	5 05
4 M	6 55 17	13 50 13	12♍55	19 46	22 37	24 10	28 40	3 28	1 58	6 46	18 32	24 17	12 56	8 51	5 11	20 30	5 06
5 T	6 59 14	14 51 22	26 42	19 40	24 15	25 25	29 07	3 42	2 05	6 46	18 33	24 19	13 15	9 11	5 30	20 37	5 08
6 W	7 3 10	15 52 31	10≏39	19 39D	25 54	26 40	29 34	3 56	2 12	6 45	18 34	24 21	13 34	9 31	5 48	20 43	5 09
7 Th	7 7 7	16 53 40	24 45	19 39	27 32	27 56	0♉02	4 09	2 19	6 45	18 36	24 23	13 53	9 51	6 07	20 49	5 10
8 F	7 11 3	17 54 50	8♏58	19 40	29 11	29 11	0 29	4 24	2 26	6 45	18 37	24 25	14 13	10 11	6 25	20 54	5 11
9 Sa	7 15 0	18 56 00	23 16	19 42	0≈49	0♑26	0 57	4 38	2 33	6 44	18 38	24 27	14 32	10 31	6 43	20 59	5 12
10 Su	7 18 56	19 57 09	7♐38	19 43R	2 27	1 41	1 25	4 52	2 40	6 44	18 40	24 29	14 52	10 51	7 01	21 04	5 14
11 M	7 22 53	20 58 19	21 58	19 44	4 05	2 56	1 54	5 06	2 47	6 44	18 41	24 31	15 11	11 11	7 19	21 08	5 15
12 T	7 26 50	21 59 29	6♑13	19 43	5 43	4 12	2 22	5 20	2 54	6 43	18 42	24 33	15 31	11 31	7 37	21 11	5 16
13 W	7 30 46	23 00 39	20 19	19 40	7 20	5 27	2 51	5 34	3 01	6 43	18 44	24 35	15 51	11 51	7 55	21 14	5 18
14 Th	7 34 43	24 01 48	4≈10	19 35	8 56	6 42	3 20	5 48	3 08	6 43D	18 45	24 37	16 11	12 12	8 13	21 17	5 19
15 F	7 38 39	25 02 57	17 43	19 30	10 30	7 57	3 49	6 02	3 15	6 43	18 47	24 39	16 31	12 32	8 31	21 19	5 21
16 Sa	7 42 36	26 04 05	0♓56	19 23	12 04	9 13	4 19	6 16	3 22	6 43	18 48	24 41	16 52	12 52	8 49	21 21	5 23
17 Su	7 46 32	27 05 12	13 48	19 17	13 35	10 28	4 48	6 30	3 30	6 43	18 50	24 43	17 12	13 12	9 06	21 22	5 24
18 M	7 50 29	28 06 19	26 20	19 11	15 05	11 43	5 18	6 44	3 37	6 44	18 52	24 45	17 32	13 33	9 24	21 23	5 26
19 T	7 54 25	29 07 24	8♈35	19 07	16 32	12 58	5 48	6 59	3 44	6 44	18 53	24 47	17 53	13 53	9 41	21 24R	5 28
20 W	7 58 22	0≈08 29	20 37	19 05D	17 55	14 13	6 18	7 13	3 51	6 44	18 55	24 49	18 14	14 13	9 58	21 24	5 30
21 Th	8 2 19	1 09 34	2♉30	19 04	19 15	15 29	6 49	7 27	3 58	6 44	18 56	24 51	18 34	14 34	10 15	21 23	5 31
22 F	8 6 15	2 10 37	14 19	19 04	20 31	16 44	7 19	7 41	4 05	6 45	18 58	24 53	18 55	14 54	10 32	21 22	5 33
23 Sa	8 10 12	3 11 39	26 10	19 07	21 42	17 59	7 50	7 55	4 12	6 45	19 00	24 55	19 16	15 14	10 49	21 21	5 35
24 Su	8 14 8	4 12 40	8♊08	19 08R	22 47	19 14	8 21	8 10	4 19	6 46	19 02	24 57	19 37	15 34	11 06	21 19	5 37
25 M	8 18 5	5 13 41	20 17	19 09	23 45	20 30	8 52	8 24	4 27	6 46	19 03	24 59	19 58	15 55	11 23	21 16	5 39
26 T	8 22 1	6 14 40	2♋41	19 07	24 35	21 45	9 23	8 38	4 34	6 47	19 05	25 01	20 19	16 15	11 39	21 13	5 41
27 W	8 25 58	7 15 39	15 23	19 04	25 18	23 00	9 54	8 52	4 41	6 48	19 07	25 03	20 41	16 36	11 56	21 10	5 44
28 Th	8 29 54	8 16 36	28 24	19 00	25 51	24 15	10 26	9 07	4 48	6 48	19 09	25 05	21 02	16 56	12 12	21 06	5 46
29 F	8 33 51	9 17 33	11♌45	18 51	26 14	25 30	10 57	9 21	4 55	6 49	19 10	25 07	21 23	17 16	12 29	21 02	5 48
30 Sa	8 37 48	10 18 28	25 23	18 42	26 27R	26 45	11 29	9 35	5 02	6 50	19 12	25 09	21 45	17 37	12 45	20 57	5 50
31 Su	8 41 44	11 19 23	9♍15	18 33	26 29	28 01	12 01	9 49	5 09	6 51	19 14	25 11	22 07	17 57	13 01	20 52	5 53

EPHEMERIS CALCULATED FOR 12 MIDNIGHT GREENWICH MEAN TIME. ALL OTHER DATA AND FACING ASPECTARIAN PAGE IN **EASTERN TIME (BOLD)** AND PACIFIC TIME (REGULAR).

FEBRUARY 2021

☽ Last Aspect day	ET / hr:mn / PT	asp	☽ Ingress sign day	ET / hr:mn / PT
1	**6:10 am** 3:10 am	△♀	♎ 1	**6:25 am** 3:25 am
2	10:15 pm	△☿	♏ 3	**9:15 am** 6:15 am
3	**1:15 am**	△☿	♏ 3	**9:15 am** 6:15 am
5	**4:20 am** 1:20 am	⚹♇	♐ 5	**12:16 pm** 9:16 am
6	10:16 pm	⚹☿	♑ 7	**3:52 pm** 12:52 pm
7	**1:16 am**	⚹☿	♑ 7	**3:52 pm** 12:52 pm
9	**12:22 pm** 9:22 am	☌♇	♒ 9	**8:20 pm** 5:20 pm
11	**2:06 pm** 11:06 am	☌☉	♓ 11	11:23 pm
11	**2:06 pm** 11:06 am	☌☉	♓ 12	**2:23 am**
13	11:29 pm	⚹♇	♈ 14	**10:54 am** 7:54 am

☽ Last Aspect day	ET / hr:mn / PT	asp	☽ Ingress sign day	ET / hr:mn / PT
14	**2:29 am**	⚹♇	♈ 14	**10:54 am** 7:54 am
16	**7:17 pm** 4:17 pm	⚹☉	♉ 16	**10:12 pm** 7:12 pm
18	11:28 pm	△♇	♊ 19	**11:04 am** 8:04 am
19	**2:28 am**	△♇	♊ 19	**11:04 am** 8:04 am
21	**1:39 pm** 10:39 am	△♀	♋ 21	**10:53 pm** 7:53 pm
23	**11:54 pm** 8:54 pm	☍♇	♌ 24	**7:23 am** 4:23 am
26	**6:32 am** 3:32 am	□♂	♍ 26	**12:07 pm** 9:07 am
28	**10:58 am** 7:58 am	△♂	♎ 28	**2:17 pm** 11:17 am

☽ Phases & Eclipses phase	day	ET / hr:mn / PT
4th Quarter	4	**12:37 pm** 9:37 am
New Moon	11	**2:06 pm** 11:06 am
2nd Quarter	19	**1:47 pm** 10:47 am
Full Moon	27	**3:17 am** 12:17 am

Planet Ingress	day	ET / hr:mn / PT
♀ ♒	1	**9:05 am** 6:05 am
☉ ♓	18	**5:44 am** 2:44 am
⚳ ♈	20	9:23 pm
⚳ ♈	21	**12:23 am**
♀ ♓	25	**8:11 am** 5:11 am

Planetary Motion	day	ET / hr:mn / PT
☿ D	20	**7:52 pm** 4:52 pm

1 MONDAY
☽ ⚻ ☿ **12:05 am**
☉ □ ♂ **5:34 am** 2:34 am
☽ △ ♀ **6:10 am** 3:10 am
☽ △ ♄ **3:32 pm** 12:32 pm
☽ ⚻ ♅ **6:05 pm** 3:05 pm
☽ △ ♃ **11:58 pm** 8:58 pm

2 TUESDAY
☽ ⚻ ♂ **4:59 am** 1:59 am
☽ △ ☉ **5:50 am** 2:50 am
☽ ⚻ ♆ **3:10 pm** 12:10 pm
☽ □ ♇ 10:15 pm
☽ △ ☿ 10:15 pm
☿ ⚺ ♇ 10:22 pm

3 WEDNESDAY
☽ □ ♇ **1:15 am**
☽ △ ☿ **1:15 am**
☿ ⚺ ♇ **1:22 am**
☽ □ ♀ **1:55 pm** 10:55 am
☽ □ ♄ **6:47 pm** 3:47 pm
☽ ☍ ♅ **8:57 pm** 5:57 pm

4 THURSDAY
☽ □ ♃ **3:40 am** 12:40 am
☽ ☍ ♂ **9:51 am** 6:51 am
☽ □ ☉ **12:37 pm** 9:37 am
☽ △ ♆ **6:11 pm** 3:11 pm
☽ □ ☿ 10:27 pm

5 FRIDAY
☽ □ ☿ **1:27 am**
☽ ⚹ ♇ **4:20 am** 1:20 am
☽ ⚹ ♀ **10:00 pm** 7:00 pm
☽ ⚹ ♄ **10:20 pm** 7:20 pm
☽ ⚻ ♅ 9:10 pm
♀ ☌ ♄ 11:07 pm

6 SATURDAY
☽ ⚻ ♅ **12:10 am**
♀ ☌ ♄ **2:07 am**
☽ ⚹ ♃ **7:45 am** 4:45 am
☽ ⚻ ♂ **3:12 pm** 12:12 pm
☽ ⚹ ☉ **7:56 pm** 4:56 pm
☽ □ ♆ **9:40 pm** 6:40 pm
♀ □ ♅ **10:33 pm** 7:33 pm
☽ ⚹ ☿ 10:16 pm

7 SUNDAY
☽ ⚹ ☿ **1:16 am**
☽ ⚺ ♇ **7:56 am** 4:56 am
☉ ⚺ ♆ **8:32 pm** 5:32 pm
☽ ⚺ ♄ 11:31 pm

8 MONDAY
☽ ⚺ ♄ **2:31 am**
☽ △ ♅ **4:00 am** 1:00 am
☽ ⚺ ♀ **6:53 am** 3:53 am
☉ ☌ ☿ **8:48 am** 5:48 am
☽ ⚺ ♃ **12:32 pm** 9:32 am
☿ ⚺ ♆ **6:35 pm** 3:35 pm
☽ △ ♂ **9:21 pm** 6:21 pm
☽ ⚺ ☿ 10:18 pm
☽ ⚹ ♆ 10:55 pm

9 TUESDAY
☽ ⚺ ☿ **1:18 am**
☽ ⚹ ♆ **1:55 am**
☽ ⚺ ☉ **4:11 am** 1:11 am
☽ ☌ ♇ **12:22 pm** 9:22 am

10 WEDNESDAY
☿ □ ♂ **7:16 am** 4:16 am
☽ ☌ ♄ **7:42 am** 4:42 am
☽ □ ♅ **8:51 am** 5:51 am
☽ ☌ ♀ **5:11 pm** 2:11 pm
☽ ☌ ♃ **6:29 pm** 3:29 pm
☽ ☌ ☿ 11:22 pm

11 THURSDAY
☽ ☌ ☿ **2:22 am**
☽ □ ♂ **4:55 am** 1:55 am
☽ ⚺ ♆ **7:27 am** 4:27 am
♀ ☌ ♃ **10:00 am** 7:00 am
☽ ☌ ☉ **2:06 pm** 11:06 am
☽ ⚺ ♇ **6:14 pm** 3:14 pm

12 FRIDAY
☽ ⚺ ♄ **2:42 pm** 11:42 am
☽ ⚹ ♅ **3:30 pm** 12:30 pm
☽ ⚺ ♃ 11:29 pm
☿ ☌ ♀ 11:48 pm

13 SATURDAY
☽ ⚺ ♃ **2:29 am**
☿ ☌ ♀ **2:48 am**
☽ ⚺ ☿ **5:32 am** 2:32 am
☽ ⚺ ♀ **6:03 am** 3:03 am
☽ ⚹ ♂ **2:55 pm** 11:55 am
☽ ☌ ♆ **3:11 pm** 12:11 pm
♂ ⚹ ♆ **9:13 pm** 6:13 pm
☉ ⚺ ♇ **9:34 pm** 6:34 pm
☽ ⚹ ♇ 11:29 pm
☽ ⚺ ☉ 11:54 pm

14 SUNDAY
☽ ⚹ ♇ **2:29 am**
☽ ⚺ ☉ **2:54 am**
☿ ☌ ♃ **4:40 pm** 1:40 pm
☽ ⚹ ♄ 9:23 pm
☽ ⚺ ♅ 9:49 pm

15 MONDAY
☽ ⚹ ♄ **12:23 am**
☽ ⚺ ♅ **12:49 am**
☽ ⚹ ☿ **11:50 am** 8:50 am
☽ ⚹ ♃ **1:22 pm** 10:22 am
☽ ⚹ ♀ **10:40 pm** 7:40 pm
☽ ⚺ ♆ 10:44 pm

16 TUESDAY
☽ ⚺ ♆ **1:44 am**
☽ ⚺ ♂ **4:08 am** 1:08 am
☽ □ ♇ **1:32 pm** 10:32 am
☽ ⚹ ☉ **7:17 pm** 4:17 pm

17 WEDNESDAY
♀ ⚺ ♆ **5:00 am** 2:00 am
☽ □ ♄ **12:48 pm** 9:48 am
☽ ☌ ♅ **12:48 pm** 9:48 am
♄ □ ♅ **2:08 pm** 11:08 am
☽ □ ☿ **9:32 pm** 6:32 pm
☽ □ ♃ 11:51 pm

18 THURSDAY
☽ □ ♃ **2:51 am**
☽ ⚹ ♆ **2:30 pm** 11:30 am
☽ □ ♀ **6:21 pm** 3:21 pm
☽ ☌ ♂ **7:48 pm** 4:48 pm
☽ △ ♇ 11:28 pm

19 FRIDAY
☽ △ ♇ **2:28 am**
☽ □ ☉ **1:47 pm** 10:47 am
♀ □ ♂ **6:04 pm** 3:04 pm
☽ ⚺ ♅ 10:50 pm
☽ △ ♄ 11:15 pm

20 SATURDAY
☽ ⚺ ♅ **1:50 am**
☽ △ ♄ **2:15 am**
☽ △ ☿ **9:20 am** 6:20 am
☽ △ ♃ **4:46 pm** 1:46 pm

21 SUNDAY
☽ □ ♆ **3:10 am** 12:10 am
☽ ⚺ ♂ **11:06 am** 8:06 am
☽ △ ♀ **1:39 pm** 10:39 am
☽ ⚻ ♇ **2:45 pm** 11:45 am
♀ ⚺ ♇ 9:31 pm

22 MONDAY
♀ ⚺ ♇ **12:31 am**
☽ △ ☉ **6:47 am** 3:47 am
☽ ⚹ ♅ **1:09 pm** 10:09 am
☽ ⚻ ♄ **1:55 pm** 10:55 am
☽ ⚻ ☿ **8:31 pm** 5:31 pm

23 TUESDAY
☽ ⚻ ♃ **4:14 am** 1:14 am
☽ △ ♆ **1:06 pm** 10:06 am
☽ ⚹ ♂ **10:59 pm** 7:59 pm
☽ ☍ ♇ **11:54 pm** 8:54 pm

24 WEDNESDAY
☽ ⚻ ♀ **4:47 am** 1:47 am
☽ ⚻ ☉ **7:18 pm** 4:18 pm
☽ □ ♅ **8:49 pm** 5:49 pm
♂ △ ♇ **8:52 pm** 5:52 pm
☽ ☍ ♄ **9:52 pm** 6:52 pm

25 THURSDAY
☽ ☍ ☿ **4:56 am** 1:56 am
☽ ☍ ♃ **11:40 am** 8:40 am
☉ ⚹ ♅ **4:13 pm** 1:13 pm
☽ ⚻ ♆ **7:09 pm** 4:09 pm

26 FRIDAY
☽ ⚻ ♇ **5:12 am** 2:12 am
☽ □ ♂ **6:32 am** 3:32 am
☉ ⚺ ♄ **9:25 am** 6:25 am
☽ ☍ ♀ **2:50 pm** 11:50 am
☽ △ ♅ 9:54 pm
☽ ⚻ ♄ 11:09 pm

27 SATURDAY
☽ △ ♅ **12:54 am**
☽ ⚻ ♄ **2:09 am**
☽ ☍ ☉ **3:17 am** 12:17 am
☽ ⚻ ☿ **10:25 am** 7:25 am
☽ ⚻ ♃ **3:40 pm** 12:40 pm
☽ ☍ ♆ **10:06 pm** 7:06 pm

28 SUNDAY
☽ △ ♇ **7:42 am** 4:42 am
☽ △ ♂ **10:58 am** 7:58 am
☽ ⚻ ♀ **9:36 pm** 6:36 pm
☽ ⚻ ♅ 11:49 pm

Eastern time in bold type
Pacific time in medium type

FEBRUARY 2021

DATE	SID.TIME	SUN	MOON	NODE	MERCURY	VENUS	MARS	JUPITER	SATURN	URANUS	NEPTUNE	PLUTO	CERES	PALLAS	JUNO	VESTA	CHIRON
1 M	8 45 41	12≈20 16	23♍17	18Ⅱ25℞	26≈19℞	29♑16	12♉33	10≈04	5≈17	6♉51	19♓16	25♑13	22♈28	18≈17	13♐17	20♍46℞	5♈55
2 T	8 49 37	13 21 09	7≏25	18 18	25 59	0≈31	13 05	10 18	5 24	6 52	19 18	25 15	22 50	18 38	13 33	20 40	5 57
3 W	8 53 34	14 22 01	21 36	18 13	25 27	1 46	13 37	10 32	5 31	6 53	19 20	25 16	23 12	18 58	13 48	20 33	6 00
4 Th	8 57 30	15 22 52	5♏45	18 11D	24 45	3 01	14 10	10 46	5 38	6 54	19 22	25 18	23 34	19 19	14 04	20 26	6 02
5 F	9 01 27	16 23 43	19 52	18 10	23 54	4 17	14 42	11 00	5 45	6 56	19 24	25 20	23 56	19 39	14 19	20 18	6 05
6 Sa	9 05 23	17 24 32	3♐56	18 11	22 56	5 32	15 15	11 15	5 52	6 57	19 26	25 22	24 18	19 59	14 34	20 10	6 07
7 Su	9 09 20	18 25 21	17 55	18 12℞	21 51	6 47	15 47	11 29	5 59	6 58	19 28	25 24	24 40	20 20	14 50	20 02	6 10
8 M	9 13 17	19 26 09	1♑49	18 11	20 42	8 02	16 20	11 43	6 06	6 59	19 30	25 26	25 02	20 40	15 05	19 53	6 12
9 T	9 17 13	20 26 56	15 36	18 08	19 31	9 17	16 53	11 57	6 13	7 00	19 32	25 28	25 24	21 00	15 19	19 43	6 15
10 W	9 21 10	21 27 42	29 15	18 02	18 19	10 32	17 26	12 12	6 20	7 02	19 34	25 30	25 46	21 21	15 34	19 33	6 18
11 Th	9 25 6	22 28 26	12≈43	17 53	17 09	11 48	17 59	12 26	6 27	7 03	19 36	25 31	26 09	21 41	15 49	19 23	6 20
12 F	9 29 3	23 29 09	25 58	17 42	16 03	13 03	18 33	12 40	6 34	7 05	19 38	25 33	26 31	22 01	16 03	19 12	6 23
13 Sa	9 32 59	24 29 51	8♓58	17 30	15 01	14 18	19 06	12 54	6 41	7 06	19 40	25 35	26 53	22 22	16 17	19 01	6 26
14 Su	9 36 56	25 30 31	21 43	17 18	14 05	15 33	19 39	13 08	6 48	7 08	19 42	25 37	27 16	22 42	16 31	18 50	6 29
15 M	9 40 52	26 31 10	4♈11	17 06	13 16	16 48	20 13	13 22	6 55	7 09	19 44	25 39	27 38	23 02	16 45	18 38	6 32
16 T	9 44 49	27 31 47	16 24	16 57	12 35	18 03	20 47	13 36	7 02	7 11	19 47	25 40	28 01	23 22	16 59	18 26	6 35
17 W	9 48 46	28 32 22	28 25	16 50	12 01	19 18	21 20	13 50	7 08	7 13	19 49	25 42	28 24	23 43	17 13	18 13	6 37
18 Th	9 52 42	29 32 56	10♉17	16 46	11 35	20 33	21 54	14 04	7 15	7 14	19 51	25 44	28 46	24 03	17 26	18 00	6 40
19 F	9 56 39	0♓33 28	22 06	16 44D	11 16	21 49	22 28	14 18	7 22	7 16	19 53	25 46	29 09	24 23	17 39	17 47	6 43
20 Sa	10 0 35	1 33 58	3Ⅱ55	16 44	11 05	23 04	23 02	14 32	7 29	7 18	19 55	25 47	29 32	24 43	17 52	17 34	6 46
21 Su	10 4 32	2 34 26	15 52	16 44℞	11 01D	24 19	23 36	14 46	7 36	7 20	19 57	25 49	29 55	25 03	18 05	17 20	6 49
22 M	10 8 28	3 34 52	28 01	16 44	11 05	25 34	24 10	15 00	7 42	7 22	20 00	25 51	0♉18	25 24	18 18	17 06	6 52
23 T	10 12 25	4 35 17	10♋27	16 41	11 14	26 49	24 44	15 14	7 49	7 23	20 02	25 52	0 41	25 44	18 31	16 52	6 55
24 W	10 16 21	5 35 40	23 15	16 37	11 30	28 04	25 19	15 28	7 55	7 25	20 04	25 54	1 04	26 04	18 43	16 37	6 59
25 Th	10 20 18	6 36 00	6♌27	16 33	11 51	29 19	25 53	15 42	8 02	7 28	20 06	25 55	1 27	26 24	18 55	16 22	7 02
26 F	10 24 15	7 36 19	20 03	16 20	12 18	0♓34	26 27	15 56	8 09	7 30	20 09	25 57	1 50	26 44	19 07	16 07	7 05
27 Sa	10 28 11	8 36 36	4♍03	16 08	12 50	1 49	27 02	16 09	8 15	7 32	20 11	25 59	2 13	27 04	19 19	15 52	7 08
28 Su	10 32 8	9 36 52	18 21	15 56	13 26	3 04	27 36	16 23	8 22	7 34	20 13	26 00	2 36	27 24	19 31	15 37	7 11

EPHEMERIS CALCULATED FOR 12 MIDNIGHT GREENWICH MEAN TIME. ALL OTHER DATA AND FACING ASPECTARIAN PAGE IN **EASTERN TIME (BOLD)** AND PACIFIC TIME (REGULAR).

MARCH 2021

☽ Last Aspect day	ET / hr:mn / PT	asp	☽ Ingress sign day	ET / hr:mn / PT
2	**9:09 am** 6:09 am	□♇	♏ 2	**3:38 pm** 12:38 pm
4	**11:10 am** 8:10 am	⚹♇	♐ 4	**5:43 pm** 2:43 pm
6	**4:44 am** 1:44 am	□♆	♑ 6	**9:20 pm** 6:20 pm
8	**7:52 pm** 4:52 pm	☌♇	♒ 8	11:41 pm
8	**7:52 pm** 4:52 pm	☌♇	♒ 9	**2:41 am**
10	**10:32 pm** 7:32 pm	☌☿	♓ 11	**9:44 am** 6:44 am
13	**11:38 am** 8:38 am	⚹♇	♈ 13	**6:44 pm** 3:44 pm
15	**11:40 pm** 8:40 pm	□♇	♉ 16	**6:56 am** 3:56 am
18	**4:40 pm** 1:40 pm	⚹☉	♊ 18	**7:47 pm** 4:47 pm
21	**8:04 am** 5:04 am	□♀	♋ 21	**8:18 am** 5:18 am

☽ Last Aspect day	ET / hr:mn / PT	asp	☽ Ingress sign day	ET / hr:mn / PT
23	**11:26 am** 8:26 am	☍♇	♌ 23	**5:56 pm** 2:56 pm
25	**9:27 am** 6:27 am	☍♃	♍ 25	**11:25 pm** 8:25 pm
27	**7:48 pm** 4:48 pm	△♇	♎ 27	10:22 pm
27	**7:48 pm** 4:48 pm	△♇	♎ 28	**1:22 am**
29	**8:08 pm** 5:08 pm	□♇	♏ 29	10:33 pm
29	**8:08 pm** 5:08 pm	□♇	♏ 30	**1:33 am**
31	**8:29 pm** 5:29 pm	⚹♇	♐ 31	10:59 pm
31	**8:29 pm** 5:29 pm	⚹♇	♐ 4/1	**1:59 am**

☽ Phases & Eclipses phase	day	ET / hr:mn / PT
4th Quarter	5	**8:30 pm** 5:30 pm
New Moon	13	**5:21 am** 2:21 am
2nd Quarter	21	**10:40 am** 7:40 am
Full Moon	28	**2:48 pm** 11:48 am

Planet Ingress	day	ET / hr:mn / PT
♂ ♊	3	**10:30 pm** 7:30 pm
♀ ♓	7	**4:06 pm** 1:06 pm
☿ ♓	15	**6:26 pm** 3:26 pm
☉ ♈	20	**5:37 am** 2:37 am
♀ ♈	21	**10:16 am** 7:16 am

Planetary Motion	day	ET / hr:mn / PT

1 MONDAY
☽ ⚻ ♅ **2:49 am**
☽ △ ♄ **4:17 am** 1:17 am
☽ ⚻ ☉ **8:42 am** 5:42 am
☽ △ ☿ **2:27 pm** 11:27 am
☽ △ ♃ **5:57 pm** 2:57 pm
☽ ⚻ ♆ **11:40 pm** 8:40 pm

2 TUESDAY
☽ □ ♇ **9:09 am** 6:09 am
☽ ⚻ ♂ **2:22 pm** 11:22 am

3 WEDNESDAY
☽ △ ♀ **3:39 am** 12:39 am
☽ ☍ ♅ **4:22 am** 1:22 am
☽ □ ♄ **6:05 am** 3:05 am
♀ ⚹ ♅ **12:09 pm** 9:09 am
☽ △ ☉ **1:52 pm** 10:52 am
☽ □ ☿ **7:01 pm** 4:01 pm
☽ □ ♃ **8:22 pm** 5:22 pm
☽ △ ♆ 10:30 pm

4 THURSDAY
☽ △ ♆ **1:30 am**
♀ ⚺ ♄ **10:14 am** 7:14 am
☽ ⚹ ♇ **11:10 am** 8:10 am
☽ ☍ ♂ **6:32 pm** 3:32 pm
☿ ☌ ♃ **10:27 pm** 7:27 pm

5 FRIDAY
☽ ⚻ ♅ **6:55 am** 3:55 am
☽ ⚹ ♄ **8:56 am** 5:56 am
☽ □ ♀ **10:58 am** 7:58 am
☽ □ ☉ **8:30 pm** 5:30 pm
☽ ⚹ ♃ 9:07 pm
☽ ⚹ ☿ 10:36 pm

6 SATURDAY
☽ ⚹ ♃ **12:07 am**
☽ ⚹ ☿ **1:36 am**
☽ □ ♆ **4:44 am** 1:44 am
☽ ⚺ ♇ **2:39 pm** 11:39 am
☽ ⚻ ♂ 9:29 pm

7 SUNDAY
☽ ⚻ ♂ **12:29 am**
☽ △ ♅ **11:09 am** 8:09 am
☽ ⚺ ♄ **1:28 pm** 10:28 am
☽ ⚹ ♀ **8:29 pm** 5:29 pm
☿ ⚺ ♆ **9:12 pm** 6:12 pm

8 MONDAY
☽ ⚹ ☉ **5:15 am** 2:15 am
☽ ⚺ ♃ **5:39 am** 2:39 am
☽ ⚹ ♆ **9:41 am** 6:41 am
☽ ⚺ ☿ **10:44 am** 7:44 am
☉ ⚺ ♃ **12:04 pm** 9:04 am
☽ ☌ ♇ **7:52 pm** 4:52 pm

9 TUESDAY
☽ △ ♂ **8:23 am** 5:23 am
☽ □ ♅ **5:06 pm** 2:06 pm
☽ ☌ ♄ **7:45 pm** 4:45 pm

10 WEDNESDAY
☽ ⚺ ♀ **8:16 am** 5:16 am
☽ ☌ ♃ **12:58 pm** 9:58 am
☽ ⚺ ☉ **4:08 pm** 1:08 pm
☽ ⚺ ♆ **4:21 pm** 1:21 pm
☉ ☌ ♆ **7:01 pm** 4:01 pm
☽ ☌ ☿ **10:32 pm** 7:32 pm
☽ ⚺ ♇ 11:48 pm

11 THURSDAY
☽ ⚺ ♇ **2:48 am**
☽ □ ♂ **6:16 pm** 3:16 pm
☽ ⚹ ♅ 9:50 pm

12 FRIDAY
☽ ⚹ ♅ **12:50 am**
☽ ⚺ ♄ **3:49 am** 12:49 am
♀ ⚺ ♃ **6:53 pm** 3:53 pm
☿ ⚺ ♇ **8:41 pm** 5:41 pm
☽ ⚺ ♃ **10:11 pm** 7:11 pm
☽ ☌ ♀ **10:29 pm** 7:29 pm
☽ ☌ ♆ 9:52 pm

13 SATURDAY
☽ ☌ ♆ **12:52 am**
☽ ☌ ☉ **5:21 am** 2:21 am
☽ ⚹ ♇ **11:38 am** 8:38 am
☽ ⚺ ☿ **1:17 pm** 10:17 am
♀ ☌ ♆ **11:08 pm** 8:08 pm

14 SUNDAY
☽ ⚹ ♂ **7:28 am** 4:28 am
☽ ⚺ ♅ **11:37 am** 8:37 am
☽ ⚹ ♄ **2:58 pm** 11:58 am

15 MONDAY
☽ ⚹ ♃ **10:40 am** 7:40 am
☽ ⚺ ♆ **12:35 pm** 9:35 am
☽ ⚺ ♀ **4:39 pm** 1:39 pm
☽ ⚺ ☉ **10:22 pm** 7:22 pm
☽ □ ♇ **11:40 pm** 8:40 pm

16 TUESDAY
☽ ⚹ ☿ **8:31 am** 5:31 am
☉ ⚹ ♇ **2:26 pm** 11:26 am
☽ ⚺ ♂ **10:12 pm** 7:12 pm
☽ ☌ ♅ **11:37 pm** 8:37 pm

17 WEDNESDAY
☽ □ ♄ **3:20 am** 12:20 am
☽ □ ♃ 9:14 pm
☽ ⚹ ♆ 10:16 pm

18 THURSDAY
☽ □ ♃ **12:14 am**
☽ ⚹ ♆ **1:16 am**
♂ ⚺ ♅ **4:48 am** 1:48 am
☽ ⚹ ♀ **12:24 pm** 9:24 am
☽ △ ♇ **12:30 pm** 9:30 am
♀ ⚹ ♇ **1:20 pm** 10:20 am
☽ ⚹ ☉ **4:40 pm** 1:40 pm

19 FRIDAY
☽ □ ☿ **5:28 am** 2:28 am
☽ ⚺ ♅ **12:52 pm** 9:52 am
☽ ☌ ♂ **2:25 pm** 11:25 am
☽ △ ♄ **4:50 pm** 1:50 pm

20 SATURDAY
☽ △ ♃ **2:14 pm** 11:14 am
☽ □ ♆ **2:20 pm** 11:20 am
♃ ⚺ ♆ **9:51 pm** 6:51 pm
☽ ⚻ ♇ 10:17 pm

21 SUNDAY
☽ ⚻ ♇ **1:17 am**
☽ □ ♀ **8:04 am** 5:04 am
☽ □ ☉ **10:40 am** 7:40 am
☿ ⚹ ♅ **7:35 pm** 4:35 pm
♂ △ ♄ **10:35 pm** 7:35 pm
☽ ⚹ ♅ 10:02 pm
☽ △ ☿ 10:46 pm

22 MONDAY
☽ ⚹ ♅ **1:02 am**
☽ △ ☿ **1:46 am**
☽ ⚻ ♄ **5:02 am** 2:02 am
☽ ⚺ ♂ **5:19 am** 2:19 am
☽ △ ♆ 10:14 pm
☽ ⚻ ♃ 10:56 pm

23 TUESDAY
☽ △ ♆ **1:14 am**
☽ ⚻ ♃ **1:56 am**
☿ ⚺ ♄ **6:12 am** 3:12 am
☽ ☍ ♇ **11:26 am** 8:26 am
☿ □ ♂ **11:26 pm** 8:26 pm
☽ △ ♀ **11:50 pm** 8:50 pm
☽ △ ☉ 9:54 pm

24 WEDNESDAY
☽ △ ☉ **12:54 am**
☽ □ ♅ **9:45 am** 6:45 am
☽ ☍ ♄ **1:38 pm** 10:38 am
☽ ⚹ ♂ **4:08 pm** 1:08 pm
☽ ⚻ ☿ **5:28 pm** 2:28 pm

25 THURSDAY
☽ ⚻ ♆ **8:07 am** 5:07 am
☽ ☍ ♃ **9:27 am** 6:27 am
☽ ⚻ ♇ **5:28 pm** 2:28 pm
☉ ☌ ♀ 11:58 pm

26 FRIDAY
☉ ☌ ♀ **2:58 am**
☽ ⚻ ☉ **9:52 am** 6:52 am
☽ ⚻ ♀ **10:00 am** 7:00 am
☽ △ ♅ **2:17 pm** 11:17 am
☽ ⚻ ♄ **6:00 pm** 3:00 pm
☽ □ ♂ **10:16 pm** 7:16 pm

27 SATURDAY
☽ ☍ ☿ **3:37 am** 12:37 am
☽ ☍ ♆ **11:05 am** 8:05 am
☽ ⚻ ♃ **12:55 pm** 9:55 am
☽ △ ♇ **7:48 pm** 4:48 pm

28 SUNDAY
♀ ⚺ ♅ **12:53 pm** 9:53 am
☽ ☍ ☉ **2:48 pm** 11:48 am
☽ ⚻ ♅ **3:40 pm** 12:40 pm
☽ ☍ ♀ **3:55 pm** 12:55 pm
☽ △ ♄ **7:21 pm** 4:21 pm
☽ △ ♂ 10:12 pm

29 MONDAY
☽ △ ♂ **1:12 am**
☉ ⚺ ♅ **4:34 am** 1:34 am
☽ ⚻ ☿ **10:16 am** 7:16 am
☽ ⚻ ♆ **11:42 am** 8:42 am
☽ △ ♃ **2:01 pm** 11:01 am
☽ □ ♇ **8:08 pm** 5:08 pm
☿ ☌ ♆ **11:24 pm** 8:24 pm

30 TUESDAY
♀ ⚹ ♄ **11:47 am** 8:47 am
☽ ☍ ♅ **3:54 pm** 12:54 pm
☽ ⚻ ☉ **6:16 pm** 3:16 pm
☽ □ ♄ **7:39 pm** 4:39 pm
☽ ⚻ ♀ **8:20 pm** 5:20 pm
☿ ⚺ ♃ **11:54 pm** 8:54 pm

31 WEDNESDAY
☽ ⚻ ♂ **3:17 am** 12:17 am
☽ △ ♆ **11:59 am** 8:59 am
☽ □ ♃ **2:52 pm** 11:52 am
☽ △ ☿ **4:35 pm** 1:35 pm
☉ ⚹ ♄ **5:04 pm** 2:04 pm
☽ ⚹ ♇ **8:29 pm** 5:29 pm

Eastern time in bold type
Pacific time in medium type

MARCH 2021

DATE	SID.TIME	SUN	MOON	NODE	MERCURY	VENUS	MARS	JUPITER	SATURN	URANUS	NEPTUNE	PLUTO	CERES	PALLAS	JUNO	VESTA	CHIRON
1 M	10 36 4	10♓07 05	2≈52	15Ⅱ44R	14≈06	4♓19	28Ⅱ11	16≈37	8≈28	7♉36	20♓15	26♑02	2♉59	27≈44	19♒42	15♏22R	7♈14
2 T	10 40 1	11 37 17	17 28	15 34	14 51	5 34	28 46	16 50	8 34	7 38	20 17	26 03	3 22	28 04	19 53	15 06	7 18
3 W	10 43 57	12 37 27	2♏02	15 27	15 39	6 49	29 20	17 04	8 41	7 41	20 20	26 05	3 46	28 23	20 04	14 50	7 21
4 Th	10 47 54	13 37 36	16 29	15 23	16 30	8 04	29 55	17 17	8 47	7 43	20 22	26 06	4 09	28 43	20 15	14 35	7 24
5 F	10 51 50	14 37 44	0♐46	15 22	17 25	9 18	0♋30	17 31	8 53	7 45	20 24	26 08	4 32	29 03	20 26	14 19	7 27
6 Sa	10 55 47	15 37 49	14 49	15 21	18 22	10 33	1 05	17 44	9 00	7 48	20 27	26 09	4 56	29 23	20 36	14 03	7 31
7 Su	10 59 44	16 37 54	28 40	15 21	19 23	11 48	1 40	17 58	9 06	7 50	20 29	26 11	5 19	29 43	20 46	13 48	7 34
8 M	11 3 40	17 37 57	12♑18	15 20	20 25	13 03	2 14	18 11	9 12	7 52	20 31	26 12	5 42	0♓02	20 56	13 32	7 37
9 T	11 7 37	18 37 58	25 44	15 16	21 31	14 18	2 50	18 24	9 18	7 55	20 33	26 13	6 06	0 22	21 06	13 16	7 41
10 W	11 11 33	19 37 57	9≈00	15 09	22 38	15 33	3 25	18 38	9 24	7 57	20 36	26 15	6 29	0 42	21 16	13 00	7 44
11 Th	11 15 30	20 37 55	22 04	14 59	23 48	16 48	4 00	18 51	9 30	8 00	20 38	26 16	6 53	1 01	21 25	12 45	7 48
12 F	11 19 26	21 37 51	4♓57	14 47	25 00	18 03	4 35	19 04	9 36	8 03	20 40	26 17	7 16	1 21	21 34	12 29	7 51
13 Sa	11 23 23	22 37 45	17 39	14 33	26 13	19 17	5 10	19 17	9 42	8 05	20 43	26 19	7 40	1 40	21 43	12 14	7 54
14 Su	11 27 19	23 37 37	0♈08	14 19	27 29	20 32	5 45	19 30	9 48	8 08	20 45	26 20	8 04	2 00	21 51	11 59	7 58
15 M	11 31 16	24 37 27	12 26	14 07	28 46	21 47	6 21	19 43	9 53	8 11	20 47	26 21	8 27	2 19	22 00	11 44	8 01
16 T	11 35 13	25 37 15	24 32	13 56	0♓05	23 02	6 56	19 56	9 59	8 13	20 49	26 22	8 51	2 39	22 08	11 29	8 05
17 W	11 39 9	26 37 01	6♉29	13 47	1 26	24 17	7 31	20 09	10 05	8 16	20 52	26 23	9 14	2 58	22 16	11 14	8 08
18 Th	11 43 6	27 36 44	18 19	13 42	2 48	25 31	8 07	20 22	10 10	8 19	20 54	26 25	9 38	3 17	22 23	11 00	8 12
19 F	11 47 2	28 36 26	0Ⅱ06	13 39	4 12	26 46	8 42	20 35	10 16	8 22	20 56	26 26	10 02	3 36	22 30	10 46	8 15
20 Sa	11 50 59	29 36 05	11 55	13 38R	5 37	28 01	9 18	20 47	10 21	8 25	20 58	26 27	10 25	3 56	22 38	10 32	8 19
21 Su	11 54 55	0♈35 42	23 50	13 39R	7 04	29 16	9 53	21 00	10 27	8 28	21 01	26 28	10 49	4 15	22 44	10 18	8 22
22 M	11 58 52	1 35 17	5♋56	13 39	8 32	0♈30	10 29	21 12	10 32	8 30	21 03	26 29	11 13	4 34	22 51	10 05	8 26
23 T	12 2 48	2 34 50	18 20	13 37	10 01	1 45	11 05	21 25	10 38	8 33	21 05	26 30	11 37	4 53	22 57	9 52	8 29
24 W	12 6 45	3 34 20	1♌27	13 34	11 32	3 00	11 40	21 37	10 43	8 36	21 07	26 31	12 00	5 12	23 03	9 40	8 33
25 Th	12 10 42	4 33 48	14 20	13 29	13 05	4 14	12 16	21 50	10 48	8 39	21 10	26 32	12 24	5 31	23 09	9 27	8 36
26 F	12 14 38	5 33 14	28 01	13 21	14 38	5 29	12 52	22 02	10 53	8 42	21 12	26 33	12 48	5 49	23 14	9 16	8 40
27 Sa	12 18 35	6 32 37	12♍09	13 11	16 13	6 43	13 27	22 14	10 58	8 45	21 14	26 34	13 12	6 08	23 20	9 04	8 43
28 Su	12 22 31	7 31 58	26 42	13 01	17 50	7 58	14 03	22 26	11 03	8 48	21 16	26 35	13 36	6 27	23 24	8 53	8 47
29 M	12 26 28	8 31 17	11≏32	12 51	19 28	9 13	14 39	22 38	11 08	8 51	21 18	26 36	13 59	6 45	23 29	8 42	8 50
30 T	12 30 24	9 30 34	26 32	12 43	21 07	10 27	15 15	22 50	11 13	8 54	21 21	26 36	14 23	7 04	23 33	8 32	8 54
31 W	12 34 21	10 29 50	11♏30	12 37	22 47	11 42	15 51	23 02	11 18	8 58	21 23	26 37	14 47	7 23	23 37	8 22	8 57

APRIL 2021

☽ Last Aspect day	ET / hr:mn / PT		asp	☽ Ingress sign	day	ET / hr:mn / PT	
3/31	**8:29 pm**	5:29 pm	✶♇	♐	1	**1:59 am**	
2		10:24 pm	□☿	♑	3	**4:13 am**	1:13 am
3	**1:24 am**		□☿	♑	3	**4:13 am**	1:13 am
5	**3:05 am**	12:05 am	☌♇	♒	5	**9:04 am**	6:04 am
7	**6:05 am**	3:05 am	☌♃	♓	7	**4:30 pm**	1:30 pm
9	**7:48 pm**	4:48 pm	✶♇	♈	9		11:11 pm
9	**7:48 pm**	4:48 pm	✶♇	♈	10	**2:11 am**	
12	**8:06 am**	5:06 am	☌♀	♉	12	**1:44 pm**	10:44 am
14	**8:00 pm**	5:00 pm	△♇	♊	14		11:35 pm
14	**8:00 pm**	5:00 pm	△♇	♊	15	**2:35 am**	

☽ Last Aspect day	ET / hr:mn / PT		asp	☽ Ingress sign	day	ET / hr:mn / PT	
17	**11:03 am**	8:03 am	✶☉	♋	17	**3:25 pm**	12:25 pm
19	**8:03 pm**	5:03 pm	☍♇	♌	19		11:11 pm
19	**8:03 pm**	5:03 pm	☍♇	♌	20	**2:11 am**	
22	**8:05 am**	5:05 am	✶♂	♍	22	**9:08 am**	6:08 am
24	**6:50 am**	3:50 am	△♇	♎	24	**12:06 pm**	9:06 am
26	**8:40 am**	5:40 am	△♃	♏	26	**12:18 pm**	9:18 am
28	**8:31 am**	5:31 am	□♃	♐	28	**11:42 am**	8:42 am
30	**9:27 am**	6:27 am	✶♃	♑	30	**12:16 pm**	9:16 am

☽ Phases & Eclipses phase	day	ET / hr:mn / PT	
4th Quarter	4	**6:02 am**	3:02 am
New Moon	11	**10:31 pm**	7:31 pm
2nd Quarter	19		11:59 pm
2nd Quarter	20	**2:59 pm**	
Full Moon	26	**11:32 pm**	8:32 pm

Planet Ingress		day	ET / hr:mn / PT	
☿	♈	3	**11:41 pm**	8:41 pm
♀	♉	14	**2:22 pm**	11:22 am
☿	♉	19	**6:29 am**	3:29 am
☉	♉	19	**4:33 pm**	1:33 pm
♂	♋	23	**7:49 am**	4:49 am

Planetary Motion		day	ET / hr:mn / PT	
⚵	R	12	**6:13 am**	3:13 am
⚶	D	20	**3:06 am**	12:06 am
♇	R	27	**4:04 pm**	1:04 pm

1 THURSDAY
☽ ⚻ ♅ **4:54 pm** 1:54 pm
☽ ✶ ♄ **8:53 pm** 5:53 pm
☽ △ ☉ **10:46 pm** 7:46 pm
☽ △ ♀ 10:56 pm
☿ ✶ ♇ 11:04 pm

2 FRIDAY
☽ △ ♀ **1:56 am**
☿ ✶ ♇ **2:04 am**
☽ ☍ ♂ **6:40 am** 3:40 am
☽ □ ♆ **1:42 pm** 10:42 am
☽ ✶ ♃ **5:17 pm** 2:17 pm
☽ ⚺ ♇ **10:30 pm** 7:30 pm
☽ □ ☿ 10:24 pm

3 SATURDAY
☽ □ ☿ **1:24 am**
☽ △ ♅ **8:05 pm** 5:05 pm
☽ ⚺ ♄ 9:21 pm

4 SUNDAY
☽ ⚺ ♄ **12:21 am**
☽ □ ☉ **6:02 am** 3:02 am
☽ □ ♀ **10:33 am** 7:33 am
☽ ⚻ ♂ **12:46 pm** 9:46 am
☽ ✶ ♆ **5:55 pm** 2:55 pm
☽ ⚺ ♃ **10:18 pm** 7:18 pm

5 MONDAY
☽ ☌ ♇ **3:05 am** 12:05 am
☽ ✶ ☿ **2:19 pm** 11:19 am
☽ □ ♅ 10:58 pm

Eastern time in bold type
Pacific time in medium type

6 TUESDAY
☽ □ ♅ **1:58 am**
☽ ☌ ♄ **6:32 am** 3:32 am
♀ ✶ ♂ **7:18 am** 4:18 am
☽ ✶ ☉ **4:40 pm** 1:40 pm
☽ △ ♂ **9:55 pm** 6:55 pm
☽ ✶ ♀ **10:44 pm** 7:44 pm
☽ ⚺ ♆ 9:49 pm

7 WEDNESDAY
☽ ⚺ ♆ **12:49 am**
☽ ☌ ♃ **6:05 am** 3:05 am
☽ ⚺ ♇ **10:18 am** 7:18 am
♀ ⚺ ♆ **8:55 pm** 5:55 pm

8 THURSDAY
☽ ⚺ ☿ **7:36 am** 4:36 am
☽ ✶ ♅ **10:24 am** 7:24 am
☽ ⚺ ♄ **3:13 pm** 12:13 pm
☿ ⚺ ♅ 11:37 pm

9 FRIDAY
☿ ⚺ ♅ **2:37 am**
☽ ⚺ ☉ **6:19 am** 3:19 am
☽ □ ♂ **9:49 am** 6:49 am
☽ ☌ ♆ **10:04 am** 7:04 am
☽ ⚺ ♀ **2:05 pm** 11:05 am
♂ □ ♆ **3:18 pm** 12:18 pm
☽ ⚺ ♃ **4:15 pm** 1:15 pm
☽ ✶ ♇ **7:48 pm** 4:48 pm

10 SATURDAY
☿ ✶ ♄ **11:09 am** 8:09 am
♀ ✶ ♃ **2:53 pm** 11:53 am
☽ ⚺ ♅ **8:58 pm** 5:58 pm
☽ ✶ ♄ 11:01 pm

11 SUNDAY
☽ ✶ ♄ **2:01 am**
☽ ☌ ☿ **4:46 am** 1:46 am
☉ ⚺ ♆ **7:10 am** 4:10 am
☽ ⚺ ♆ **9:18 pm** 6:18 pm
☽ ☌ ☉ **10:31 pm** 7:31 pm
♀ □ ♇ **11:20 pm** 8:20 pm
☽ ✶ ♂ 9:00 pm

12 MONDAY
☽ ✶ ♂ **12:00 am**
☽ ✶ ♃ **4:24 am** 1:24 am
☽ □ ♇ **7:12 am** 4:12 am
☽ ☌ ♀ **8:06 am** 5:06 am

13 TUESDAY
☽ ☌ ♅ **9:18 am** 6:18 am
☽ □ ♄ **2:30 pm** 11:30 am
☉ ✶ ♂ **7:09 pm** 4:09 pm

14 WEDNESDAY
☽ ⚺ ☿ **5:14 am** 2:14 am
☽ ✶ ♆ **10:03 am** 7:03 am
☽ ⚺ ♂ **3:54 pm** 12:54 pm
☽ ⚺ ☉ **4:37 pm** 1:37 pm
☽ □ ♃ **6:02 pm** 3:02 pm
☽ △ ♇ **8:00 pm** 5:00 pm

15 THURSDAY
☽ ⚺ ♀ **4:01 am** 1:01 am
☿ ⚺ ♆ **9:32 am** 6:32 am
☉ ✶ ♃ **12:59 pm** 9:59 am
☽ ⚺ ♅ **10:38 pm** 7:38 pm

16 FRIDAY
☽ △ ♄ **3:53 am** 12:53 am
☉ □ ♇ **9:27 am** 6:27 am
☽ □ ♆ **11:15 pm** 8:15 pm
♂ △ ♃ 10:14 pm

17 SATURDAY
♂ △ ♃ **1:14 am**
☽ ✶ ☿ **7:05 am** 4:05 am
☽ △ ♃ **7:53 am** 4:53 am
☽ ☌ ♂ **8:08 am** 5:08 am
☽ ⚻ ♇ **8:58 am** 5:58 am
☽ ✶ ☉ **11:03 am** 8:03 am
☿ ✶ ♃ **12:00 pm** 9:00 am
☿ ✶ ♂ **3:09 pm** 12:09 pm
☿ □ ♇ **5:49 pm** 2:49 pm
☽ ✶ ♀ **11:49 pm** 8:49 pm
♂ ⚻ ♇ 9:26 pm

18 SUNDAY
♂ ⚻ ♇ **12:26 am**
☽ ✶ ♅ **11:19 am** 8:19 am
☽ ⚻ ♄ **4:24 pm** 1:24 pm
☉ ☌ ☿ **9:50 pm** 6:50 pm

19 MONDAY
☽ △ ♆ **10:56 am** 7:56 am
☽ ⚻ ♃ **7:49 pm** 4:49 pm
☽ ☍ ♇ **8:03 pm** 5:03 pm
☽ ⚺ ♂ **10:15 pm** 7:15 pm
☽ □ ☉ 11:59 pm

20 TUESDAY
☽ □ ☉ **2:59 am**
☽ □ ☿ **6:08 am** 3:08 am
♃ ⚺ ♇ **3:09 pm** 12:09 pm
☽ □ ♀ **4:21 pm** 1:21 pm
☽ □ ♅ **9:11 pm** 6:11 pm
☽ ☍ ♄ 10:56 pm

21 WEDNESDAY
☽ ☍ ♄ **1:56 am**
☽ ⚻ ♆ **7:07 pm** 4:07 pm

22 THURSDAY
☽ ⚻ ♇ **3:29 am** 12:29 am
☽ ☍ ♃ **3:54 am** 12:54 am
☽ ✶ ♂ **8:05 am** 5:05 am
☽ △ ☉ **2:06 pm** 11:06 am
♀ ☌ ♅ **9:01 pm** 6:01 pm
☽ △ ☿ **10:47 pm** 7:47 pm
☽ △ ♅ 11:57 pm

23 FRIDAY
☽ △ ♅ **2:57 am**
☽ △ ♀ **3:30 am** 12:30 am
☽ ⚻ ♄ **7:19 am** 4:19 am
☽ ☍ ♆ **11:10 pm** 8:10 pm
☿ ☌ ♅ 11:42 pm

24 SATURDAY
☿ ☌ ♅ **2:42 am**
☽ △ ♇ **6:50 am** 3:50 am
☽ ⚻ ♃ **7:47 am** 4:47 am
☽ □ ♂ **1:19 pm** 10:19 am
☽ ⚻ ☉ **8:19 pm** 5:19 pm
♀ □ ♄ 9:22 pm

25 SUNDAY
♀ □ ♄ **12:22 am**
☽ ⚻ ♅ **4:58 am** 1:58 am
☿ □ ♄ **7:58 am** 4:58 am
☽ △ ♄ **9:02 am** 6:02 am
☽ ⚻ ☿ **9:13 am** 6:13 am
☽ ⚻ ♀ **9:48 am** 6:48 am
☿ ☌ ♀ **6:19 pm** 3:19 pm
☽ ⚻ ♆ 9:01 pm

26 MONDAY
☽ ⚻ ♆ **12:01 am**
☽ □ ♇ **7:15 am** 4:15 am
☽ △ ♃ **8:40 am** 5:40 am
☽ △ ♂ **3:29 pm** 12:29 pm
☽ ☍ ☉ **11:32 pm** 8:32 pm

27 TUESDAY
☽ ☍ ♅ **4:51 am** 1:51 am
☽ □ ♄ **8:47 am** 5:47 am
☽ ☍ ♀ **1:35 pm** 10:35 am
☽ ☍ ☿ **4:24 pm** 1:24 pm
☽ △ ♆ **11:31 pm** 8:31 pm

28 WEDNESDAY
☽ ✶ ♇ **6:38 am** 3:38 am
☽ □ ♃ **8:31 am** 5:31 am
☽ ⚻ ♂ **4:54 pm** 1:54 pm
☽ ⚻ ☉ 11:20 pm

29 THURSDAY
☽ ⚻ ☉ **2:20 am**
☽ ⚻ ♅ **4:38 am** 1:38 am
☽ ✶ ♄ **8:36 am** 5:36 am
☽ ⚻ ♀ **5:44 pm** 2:44 pm
☿ ✶ ♆ **10:27 pm** 7:27 pm
☽ □ ♆ **11:42 pm** 8:42 pm
☽ ⚻ ☿ **11:54 pm** 8:54 pm

30 FRIDAY
☽ ⚺ ♇ **7:00 am** 4:00 am
☽ ✶ ♃ **9:27 am** 6:27 am
☉ ☌ ♅ **3:54 pm** 12:54 pm
☽ ☍ ♂ **7:51 pm** 4:51 pm

APRIL 2021

DATE	SID.TIME	SUN	MOON	NODE	MERCURY	VENUS	MARS	JUPITER	SATURN	URANUS	NEPTUNE	PLUTO	CERES	PALLAS	JUNO	VESTA	CHIRON
1 Th	12 38 17	11♈29 03	26♏20	12♊33R	24♈29	12♉56	16♊27	23♒14	11♒22	9♉01	21♓25	26♑38	15♉11	7♈41	23♑41	8♉12R	9♈01
2 F	12 42 14	12 28 14	10♐55	12 32D	26 13	14 11	17 03	23 35	11 27	9 04	21 27	26 39	15 35	7 59	23 45	8 03	9 04
3 Sa	12 46 10	13 27 24	25 12	12 33	27 57	15 25	17 38	23 37	11 32	9 07	21 29	26 40	15 59	8 18	23 48	7 55	9 08
4 Su	12 50 7	14 26 32	9♑07	12 33R	29 44	16 40	18 14	23 49	11 36	9 10	21 31	26 40	16 22	8 36	23 51	7 47	9 11
5 M	12 54 4	15 25 39	22 44	12 33	1♈31	17 54	18 50	24 00	11 41	9 13	21 34	26 41	16 46	8 54	23 53	7 39	9 15
6 T	12 58 0	16 24 43	6♒02	12 31	3 20	19 08	19 26	24 11	11 45	9 17	21 36	26 42	17 10	9 12	23 55	7 32	9 18
7 W	13 1 57	17 23 46	19 03	12 27	5 11	20 23	20 02	24 23	11 49	9 20	21 38	26 42	17 34	9 30	23 57	7 25	9 22
8 Th	13 5 53	18 22 47	1♓51	12 21	7 03	21 37	20 39	24 34	11 53	9 23	21 40	26 43	17 58	9 48	23 59	7 19	9 25
9 F	13 9 50	19 21 46	14 26	12 12	8 56	22 52	21 15	24 45	11 57	9 27	21 42	26 43	18 22	10 06	24 00	7 13	9 29
10 Sa	13 13 46	20 20 43	26 50	12 03	10 51	24 06	21 51	24 56	12 01	9 30	21 44	26 44	18 46	10 24	24 01	7 08	9 32
11 Su	13 17 43	21 19 39	9♈04	11 53	12 47	25 20	22 27	25 07	12 05	9 33	21 46	26 44	19 10	10 42	24 02	7 03	9 36
12 M	13 21 39	22 18 32	21 09	11 44	14 45	26 35	23 03	25 17	12 09	9 36	21 48	26 45	19 34	10 59	24 02R	6 58	9 39
13 T	13 25 36	23 17 23	3♉07	11 36	16 44	27 49	23 39	25 28	12 13	9 40	21 50	26 45	19 57	11 17	24 02	6 55	9 43
14 W	13 29 33	24 16 13	14 58	11 31	18 44	29 03	24 15	25 39	12 17	9 43	21 52	26 46	20 21	11 34	24 02	6 51	9 46
15 Th	13 33 29	25 15 00	26 46	11 27	20 46	0♊17	24 52	25 49	12 20	9 47	21 54	26 46	20 45	11 52	24 01	6 48	9 50
16 F	13 37 26	26 13 45	8♊33	11 26D	22 49	1 32	25 28	26 00	12 24	9 50	21 56	26 46	21 09	12 09	24 00	6 46	9 53
17 Sa	13 41 22	27 12 28	20 22	11 26	24 53	2 46	26 04	26 10	12 27	9 53	21 58	26 47	21 33	12 26	23 59	6 44	9 56
18 Su	13 45 19	28 11 09	2♋17	11 28	26 58	4 00	26 40	26 20	12 31	9 57	22 00	26 47	21 57	12 43	23 57	6 43	10 00
19 M	13 49 15	29 09 48	14 24	11 28	29 05	5 14	27 17	26 30	12 34	10 00	22 02	26 47	22 21	13 00	23 55	6 42	10 03
20 T	13 53 12	0♉08 24	26 46	11 30R	1♉12	6 28	27 53	26 40	12 37	10 04	22 04	26 48	22 44	13 17	23 53	6 42D	10 07
21 W	13 57 8	1 06 59	9♌29	11 30	3 19	7 43	28 29	26 50	12 40	10 07	22 06	26 48	23 08	13 34	23 50	6 42	10 10
22 Th	14 1 5	2 05 31	22 37	11 28	5 27	8 57	29 06	26 59	12 43	10 10	22 08	26 48	23 32	13 51	23 47	6 42	10 13
23 F	14 5 2	3 04 01	6♍13	11 24	7 35	10 11	29 42	27 09	12 46	10 14	22 09	26 48	23 56	14 07	23 44	6 43	10 16
24 Sa	14 8 58	4 02 28	20 18	11 19	9 43	11 25	0♋18	27 18	12 49	10 17	22 11	26 48	24 20	14 24	23 40	6 45	10 20
25 Su	14 12 55	5 00 54	4♎50	11 14	11 50	12 39	0 55	27 28	12 52	10 21	22 13	26 48	24 43	14 40	23 36	6 47	10 23
26 M	14 16 51	5 59 17	19 44	11 11	13 57	13 53	1 31	27 37	12 55	10 24	22 15	26 48	25 07	14 57	23 32	6 49	10 26
27 T	14 20 48	6 57 39	4♏52	11 09	16 02	15 07	2 08	27 46	12 57	10 28	22 17	26 48R	25 31	15 13	23 27	6 52	10 30
28 W	14 24 44	7 55 59	20 05	11 09	18 06	16 21	2 44	27 55	13 00	10 31	22 18	26 48	25 55	15 29	23 22	6 56	10 33
29 Th	14 28 41	8 54 17	5♐12	11 00D	20 09	17 35	3 21	28 04	13 02	10 35	22 20	26 48	26 18	15 45	23 17	7 00	10 36
30 F	14 32 37	9 52 34	20 06	11 00	22 10	18 49	3 57	28 13	13 04	10 38	22 22	26 48	26 42	16 01	23 11	7 04	10 39

EPHEMERIS CALCULATED FOR 12 MIDNIGHT GREENWICH MEAN TIME. ALL OTHER DATA AND FACING ASPECTARIAN PAGE IN **EASTERN TIME (BOLD)** AND PACIFIC TIME (REGULAR).

MAY 2021

☽ Last Aspect day	ET / hr:mn / PT	asp	☽ Ingress sign	day	ET / hr:mn / PT
2	**10:38 am** 7:38 am	△☿	♒	2	**3:31 pm** 12:31 pm
4	**8:05 pm** 5:05 pm	☌♃	♓	4	**10:09 pm** 7:09 pm
7	**3:36 am** 12:36 am	⚹♀	♈	7	**7:52 am** 4:52 am
9	**6:50 pm** 3:50 pm	⚹♃	♉	9	**7:46 pm** 4:46 pm
12	**8:23 am** 5:23 am	□♃	♊	12	**8:43 am** 5:43 am
14	**6:51 am** 3:51 am	□♆	♋	14	**9:30 pm** 6:30 pm
16	11:23 pm	☍♇	♌	17	**8:44 am** 5:44 am
17	**2:23 am**	☍♇	♌	17	**8:44 am** 5:44 am
19	**3:13 pm** 12:13 pm	□☉	♍	19	**4:59 pm** 1:59 pm
21	**3:56 pm** 12:56 pm	△♇	♎	21	**9:35 pm** 6:35 pm

☽ Last Aspect day	ET / hr:mn / PT	asp	☽ Ingress sign	day	ET / hr:mn / PT
23	**5:36 pm** 2:36 pm	□♇	♏	23	**11:00 pm** 8:00 pm
25	**5:20 pm** 2:20 pm	⚹♇	♐	25	**10:39 pm** 7:39 pm
27	**1:35 pm** 10:35 am	☍☿	♑	27	**10:23 pm** 7:23 pm
29	**6:15 pm** 3:15 pm	☌♇	♒	29	9:04 pm
29	**6:15 pm** 3:15 pm	☌♇	♒	30	**12:04 am**
31	11:14 pm	△♀	♓	6/1	**5:07 am** 2:07 am
6/1	**2:14 am**	△♀	♓	6/1	**5:07 am** 2:07 am

☽ Phases & Eclipses phase	day	ET / hr:mn / PT
4th Quarter	3	**3:50 pm** 12:50 pm
New Moon	11	**3:00 pm** 12:00 pm
2nd Quarter	19	**3:13 pm** 12:13 pm
Full Moon	26	**7:14 am** 4:14 am
●	26	5° ♐ 26'

Planet Ingress		day	ET / hr:mn / PT
☿	♊	3	**10:49 pm** 7:49 pm
⚳	♉	8	**4:54 am** 1:54 am
♀	♊	8	**10:01 pm** 7:01 pm
♃	♓	13	**6:36 pm** 3:36 pm
☉	♊	20	**3:37 pm** 12:37 pm

Planetary Motion		day	ET / hr:mn / PT
♄	℞	23	**5:21 am** 2:21 am
☿	℞	29	**6:34 pm** 3:34 pm

1 SATURDAY
- ☽ △ ♅ **6:13 am** 3:13 am
- ☽ △ ☉ **7:12 am** 4:12 am
- ☽ ⚺ ♄ **10:18 am** 7:18 am
- ☽ △ ♀ 9:42 pm
- ☽ ⚹ ♆ 11:16 pm

2 SUNDAY
- ☽ △ ♀ **12:42 am**
- ☽ ⚹ ♆ **2:16 am**
- ☿ △ ♇ **5:19 am** 2:19 am
- ☽ ☌ ♇ **9:54 am** 6:54 am
- ☽ △ ☿ **10:38 am** 7:38 am
- ☽ ⚺ ♃ **1:02 pm** 10:02 am
- ♀ ⚹ ♆ **6:38 pm** 3:38 pm
- ☽ ⚻ ♂ 11:02 pm

3 MONDAY
- ☽ ⚻ ♂ **2:02 am**
- ☿ □ ♃ **5:33 am** 2:33 am
- ☉ □ ♄ **6:02 am** 3:02 am
- ☽ □ ♅ **10:52 am** 7:52 am
- ☽ ☌ ♄ **3:08 pm** 12:08 pm
- ☽ □ ☉ **3:50 pm** 12:50 pm

4 TUESDAY
- ☽ ⚺ ♆ **8:08 am** 5:08 am
- ☽ □ ♀ **12:00 pm** 9:00 am
- ☽ ⚺ ♇ **4:09 pm** 1:09 pm
- ☽ ☌ ♃ **8:05 pm** 5:05 pm
- ☽ □ ☿ 10:54 pm

5 WEDNESDAY
- ☽ □ ☿ **1:54 am**
- ☽ △ ♂ **12:07 pm** 9:07 am
- ☽ ⚹ ♅ **6:57 pm** 3:57 pm
- ☽ ⚺ ♄ **11:21 pm** 8:21 pm

6 THURSDAY
- ☽ ⚹ ☉ **4:41 am** 1:41 am
- ♀ △ ♇ **7:25 am** 4:25 am
- ☽ ☌ ♆ **5:17 pm** 2:17 pm
- ☽ ⚹ ♇ 10:34 pm

7 FRIDAY
- ☽ ⚹ ♇ **1:34 am**
- ☽ ⚹ ♀ **3:36 am** 12:36 am
- ☽ ⚺ ♃ **6:21 am** 3:21 am
- ☽ ⚹ ☿ **9:01 pm** 6:01 pm
- ☽ □ ♂ 10:35 pm

8 SATURDAY
- ☽ □ ♂ **1:35 am**
- ☽ ⚺ ♅ **5:53 am** 2:53 am
- ♀ □ ♃ **9:38 am** 6:38 am
- ☽ ⚹ ♄ **10:18 am** 7:18 am
- ☽ ⚺ ☉ **8:54 pm** 5:54 pm

9 SUNDAY
- ☽ ⚺ ♆ **4:52 am** 1:52 am
- ☽ □ ♇ **1:16 pm** 10:16 am
- ☽ ⚹ ♃ **6:50 pm** 3:50 pm
- ☽ ⚺ ♀ **10:17 pm** 7:17 pm

10 MONDAY
- ☿ ⚺ ♂ **7:48 am** 4:48 am
- ☽ ⚹ ♂ **5:12 pm** 2:12 pm
- ☽ ⚺ ☿ **5:55 pm** 2:55 pm
- ☽ ☌ ♅ **6:35 pm** 3:35 pm
- ☽ □ ♄ **10:55 pm** 7:55 pm
- ☿ ⚺ ♅ **11:48 pm** 8:48 pm

11 TUESDAY
- ☽ ☌ ☉ **3:00 pm** 12:00 pm
- ☽ ⚹ ♆ **5:47 pm** 2:47 pm
- ♂ ⚹ ♅ **10:48 pm** 7:48 pm
- ☽ △ ♇ 11:07 pm

12 WEDNESDAY
- ☽ △ ♇ **2:07 am**
- ☽ □ ♃ **8:23 am** 5:23 am
- ☿ △ ♄ **2:34 pm** 11:34 am
- ☽ ☌ ♀ **6:20 pm** 3:20 pm
- ☉ ⚹ ♆ 10:45 pm

13 THURSDAY
- ☉ ⚹ ♆ **1:45 am**
- ☽ ⚺ ♅ **7:55 am** 4:55 am
- ☽ ⚺ ♂ **9:33 am** 6:33 am
- ☽ △ ♄ **12:03 pm** 9:03 am
- ☽ ☌ ☿ **2:32 pm** 11:32 am

14 FRIDAY
- ☽ □ ♆ **6:51 am** 3:51 am
- ☽ ⚺ ☉ **9:22 am** 6:22 am
- ☽ ⚻ ♇ **2:57 pm** 11:57 am
- ☽ △ ♃ **9:45 pm** 6:45 pm

15 SATURDAY
- ♂ ⚻ ♄ **10:49 am** 7:49 am
- ☽ ⚺ ♀ **1:53 pm** 10:53 am
- ☽ ⚹ ♅ **8:35 pm** 5:35 pm
- ☽ ⚻ ♄ 9:24 pm
- ☽ ☌ ♂ 10:06 pm

16 SUNDAY
- ☽ ⚻ ♄ **12:24 am**
- ☽ ☌ ♂ **1:06 am**
- ☽ ⚺ ☿ **8:51 am** 5:51 am
- ☽ △ ♆ **6:42 pm** 3:42 pm
- ☽ ⚹ ☉ 11:05 pm
- ☽ ☍ ♇ 11:23 pm

17 MONDAY
- ☽ ⚹ ☉ **2:05 am**
- ☽ ☍ ♇ **2:23 am**
- ☉ △ ♇ **5:49 am** 2:49 am
- ☽ ⚻ ♃ **9:29 am** 6:29 am

18 TUESDAY
- ☽ ⚹ ♀ **6:43 am** 3:43 am
- ☽ □ ♅ **7:04 am** 4:04 am
- ☽ ☍ ♄ **10:29 am** 7:29 am
- ♀ ⚺ ♅ **10:31 am** 7:31 am
- ☽ ⚺ ♂ **2:01 pm** 11:01 am
- ☽ ⚹ ☿ **10:55 pm** 7:55 pm

19 WEDNESDAY
- ☽ ⚻ ♆ **3:51 am** 12:51 am
- ☽ ⚻ ♇ **10:58 am** 7:58 am
- ☽ □ ☉ **3:13 pm** 12:13 pm
- ☽ ☍ ♃ **6:07 pm** 3:07 pm
- ♀ △ ♄ **9:58 pm** 6:58 pm

20 THURSDAY
- ☽ △ ♅ **2:09 pm** 11:09 am
- ☽ ⚻ ♄ **5:08 pm** 2:08 pm
- ☽ □ ♀ **7:01 pm** 4:01 pm
- ☽ ⚹ ♂ **10:57 pm** 7:57 pm

21 FRIDAY
- ☽ □ ☿ **7:47 am** 4:47 am
- ☽ ☍ ♆ **9:24 am** 6:24 am
- ☉ □ ♃ **11:03 am** 8:03 am
- ☽ △ ♇ **3:56 pm** 12:56 pm
- ☽ ⚻ ♃ **10:59 pm** 7:59 pm
- ☽ △ ☉ **11:46 pm** 8:46 pm

22 SATURDAY
- ☽ ⚻ ♅ **5:34 pm** 2:34 pm
- ☽ △ ♄ **8:11 pm** 5:11 pm
- ☿ □ ♆ **10:43 pm** 7:43 pm
- ☽ △ ♀ 11:36 pm

23 SUNDAY
- ☽ △ ♀ **2:36 am**
- ☽ □ ♂ **3:51 am** 12:51 am
- ☽ ⚻ ♆ **11:33 am** 8:33 am
- ☽ △ ☿ **11:59 am** 8:59 am
- ☽ □ ♇ **5:36 pm** 2:36 pm
- ☽ △ ♃ 9:37 pm

24 MONDAY
- ☽ △ ♃ **12:37 am**
- ☽ ⚻ ☉ **4:28 am** 1:28 am
- ♀ ⚺ ♂ **7:15 am** 4:15 am
- ☽ ☍ ♅ **6:15 pm** 3:15 pm
- ☽ □ ♄ **8:35 pm** 5:35 pm

25 TUESDAY
- ☽ △ ♂ **6:01 am** 3:01 am
- ☽ ⚻ ♀ **7:01 am** 4:01 am
- ☽ △ ♆ **11:30 am** 8:30 am
- ☽ ⚻ ☿ **1:13 pm** 10:13 am
- ☽ ⚹ ♇ **5:20 pm** 2:20 pm
- ☽ □ ♃ 9:30 pm

26 WEDNESDAY
- ☽ □ ♃ **12:30 am**
- ☽ ☍ ☉ **7:14 am** 4:14 am
- ☽ ⚻ ♅ **5:52 pm** 2:52 pm
- ☽ ⚹ ♄ **8:01 pm** 5:01 pm

27 THURSDAY
- ☽ ⚻ ♂ **7:31 am** 4:31 am
- ☽ ☍ ♀ **10:43 am** 7:43 am
- ☽ □ ♆ **11:06 am** 8:06 am
- ☽ ☍ ☿ **1:35 pm** 10:35 am
- ♀ □ ♆ **3:25 pm** 12:25 pm
- ☽ ⚺ ♇ **4:55 pm** 1:55 pm
- ☽ ⚹ ♃ 9:31 pm

28 FRIDAY
- ☽ ⚹ ♃ **12:31 am**
- ☽ ⚻ ☉ **10:32 am** 7:32 am
- ☽ △ ♅ **6:22 pm** 3:22 pm
- ☽ ⚺ ♄ **8:23 pm** 5:23 pm
- ☿ ☌ ♀ 10:13 pm

29 SATURDAY
- ☿ ☌ ♀ **1:13 am**
- ☽ ☍ ♂ **10:36 am** 7:36 am
- ☽ ⚹ ♆ **12:13 pm** 9:13 am
- ☽ ⚻ ☿ **3:07 pm** 12:07 pm
- ☽ ⚻ ♀ **4:23 pm** 1:23 pm
- ☽ ☌ ♇ **6:15 pm** 3:15 pm
- ☽ ⚺ ♃ 11:34 pm

30 SUNDAY
- ☽ ⚺ ♃ **2:34 am**
- ♀ ⚻ ♇ **1:47 pm** 10:47 am
- ☽ △ ☉ **4:43 pm** 1:43 pm
- ☽ □ ♅ **9:30 pm** 6:30 pm
- ☽ ☌ ♄ **11:25 pm** 8:25 pm
- ♂ △ ♆ 10:15 pm

31 MONDAY
- ♂ △ ♆ **1:15 am**
- ☽ ⚺ ♆ **4:27 pm** 1:27 pm
- ☽ ⚻ ♂ **5:11 pm** 2:11 pm
- ☽ △ ☿ **7:13 pm** 4:13 pm
- ☽ ⚺ ♇ **10:48 pm** 7:48 pm
- ☽ △ ♀ 11:14 pm

Eastern time in bold type
Pacific time in medium type

MAY 2021

DATE	SID.TIME	SUN	MOON	NODE	MERCURY	VENUS	MARS	JUPITER	SATURN	URANUS	NEPTUNE	PLUTO	CERES	PALLAS	JUNO	VESTA	CHIRON
1 Sa	14 36 34	10♉50 49	4♌39	11♊03	24♊08	20♉03	4♋33	28≈21	13≈07	10♉41	22♓25	26♑48R	27♍06	16♓17	23♐05R	7♈09	10♈42
2 Su	14 40 31	11 49 02	18 48	11 04R	26 04	21 17	5 10	28 30	13 09	10 45	22 25	26 48	27 30	16 32	22 59	7 14	10 45
3 M	14 44 27	12 47 14	2≈32	11 04	27 57	22 31	5 46	28 38	13 11	10 48	22 27	26 48	27 53	16 48	22 52	7 19	10 49
4 T	14 48 24	13 45 25	15 53	11 04	29 47	23 45	6 23	28 46	13 13	10 52	22 28	26 48	28 17	17 03	22 45	7 25	10 52
5 W	14 52 20	14 43 34	28 51	11 02	1♋34	24 58	6 59	28 54	13 14	10 55	22 30	26 48	28 40	17 19	22 38	7 32	10 55
6 Th	14 56 17	15 41 41	11♓32	10 59	3 18	26 12	7 36	29 02	13 16	10 59	22 31	26 47	29 04	17 34	22 30	7 39	10 58
7 F	15 0 13	16 39 47	23 56	10 55	4 58	27 26	8 13	29 10	13 18	11 02	22 33	26 47	29 28	17 49	22 22	7 46	11 01
8 Sa	15 4 10	17 37 52	6♈09	10 51	6 35	28 40	8 49	29 18	13 19	11 06	22 34	26 47	29 51	18 04	22 14	7 54	11 04
9 Su	15 8 6	18 35 55	18 11	10 48	8 08	29 54	9 26	29 25	13 21	11 09	22 36	26 47	0♎15	18 19	22 06	8 02	11 07
10 M	15 12 3	19 33 57	0♉07	10 45	9 38	1♊08	10 02	29 32	13 22	11 13	22 37	26 46	0 38	18 34	21 57	8 10	11 10
11 T	15 16 0	20 31 57	11 57	10 43	11 03	2 21	10 39	29 40	13 24	11 16	22 39	26 46	1 02	18 48	21 48	8 19	11 12
12 W	15 19 56	21 29 56	23 45	10 42D	12 25	3 35	11 15	29 47	13 25	11 19	22 40	26 46	1 25	19 03	21 38	8 29	11 15
13 Th	15 23 53	22 27 53	5♊33	10 42	13 43	4 49	11 52	29 54	13 26	11 23	22 41	26 45	1 49	19 17	21 29	8 38	11 18
14 F	15 27 49	23 25 49	17 22	10 42	14 57	6 03	12 29	0♓00	13 27	11 26	22 43	26 45	2 12	19 31	21 19	8 49	11 21
15 Sa	15 31 46	24 23 43	29 15	10 43	16 06	7 16	13 05	0 07	13 28	11 30	22 44	26 44	2 36	19 45	21 09	8 59	11 24
16 Su	15 35 42	25 21 35	11♋16	10 44	17 12	8 30	13 42	0 13	13 28	11 33	22 45	26 44	2 59	19 59	20 58	9 10	11 27
17 M	15 39 39	26 19 26	23 27	10 46	18 13	9 44	14 19	0 20	13 29	11 36	22 47	26 43	3 22	20 13	20 48	9 21	11 29
18 T	15 43 35	27 17 15	5♌52	10 47	19 10	10 57	14 55	0 26	13 30	11 40	22 48	26 43	3 46	20 26	20 37	9 33	11 32
19 W	15 47 32	28 15 03	18 35	10 47R	20 03	12 11	15 32	0 32	13 31	11 43	22 50	26 42	4 09	20 40	20 25	9 44	11 35
20 Th	15 51 29	29 12 48	1♍40	10 47	20 52	13 25	16 09	0 38	13 30	11 46	22 51	26 42	4 32	20 53	20 14	9 57	11 37
21 F	15 55 25	0♊10 32	15 09	10 47	21 36	14 38	16 46	0 43	13 31R	11 50	22 51	26 41	4 55	21 06	20 02	10 09	11 40
22 Sa	15 59 22	1 08 15	29 04	10 46	22 15	15 52	17 22	0 49	13 31	11 53	22 53	26 40	5 18	21 19	19 51	10 22	11 42
23 Su	16 3 18	2 05 55	13♎24	10 46	22 50	17 05	17 59	0 54	13 31	11 56	22 54	26 40	5 42	21 32	19 39	10 36	11 45
24 M	16 7 15	3 03 35	28 08	10 45	23 20	18 19	18 36	0 59	13 31	12 00	22 55	26 38	6 05	21 44	19 27	10 49	11 47
25 T	16 11 11	4 01 12	13♏09	10 44D	23 46	19 32	19 13	1 04	13 31	12 03	22 56	26 38	6 28	21 57	19 14	11 03	11 50
26 W	16 15 8	4 58 49	28 19	10 44	24 07	20 46	19 49	1 09	13 31	12 06	22 57	26 37	6 51	22 09	19 02	11 17	11 52
27 Th	16 19 4	5 56 24	13♐30	10 44	24 23	21 59	20 26	1 14	13 30	12 09	22 58	26 37	7 14	22 21	18 49	11 32	11 54
28 F	16 23 1	6 53 58	28 31	10 44	24 34	23 12	21 03	1 18	13 30	12 13	22 59	26 36	7 37	22 33	18 36	11 47	11 57
29 Sa	16 26 58	7 51 31	13♑15	10 44	24 41R	24 26	21 40	1 22	13 30	12 16	23 00	26 35	8 00	22 45	18 23	12 02	11 59
30 Su	16 30 54	8 49 04	27 36	10 44	24 43	25 39	22 17	1 27	13 29	12 19	23 00	26 34	8 23	22 57	18 10	12 17	12 01
31 M	16 34 51	9 46 35	11≈31	10 44	24 40	26 53	22 53	1 31	13 28	12 22	23 01	26 33	8 45	23 08	17 57	12 33	12 04

EPHEMERIS CALCULATED FOR 12 MIDNIGHT GREENWICH MEAN TIME. ALL OTHER DATA AND FACING ASPECTARIAN PAGE IN **EASTERN TIME (BOLD)** AND PACIFIC TIME (REGULAR).

JUNE 2021

☽ Last Aspect day	ET / hr:mn / PT	asp	☽ Ingress sign	day	ET / hr:mn / PT
1	**2:14 am**	△♀	♓	1	**5:07 am** 2:07 am
3	**7:10 am** 4:10 am	⚹♇	♈	3	**1:59 pm** 10:59 am
5	**6:47 pm** 3:47 pm	□♂	♉	5	10:46 pm
5	**6:47 pm** 3:47 pm	□♂	♉	6	**1:46 am**
8	**11:07 am** 8:07 am	⚹♂	♊	8	**2:47 pm** 11:47 am
10	**1:38 pm** 10:38 am	□♆	♋	11	**3:23 am** 12:23 am
13	**7:16 am** 4:16 am	☍♇	♌	13	**2:22 pm** 11:22 am
15	**1:27 pm** 10:27 am	⚹☉	♍	15	**11:02 pm** 8:02 pm
17	**11:54 pm** 8:54 pm	□☉	♎	18	**4:54 am** 1:54 am
20	**6:52 am** 3:52 am	△☉	♏	20	**7:58 am** 4:58 am

☽ Last Aspect day	ET / hr:mn / PT	asp	☽ Ingress sign	day	ET / hr:mn / PT
21	11:43 pm	⚹♇	♐	22	**8:55 am** 5:55 am
22	**2:43 am**	⚹♇	♐	22	**8:55 am** 5:55 am
23	**10:09 pm** 7:09 pm	□♆	♑	24	**9:05 am** 6:05 am
26	**8:49 am** 5:49 am	☍♀	♒	26	**10:09 am** 7:09 am
27	**3:08 pm** 12:08 pm	△☿	♓	28	**1:51 pm** 10:51 am
30	**1:40 pm** 10:40 am	⚹♇	♈	30	**9:21 pm** 6:21 pm

☽ Phases & Eclipses phase	day	ET / hr:mn / PT
4th Quarter	2	**3:24 am** 12:24 am
New Moon	10	**6:53 am** 3:53 am
●	10	19° ♊ 47'
2nd Quarter	17	**11:54 pm** 8:54 pm
Full Moon	24	**2:40 pm** 11:40 am

Planet Ingress	day	ET / hr:mn / PT
♀ ♋	2	**9:19 am** 6:19 am
♂ ♌	11	**9:34 am** 6:34 am
☉ ♋	20	**11:32 pm** 8:32 pm
♀ ♌	26	9:27 pm
♀ ♌	27	**12:27 am**

Planetary Motion	day	ET / hr:mn / PT
♃ ℞	20	**11:06 am** 8:06 am
☿ D	22	**6:00 pm** 3:00 pm
♆ ℞	25	**3:21 pm** 12:21 pm

1 TUESDAY

☽△♀	**2:14 am**	
☽☌♃	**8:04 am**	5:04 am

2 WEDNESDAY

☿⚺♂	**3:14 am**	12:14 am
☽□☉	**3:24 am**	12:24 am
☽⚹♅	**4:22 am**	1:22 am
☽⚺♄	**6:08 am**	3:08 am
☉⚺♅	**4:43 pm**	1:43 pm
☽☌♆		9:31 pm
☽□☿		11:24 pm

3 THURSDAY

☽☌♆	**12:31 am**	
☽□☿	**2:24 am**	
☽△♂	**4:08 am**	1:08 am
☽⚹♇	**7:10 am**	4:10 am
☉△♄	**3:05 pm**	12:05 pm
☽□♀	**5:09 pm**	2:09 pm
☽⚺♃	**5:23 pm**	2:23 pm
♀△♃	**7:33 pm**	4:33 pm

4 FRIDAY

☽⚺♅	**2:52 pm**	11:52 am
☽⚹♄	**4:24 pm**	1:24 pm
☽⚹☉	**6:38 pm**	3:38 pm

5 SATURDAY

☽⚺♆	**11:49 am**	8:49 am
☽⚹☿	**11:56 am**	8:56 am
☿□♆	**3:05 pm**	12:05 pm
♂☍♇	**3:45 pm**	12:45 pm
☽□♇	**6:37 pm**	3:37 pm
☽□♂	**6:47 pm**	3:47 pm

Eastern time in bold type
Pacific time in medium type

6 SUNDAY

☽⚹♃	**5:32 am**	2:32 am
☽⚹♀	**11:57 am**	8:57 am

7 MONDAY

☽☌♅	**3:39 am**	12:39 am
☽□♄	**4:51 am**	1:51 am
☽⚺☉	**12:36 pm**	9:36 am
☽⚺☿	**10:27 pm**	7:27 pm
☽⚹♆		9:47 pm

8 TUESDAY

☽⚹♆	**12:47 am**	
☽△♇	**7:30 am**	4:30 am
☽⚹♂	**11:07 am**	8:07 am
☽□♃	**6:47 pm**	3:47 pm

9 WEDNESDAY

☽⚺♀	**8:01 am**	5:01 am
☽⚺♅	**4:55 pm**	1:55 pm
☽△♄	**5:44 pm**	2:44 pm

10 THURSDAY

☽☌☉	**6:53 am**	3:53 am
☽☌☿	**8:37 am**	5:37 am
☽□♆	**1:38 pm**	10:38 am
☽⚻♇	**8:07 pm**	5:07 pm
☉☌☿	**9:13 pm**	6:13 pm

11 FRIDAY

☽⚺♂	**3:02 am**	12:02 am
☽△♃	**7:28 am**	4:28 am
☽☌♀		11:59 pm

12 SATURDAY

☽☌♀	**2:59 am**	
☽⚹♅	**5:11 am**	2:11 am
☽⚻♄	**5:35 am**	2:35 am
☽⚺☿	**5:38 pm**	2:38 pm
☽⚺☉	**11:33 pm**	8:33 pm
☽△♆		10:06 pm
♀⚹♅		10:38 pm

13 SUNDAY

☽△♆	**1:06 am**	
♀⚹♅	**1:38 am**	
♀⚻♄	**4:15 am**	1:15 am
☽☍♇	**7:16 am**	4:16 am
☽☌♂	**5:08 pm**	2:08 pm
☽⚻♃	**6:27 pm**	3:27 pm
☉□♆	**7:40 pm**	4:40 pm

14 MONDAY

☽□♅	**3:27 pm**	12:27 pm
☽☍♄	**3:28 pm**	12:28 pm
♄□♅	**6:01 pm**	3:01 pm
☽⚺♀	**7:19 pm**	4:19 pm
♂⚻♃	**8:39 pm**	5:39 pm
☽⚹☿		9:58 pm

15 TUESDAY

☽⚹☿	**12:58 am**	
☽⚻♆	**10:22 am**	7:22 am
☽⚹☉	**1:27 pm**	10:27 am
☽⚻♇	**4:10 pm**	1:10 pm

16 WEDNESDAY

☽☍♃	**3:00 am**	12:00 am
☽⚺♂	**4:28 am**	1:28 am
☿⚺♀	**4:11 pm**	1:11 pm
☽⚻♄	**10:47 pm**	7:47 pm
☽△♅	**11:07 pm**	8:07 pm
☉⚻♇		10:24 pm

17 THURSDAY

☉⚻♇	**1:24 am**	
☽□☿	**6:16 am**	3:16 am
☽⚹♀	**8:07 am**	5:07 am
☽☍♆	**4:55 pm**	1:55 pm
☽△♇	**10:18 pm**	7:18 pm
☽□☉	**11:54 pm**	8:54 pm

18 FRIDAY

☽⚻♃	**8:41 am**	5:41 am
☽⚹♂	**12:32 pm**	9:32 am

19 SATURDAY

☽△♄	**3:15 am**	12:15 am
☽⚻♅	**3:53 am**	12:53 am
☽△☿	**9:22 am**	6:22 am
☽□♀	**5:07 pm**	2:07 pm
☽⚻♆	**8:36 pm**	5:36 pm
☽□♇		10:37 pm

20 SUNDAY

☽□♇	**1:37 am**	
☽△☉	**6:52 am**	3:52 am
☽△♃	**11:35 am**	8:35 am
☽□♂	**5:29 pm**	2:29 pm

21 MONDAY

☽□♄	**5:09 am**	2:09 am
☽☍♅	**6:02 am**	3:02 am
♀△♆	**9:57 am**	6:57 am
☽⚻☿	**10:35 am**	7:35 am
☽△♆	**9:57 pm**	6:57 pm
☽△♀	**11:01 pm**	8:01 pm
☽⚹♇		11:43 pm

22 TUESDAY

☽⚹♇	**2:43 am**	
☽⚻☉	**11:12 am**	8:12 am
☽□♃	**12:26 pm**	9:26 am
☽△♂	**8:17 pm**	5:17 pm

23 WEDNESDAY

☽⚹♄	**5:25 am**	2:25 am
☉△♃	**6:11 am**	3:11 am
☽⚻♅	**6:35 am**	3:35 am
☽☍☿	**10:50 am**	7:50 am
♀☍♇	**7:39 pm**	4:39 pm
☽□♆	**10:09 pm**	7:09 pm
☽⚺♇		11:49 pm

24 THURSDAY

☽⚺♇	**2:49 am**	
☽⚻♀	**3:28 am**	12:28 am
☽⚹♃	**12:33 pm**	9:33 am
☽☍☉	**2:40 pm**	11:40 am
☽⚻♂	**10:35 pm**	7:35 pm

25 FRIDAY

☽⚺♄	**5:35 am**	2:35 am
☽△♅	**7:04 am**	4:04 am
☽⚻☿	**11:42 am**	8:42 am
☽⚹♆	**10:51 pm**	7:51 pm

26 SATURDAY

☽☌♇	**3:36 am**	12:36 am
☽☍♀	**8:49 am**	5:49 am
☽⚺♃	**1:42 pm**	10:42 am
☽⚻☉	**7:29 pm**	4:29 pm
☽☍♂		11:30 pm

27 SUNDAY

☽☍♂	**2:30 am**	
☽☌♄	**7:23 am**	4:23 am
☽□♅	**9:16 am**	6:16 am
☽△☿	**3:08 pm**	12:08 pm
☽⚺♆		10:49 pm

28 MONDAY

☽⚺♆	**1:49 am**	
☽⚺♇	**6:47 am**	3:47 am
♀⚻♃	**5:31 pm**	2:31 pm
☽☌♃	**5:33 pm**	2:33 pm
☽⚻♀	**5:34 pm**	2:34 pm

29 TUESDAY

☽△☉	**3:54 am**	12:54 am
☽⚻♂	**9:58 am**	6:58 am
☽⚺♄	**12:24 pm**	9:24 am
☽⚹♅	**2:47 pm**	11:47 am
☽□☿	**11:00 pm**	8:00 pm

30 WEDNESDAY

☽☌♆	**8:25 am**	5:25 am
☽⚹♇	**1:40 pm**	10:40 am
☽⚺♃		10:12 pm

JUNE 2021

DATE	SID.TIME	SUN	MOON	NODE	MERCURY	VENUS	MARS	JUPITER	SATURN	URANUS	NEPTUNE	PLUTO	CERES	PALLAS	JUNO	VESTA	CHIRON
1 T	16 38 47	10Ⅱ44 05	25≈00	10Ⅱ44Rx	24Ⅱ34Rx	28Ⅱ06	23♋30	1♓34	13≈27Rx	12♉25	23♓02	26♑33Rx	9♋08	23♈19	17♐44Rx	12♍49	12♈06
2 W	16 42 44	11 41 35	8♓02	10 44	24 22	29 19	24 07	1 38	13 27	12 29	23 03	26 32	9 31	23 30	17 30	13 05	12 08
3 Th	16 46 40	12 39 04	20 43	10 44	24 07	0♋33	24 44	1 41	13 26	12 32	23 04	26 31	9 54	23 41	17 17	13 22	12 10
4 F	16 50 37	13 36 32	3♈05	10 44	23 48	1 46	25 21	1 45	13 25	12 35	23 04	26 30	10 16	23 52	17 03	13 38	12 12
5 Sa	16 54 33	14 33 59	15 12	10 45	23 26	2 59	25 58	1 48	13 23	12 38	23 05	26 29	10 39	24 02	16 50	13 55	12 14
6 Su	16 58 30	15 31 26	27 09	10 45	23 00	4 13	26 34	1 51	13 22	12 41	23 06	26 28	11 02	24 13	16 36	14 13	12 16
7 M	17 2 27	16 28 52	8♉59	10 46	22 32	5 26	27 11	1 53	13 21	12 44	23 06	26 27	11 24	24 23	16 23	14 30	12 18
8 T	17 6 23	17 26 17	20 46	10 46	22 02	6 39	27 48	1 56	13 19	12 47	23 07	26 27	11 47	24 33	16 09	14 48	12 20
9 W	17 10 20	18 23 42	2Ⅱ34	10 46	21 30	7 52	28 25	1 58	13 18	12 50	23 07	26 26	12 09	24 42	15 55	15 06	12 22
10 Th	17 14 16	19 21 06	14 24	10 47	20 57	9 05	29 02	2 00	13 16	12 53	23 08	26 25	12 31	24 52	15 42	15 25	12 23
11 F	17 18 13	20 18 29	26 19	10 46	20 23	10 19	29 39	2 02	13 14	12 56	23 08	26 24	12 54	25 01	15 28	15 43	12 25
12 Sa	17 22 9	21 15 51	8♋21	10 46	19 50	11 32	0♌16	2 04	13 13	12 59	23 09	26 23	13 16	25 10	15 15	16 02	12 27
13 Su	17 26 6	22 13 13	20 33	10 44	19 17	12 45	0 53	2 05	13 11	13 01	23 09	26 21	13 38	25 19	15 01	16 21	12 28
14 M	17 30 2	23 10 33	2♌55	10 43	18 45	13 58	1 30	2 07	13 09	13 04	23 10	26 20	14 00	25 27	14 48	16 40	12 30
15 T	17 33 59	24 07 53	15 31	10 41	18 15	15 11	2 07	2 08	13 07	13 07	23 10	26 19	14 22	25 36	14 34	17 00	12 32
16 W	17 37 56	25 05 12	28 21	10 39	17 47	16 24	2 44	2 09	13 05	13 10	23 10	26 18	14 44	25 44	14 21	17 20	12 33
17 Th	17 41 52	26 02 30	11♍29	10 38	17 22	17 37	3 21	2 10	13 02	13 13	23 11	26 17	15 06	25 52	14 08	17 40	12 35
18 F	17 45 49	26 59 47	24 56	10 38	17 00	18 50	3 58	2 10	13 00	13 15	23 11	26 16	15 28	25 59	13 55	18 00	12 36
19 Sa	17 49 45	27 57 04	8≏43	10 38	16 41	20 03	4 35	2 11	12 58	13 18	23 11	26 14	15 50	26 07	13 42	18 20	12 37
20 Su	17 53 42	28 54 19	22 50	10 39	16 27	21 16	5 12	2 11Rx	12 55	13 21	23 11	26 13	16 12	26 14	13 29	18 41	12 39
21 M	17 57 38	29 51 34	7♏17	10 40	16 16	22 29	5 49	2 11	12 53	13 23	23 11	26 12	16 34	26 21	13 16	19 01	12 40
22 T	18 1 35	0♋48 48	22 04	10 41	16 10	23 42	6 26	2 11	12 50	13 26	23 12Rx	26 11	16 55	26 27	13 04	19 22	12 41
23 W	18 5 32	1 46 02	6♐53	10 42Rx	16 08	24 55	7 03	2 11	12 47	13 29	23 12	26 09	17 17	26 34	12 52	19 44	12 42
24 Th	18 9 28	2 43 15	21 52	10 41	16 10	26 08	7 40	2 10	12 44	13 31	23 12	26 08	17 38	26 40	12 39	20 05	12 44
25 F	18 13 25	3 40 28	6♑46	10 40	16 18	27 21	8 18	2 09	12 41	13 34	23 12	26 07	18 00	26 46	12 28	20 26	12 45
26 Sa	18 17 21	4 37 40	21 28	10 38	16 30	28 34	8 55	2 08	12 39	13 36	23 12	26 06	18 21	26 52	12 16	20 48	12 46
27 Su	18 21 18	5 34 52	5≈52	10 34	16 47	29 47	9 32	2 07	12 35	13 38	23 12	26 04	18 43	26 57	12 04	21 10	12 47
28 M	18 25 14	6 32 04	19 52	10 31	17 09	0♌59	10 09	2 06	12 32	13 41	23 12	26 03	19 04	27 02	11 53	21 32	12 48
29 T	18 29 11	7 29 16	3♓26	10 27	17 35	2 12	10 46	2 04	12 29	13 43	23 12	26 02	19 25	27 07	11 42	21 54	12 49
30 W	18 33 7	8 26 28	16 34	10 25	18 06	3 25	11 23	2 03	12 26	13 46	23 12	**25 59**	19 46	27 11	11 31	22 17	12 49

EPHEMERIS CALCULATED FOR 12 MIDNIGHT GREENWICH MEAN TIME. ALL OTHER DATA AND FACING ASPECTARIAN PAGE IN **EASTERN TIME (BOLD)** AND PACIFIC TIME (REGULAR).

JULY 2021

☽ Last Aspect / ☽ Ingress

day	ET / hr:mn / PT		asp	sign	day	ET / hr:mn / PT	
2		9:15 pm	□♇	♉	3	**8:28 am**	5:28 am
3	**12:15 am**		□♇	♉	3	**8:28 am**	5:28 am
5	**12:57 pm**	9:57 am	△♇	♊	5	**9:24 pm**	6:24 pm
7		9:20 pm	☌☿	♋	8	**9:51 am**	6:51 am
8	**12:20 am**		☌☿	♋	8	**9:51 am**	6:51 am
10	**12:10 pm**	9:10 am	☍♇	♌	10	**8:21 pm**	5:21 pm
12	**8:29 am**	5:29 am	☌♂	♍	13	**4:30 am**	1:30 am
14		11:46 pm	△♇	♎	15	**10:32 am**	7:32 am
15	**2:46 am**		△♇	♎	15	**10:32 am**	7:32 am
17	**7:03 am**	4:03 am	□♇	♏	17	**2:38 pm**	11:38 am
19	**12:30 pm**	9:30 am	△☉	♐	19	**5:08 pm**	2:08 pm
21	**6:26 pm**	3:26 pm	△♀	♑	21	**6:36 pm**	3:36 pm
23	**12:34 pm**	9:34 am	☌♇	♒	23	**8:12 pm**	5:12 pm
25	**7:14 pm**	4:14 pm	☍♂	♓	25	**11:30 pm**	8:30 pm
27	**9:13 pm**	6:13 pm	⚹♇	♈	28	**5:58 am**	2:58 am
30	**3:38 pm**	12:38 pm	⚹♃	♉	30	**4:08 pm**	1:08 pm

☽ Phases & Eclipses

phase	day	ET / hr:mn / PT	
4th Quarter	1	**5:11 pm**	2:11 pm
New Moon	9	**9:17 pm**	6:17 pm
2nd Quarter	17	**6:11 am**	3:11 am
Full Moon	23	**10:37 pm**	7:37 pm
4th Quarter	31	**9:16 am**	6:16 am

Planet Ingress

		day	ET / hr:mn / PT	
☿	♋	11	**4:35 pm**	1:35 pm
⚵	♎	18		11:31 pm
⚵	♎	19	**2:31 am**	
♀	♍	21	**8:37 pm**	5:37 pm
☉	♌	22	**10:26 am**	7:26 am
☿	♌	27	**9:12 pm**	6:12 pm
♃	♒	28	**8:43 am**	5:43 am
♂	♍	29	**4:32 pm**	1:32 pm
⚳	♊	31	**4:13 am**	1:13 am

Planetary Motion

		day	ET / hr:mn / PT	
♀	R	14	**3:40 am**	12:40 am
⚷	R	15	**12:41 pm**	9:41 am

1 THURSDAY
☽ ⚺ ♃ **1:12 am**
☽ △ ♀ **7:22 am** 4:22 am
♂ ☍ ♄ **9:08 am** 6:08 am
☽ □ ☉ **5:11 pm** 2:11 pm
☽ ⚹ ♄ **9:16 pm** 6:16 pm
☽ △ ♂ **9:58 pm** 6:58 pm
☽ ⚺ ♅ 9:15 pm

2 FRIDAY
☽ ⚺ ♅ **12:15 am**
☽ ⚹ ☿ **12:12 pm** 9:12 am
☽ ⚺ ♆ **6:48 pm** 3:48 pm
☽ □ ♇ 9:15 pm

3 SATURDAY
☽ □ ♇ **12:15 am**
☽ ⚹ ♃ **12:19 pm** 9:19 am
☉ ⚻ ♄ **6:51 pm** 3:51 pm
♂ □ ♅ **9:40 pm** 6:40 pm
☽ □ ♀ 10:44 pm

4 SUNDAY
☽ □ ♀ **1:44 am**
☽ □ ♄ **9:06 am** 6:06 am
☽ ⚹ ☉ **10:26 am** 7:26 am
☽ ☌ ♅ **12:41 pm** 9:41 am
☽ □ ♂ **1:28 pm** 10:28 am

5 MONDAY
☽ ⚺ ☿ **5:36 am** 2:36 am
☽ ⚹ ♆ **7:30 am** 4:30 am
☽ △ ♇ **12:57 pm** 9:57 am

☉ ⚹ ♅ **3:14 pm** 12:14 pm
☽ □ ♃ 10:03 pm

6 TUESDAY
☽ □ ♃ **1:03 am**
☿ □ ♆ **3:39 am** 12:39 am
☽ ⚹ ♀ **9:41 pm** 6:41 pm
☽ △ ♄ **9:47 pm** 6:47 pm
♀ ☍ ♄ **10:36 pm** 7:36 pm
☽ ⚺ ♅ 10:50 pm

7 WEDNESDAY
☽ ⚺ ♅ **1:50 am**
☽ ⚺ ☉ **4:44 am** 1:44 am
☽ ⚹ ♂ **5:47 am** 2:47 am
☽ □ ♆ **8:12 pm** 5:12 pm
☽ ☌ ☿ 9:20 pm
☽ ⚻ ♇ 10:28 pm

8 THURSDAY
☽ ☌ ☿ **12:20 am**
☽ ⚻ ♇ **1:28 am**
☿ ⚻ ♇ **11:36 am** 8:36 am
☽ △ ♃ **1:09 pm** 10:09 am
♀ □ ♅ **3:25 pm** 12:25 pm
☉ ⚺ ♂ **4:29 pm** 1:29 pm

9 FRIDAY
☽ ⚻ ♄ **9:15 am** 6:15 am
☽ ⚹ ♅ **1:38 pm** 10:38 am
☽ ⚺ ♀ **3:59 pm** 12:59 pm
☽ ⚺ ♂ **8:28 pm** 5:28 pm
☽ ☌ ☉ **9:17 pm** 6:17 pm

10 SATURDAY
☽ △ ♆ **7:11 am** 4:11 am
☽ ☍ ♇ **12:10 pm** 9:10 am
☽ ⚺ ☿ **5:49 pm** 2:49 pm
☽ ⚻ ♃ **11:14 pm** 8:14 pm

11 SUNDAY
☽ ☍ ♄ **6:32 pm** 3:32 pm
☽ □ ♅ **11:11 pm** 8:11 pm

12 MONDAY
☽ ☌ ♀ **7:14 am** 4:14 am
☽ ☌ ♂ **8:29 am** 5:29 am
☽ ⚺ ☉ **10:56 am** 7:56 am
☿ △ ♃ **3:45 pm** 12:45 pm
☽ ⚻ ♆ **3:50 pm** 12:50 pm
☽ ⚻ ♇ **8:33 pm** 5:33 pm

13 TUESDAY
☽ ☍ ♃ **7:00 am** 4:00 am
☽ ⚹ ☿ **9:05 am** 6:05 am
♀ ☌ ♂ **9:33 am** 6:33 am
☽ ⚻ ♄ 10:33 pm

14 WEDNESDAY
☽ ⚻ ♄ **1:33 am**
☽ △ ♅ **6:25 am** 3:25 am
☽ ⚺ ♂ **5:55 pm** 2:55 pm
☽ ⚺ ♀ **7:28 pm** 4:28 pm
☽ ⚹ ☉ **9:46 pm** 6:46 pm
☽ ☍ ♆ **10:17 pm** 7:17 pm
☽ △ ♇ 11:46 pm

15 THURSDAY
☽ △ ♇ **2:46 am**
☉ △ ♆ **4:49 am** 1:49 am
☽ ⚻ ♃ **12:38 pm** 9:38 am
☽ □ ☿ **10:09 pm** 7:09 pm
♀ ⚻ ♆ 11:41 pm

16 FRIDAY
♀ ⚻ ♆ **2:41 am**
☽ △ ♄ **6:33 am** 3:33 am
☽ ⚻ ♅ **11:37 am** 8:37 am
☽ ⚹ ♂ 10:04 pm
☽ ⚻ ♆ 11:46 pm

17 SATURDAY
☽ ⚹ ♂ **1:04 am**
☽ ⚻ ♆ **2:46 am**
☽ ⚹ ♀ **5:04 am** 2:04 am
☽ □ ☉ **6:11 am** 3:11 am
☽ □ ♇ **7:03 am** 4:03 am
☽ △ ♃ **4:23 pm** 1:23 pm
☉ ☍ ♇ **6:46 pm** 3:46 pm

18 SUNDAY
♀ ⚻ ♇ **3:48 am** 12:48 am
☽ △ ☿ **9:13 am** 6:13 am
☽ □ ♄ **9:45 am** 6:45 am
☿ ⚻ ♄ **1:13 pm** 10:13 am
♂ ⚻ ♆ **2:22 pm** 11:22 am
☽ ☍ ♅ **3:00 pm** 12:00 pm

19 MONDAY
☽ △ ♆ **5:33 am** 2:33 am
☽ □ ♂ **6:15 am** 3:15 am
☽ ⚹ ♇ **9:40 am** 6:40 am

☽ □ ♀ **12:27 pm** 9:27 am
☽ △ ☉ **12:30 pm** 9:30 am
☉ ⚺ ♀ **3:17 pm** 12:17 pm
☽ □ ♃ **6:32 pm** 3:32 pm

20 TUESDAY
☿ ⚹ ♅ **5:38 am** 2:38 am
☽ ⚹ ♄ **11:31 am** 8:31 am
☽ ⚻ ♅ **4:59 pm** 1:59 pm
☽ ⚻ ☿ **6:42 pm** 3:42 pm

21 WEDNESDAY
☽ □ ♆ **7:08 am** 4:08 am
☽ △ ♂ **10:06 am** 7:06 am
☽ ⚺ ♇ **11:10 am** 8:10 am
☽ ⚻ ☉ **5:30 pm** 2:30 pm
☽ △ ♀ **6:26 pm** 3:26 pm
☽ ⚹ ♃ **7:41 pm** 4:41 pm

22 THURSDAY
♀ ☍ ♃ **8:45 am** 5:45 am
♂ ⚻ ♇ **10:09 am** 7:09 am
☽ ⚺ ♄ **12:38 pm** 9:38 am
☽ △ ♅ **6:25 pm** 3:25 pm
☉ ⚻ ♃ 9:10 pm

23 FRIDAY
☉ ⚻ ♃ **12:10 am**
☽ ☍ ☿ **3:53 am** 12:53 am
☽ ⚹ ♆ **8:32 am** 5:32 am
☽ ☌ ♇ **12:34 pm** 9:34 am
☽ ⚻ ♂ **1:49 pm** 10:49 am
☽ ⚺ ♃ **8:59 pm** 5:59 pm
☽ ☍ ☉ **10:37 pm** 7:37 pm
☽ ⚻ ♀ 9:34 pm

24 SATURDAY
☽ ⚻ ♀ **12:34 am**
☿ △ ♆ **12:35 pm** 9:35 am
☽ ☌ ♄ **2:25 pm** 11:25 am
☽ □ ♅ **8:43 pm** 5:43 pm

25 SUNDAY
☽ ⚺ ♆ **11:14 am** 8:14 am
☽ ⚻ ☿ **3:15 pm** 12:15 pm
☽ ⚺ ♇ **3:25 pm** 12:25 pm
☿ ☍ ♇ **4:15 pm** 1:15 pm
☽ ☍ ♂ **7:14 pm** 4:14 pm
☽ ☌ ♃ **11:56 pm** 8:56 pm

26 MONDAY
☽ ⚻ ☉ **5:55 am** 2:55 am
☽ ☍ ♀ **9:04 am** 6:04 am
☽ ⚺ ♄ **6:25 pm** 3:25 pm
☽ ⚹ ♅ 10:28 pm
☿ ⚺ ♂ 11:48 pm

27 TUESDAY
☽ ⚹ ♅ **1:28 am**
☿ ⚺ ♂ **2:48 am**
☽ ☌ ♆ **4:47 pm** 1:47 pm
☽ ⚹ ♇ **9:13 pm** 6:13 pm
☿ ⚻ ♃ **9:45 pm** 6:45 pm

28 WEDNESDAY
☽ ⚻ ♂ **4:11 am** 1:11 am
☽ ⚺ ♃ **5:59 am** 2:59 am
☽ △ ☿ **7:42 am** 4:42 am
☽ △ ☉ **5:19 pm** 2:19 pm
☽ ⚻ ♀ **10:00 pm** 7:00 pm
☽ ⚹ ♄ 10:53 pm

29 THURSDAY
☽ ⚹ ♄ **1:53 am**
☽ ⚺ ♅ **9:51 am** 6:51 am
♂ ☍ ♃ **11:50 am** 8:50 am
☽ ⚺ ♆ 11:03 pm

30 FRIDAY
☽ ⚺ ♆ **2:03 am**
☽ □ ♇ **6:44 am** 3:44 am
♀ ⚻ ♄ **12:27 pm** 9:27 am
☽ ⚹ ♃ **3:38 pm** 12:38 pm
☽ △ ♂ **5:26 pm** 2:26 pm

31 SATURDAY
☽ □ ☿ **6:24 am** 3:24 am
☽ □ ☉ **9:16 am** 6:16 am
☽ □ ♄ **12:48 pm** 9:48 am
☽ △ ♀ **3:41 pm** 12:41 pm
☽ ☌ ♅ **9:34 pm** 6:34 pm

Eastern time in bold type
Pacific time in medium type

JULY 2021

DATE	SID.TIME	SUN	MOON	NODE	MERCURY	VENUS	MARS	JUPITER	SATURN	URANUS	NEPTUNE	PLUTO	CERES	PALLAS	JUNO	VESTA	CHIRON
1 Th	18 37 4	9♋23 40	29♈18	10♊23D	18♊42	4♋37	12♋00	2♓01R	12≈23R	13♉48	23♓12R	25♑58R	20♑07	27♈16	11♊20R	22♍40	12♈50
2 F	18 41 1	10 20 52	11♈41	10 23	19 23	5 50	12 38	1 59	12 19	13 50	23 11	25 56	20 28	27 20	11 00	23 02	12 51
3 Sa	18 44 57	11 18 05	23 47	10 23	20 08	7 03	13 15	1 56	12 16	13 52	23 11	25 55	20 49	27 23	11 00	23 25	12 52
4 Su	18 48 54	12 15 17	5♉43	10 25	20 58	8 15	13 52	1 54	12 12	13 55	23 11	25 53	21 10	27 27	10 50	23 48	12 52
5 M	18 52 50	13 12 30	17 32	10 25	21 52	9 28	14 29	1 51	12 09	13 57	23 11	25 52	21 30	27 30	10 40	24 12	12 53
6 T	18 56 47	14 09 43	29 19	10 26R	22 51	10 41	15 07	1 48	12 05	13 59	23 10	25 51	21 51	27 33	10 31	24 35	12 53
7 W	19 0 43	15 06 56	11♊08	10 28	23 54	11 53	15 44	1 45	12 02	14 01	23 10	25 49	22 12	27 35	10 22	24 59	12 54
8 Th	19 4 40	16 04 10	23 04	10 28	25 01	13 06	16 21	1 42	11 58	14 03	23 10	25 48	22 32	27 37	10 13	25 22	12 54
9 F	19 8 36	17 01 23	5♋07	10 25	26 12	14 18	16 58	1 39	11 54	14 05	23 09	25 46	22 52	27 39	10 05	25 46	12 55
10 Sa	19 12 33	17 58 37	17 22	10 21	27 28	15 31	17 36	1 35	11 50	14 07	23 09	25 45	23 13	27 41	9 57	26 10	12 55
11 Su	19 16 30	18 55 52	29 49	10 15	28 46	16 43	18 13	1 32	11 46	14 09	23 08	25 44	23 33	27 42	9 49	26 35	12 55
12 M	19 20 26	19 53 06	12♌29	10 09	0♋14	17 56	18 50	1 29	11 42	14 11	23 08	25 42	23 53	27 43	9 42	26 59	12 55
13 T	19 24 23	20 50 20	25 23	10 02	1 40	19 08	19 28	1 24	11 38	14 12	23 07	25 41	24 13	27 43	9 34	27 23	12 56
14 W	19 28 19	21 47 34	8♍29	9 56	3 12	20 20	20 05	1 19	11 34	14 14	23 06	25 39	24 33	27 44R	9 28	27 48	12 56
15 Th	19 32 16	22 44 49	21 49	9 50	4 48	21 33	20 43	1 15	11 30	14 16	23 06	25 38	24 53	27 44	9 21	28 13	12 56R
16 F	19 36 12	23 42 03	5≏23	9 47	6 27	22 45	21 20	1 10	11 26	14 18	23 05	25 36	25 12	27 43	9 15	28 38	12 56
17 Sa	19 40 9	24 39 18	19 09	9 46D	8 04	23 57	21 57	1 06	11 22	14 19	23 05	25 35	25 32	27 43	9 09	29 03	12 56
18 Su	19 44 5	25 36 32	3♏09	9 46	9 56	25 10	22 35	1 01	11 18	14 21	23 04	25 34	25 51	27 41	9 03	29 28	12 56
19 M	19 48 2	26 33 47	17 21	9 47	11 48	26 22	23 12	0 56	11 14	14 22	23 03	25 32	26 11	27 40	8 58	29 53	12 56
20 T	19 51 59	27 31 02	1♐44	9 48R	13 39	27 34	23 50	0 50	11 09	14 24	23 03	25 31	26 30	27 38	8 53	0≏19	12 55
21 W	19 55 55	28 28 17	16 15	9 48	15 34	28 46	24 27	0 45	11 05	14 25	23 02	25 29	26 49	27 36	8 49	0 44	12 55
22 Th	19 59 52	29 25 33	0♑51	9 46	17 32	29 58	25 05	0 39	11 01	14 27	23 01	25 28	27 08	27 34	8 45	1 10	12 55
23 F	20 3 48	0♌22 49	15 25	9 42	19 32	1♌10	25 42	0 34	10 56	14 28	23 00	25 26	27 27	27 31	8 41	1 35	12 54
24 Sa	20 7 45	1 20 05	29 53	9 36	21 34	2 22	26 20	0 28	10 52	14 30	22 59	25 25	27 46	27 28	8 37	2 01	12 54
25 Su	20 11 41	2 17 22	14≈06	9 29	23 37	3 34	26 57	0 22	10 48	14 31	22 59	25 23	28 04	27 25	8 34	2 27	12 54
26 M	20 15 38	3 14 40	28 00	9 20	25 42	4 46	27 35	0 16	10 43	14 32	22 58	25 22	28 23	27 21	8 31	2 54	12 53
27 T	20 19 34	4 11 58	11♓32	9 11	27 47	5 58	28 13	0 10	10 39	14 33	22 57	25 21	28 41	27 17	8 29	3 20	12 53
28 W	20 23 31	5 09 17	24 40	9 04	29 54	7 10	28 50	0 03	10 34	14 34	22 56	25 19	29 00	27 12	8 26	3 46	12 52
29 Th	20 27 28	6 06 37	7♈25	8 58	2♌06	8 22	29 28	29♈57	10 30	14 36	22 54	25 18	29 18	27 07	8 25	4 13	12 51
30 F	20 31 24	7 03 58	19 49	8 55	4 07	9 33	0♌07	29 50	10 26	14 37	22 53	25 16	29 36	27 02	8 23	4 39	12 51
31 Sa	20 35 21	8 01 21	1♉56	8 53D	6 13	10 45	0 43	29 44	10 21	14 38	22 53	25 15	29 54	26 57	8 22	5 06	12 50

EPHEMERIS CALCULATED FOR 12 MIDNIGHT GREENWICH MEAN TIME. ALL OTHER DATA AND FACING ASPECTARIAN PAGE IN **EASTERN TIME (BOLD)** AND PACIFIC TIME (REGULAR).

AUGUST 2021

☽ Last Aspect day	ET / hr:mn / PT		asp	☽ Ingress sign	day	ET / hr:mn / PT	
2	3:41 am	12:41 am	□ ♃	♊	2	4:46 am	1:46 am
4	3:38 pm	12:38 pm	△ ♃	♋	4	5:17 pm	2:17 pm
6	6:12 pm	3:12 pm	☍ ♇	♌	7	3:31 am	12:31 am
9	8:23 am	5:23 am	☍ ♃	♍	9	10:56 am	7:56 am
11	7:22 am	4:22 am	△ ♇	♎	11	4:08 pm	1:08 pm
13	4:39 pm	1:39 pm	△ ♃	♏	13	8:01 pm	5:01 pm
15	11:05 pm	8:05 pm	✶ ♀	♐	15	11:12 pm	8:12 pm
17	9:43 pm	6:43 pm	✶ ♃	♑	17		10:58 pm
17	9:43 pm	6:43 pm	✶ ♃	♑	18	1:58 am	
19	7:59 pm	4:59 pm	☌ ♇	♒	20	4:49 am	1:49 am
22	8:02 am	5:02 am	☍ ☉	♓	22	8:43 am	5:43 am
24	5:12 am	2:12 am	✶ ♇	♈	24	2:57 pm	11:57 am
26	5:14 pm	2:14 pm	✶ ♃	♉	26		9:27 pm
26	5:14 pm	2:14 pm	✶ ♃	♉	27	12:27 am	
29	10:59 am	7:59 am	△ ☿	♊	29	12:42 pm	9:42 am
31	4:48 pm	1:48 pm	△ ♃	♋	31		10:26 pm

☽ Phases & Eclipses phase	day	ET / hr:mn / PT	
New Moon	8	9:50 am	6:50 am
2nd Quarter	15	11:20 am	8:20 am
Full Moon	22	8:02 am	5:02 am
4th Quarter	30	3:13 am	12:13 am

Planet Ingress		day	ET / hr:mn / PT	
☿	♍	11	5:57 pm	2:57 pm
♀	♎	15		9:27 pm
♀	♎	16	12:27 am	
☉	♍	22	5:35 pm	2:35 pm
☿	♎	29		10:10 pm
☿	♎	30	1:10 am	

Planetary Motion		day	ET / hr:mn / PT	
⚵	D	2	7:43 pm	4:43 pm
♅	℞	19	9:40 pm	6:40 pm

1 SUNDAY
☉☌☿ 10:08 am 7:08 am
☽✶♆ 2:13 pm 11:13 am
☿☍♄ 5:50 pm 2:50 pm
☽△♇ 7:01 pm 4:01 pm
☉☍♄ 11:14 pm

2 MONDAY
☉☍♄ 2:14 am
☽□♃ 3:41 am 12:41 am
☽□♂ 9:30 am 6:30 am
☽△♄ 10:19 pm
♀△♅ 11:53 pm

3 TUESDAY
☽△♄ 1:19 am
♀△♅ 2:53 am
☽✶☉ 3:30 am 12:30 am
☽✶☿ 8:12 am 5:12 am
☽⊻♅ 10:34 am 7:34 am
☽□♀ 11:25 am 8:25 am
☿□♅ 9:57 pm 6:57 pm
☽□♆ 11:55 pm

4 WEDNESDAY
☽□♆ 2:55 am
☽⊼♇ 7:37 am 4:37 am
☽△♃ 3:38 pm 12:38 pm
☿⊻♀ 9:43 pm
☽✶♂ 10:12 pm

5 THURSDAY
☿⊻♀ 12:43 am
☽✶♂ 1:12 am
☽⊼♄ 12:52 pm 9:52 am
☽⊻☉ 8:24 pm 5:24 pm
☽✶♅ 10:12 pm 7:12 pm

6 FRIDAY
☽✶♀ 5:17 am 2:17 am
☽⊻☿ 7:31 am 4:31 am
☽△♆ 1:43 pm 10:43 am
☽☍♇ 6:12 pm 3:12 pm
☉□♅ 7:57 pm 4:57 pm
☽⊼♃ 10:23 pm

7 SATURDAY
☽⊼♃ 1:23 am
☽⊻♂ 2:04 pm 11:04 am
☽☍♄ 9:50 pm 6:50 pm
☿⊼♆ 10:24 pm 7:24 pm

8 SUNDAY
☽□♅ 7:04 am 4:04 am
☽☌☉ 9:50 am 6:50 am
☽⊻♀ 7:24 pm 4:24 pm
☽⊼♆ 9:42 pm 6:42 pm
☽☌☿ 10:45 pm
☽⊼♇ 10:57 pm

9 MONDAY
☽☌☿ 1:45 am
☽⊼♇ 1:57 am
☿⊼♇ 3:03 am 12:03 am
☽☍♃ 8:23 am 5:23 am
♀☍♆ 8:20 pm 5:20 pm
☽☌♂ 11:42 pm 8:42 pm

10 TUESDAY
☽⊼♄ 4:07 am 1:07 am
☽△♅ 1:19 pm 10:19 am
☽⊻☉ 8:03 pm 5:03 pm
☿☍♃ 9:20 pm 6:20 pm

11 WEDNESDAY
☽☍♆ 3:16 am 12:16 am
☽☌♀ 6:15 am 3:15 am
☽△♇ 7:22 am 4:22 am
☽⊼♃ 1:10 pm 10:10 am
☽⊻☿ 3:51 pm 12:51 pm
♀△♇ 6:46 pm 3:46 pm

12 THURSDAY
☽⊻♂ 7:03 am 4:03 am
☽△♄ 8:32 am 5:32 am
☽⊼♅ 5:48 pm 2:48 pm

13 FRIDAY
☽✶☉ 4:13 am 1:13 am
☽⊼♆ 7:19 am 4:19 am
☽□♇ 11:20 am 8:20 am
♂⊼♄ 12:27 pm 9:27 am
☽⊻♀ 3:10 pm 12:10 pm
☽△♃ 4:39 pm 1:39 pm

14 SATURDAY
☽✶☿ 3:33 am 12:33 am
♀⊼♃ 6:58 am 3:58 am
☽□♄ 11:54 am 8:54 am
☽✶♂ 1:08 pm 10:08 am
☽☍♅ 9:18 pm 6:18 pm
☉⊼♆ 9:14 pm

15 SUNDAY
☉⊼♆ 12:14 am
☽△♆ 10:33 am 7:33 am
☽□☉ 11:20 am 8:20 am
☽✶♇ 2:32 pm 11:32 am
☽□♃ 7:23 pm 4:23 pm
☽✶♀ 11:05 pm 8:05 pm

16 MONDAY
☽□☿ 1:57 pm 10:57 am
☽✶♄ 2:40 pm 11:40 am
☽□♂ 6:31 pm 3:31 pm
☿⊼♄ 7:35 pm 4:35 pm
☽⊼♅ 9:15 pm

17 TUESDAY
☽⊼♅ 12:15 am
☉⊼♇ 9:31 am 6:31 am
☽□♆ 1:19 pm 10:19 am
☽⊻♇ 5:17 pm 2:17 pm
☽△☉ 5:51 pm 2:51 pm
☽✶♃ 9:43 pm 6:43 pm

18 WEDNESDAY
☽□♀ 6:27 am 3:27 am
☽⊻♄ 5:08 pm 2:08 pm
☿☌♂ 11:28 pm 8:28 pm
☽△♂ 11:37 pm 8:37 pm
☽△☿ 11:38 pm 8:38 pm
☽△♅ 11:59 pm

19 THURSDAY
☽△♅ 2:59 am
☽✶♆ 3:59 pm 12:59 pm
☽☌♇ 7:59 pm 4:59 pm
☉☍♃ 8:29 pm 5:29 pm
☽⊻♃ 9:03 pm
☽⊼☉ 9:21 pm

20 FRIDAY
☽⊻♃ 12:03 am
☽⊼☉ 12:21 am
☿△♅ 4:06 am 1:06 am
☽△♀ 2:01 pm 11:01 am
☽☌♄ 7:55 pm 4:55 pm

21 SATURDAY
☽⊼♂ 5:13 am 2:13 am
☽□♅ 6:12 am 3:12 am
☽⊼☿ 9:41 am 6:41 am
☽⊻♆ 7:24 pm 4:24 pm
☽⊻♇ 11:32 pm 8:32 pm
♂△♅ 11:38 pm

22 SUNDAY
♂△♅ 2:38 am
☽☌♃ 3:19 am 12:19 am
☽☍☉ 8:02 am 5:02 am
☽⊼♀ 11:14 pm 8:14 pm
☽⊻♄ 9:07 pm

23 MONDAY
☽⊻♄ 12:07 am
♀△♄ 8:48 am 5:48 am
☽✶♅ 11:04 am 8:04 am
☽☍♂ 12:43 pm 9:43 am
☽☍☿ 10:03 pm 7:03 pm
☽☌♆ 9:50 pm

24 TUESDAY
☽☌♆ 12:50 am
☽✶♇ 5:12 am 2:12 am
☽⊻♃ 8:43 am 5:43 am
☽⊼☉ 6:37 pm 3:37 pm
☿☍♆ 9:14 pm 6:14 pm

25 WEDNESDAY
☽✶♄ 6:58 am 3:58 am
☽☍♀ 11:57 am 8:57 am
☽⊻♅ 6:51 pm 3:51 pm
☽⊼♂ 11:37 pm 8:37 pm

26 THURSDAY
☽⊻♆ 9:22 am 6:22 am
☿△♇ 10:23 am 7:23 am
☽□♇ 2:02 pm 11:02 am
☽⊼☿ 2:33 pm 11:33 am
☽✶♃ 5:14 pm 2:14 pm

27 FRIDAY
☽△☉ 9:19 am 6:19 am
☿⊼♃ 11:05 am 8:05 am
☽□♄ 5:04 pm 2:04 pm

28 SATURDAY
☽⊼♀ 5:00 am 2:00 am
☽☌♅ 5:52 am 2:52 am
♀⊼♅ 1:43 pm 10:43 am
☽△♂ 2:14 pm 11:14 am
☽✶♆ 8:56 pm 5:56 pm
☽△♇ 10:50 pm

29 SUNDAY
☽△♇ 1:50 am
☽□♃ 4:36 am 1:36 am
☽△☿ 10:59 am 7:59 am

30 MONDAY
☽□☉ 3:13 am 12:13 am
☽△♄ 5:26 am 2:26 am
☽⊻♅ 6:40 pm 3:40 pm
☽△♀ 9:30 pm

31 TUESDAY
☽△♀ 12:30 am
☉⊼♄ 4:46 am 1:46 am
☽□♂ 6:36 am 3:36 am
☽□♆ 9:41 am 6:41 am
☽⊼♇ 2:37 pm 11:37 am
☽△♃ 4:48 pm 1:48 pm

Eastern time in bold type
Pacific time in medium type

AUGUST 2021

DATE	SID. TIME	SUN	MOON	NODE	MERCURY	VENUS	MARS	JUPITER	SATURN	URANUS	NEPTUNE	PLUTO	CERES	PALLAS	JUNO	VESTA	CHIRON
1 Su	20 39 17	8♌58 44	13♋52	8♊53	8♌19	11♍57	1♍21	29♒37℞	10♒17℞	14♉39	22♓52℞	25♑14℞	0♊12	26♓51℞	8♈21℞	5♋33	12♈49℞
2 M	20 43 14	9 56 08	25 41	8 54	10 24	13 08	1 58	29 30	10 12	14 40	22 51	25 12	0 29	26 44	8 21D	5 59	12 48
3 T	20 47 10	10 53 34	7♌29	8 54℞	12 28	14 20	2 36	29 23	10 08	14 40	22 49	25 11	0 47	26 38	8 20	6 26	12 47
4 W	20 51 7	11 51 01	19 22	8 53	14 31	15 32	3 14	29 16	10 03	14 41	22 48	25 11	1 04	26 31	8 21	6 54	12 46
5 Th	20 55 3	12 48 29	1♍22	8 51	16 33	16 43	3 52	29 09	9 59	14 42	22 47	25 09	1 21	26 24	8 21	7 21	12 45
6 F	20 59 0	13 45 58	13 35	8 46	18 34	17 55	4 29	29 01	9 54	14 43	22 46	25 08	1 39	26 16	8 22	7 48	12 44
7 Sa	21 2 57	14 43 28	26 02	8 39	20 34	19 06	5 07	28 54	9 50	14 43	22 45	25 07	1 55	26 08	8 23	8 15	12 43
8 Su	21 6 53	15 40 59	8♎46	8 29	22 32	20 17	5 45	28 47	9 46	14 44	22 44	25 05	2 12	25 59	8 25	8 43	12 42
9 M	21 10 50	16 38 32	21 47	8 18	24 28	21 29	6 23	28 39	9 41	14 45	22 42	25 04	2 29	25 51	8 26	9 10	12 41
10 T	21 14 46	17 36 05	5♏03	8 07	26 24	22 40	7 01	28 32	9 37	14 45	22 41	25 03	2 45	25 42	8 29	9 38	12 40
11 W	21 18 43	18 33 39	18 32	7 56	28 17	23 51	7 39	28 24	9 32	14 46	22 40	25 03	3 02	25 32	8 31	10 06	12 38
12 Th	21 22 39	19 31 15	2♐17	7 47	0♍10	25 03	8 17	28 16	9 28	14 46	22 39	25 00	3 18	25 23	8 34	10 34	12 37
13 F	21 26 36	20 28 51	16 03	7 41	2 00	26 14	8 55	28 09	9 24	14 46	22 37	24 59	3 34	25 13	8 37	11 02	12 36
14 Sa	21 30 32	21 26 28	29 59	7 37	3 50	27 25	9 33	28 01	9 19	14 47	22 36	24 56	3 49	25 02	8 40	11 30	12 34
15 Su	21 34 29	22 24 06	14♑01	7 36D	5 37	28 36	10 11	27 53	9 15	14 47	22 34	24 55	4 05	24 52	8 44	11 58	12 33
16 M	21 38 26	23 21 45	28 07	7 35℞	7 22	29 47	10 49	27 45	9 11	14 47	22 33	24 54	4 20	24 41	8 48	12 26	12 31
17 T	21 42 22	24 19 25	12♒17	7 35	9 06	0♎58	11 27	27 37	9 06	14 47	22 32	24 53	4 36	24 29	8 52	12 54	12 30
18 W	21 46 19	25 17 07	26 28	7 34	10 52	2 09	12 05	27 30	9 02	14 47	22 30	24 51	4 51	24 18	8 57	13 23	12 28
19 Th	21 50 15	26 14 49	10♓49	7 31	12 34	3 19	12 43	27 22	8 58	14 47	22 29	24 50	5 06	24 06	9 02	13 51	12 26
20 F	21 54 12	27 12 32	24 49	7 25	14 14	4 30	13 21	27 14	8 54	14 48℞	22 27	24 49	5 20	23 54	9 07	14 20	12 25
21 Sa	21 58 8	28 10 17	8♈53	7 17	15 53	5 41	13 59	27 06	8 50	14 48	22 26	24 48	5 35	23 41	9 13	14 48	12 23
22 Su	22 2 5	29 08 02	22 45	7 06	17 31	6 52	14 37	26 58	8 46	14 47	22 25	24 47	5 49	23 29	9 18	15 17	12 21
23 M	22 6 1	0♍05 49	6♉23	6 54	19 07	8 02	15 15	26 50	8 42	14 47	22 23	24 46	6 03	23 16	9 24	15 46	12 19
24 T	22 9 58	1 03 38	19 43	6 42	20 42	9 13	15 53	26 42	8 38	14 47	22 22	24 45	6 17	23 03	9 31	16 15	12 18
25 W	22 13 55	2 01 28	2♊43	6 31	22 15	10 23	16 31	26 35	8 34	14 47	22 20	24 43	6 31	22 49	9 37	16 44	12 16
26 Th	22 17 51	2 59 19	15 23	6 22	23 47	11 33	17 10	26 27	8 30	14 46	22 18	24 42	6 44	22 36	9 44	17 13	12 14
27 F	22 21 48	3 57 13	27 44	6 15	25 18	12 44	17 48	26 19	8 26	14 46	22 17	24 41	6 58	22 22	9 51	17 42	12 12
28 Sa	22 25 44	4 55 08	9♋51	6 11	26 47	13 54	18 26	26 11	8 23	14 46	22 15	24 40	7 11	22 08	9 59	18 11	12 10
29 Su	22 29 41	5 53 05	21 46	6 10	28 15	15 04	19 04	26 04	8 19	14 46	22 14	24 39	7 23	21 53	10 07	18 40	12 08
30 M	22 33 37	6 51 03	3♌36	6 09	29 42	16 14	19 43	25 56	8 15	14 45	22 12	24 38	7 36	21 39	10 15	19 09	12 06
31 T	22 37 34	7 49 04	15 24	6 09	1♎07	17 24	20 21	25 48	8 12	14 45	22 11	24 37	7 48	21 24	10 23	19 38	12 04

EPHEMERIS CALCULATED FOR 12 MIDNIGHT GREENWICH MEAN TIME. ALL OTHER DATA AND FACING ASPECTARIAN PAGE IN **EASTERN TIME (BOLD)** AND PACIFIC TIME (REGULAR).

SEPTEMBER 2021

Last Aspect / Ingress

☽ Last Aspect			☽ Ingress		
day	ET / hr:mn / PT	asp	sign day	ET / hr:mn / PT	
2	4:48 am 1:48 am	△♇	♎ 2	1:26 am	
	10:37 pm			10:40 am 8:58 am	
5	1:37 am	☐♇	♏ 5	11:58 am 8:58 am	
5	5:14 am 2:14 am	☐♀	♐ 7	7:06 pm 4:06 pm	
7	10:22 am 7:22 am	♂♄	♑ 9	11:20 pm 8:20 pm	
7	3:24 pm 12:24 pm	♂♂		11:05 pm	
9	9:48 pm				
10	12:48 am				

Planet Ingress

Planet Ingress		
	ET / hr:mn / PT	
♀ ♏,	4:39 pm 1:39 pm	
☉ ♎,	8:14 am 5:14 am	
♇ ♏,	12:57 pm 9:57 am	
☿ ♎	3:21 pm 12:21 pm	

Planetary Motion

Planetary Motion		
	day	ET / hr:mn / PT
☿ R₍	26	1:10 am
♇ R₍	27	

Phases & Eclipses

☽ Phases & Eclipses			
phase	day	ET / hr:mn / PT	
New Moon	6	8:52 pm 5:52 pm	
2nd Quarter	13	4:39 pm 1:39 pm	
Full Moon	20	7:55 pm 4:55 pm	
4th Quarter	28	9:57 pm 6:57 pm	

Eastern time in bold type
Pacific time in medium type

SEPTEMBER 2021

DATE	SID.TIME	SUN	MOON	NODE	MERCURY	VENUS	MARS	JUPITER	SATURN	URANUS	NEPTUNE	PLUTO	CERES	PALLAS	JUNO	VESTA	CHIRON
1 W	22 41 30	8♍47 07	27♏17	6♊08℞	2≏30	18♍34	20♍59	25≈41℞	8≈05℞	14♉44℞	22♓08℞	24♑36℞	8♊01	21♋09℞	10♐31	20≏08	12♈01℞
2 Th	22 45 27	9 45 11	9♐21	6 06	3 52	19 44	21 38	25 34	8 04	14 43	22 07	24 35	8 12	20 54	10 40	20 37	11 59
3 F	22 49 24	10 43 17	21 39	6 01	5 13	20 54	22 16	25 26	8 01	14 43	22 06	24 34	8 24	20 39	10 49	21 07	11 57
4 Sa	22 53 20	11 41 26	4♑15	5 53	6 32	22 04	22 55	25 19	7 58	14 42	22 04	24 34	8 36	20 24	10 58	21 37	11 55
5 Su	22 57 17	12 39 36	17 12	5 43	7 50	23 13	23 33	25 12	7 55	14 41	22 03	24 33	8 47	20 09	11 08	22 06	11 53
6 M	23 1 13	13 37 47	0♒31	5 31	9 05	24 23	24 12	25 05	7 51	14 41	22 01	24 32	8 58	19 53	11 18	22 36	11 50
7 T	23 5 10	14 36 01	14 08	5 19	10 20	25 32	24 50	24 58	7 48	14 40	21 59	24 31	9 08	19 38	11 27	23 06	11 48
8 W	23 9 6	15 34 16	28 03	5 07	11 32	26 42	25 29	24 51	7 45	14 39	21 58	24 30	9 19	19 22	11 38	23 36	11 46
9 Th	23 13 3	16 32 33	12♓14	4 58	12 42	27 51	26 07	24 44	7 42	14 38	21 56	24 30	9 29	19 06	11 48	24 06	11 43
10 F	23 16 59	17 30 52	26 23	4 50	13 51	29 00	26 46	24 37	7 39	14 37	21 54	24 29	9 39	18 51	11 59	24 35	11 41
11 Sa	23 20 56	18 29 12	10♈40	4 46	14 57	0♎10	27 25	24 31	7 36	14 36	21 53	24 28	9 48	18 35	12 10	25 06	11 38
12 Su	23 24 53	19 27 34	24 55	4 44D	16 02	1 19	28 03	24 24	7 34	14 35	21 51	24 27	9 58	18 19	12 21	25 36	11 36
13 M	23 28 49	20 25 58	9♉07	4 44℞	17 05	2 28	28 42	24 18	7 31	14 34	21 49	24 27	10 07	18 03	12 32	26 06	11 34
14 T	23 32 46	21 24 23	23 14	4 44	18 03	3 37	29 21	24 12	7 28	14 32	21 48	24 26	10 15	17 47	12 44	26 36	11 31
15 W	23 36 42	22 22 49	7♊15	4 43	19 00	4 45	0≏00	24 06	7 26	14 31	21 46	24 26	10 24	17 31	12 56	27 06	11 29
16 Th	23 40 39	23 21 17	21 09	4 41	19 54	5 54	0 38	24 00	7 24	14 30	21 44	24 25	10 32	17 16	13 08	27 37	11 26
17 F	23 44 35	24 19 47	4♋56	4 35	20 45	7 03	1 17	23 54	7 21	14 29	21 43	24 24	10 40	17 00	13 20	28 07	11 23
18 Sa	23 48 32	25 18 19	18 34	4 27	21 33	8 11	1 56	23 48	7 19	14 27	21 41	24 24	10 47	16 45	13 32	28 37	11 21
19 Su	23 52 28	26 16 52	2♌01	4 17	22 17	9 20	2 35	23 43	7 17	14 26	21 40	24 23	10 55	16 29	13 45	29 08	11 18
20 M	23 56 25	27 15 26	15 16	4 06	22 58	10 28	3 14	23 37	7 15	14 25	21 38	24 23	11 01	16 14	13 58	29 38	11 16
21 T	0 0 22	28 14 03	28 17	3 55	23 36	11 36	3 53	23 32	7 13	14 23	21 36	24 22	11 08	15 58	14 11	0♏09	11 13
22 W	0 4 18	29 12 42	11♍02	3 44	24 06	12 44	4 32	23 27	7 11	14 22	21 35	24 22	11 14	15 43	14 24	0 40	11 10
23 Th	0 8 15	0≏11 22	23 31	3 36	24 33	13 52	5 11	23 22	7 09	14 20	21 33	24 22	11 20	15 28	14 37	1 10	11 08
24 F	0 12 11	1 10 05	5♎46	3 30	24 56	15 00	5 50	23 18	7 07	14 18	21 31	24 21	11 26	15 13	14 51	1 41	11 05
25 Sa	0 16 8	2 08 50	17 49	3 26	25 13	16 07	6 29	23 13	7 06	14 17	21 30	24 21	11 31	14 59	15 05	2 12	11 03
26 Su	0 20 4	3 07 37	29 42	3 25D	25 24	17 15	7 08	23 09	7 04	14 15	21 28	24 21	11 36	14 44	15 19	2 43	11 00
27 M	0 24 1	4 06 26	11♏30	3 25	25 28℞	18 22	7 47	23 04	7 03	14 13	21 26	24 20	11 41	14 30	15 33	3 13	10 57
28 T	0 27 57	5 05 18	23 18	3 26	25 25	19 30	8 26	23 00	7 01	14 12	21 25	24 20	11 45	14 16	15 47	3 44	10 54
29 W	0 31 54	6 04 11	5♐11	3 26℞	25 17	20 37	9 05	22 57	7 00	14 10	21 23	24 20	11 49	14 02	16 01	4 15	10 52
30 Th	0 35 51	7 03 07	17 14	3 26	25 01	21 44	9 44	22 53	6 59	14 08	21 22	24 20	11 53	13 48	16 16	4 46	10 49

EPHEMERIS CALCULATED FOR 12 MIDNIGHT GREENWICH MEAN TIME. ALL OTHER DATA AND FACING ASPECTARIAN PAGE IN EASTERN TIME (BOLD) AND PACIFIC TIME (REGULAR).

OCTOBER 2021

☽ Last Aspect day	ET / hr:mn / PT		asp	☽ Ingress sign	day	ET / hr:mn / PT	
2	**7:43 pm**	4:43 pm	□♀	♍	3	**4:38 am**	1:38 am
5	**4:46 am**	1:46 am	⚹♀	♎	5	**8:41 am**	5:41 am
6		10:03 pm	□♇	♏	7	**10:22 am**	7:22 am
7	**1:03 am**		□♇	♏	7	**10:22 am**	7:22 am
8		11:05 pm	⚹♇	♐	9	**11:24 am**	8:24 am
9	**2:05 am**		⚹♇	♐	9	**11:24 am**	8:24 am
10		9:30 pm	⚹♃	♑	11	**1:15 pm**	10:15 am
11	**12:30 am**		⚹♃	♑	11	**1:15 pm**	10:15 am
13	**6:53 am**	3:53 am	☌♇	♒	13	**4:47 pm**	1:47 pm
15	**8:33 am**	5:33 am	△☉	♓	15	**10:22 pm**	7:22 pm

☽ Last Aspect day	ET / hr:mn / PT		asp	☽ Ingress sign	day	ET / hr:mn / PT	
17	**7:24 pm**	4:24 pm	⚹♇	♈	18	**6:04 am**	3:04 am
20	**10:57 am**	7:57 am	☍☉	♉	20	**3:59 pm**	12:59 pm
22	**4:35 pm**	1:35 pm	△♇	♊	23	**3:57 am**	12:57 am
25	**10:11 am**	7:11 am	△♂	♋	25	**5:00 pm**	2:00 pm
27		11:02 pm	□♂	♌	28	**5:07 am**	2:07 am
28	**2:02 am**		□♂	♌	28	**5:07 am**	2:07 am
30	**3:05 am**	12:05 am	△♀	♍	30	**2:09 pm**	11:09 am

☽ Phases & Eclipses phase	day	ET / hr:mn / PT	
New Moon	6	**7:05 am**	4:05 am
2nd Quarter	12	**11:25 pm**	8:25 pm
Full Moon	20	**10:57 am**	7:57 am
4th Quarter	28	**4:05 pm**	1:05 pm

Planet Ingress	day	ET / hr:mn / PT	
♀ ♐	7	**7:21 am**	4:21 am
☉ ♏	22		9:51 pm
☉ ♏	23	**12:51 am**	
♂ ♏	30	**10:21 am**	7:21 am

Planetary Motion	day	ET / hr:mn / PT	
♇ D	6	**2:29 pm**	11:29 am
⚳ ℞	8	**9:31 pm**	6:31 pm
♄ D	10	**10:17 pm**	7:17 pm
♃ D	17		10:30 pm
♃ D	18	**1:30 am**	
☿ D	18	**11:17 am**	8:17 am

1 FRIDAY
☽☍♄ **10:10 am** 7:10 am
☿□♇ **10:26 am** 7:26 am
☽⚹☉ **1:34 pm** 10:34 am
☽⚹♂ **5:46 pm** 2:46 pm
☿⚺♀ **9:56 pm** 6:56 pm
☽□♅ **11:32 pm** 8:32 pm

2 SATURDAY
♀⚹♇ **3:48 am** 12:48 am
☽⚻♆ **12:51 pm** 9:51 am
☽☍♃ **3:29 pm** 12:29 pm
☽⚹☿ **4:57 pm** 1:57 pm
☽⚻♇ **6:22 pm** 3:22 pm
☽□♀ **7:43 pm** 4:43 pm

3 SUNDAY
☽⚻♄ **4:56 pm** 1:56 pm
☿△♃ **8:05 pm** 5:05 pm
☽⚺☉ 9:23 pm
☽⚺♂ 11:47 pm

4 MONDAY
☽⚺☉ **12:23 am**
☽⚺♂ **2:47 am**
☽△♅ **5:19 am** 2:19 am
☽☍♆ **5:48 pm** 2:48 pm
☽⚺☿ **6:48 pm** 3:48 pm
☽⚻♃ **8:10 pm** 5:10 pm
☽△♇ **11:03 pm** 8:03 pm

5 TUESDAY
☽⚹♀ **4:46 am** 1:46 am
☿⚻♆ **9:53 am** 6:53 am
☽△♄ **8:16 pm** 5:16 pm

6 WEDNESDAY
♂⚻♅ **5:27 am** 2:27 am
☽☌☉ **7:05 am** 4:05 am
☽⚻♅ **7:56 am** 4:56 am
☽☌♂ **8:04 am** 5:04 am
☽☌☿ **5:40 pm** 2:40 pm
☉⚻♅ **7:11 pm** 4:11 pm
☽⚻♆ **7:54 pm** 4:54 pm
☽△♃ **10:08 pm** 7:08 pm
☽□♇ 10:03 pm

7 THURSDAY
☽□♇ **1:03 am**
☽⚺♀ **10:37 am** 7:37 am
☽□♄ **9:37 pm** 6:37 pm
☉☌♂ 9:01 pm

8 FRIDAY
☉☌♂ **12:01 am**
☽☍♅ **9:00 am** 6:00 am
☽⚺♂ **11:32 am** 8:32 am
☽⚺☉ **11:49 am** 8:49 am
☽⚺☿ **3:10 pm** 12:10 pm
☽△♆ **8:53 pm** 5:53 pm
☽□♃ **11:04 pm** 8:04 pm
☽⚹♇ 11:05 pm

9 SATURDAY
☽⚹♇ **2:05 am**
☉☌☿ **12:18 pm** 9:18 am
☽☌♀ **3:37 pm** 12:37 pm
☿☌♂ **6:48 pm** 3:48 pm
☽⚹♄ **10:43 pm** 7:43 pm

10 SUNDAY
☽⚻♅ **10:08 am** 7:08 am
☽⚹☿ **12:49 pm** 9:49 am
☽⚹♂ **3:12 pm** 12:12 pm
☽⚹☉ **4:45 pm** 1:45 pm
☽□♆ **10:17 pm** 7:17 pm
☽⚹♃ 9:30 pm

11 MONDAY
☽⚹♃ **12:30 am**
☽⚺♇ **3:42 am** 12:42 am
☽⚺♀ **9:43 pm** 6:43 pm
☽⚺♄ 9:54 pm
☿⚻♅ 10:29 pm

12 TUESDAY
☽⚺♄ **12:54 am**
☿⚻♅ **1:29 am**
☽□☿ **11:51 am** 8:51 am
☽△♅ **12:34 pm** 9:34 am
☽□♂ **8:27 pm** 5:27 pm
☽□☉ **11:25 pm** 8:25 pm
☽⚹♆ 10:11 pm

13 WEDNESDAY
☽⚹♆ **1:11 am**
☽⚺♃ **3:30 am** 12:30 am
☽☌♇ **6:53 am** 3:53 am
♀⚹♄ **3:26 pm** 12:26 pm
☉⚻♆ **11:32 pm** 8:32 pm

14 THURSDAY
☽☌♄ **4:54 am** 1:54 am
☽⚹♀ **6:03 am** 3:03 am
☽△☿ **1:09 pm** 10:09 am
☽□♅ **4:52 pm** 1:52 pm

15 FRIDAY
☽△♂ **3:58 am** 12:58 am
☽⚺♆ **6:02 am** 3:02 am
☉△♃ **7:46 am** 4:46 am
☽☌♃ **8:29 am** 5:29 am
☽△☉ **8:33 am** 5:33 am
☽⚺♇ **12:05 pm** 9:05 am

16 SATURDAY
☽⚺♄ **10:59 am** 7:59 am
☽□♀ **4:59 pm** 1:59 pm
☽⚻☿ **5:27 pm** 2:27 pm
♂⚻♆ **8:32 pm** 5:32 pm
☿⚹♀ **9:24 pm** 6:24 pm
☽⚹♅ **11:14 pm** 8:14 pm

17 SUNDAY
☉□♇ **8:12 am** 5:12 am
☽☌♆ **1:00 pm** 10:00 am
☽⚻♂ **1:56 pm** 10:56 am
☽⚺♃ **3:37 pm** 12:37 pm
☽⚹♇ **7:24 pm** 4:24 pm
☽⚻☉ **8:20 pm** 5:20 pm

18 MONDAY
☽⚹♄ **7:15 pm** 4:15 pm
♂△♃ **10:36 pm** 7:36 pm
☽☍☿ 10:26 pm

19 TUESDAY
☽☍☿ **1:26 am**
☽△♀ **6:40 am** 3:40 am
☽⚺♅ **7:46 am** 4:46 am
♀⚻♅ **7:15 pm** 4:15 pm
☽⚺♆ **10:09 pm** 7:09 pm
☽⚹♃ 9:59 pm
☽☍♂ 11:28 pm

20 WEDNESDAY
☽⚹♃ **12:59 am**
☽☍♂ **2:28 am**
☽□♇ **4:56 am** 1:56 am
☽☍☉ **10:57 am** 7:57 am

21 THURSDAY
☽□♄ **5:45 am** 2:45 am
☽⚻☿ **1:44 pm** 10:44 am
☽☌♅ **6:28 pm** 3:28 pm
☽⚻♀ **11:08 pm** 8:08 pm
♂□♇ 9:20 pm

22 FRIDAY
♂□♇ **12:20 am**
☽⚹♆ **9:26 am** 6:26 am
☽□♃ **12:32 pm** 9:32 am
☽△♇ **4:35 pm** 1:35 pm
☽⚻♂ **5:33 pm** 2:33 pm

23 SATURDAY
☽⚻☉ **4:14 am** 1:14 am
☽△♄ **6:12 pm** 3:12 pm

24 SUNDAY
☽△☿ **6:17 am** 3:17 am
☽⚺♅ **6:54 am** 3:54 am
☿⚻♅ **1:45 pm** 10:45 am
☽☍♀ **5:42 pm** 2:42 pm
☽□♆ **10:14 pm** 7:14 pm
☽△♃ 10:33 pm

25 MONDAY
☽△♃ **1:33 am**
☽⚻♇ **5:36 am** 2:36 am
☽△♂ **10:11 am** 7:11 am
☽△☉ **10:54 pm** 7:54 pm

26 TUESDAY
☽⚻♄ **7:21 am** 4:21 am
☽⚹♅ **7:37 pm** 4:37 pm
♀□♆ **9:06 pm** 6:06 pm
☽□☿ 10:10 pm

27 WEDNESDAY
☽□☿ **1:10 am**
☽△♆ **10:48 am** 7:48 am
☽⚻♀ **12:04 pm** 9:04 am
☽⚻♃ **2:16 pm** 11:16 am
☽☍♇ **6:08 pm** 3:08 pm
☽□♂ 11:02 pm

28 THURSDAY
☽□♂ **2:02 am**
♀⚹♃ **3:15 pm** 12:15 pm
☽□☉ **4:05 pm** 1:05 pm
☽☍♄ **7:03 pm** 4:03 pm

29 FRIDAY
☽□♅ **6:25 am** 3:25 am
☽⚹☿ **6:32 pm** 3:32 pm
☽⚻♆ **8:53 pm** 5:53 pm
☽☍♃ 9:24 pm

30 SATURDAY
☽☍♃ **12:24 am**
☽△♀ **3:05 am** 12:05 am
☽⚻♇ **3:54 am** 12:54 am
☉□♄ **5:53 am** 2:53 am
♀⚺♇ **1:54 pm** 10:54 am
☽⚹♂ **2:22 pm** 11:22 am
☿⚻♆ **3:40 pm** 12:40 pm

31 SUNDAY
☽⚻♄ **3:17 am** 12:17 am
☽⚹☉ **4:58 am** 1:58 am
☽△♅ **1:33 pm** 10:33 am
☿△♃ 9:18 pm

Eastern time in bold type
Pacific time in medium type

OCTOBER 2021

DATE	SID.TIME	SUN	MOON	NODE	MERCURY	VENUS	MARS	JUPITER	SATURN	URANUS	NEPTUNE	PLUTO	CERES	PALLAS	JUNO	VESTA	CHIRON
1 F	0 39 47	8≏02 06	29♍32	3♊23R	24≏37R	22♏51	10≏24	22≈49R	6≈58R	14♉06R	21♓20R	24♑19R	11♊56	13♋34R	16✗31R	5♏17	10♈46R
2 Sa	0 43 44	9 01 06	12♎11	3 19	24 06	23 58	11 03	22 46	6 57	14 04	21 19	24 19	11 59	13 21	16 46	5 48	10 44
3 Su	0 47 40	10 00 09	25 13	3 12	23 27	25 04	11 42	22 43	6 56	14 03	21 17	24 19	12 01	13 08	17 01	6 20	10 41
4 M	0 51 37	10 59 14	8♏40	3 04	22 40	26 11	12 22	22 40	6 56	14 01	21 15	24 19	12 03	12 55	17 17	6 51	10 38
5 T	0 55 33	11 58 22	22 32	2 55	21 47	27 17	13 01	22 37	6 55	13 59	21 14	24 19	12 05	12 43	17 32	7 22	10 36
6 W	0 59 30	12 57 31	6✗45	2 47	20 47	28 23	13 40	22 35	6 54	13 57	21 12	24 19D	12 06	12 31	17 48	7 53	10 33
7 Th	1 3 26	13 56 42	21 14	2 40	19 43	29 29	14 20	22 32	6 54	13 55	21 11	24 19	12 07	12 19	18 04	8 25	10 30
8 F	1 7 23	14 55 56	5♑54	2 35	18 34	0✗37	14 59	22 30	6 53	13 53	21 09	24 19	12 08R	12 07	18 20	8 56	10 27
9 Sa	1 11 19	15 55 11	20 36	2 33D	17 24	1 40	15 39	22 28	6 53	13 50	21 08	24 19	12 08	11 56	18 36	9 27	10 25
10 Su	1 15 16	16 54 28	5♒14	2 32	16 13	2 46	16 18	22 27	6 53	13 48	21 07	24 19	12 08	11 45	18 52	9 59	10 22
11 M	1 19 13	17 53 48	19 43	2 33	15 04	3 51	16 58	22 25	6 53D	13 46	21 05	24 19	12 08	11 34	19 08	10 30	10 19
12 T	1 23 9	18 53 08	4♓00	2 34	13 58	4 56	17 37	22 24	6 53	13 44	21 04	24 19	12 07	11 24	19 25	11 02	10 17
13 W	1 27 6	19 52 31	18 02	2 35R	12 58	6 01	18 17	22 23	6 53	13 42	21 02	24 19	12 05	11 14	19 42	11 33	10 14
14 Th	1 31 2	20 51 56	1♈50	2 35	12 05	7 05	18 57	22 22	6 53	13 40	21 01	24 20	12 04	11 04	19 59	12 05	10 11
15 F	1 34 59	21 51 22	15 23	2 32	11 21	8 10	19 36	22 21	6 53	13 37	20 59	24 20	12 02	10 55	20 16	12 36	10 09
16 Sa	1 38 55	22 50 49	28 42	2 28	10 46	9 14	20 16	22 20	6 54	13 35	20 58	24 20	11 59	10 46	20 33	13 08	10 06
17 Su	1 42 52	23 50 19	11♉48	2 22	10 23	10 18	20 56	22 20	6 54	13 33	20 57	24 20	11 56	10 38	20 50	13 40	10 03
18 M	1 46 48	24 49 50	24 40	2 16	10 10D	11 21	21 36	22 20D	6 55	13 31	20 55	24 21	11 53	10 29	21 08	14 11	10 01
19 T	1 50 45	25 49 23	7♊19	2 09	10 08	12 25	22 16	22 20	6 56	13 28	20 54	24 21	11 49	10 22	21 25	14 43	9 58
20 W	1 54 42	26 48 58	19 47	2 03	10 18	13 28	22 55	22 20	6 57	13 26	20 53	24 21	11 45	10 14	21 43	15 15	9 56
21 Th	1 58 38	27 48 35	2♋02	1 58	10 38	14 31	23 35	22 21	6 58	13 24	20 52	24 22	11 40	10 07	22 01	15 46	9 53
22 F	2 2 35	28 48 14	14 08	1 55	11 08	15 33	24 15	22 21	6 59	13 21	20 50	24 22	11 36	10 00	22 19	16 18	9 51
23 Sa	2 6 31	29 47 56	26 04	1 54D	11 47	16 36	24 55	22 22	7 00	13 19	20 49	24 23	11 30	9 54	22 37	16 50	9 48
24 Su	2 10 28	0♏47 39	7♌54	1 54	12 35	17 38	25 35	22 23	7 01	13 16	20 48	24 23	11 25	9 48	22 55	17 22	9 46
25 M	2 14 24	1 47 25	19 41	1 55	13 32	18 39	26 15	22 24	7 02	13 14	20 47	24 24	11 19	9 42	23 13	17 54	9 43
26 T	2 18 21	2 47 12	1♍29	1 57	14 32	19 41	26 55	22 26	7 04	13 12	20 46	24 24	11 12	9 37	23 32	18 26	9 41
27 W	2 22 17	3 47 02	13 21	1 58	15 40	20 42	27 35	22 27	7 05	13 09	20 45	24 25	11 05	9 32	23 50	18 58	9 38
28 Th	2 26 14	4 46 54	25 22	2 00	16 53	21 43	28 16	22 29	7 07	13 07	20 44	24 26	10 58	9 28	24 09	19 30	9 36
29 F	2 30 11	5 46 48	7♎38	2 00R	18 10	22 43	28 56	22 31	7 09	13 04	20 43	24 26	10 51	9 24	24 28	20 02	9 33
30 Sa	2 34 7	6 46 45	20 13	1 59	19 32	23 43	29 36	22 34	7 11	13 02	20 41	24 27	10 43	9 20	24 47	20 34	9 31
31 Su	2 38 4	7 46 43	3♏12	1 57	20 56	24 42	0♏16	22 36	7 13	12 59	20 40	24 28	10 35	9 17	25 06	21 06	9 29

EPHEMERIS CALCULATED FOR 12 MIDNIGHT GREENWICH MEAN TIME. ALL OTHER DATA AND FACING ASPECTARIAN PAGE IN **EASTERN TIME (BOLD)** AND PACIFIC TIME (REGULAR).

NOVEMBER 2021

☽ Last Aspect day	ET / hr:mn / PT		asp	☽ Ingress sign	day	ET / hr:mn / PT	
1	**1:00 pm**	10:00 am	□♀	♎	1	**7:11 pm**	4:11 pm
3	**6:32 pm**	3:32 pm	✶♀	♏	3	**8:52 pm**	5:52 pm
5	**12:10 pm**	9:10 am	✶♇	♐	5	**8:52 pm**	5:52 pm
7	**8:44 am**	5:44 am	✶♃	♑	7	**8:03 pm**	5:03 pm
9	**12:51 pm**	9:51 am	☌♇	♒	9	**10:03 pm**	7:03 pm
11	**2:52 pm**	11:52 am	☌♃	♓	11		11:54 pm
11	**2:52 pm**	11:52 am	☌♃	♓	12	**2:54 am**	
13		9:40 pm	✶♇	♈	14	**10:48 am**	7:48 am
14	**12:40 am**		✶♇	♈	14	**10:48 am**	7:48 am
16	**10:51 am**	7:51 am	□♇	♉	16	**9:18 pm**	6:18 pm

☽ Last Aspect day	ET / hr:mn / PT		asp	☽ Ingress sign	day	ET / hr:mn / PT	
19	**3:57 am**	12:57 am	☍☉	♊	19	**9:33 am**	6:33 am
21	**10:52 am**	7:52 am	△♃	♋	21	**10:33 pm**	7:33 pm
23		9:46 pm	☍♇	♌	24	**10:59 am**	7:59 am
24	**12:46 am**		☍♇	♌	24	**10:59 am**	7:59 am
26	**11:24 am**	8:24 am	☍♃	♍	26	**9:12 pm**	6:12 pm
28	**7:02 pm**	4:02 pm	△♇	♎	29	**3:55 am**	12:55 am
30	**11:20 pm**	8:20 pm	△♃	♏	12/1	**6:55 am**	3:55 am

☽ Phases & Eclipses phase	day	ET / hr:mn / PT	
New Moon	4	**5:15 pm**	2:15 pm
2nd Quarter	11	**7:46 am**	4:46 am
Full Moon	19	**3:57 am**	12:57 am
●	19	27° ♉ 14'	
4th Quarter	27	**7:28 am**	4:28 am

Planet Ingress		day	ET / hr:mn / PT	
♀	♑	5	**6:44 am**	3:44 am
⚵	♑	14	**3:23 pm**	12:23 pm
⚶	♐	16	**9:07 am**	6:07 am
☉	♐	21	**9:34 pm**	6:34 pm
☿	♐	24	**10:36 am**	7:36 am

Planetary Motion		day	ET / hr:mn / PT	
⚴	D	8	**4:23 am**	1:23 am

1 MONDAY
☿ △ ♃ **12:18 am**
☽ ☍ ♆ **3:05 am** 12:05 am
☽ ⚻ ♃ **6:35 am** 3:35 am
☽ ⚺ ☿ **7:18 am** 4:18 am
☽ △ ♇ **9:43 am** 6:43 am
☽ □ ♀ **1:00 pm** 10:00 am
☽ ⚺ ♂ **10:01 pm** 7:01 pm

2 TUESDAY
☿ □ ♇ **5:39 am** 2:39 am
☽ △ ♄ **7:31 am** 4:31 am
☽ ⚺ ☉ **12:51 pm** 9:51 am
☽ ⚻ ♅ **4:50 pm** 1:50 pm

3 WEDNESDAY
☽ ⚻ ♆ **5:36 am** 2:36 am
☽ △ ♃ **9:08 am** 6:08 am
☽ □ ♇ **11:57 am** 8:57 am
☽ ☌ ☿ **3:27 pm** 12:27 pm
☽ ✶ ♀ **6:32 pm** 3:32 pm
☽ ☌ ♂ 10:55 pm

4 THURSDAY
☽ ☌ ♂ **1:55 am**
☽ □ ♄ **8:46 am** 5:46 am
☽ ☌ ☉ **5:15 pm** 2:15 pm
☽ ☍ ♅ **5:26 pm** 2:26 pm
☉ ☍ ♅ **7:58 pm** 4:58 pm

5 FRIDAY
☽ △ ♆ **5:53 am** 2:53 am
☽ □ ♃ **9:33 am** 6:33 am
☽ ✶ ♇ **12:10 pm** 9:10 am
☽ ⚺ ☿ **9:09 pm** 6:09 pm
☽ ⚺ ♀ **9:49 pm** 6:49 pm

6 SATURDAY
☽ ⚺ ♂ **4:06 am** 1:06 am
☽ ✶ ♄ **8:46 am** 5:46 am
☿ ✶ ♀ **11:59 am** 8:59 am
☽ ⚻ ♅ **5:09 pm** 2:09 pm
☽ ⚺ ☉ **8:32 pm** 5:32 pm

7 SUNDAY
☽ □ ♆ **4:47 am** 1:47 am
☽ ✶ ♃ **8:44 am** 5:44 am
☽ ⚺ ♇ **11:14 am** 8:14 am
☽ ☌ ♀ 9:19 pm
☽ ✶ ☿ 11:13 pm

8 MONDAY
☽ ☌ ♀ **12:19 am**
☽ ✶ ☿ **2:13 am**
☽ ✶ ♂ **5:49 am** 2:49 am
☽ ⚺ ♄ **8:25 am** 5:25 am
☽ △ ♅ **4:48 pm** 1:48 pm
☽ ✶ ☉ 9:06 pm

9 TUESDAY
☽ ✶ ☉ **12:06 am**
☽ ✶ ♆ **6:01 am** 3:01 am
☽ ⚺ ♃ **10:26 am** 7:26 am
☽ ☌ ♇ **12:51 pm** 9:51 am

10 WEDNESDAY
☽ ⚺ ♀ **6:04 am** 3:04 am
☿ ☌ ♂ **7:57 am** 4:57 am
☽ □ ♂ **10:55 am** 7:55 am
☽ □ ☿ **11:08 am** 8:08 am
☽ ☌ ♄ **11:15 am** 8:15 am
☿ □ ♄ **12:04 pm** 9:04 am
♂ □ ♄ **6:14 pm** 3:14 pm
☽ □ ♅ **7:45 pm** 4:45 pm

11 THURSDAY
☽ □ ☉ **7:46 am** 4:46 am
☽ ⚺ ♆ **9:51 am** 6:51 am
☽ ☌ ♃ **2:52 pm** 11:52 am
☽ ⚺ ♇ **5:13 pm** 2:13 pm

12 FRIDAY
☉ △ ♆ **11:24 am** 8:24 am
☽ ✶ ♀ **3:18 pm** 12:18 pm
☽ ⚺ ♄ **5:05 pm** 2:05 pm
☽ △ ♂ **7:28 pm** 4:28 pm
☽ △ ☿ 9:23 pm
☽ ✶ ♅ 10:44 pm

13 SATURDAY
☽ △ ☿ **12:23 am**
☽ ✶ ♅ **1:44 am**
☿ ☍ ♅ **10:57 am** 7:57 am
☽ ☌ ♆ **4:46 pm** 1:46 pm
☽ △ ☉ **7:19 pm** 4:19 pm
♀ ⚺ ♄ **7:43 pm** 4:43 pm
☽ ⚺ ♃ **10:29 pm** 7:29 pm
☽ ✶ ♇ 9:40 pm

14 SUNDAY
☽ ✶ ♇ **12:40 am**
☽ ✶ ♄ 10:59 pm

15 MONDAY
☽ ✶ ♄ **1:59 am**
☽ □ ♀ **4:06 am** 1:06 am
☽ ⚻ ♂ **7:32 am** 4:32 am
☽ ⚺ ♅ **10:36 am** 7:36 am
☉ □ ♃ **2:58 pm** 11:58 am
☽ ⚻ ☿ **5:58 pm** 2:58 pm
☽ ⚺ ♆ 11:29 pm

16 TUESDAY
☽ ⚺ ♆ **2:29 am**
☽ ✶ ♃ **8:55 am** 5:55 am
☽ ⚻ ☉ **10:23 am** 7:23 am
☽ □ ♇ **10:51 am** 7:51 am
☉ ✶ ♇ **4:01 pm** 1:01 pm

17 WEDNESDAY
♂ ☍ ♅ **12:23 pm** 9:23 am
☽ □ ♄ **1:19 pm** 10:19 am
☽ △ ♀ **7:39 pm** 4:39 pm
☽ ☌ ♅ **9:44 pm** 6:44 pm
☽ ☍ ♂ **10:20 pm** 7:20 pm

18 THURSDAY
☿ △ ♆ **10:38 am** 7:38 am
☽ ✶ ♆ **2:14 pm** 11:14 am
☽ ☍ ☿ **2:48 pm** 11:48 am
☽ □ ♃ **9:23 pm** 6:23 pm
☽ △ ♇ **10:57 pm** 7:57 pm
♀ △ ♅ 10:08 pm

19 FRIDAY
♀ △ ♅ **1:08 am**
☽ ☍ ☉ **3:57 am** 12:57 am
☽ △ ♄ 11:12 pm

20 SATURDAY
☽ △ ♄ **2:12 am**
☽ ⚺ ♅ **10:14 am** 7:14 am
☽ ⚻ ♀ **12:43 pm** 9:43 am
☽ ⚻ ♂ **2:46 pm** 11:46 am
☿ □ ♃ **6:43 pm** 3:43 pm

21 SUNDAY
☽ □ ♆ **3:05 am** 12:05 am
☿ ✶ ♇ **4:14 am** 1:14 am
☽ △ ♃ **10:52 am** 7:52 am
☽ ⚻ ♇ **12:01 pm** 9:01 am
☽ ⚻ ☿ **1:13 pm** 10:13 am
☽ ⚻ ☉ **10:38 pm** 7:38 pm

22 MONDAY
☽ ⚻ ♄ **3:32 pm** 12:32 pm
☽ ✶ ♅ **10:59 pm** 7:59 pm

23 TUESDAY
☽ ☍ ♀ **5:49 am** 2:49 am
☽ △ ♂ **7:24 am** 4:24 am
☽ △ ♆ **3:50 pm** 12:50 pm
☽ ⚻ ♃ 9:06 pm
☽ ☍ ♇ 9:46 pm

24 WEDNESDAY
☽ ⚻ ♃ **12:06 am**
☽ ☍ ♇ **12:46 am**
☽ △ ☿ **11:02 am** 8:02 am
☽ △ ☉ **4:34 pm** 1:34 pm

25 THURSDAY
☽ ☍ ♄ **3:52 am** 12:52 am
☽ □ ♅ **10:32 am** 7:32 am
☽ ⚻ ♀ **8:57 pm** 5:57 pm
☽ □ ♂ **10:19 pm** 7:19 pm
☽ ⚻ ♆ 11:55 pm

26 FRIDAY
☽ ⚻ ♆ **2:55 am**
☽ ☍ ♃ **11:24 am** 8:24 am
☽ ⚻ ♇ **11:35 am** 8:35 am

27 SATURDAY
☽ □ ☿ **5:27 am** 2:27 am
☽ □ ☉ **7:28 am** 4:28 am
♃ ⚺ ♇ **11:16 am** 8:16 am
☽ ⚻ ♄ **1:30 pm** 10:30 am
☽ △ ♅ **7:18 pm** 4:18 pm

28 SUNDAY
☽ △ ♀ **8:15 am** 5:15 am
☽ ✶ ♂ **9:37 am** 6:37 am
☽ ☍ ♆ **10:50 am** 7:50 am
☽ △ ♇ **7:02 pm** 4:02 pm
☽ ⚻ ♃ **7:17 pm** 4:17 pm
☉ ☌ ☿ **11:39 pm** 8:39 pm

29 MONDAY
♂ △ ♆ **9:10 am** 6:10 am
☽ ✶ ☉ **5:44 pm** 2:44 pm
☽ ✶ ☿ **6:33 pm** 3:33 pm
☽ △ ♄ **7:24 pm** 4:24 pm
☽ ⚻ ♅ 9:22 pm
☽ ✶ ♄ 11:19 pm

30 TUESDAY
☽ ⚻ ♅ **12:22 am**
☿ ✶ ♄ **2:19 am**
☽ □ ♀ **2:56 pm** 11:56 am
☽ ⚻ ♆ **2:58 pm** 11:58 am
♀ ✶ ♆ **3:46 pm** 12:46 pm
☽ ⚺ ♂ **4:29 pm** 1:29 pm
☉ ✶ ♄ **6:14 pm** 3:14 pm
☽ □ ♇ **10:43 pm** 7:43 pm
☽ △ ♃ **11:20 pm** 8:20 pm

Eastern time in bold type
Pacific time in medium type

NOVEMBER 2021

DATE	SID.TIME	SUN	MOON	NODE	MERCURY	VENUS	MARS	JUPITER	SATURN	URANUS	NEPTUNE	PLUTO	CERES	PALLAS	JUNO	VESTA	CHIRON
1 T	2 42 0	8♏46 44	16♉37	1Ⅱ56R	22≏23	25✗42	0♏56	22≈39	7≈15	12♉57R	20✕39R	24✗28	10♑26R	9✕14R	25✗25	21♏38	9Υ27R
2 T	2 45 57	9 46 47	0≏57	1 51	23 53	26 41	1 37	22 42	7 17	12 52	20 38	24 29	10 17	9 11	25 44	22 10	9 24
3 W	2 49 53	10 46 52	14 47	1 48	25 24	27 39	2 17	22 45	7 19	12 52	20 38	24 30	10 08	9 09	26 03	22 42	9 22
4 Th	2 53 50	11 46 58	29 28	1 46	25 57	28 37	2 58	22 48	7 21	12 50	20 37	24 31	9 58	9 07	26 23	23 14	9 20
5 F	2 57 46	12 47 07	14♍24	1 44	28 31	29 34	3 38	22 51	7 24	12 47	20 37	24 31	9 48	9 06	26 42	23 46	9 18
6 Sa	3 1 43	13 47 18	29 27	1 43D	0♏06	0♑31	4 19	22 55	7 26	12 45	20 35	24 32	9 38	9 04	27 02	24 18	9 16
7 Su	3 5 40	14 47 30	14≏29	1 44	1 41	1 28	4 59	22 59	7 29	12 42	20 34	24 33	9 27	9 04	27 22	24 51	9 13
8 M	3 9 36	15 47 45	29 21	1 45	3 17	2 24	5 40	23 03	7 32	12 40	20 34	24 34	9 16	9 03D	27 41	25 23	9 11
9 T	3 13 33	16 48 00	13♏57	1 46	4 54	3 20	6 20	23 07	7 34	12 37	20 33	24 35	9 05	9 03	28 01	25 55	9 09
10 W	3 17 29	17 48 17	28 13	1 47	6 31	4 15	7 01	23 11	7 37	12 35	20 32	24 36	8 53	9 04	28 21	26 27	9 07
11 Th	3 21 26	18 48 36	12♐06	1 48R	8 07	5 09	7 42	23 16	7 40	12 32	20 31	24 37	8 42	9 05	28 42	26 59	9 05
12 F	3 25 22	19 48 56	25 38	1 48	9 44	6 03	8 22	23 21	7 43	12 30	20 31	24 38	8 30	9 06	29 02	27 32	9 04
13 Sa	3 29 19	20 49 17	8♑48	1 47	11 21	6 56	9 03	23 25	7 47	12 27	20 30	24 39	8 17	9 07	29 22	28 04	9 02
14 Su	3 33 15	21 49 39	21 41	1 46	12 58	7 48	9 44	23 31	7 50	12 25	20 29	24 40	8 05	9 09	29 43	28 36	9 00
15 M	3 37 12	22 50 03	4≈17	1 45	14 35	8 40	10 25	23 36	7 53	12 22	20 29	24 41	7 52	9 11	0♑03	29 09	8 58
16 T	3 41 9	23 50 28	16 39	1 44	16 12	9 31	11 05	23 41	7 57	12 20	20 28	24 42	7 39	9 14	0 24	29 41	8 56
17 W	3 45 5	24 50 55	28 51	1 43	17 48	10 22	11 46	23 47	8 00	12 18	20 28	24 44	7 26	9 17	0 44	0✗13	8 55
18 Th	3 49 2	25 51 23	10✕53	1 42	19 24	11 11	12 27	23 53	8 04	12 15	20 27	24 45	7 13	9 20	1 05	0 46	8 53
19 F	3 52 58	26 51 53	22 49	1 42D	21 00	12 00	13 08	23 59	8 07	12 13	20 27	24 46	7 00	9 24	1 26	1 18	8 51
20 Sa	3 56 55	27 52 25	4♈48	1 41	22 36	12 48	13 49	24 05	8 11	12 10	20 26	24 47	6 46	9 27	1 47	1 50	8 50
21 Su	4 0 51	28 52 57	16 28	1 42	24 12	13 35	14 30	24 11	8 15	12 08	20 26	24 48	6 32	9 32	2 08	2 23	8 48
22 M	4 4 48	29 53 32	28 15	1 42	25 48	14 21	15 11	24 18	8 19	12 06	20 26	24 50	6 19	9 36	2 29	2 55	8 47
23 T	4 8 44	0✗54 08	10♉05	1 42R	27 23	15 06	15 52	24 24	8 23	12 03	20 25	24 51	6 05	9 41	2 50	3 28	8 45
24 W	4 12 41	1 54 46	22 00	1 42	28 58	15 50	16 33	24 31	8 27	12 01	20 25	24 52	5 51	9 46	3 11	4 00	8 44
25 Th	4 16 38	2 55 25	4Ⅱ03	1 42	0✗33	16 34	17 15	24 38	8 31	11 59	20 25	24 54	5 37	9 52	3 33	4 32	8 43
26 F	4 20 34	3 56 06	16 18	1 42D	2 08	17 16	17 56	24 45	8 36	11 57	20 25	24 55	5 23	9 58	3 54	5 05	8 41
27 Sa	4 24 31	4 56 48	28 50	1 42	3 43	17 57	18 37	24 52	8 40	11 54	20 25	24 56	5 09	10 04	4 15	5 37	8 40
28 Su	4 28 27	5 57 32	11♍42	1 42	5 17	18 37	19 18	25 00	8 44	11 52	20 24	24 58	4 55	10 10	4 37	6 10	8 39
29 M	4 32 24	6 58 18	24 58	1 42	6 52	19 15	20 00	25 07	8 49	11 50	20 24	24 59	4 40	10 17	4 58	6 42	8 38
30 T	4 36 20	7 59 05	8≏32	1 42	8 26	19 53	20 41	25 15	8 53	11 48	20 24	25 01	4 26	10 24	5 20	7 15	8 37

EPHEMERIS CALCULATED FOR 12 MIDNIGHT GREENWICH MEAN TIME. ALL OTHER DATA AND FACING ASPECTARIAN PAGE IN **EASTERN TIME (BOLD)** AND PACIFIC TIME (REGULAR).

DECEMBER 2021

D Last Aspect				D Ingress		
day	ET / hr:mn / PT		asp	sign	day	ET / hr:mn / PT
11/30 11:20 pm 8:20 pm			△	♏	2	6:55 am 3:55 am
1	9:22 am		△	✗	3	7:13 am 4:13 am
4	9:08 am		⚹	✗	5	7:13 am 4:13 am
			△	♈	7	6:31 am 3:31 am
7 12:08 am			⚹	♒	9	6:31 am 3:31 am
9	6:49 am		□	♈	9	6:49 am 3:49 am
11 11:42 am 8:42 am			△	♉	11	9:53 am 6:53 am
13	5:00 am 2:00 am		□	♊	13	4:46 pm 1:46 pm
15	2:40 am 11:40 pm		⚹	♋	16	3:11 am 12:11 am
16 11:08 am 8:08 am			□	♌	18	3:43 pm 12:43 pm

D Last Aspect				D Ingress		
day	ET / hr:mn / PT		asp	sign	day	ET / hr:mn / PT
18	10:02 pm		△	♍	19	4:42 am 1:42 am
19 1:02 am			△	♍	19	4:42 am 1:42 am
21	9:44 am 6:44 am		⚹	♎	21	4:54 pm 1:54 pm
23	10:39 pm		△	♏	24	3:24 am 12:24 am
24 1:39 am			□	✗	24	3:24 am 12:24 am
26 2:39 am 12:39 am			⚹	♑	26	11:24 am 8:24 am
28 4:11 pm 1:16 pm			△	♒	28	4:16 pm 1:16 pm
30 12:10 pm 9:10 am			△	♓	30	6:08 pm 3:08 pm

D Phases & Eclipses			
phase	day	ET / hr:mn / PT	
New Moon	3		11:43 pm
New Moon	4	2:43 am	
2nd Quarter	10	8:36 am	5:36 am
Full Moon	18	11:36 am	8:36 am
4th Quarter	26	9:24 am	6:24 am

Planet Ingress			
	day	ET / hr:mn / PT	
♂ ✗	13	4:53 am	1:53 am
♀ ✗	13	12:52 pm	9:52 am
⊙ ♑	21	5:38 am	2:38 am
♀ ♑	21	5:38 pm	2:38 pm
2 ♒	21	10:59 am	7:59 am
2 ♓	28	11:09 pm	8:09 pm

Planetary Motion			
	day	ET / hr:mn / PT	
♀ D	1	8:22 am	5:22 am
Ψ R	19		
♀ R	19	5:36 am	2:36 am
♂ D	19	11:33 am	8:33 am

---

1 WEDNESDAY
☐ ⚹ ♀ 9:15 am 6:15 am
☐ ☐ ♂ 9:43 pm 6:43 pm
☐ ⚹ ♀ 11:35 am 8:35 am
☐ 11:01 pm
☐ 11:36 pm

2 THURSDAY
☐ 2:01 am
☐ 2:36 am 12:58 am
△ 2:52 pm
☐ 3:58 am 5:52 am
☐ 5:52 am 7:45 pm
8:26 am
11:26 9:22 pm

3 FRIDAY
☐ 12:22 am
☐ 10:14 am 7:14 am
☐ 9:46 6:46 pm

4 SATURDAY
☐ 1:35 am
☐ 2:43 am 4:43 am
☐ 12:22 am
☐ 6:55 am 3:55 am
☐ 9:22 am 6:22 pm
☐ 10:50 7:50 pm

5 SUNDAY
☐ 2 12:08 pm 9:25 pm

6 MONDAY
☐ 5:39 am 2:39 am
☐ 6:41 am 3:41 am
☐ 12:53 9:53 am
9:21 pm

7 TUESDAY
☐ 2 12:40 am
☐ 10:16 7:16 am
☐ 10:43 7:43 pm

8 WEDNESDAY
☐ 1:21 am
☐ 10:57 7:57 am
☐ 5:11 2:11 pm
☐ 9:07 6:07 pm

9 THURSDAY
☐ 12:15 am
☐ 1:34 am

10 FRIDAY
☐ 3:53 am 12:53 am
☐ 5:00 am 2:00 am
☐ 3:18 am 12:18 am
☐ 6:22 am 3:22 am
☐ 7:50 am 4:50 am
☐ 9:56 am 6:56 am
☐ 8:35 am 5:36 am
☐ 7:50 pm

11 SATURDAY
☐ 7:52 am 4:52 am
☐ 7:56 am 4:56 am
☐ 10:33 am 7:33 am
☐ 11:29 am 8:29 am
☐ 2:24 pm 11:24 am
☐ 2:40 pm 11:40 am
10:21 pm

12 SUNDAY
☐ 1:21 am
☐ 11:50 am 8:50 am
☐ 2:34 11:34 am

13 MONDAY
☐ 8:16 am 5:16 am
☐ 11:03 am 8:03 am
☐ 5:11 pm 2:11 pm
☐ 7:02 4:02 pm
☐ 7:16 4:16 pm
☐ 9:52 6:52 pm

14 TUESDAY
☐ 4:33 am 1:33 am
☐ 5:20 am 2:20 am
☐ 11:36 am 8:36 am
10:51 pm

15 WEDNESDAY
☐ 1:51 am
☐ 8:21 am 5:21 am

16 THURSDAY
☐ 4:50 am 1:50 am
☐ 6:29 am 3:29 am
☐ 8:14 am 5:14 am
☐ 11:08 am 8:08 am
☐ 8:56 5:56 pm

17 FRIDAY
☐ 12:21 am
☐ 3:14 am 12:14 am
☐ 12:57 9:57 am
☐ 11:29 8:28 pm

18 SATURDAY
☐ 9:24 am 6:24 am
☐ 7:38 am 4:38 am
☐ 9:35 am 6:35 am
☐ 11:36 8:36 pm
10:02 pm

19 SUNDAY
☐ 1:02 am
☐ 1:43 10:43 am

20 MONDAY
☐ 1:25 am
☐ 12:27 am
☐ 5:22 am
☐ 8:22 am
☐ 3:18 12:18 pm
7:00 pm

21 TUESDAY
☐ 8:10 am 5:10 am
☐ 9:44 am 6:44 am
☐ 2:12 pm 11:12 am
☐ 5:26 2:26 pm

22 WEDNESDAY
☐ 5:24 am 2:24 am
☐ 2:28 am
☐ 2:50 11:50 am
☐ 9:54 6:54 am

23 THURSDAY
☐ 6:24 am
☐ 4:38 pm
☐ 7:50 4:50 pm
11:17 pm

24 FRIDAY
☐ 1:39 am
☐ 3:17 am
☐ 9:05 6:05 am

25 SATURDAY
☐ 12:24 am
☐ 12:37 am
☐ 7:02 am 4:02 am
☐ 3:08 am 12:08 am
☐ 6:07 3:07 pm

26 SUNDAY
☐ 3:12 am 12:12 am
☐ 3:39 am 12:39 am
☐ 10:32 am 7:32 am
☐ 4:29 pm 1:29 pm
☐ 9:24 6:24 pm

27 MONDAY
☐ 5:07 am 2:07 am
☐ 7:13 am 4:13 am
☐ 7:55 am 4:55 am
9:04 pm

28 TUESDAY
☐ 12:04 am
☐ 3:57 am 12:57 am
☐ 7:19 am 4:19 am
☐ 9:06 am 6:06 am
☐ 4:11 pm 1:11 pm
☐ 8:04 5:04 pm

29 WEDNESDAY
☐ 5:27 am 2:27 am
☐ 5:43 am 2:43 am

30 THURSDAY
☐ 2:51 am
☐ 4:54 am 1:54 am
☐ 8:19 am 5:19 am
☐ 11:27 am 8:27 am
☐ 12:10 9:10 am
☐ 6:42 3:42 pm

31 FRIDAY
☐ 10:31 am 7:31 am
☐ 11:47 am 8:47 am
☐ 1:15 pm 10:15 am
☐ 3:01 12:01 pm

Eastern time in bold type
Pacific time in medium type

DECEMBER 2021

DATE	SID.TIME	SUN	MOON	NODE	MERCURY	VENUS	MARS	JUPITER	SATURN	URANUS	NEPTUNE	PLUTO	CERES	PALLAS	JUNO	VESTA	CHIRON
1 W	4 40 17	8♐59 53	22♎49	1♊43	10♐00	20♑29	21♏23	25≈23	8≈58	11♉46℞	20♓24D	25♑02	4♊12℞	10♓31	5♑42	7♐47	8♈36℞
2 Th	4 44 13	10 00 43	7♏23	1 44	11 35	21 04	22 04	25 31	9 03	11 44	20 24	25 04	3 58	10 39	6 04	8 20	8 35
3 F	4 48 10	11 01 35	22 18	1 44℞	13 09	21 37	22 46	25 39	9 08	11 42	20 24	25 05	3 44	10 47	6 26	8 52	8 34
4 Sa	4 52 7	12 02 27	7♐28	1 44	14 43	22 09	23 27	25 48	9 13	11 39	20 24	25 06	3 31	10 55	6 47	9 25	8 33
5 Su	4 56 3	13 03 21	22 43	1 44	16 17	22 40	24 09	25 56	9 17	11 37	20 24	25 08	3 17	11 04	7 09	9 57	8 32
6 M	5 0 0	14 04 16	7♑52	1 43	17 51	23 08	24 50	26 05	9 23	11 35	20 25	25 10	3 03	11 13	7 32	10 29	8 31
7 T	5 3 56	15 05 12	22 47	1 41	19 25	23 36	25 32	26 13	9 28	11 34	20 25	25 11	2 50	11 22	7 54	11 02	8 31
8 W	5 7 53	16 06 09	7≈21	1 39	20 59	24 01	26 14	26 22	9 33	11 32	20 25	25 13	2 36	11 31	8 16	11 34	8 30
9 Th	5 11 49	17 07 06	21 28	1 37	22 33	24 25	26 55	26 31	9 38	11 30	20 25	25 15	2 23	11 41	8 38	12 07	8 29
10 F	5 15 46	18 08 04	5♓08	1 36	24 07	24 47	27 37	26 41	9 43	11 28	20 25	25 16	2 10	11 50	9 00	12 39	8 29
11 Sa	5 19 43	19 09 03	18 21	1 36D	25 41	25 07	28 19	26 50	9 49	11 26	20 26	25 18	1 58	12 01	9 23	13 12	8 28
12 Su	5 23 39	20 10 02	1♈11	1 36	27 16	25 25	29 01	26 59	9 54	11 24	20 26	25 20	1 45	12 11	9 45	13 44	8 28
13 M	5 27 36	21 11 01	13 40	1 37	28 50	25 40	29 43	27 09	10 00	11 23	20 26	25 21	1 33	12 22	10 08	14 17	8 27
14 T	5 31 32	22 12 01	25 53	1 39	0♑25	25 54	0♐25	27 19	10 05	11 21	20 27	25 23	1 21	12 33	10 30	14 49	8 27
15 W	5 35 29	23 13 02	7♉54	1 41	1 58	26 06	1 07	27 28	10 11	11 19	20 27	25 25	1 09	12 44	10 53	15 22	8 27
16 Th	5 39 25	24 14 03	19 48	1 42	3 33	26 15	1 49	27 38	10 16	11 17	20 28	25 27	0 57	12 55	11 15	15 54	8 27
17 F	5 43 22	25 15 05	1♊37	1 42℞	5 07	26 22	2 31	27 48	10 22	11 16	20 28	25 28	0 46	13 07	11 38	16 26	8 26
18 Sa	5 47 18	26 16 08	13 25	1 42	6 42	26 27	3 13	27 59	10 28	11 14	20 29	25 30	0 35	13 19	12 01	16 59	8 26
19 Su	5 51 15	27 17 11	25 13	1 40	8 16	26 29℞	3 55	28 09	10 34	11 13	20 29	25 32	0 25	13 31	12 23	17 31	8 26D
20 M	5 55 12	28 18 14	7♋05	1 37	9 50	26 28	4 37	28 19	10 40	11 11	20 30	25 34	0 14	13 43	12 46	18 04	8 26
21 T	5 59 8	29 19 19	19 01	1 32	11 25	26 26	5 19	28 30	10 46	11 10	20 31	25 35	0 04	13 56	13 09	18 36	8 26
22 W	6 3 5	0♑20 24	1♌04	1 27	12 59	26 21	6 01	28 41	10 52	11 09	20 31	25 37	29♉56	14 08	13 32	19 08	8 26
23 Th	6 7 1	1 21 29	13 15	1 21	14 33	26 14	6 44	28 51	10 58	11 07	20 32	25 39	29 45	14 21	13 55	19 41	8 26
24 F	6 10 58	2 22 35	25 37	1 16	16 06	26 04	7 26	29 02	11 04	11 06	20 33	25 41	29 36	14 34	14 18	20 13	8 26
25 Sa	6 14 54	3 23 42	8♍12	1 13	17 40	25 51	8 08	29 13	11 10	11 05	20 34	25 43	29 28	14 48	14 41	20 46	8 27
26 Su	6 18 51	4 24 49	21 03	1 10	19 13	25 36	8 51	29 24	11 16	11 03	20 35	25 45	29 19	15 02	15 04	21 18	8 27
27 M	6 22 47	5 25 57	4♎12	1 09D	20 45	25 18	9 33	29 35	11 22	11 02	20 36	25 47	29 12	15 15	15 27	21 50	8 28
28 T	6 26 44	6 27 05	17 43	1 10	22 16	24 59	10 16	29 47	11 29	11 01	20 37	25 48	29 04	15 29	15 50	22 22	8 28
29 W	6 30 41	7 28 14	1♏36	1 11	23 47	24 37	10 58	29 58	11 35	11 00	20 38	25 50	28 57	15 44	16 13	22 55	8 29
30 Th	6 34 37	8 29 24	15 53	1 12	25 17	24 12	11 41	0♓09	11 41	10 59	20 39	25 52	28 50	15 58	16 36	23 27	8 29
31 F	6 38 34	9 30 34	0♐32	1 13℞	26 45	23 46	12 23	0 21	11 48	10 58	20 40	25 54	28 44	16 13	17 00	23 59	8 30

EPHEMERIS CALCULATED FOR 12 MIDNIGHT GREENWICH MEAN TIME. ALL OTHER DATA AND FACING ASPECTARIAN PAGE IN **EASTERN TIME (BOLD)** AND PACIFIC TIME (REGULAR).

JANUARY 2022

☽ Last Aspect day	ET / hr:mn / PT		asp	☽ Ingress sign	day	ET / hr:mn / PT	
1	**3:16 am**	12:16 am	□♆	♑	1	**6:02 pm**	3:02 pm
3	**11:21 am**	8:21 am	☌♇	♒	3	**5:44 pm**	2:44 pm
4	**7:45 pm**	4:45 pm	✶♂	♓	5	**7:17 pm**	4:17 pm
7	**5:23 pm**	2:23 pm	✶♇	♈	7		9:26 pm
7	**5:23 pm**	2:23 pm	✶♇	♈	8	**12:26 am**	
9		11:23 pm	□♇	♉	10	**9:47 am**	6:47 am
10	**2:23 am**		□♇	♉	10	**9:47 am**	6:47 am
12	**2:39 pm**	11:39 am	△♇	♊	12	**10:08 pm**	7:08 pm
14	**9:22 pm**	6:22 pm	☍♂	♋	15	**11:11 am**	8:11 am
17	**6:48 pm**	3:48 pm	☍☉	♌	17	**11:03 pm**	8:03 pm

☽ Last Aspect day	ET / hr:mn / PT		asp	☽ Ingress sign	day	ET / hr:mn / PT	
20	**3:15 am**	12:15 am	△♂	♍	20	**9:02 am**	6:02 am
22	**2:46 pm**	11:46 am	□♂	♎	22	**5:03 pm**	2:03 pm
24	**5:10 pm**	2:10 pm	□♇	♏	24	**10:57 pm**	7:57 pm
26		9:28 pm	✶☿	♐	26		11:34 pm
27	**12:28 am**		✶☿	♐	27	**2:34 am**	
28	**2:00 pm**	11:00 am	□♆	♑	29	**4:09 am**	1:09 am
30	**11:44 pm**	8:44 pm	☌♇	♒	31	**4:43 am**	1:43 am

☽ Phases & Eclipses phase	day	ET / hr:mn / PT	
New Moon	2	**1:33 pm**	10:33 am
2nd Quarter	9	**1:11 pm**	10:11 am
Full Moon	17	**6:48 pm**	3:48 pm
4th Quarter	25	**8:41 am**	5:41 am
New Moon	31		9:46 pm
New Moon	2/1	**12:46 am**	

Planet Ingress		day	ET / hr:mn / PT	
☿	♒	1		11:10 pm
☿	♒	2	**2:10 am**	
⚶	♑	10		9:19 pm
⚶	♑	11	**12:19 am**	
☉	♒	19	**9:39 pm**	6:39 pm
♂	♑	24	**7:53 am**	4:53 am
☿	♑	25	**10:05 pm**	7:05 pm

Planetary Motion		day	ET / hr:mn / PT	
☿	℞	14	**6:41 am**	3:41 am
⚳	D	14	**4:20 pm**	1:20 pm
♅	D	18	**10:27 am**	7:27 am
♀	D	29	**3:46 am**	12:46 am

1 SATURDAY
☽ □ ♆ **3:16 am** 12:16 am
☉ △ ♅ **4:50 am** 1:50 am
☽ ⚺ ♀ **7:02 am** 4:02 am
☽ ⚺ ♇ **11:38 am** 8:38 am
☽ ⚺ ☿ **5:13 pm** 2:13 pm
☽ ✶ ♃ **7:13 pm** 4:13 pm

2 SUNDAY
☉ ⚺ ♄ **7:12 am** 4:12 am
☽ △ ♅ **11:20 am** 8:20 am
☽ ⚺ ♄ **1:10 pm** 10:10 am
☽ ☌ ☉ **1:33 pm** 10:33 am
☽ ⚺ ♂ **4:56 pm** 1:56 pm
☿ ⚺ ♃ **6:44 pm** 3:44 pm
☽ ✶ ♆ 11:52 pm

3 MONDAY
☽ ✶ ♆ **2:52 am**
☽ ☌ ♀ **4:59 am** 1:59 am
☽ ☌ ♇ **11:21 am** 8:21 am
☽ ⚺ ♃ **7:34 pm** 4:34 pm
☽ ☌ ☿ **9:37 pm** 6:37 pm

4 TUESDAY
☽ □ ♅ **11:25 am** 8:25 am
☽ ☌ ♄ **1:44 pm** 10:44 am
☽ ⚺ ☉ **5:23 pm** 2:23 pm
☽ ✶ ♂ **7:45 pm** 4:45 pm

5 WEDNESDAY
☽ ⚺ ♆ **3:41 am** 12:41 am
☽ ⚺ ♀ **3:59 am** 12:59 am
♀ ✶ ♆ **11:03 am** 8:03 am
☽ ⚺ ♇ **12:39 pm** 9:39 am
☽ ☌ ♃ **9:57 pm** 6:57 pm

6 THURSDAY
☽ ⚺ ☿ **4:07 am** 1:07 am
☽ ✶ ♅ **2:04 pm** 11:04 am
☽ ⚺ ♄ **5:01 pm** 2:01 pm
☽ ✶ ☉ 9:41 pm
☽ □ ♂ 10:55 pm

7 FRIDAY
☽ ✶ ☉ **12:41 am**
☽ □ ♂ **1:55 am**
☽ ✶ ♀ **5:41 am** 2:41 am
☽ ☌ ♆ **7:40 am** 4:40 am
☽ ✶ ♇ **5:23 pm** 2:23 pm

8 SATURDAY
☽ ⚺ ♃ **4:11 am** 1:11 am
☽ ✶ ☿ **2:37 pm** 11:37 am
♀ ⚺ ♂ **5:48 pm** 2:48 pm
☉ ☌ ♀ **7:48 pm** 4:48 pm
☽ ⚺ ♅ **8:44 pm** 5:44 pm
☽ ✶ ♄ 9:27 pm

9 SUNDAY
☽ ✶ ♄ **12:27 am**
☉ ⚺ ♂ **4:32 am** 1:32 am
☽ □ ♀ **11:01 am** 8:01 am
☽ △ ♂ **12:58 pm** 9:58 am
☽ □ ☉ **1:11 pm** 10:11 am
☽ ⚺ ♆ **3:52 pm** 12:52 pm
☽ □ ♇ 11:23 pm

10 MONDAY
☽ □ ♇ **2:23 am**
☽ ✶ ♃ **2:48 pm** 11:48 am
☉ ✶ ♆ **10:28 pm** 7:28 pm

11 TUESDAY
☽ □ ☿ **4:38 am** 1:38 am
☽ ☌ ♅ **7:21 am** 4:21 am
☽ □ ♄ **11:53 am** 8:53 am
♂ □ ♆ **4:43 pm** 1:43 pm
☽ △ ♀ **7:34 pm** 4:34 pm

12 WEDNESDAY
☽ ✶ ♆ **3:38 am** 12:38 am
☽ ⚻ ♂ **4:19 am** 1:19 am
☽ △ ☉ **6:20 am** 3:20 am
☽ △ ♇ **2:39 pm** 11:39 am

13 THURSDAY
☽ □ ♃ **4:24 am** 1:24 am
☽ △ ☿ **7:10 pm** 4:10 pm
☽ ⚺ ♅ **8:12 pm** 5:12 pm
☽ △ ♄ 10:26 pm

14 FRIDAY
☽ △ ♄ **1:26 am**
☽ ⚻ ♀ **5:46 am** 2:46 am
☽ □ ♆ **4:50 pm** 1:50 pm
☽ ☍ ♂ **9:22 pm** 6:22 pm
☽ ⚻ ☉ 10:10 pm

15 SATURDAY
☽ ⚻ ☉ **1:10 am**
☽ ⚻ ♇ **3:54 am** 12:54 am
☽ △ ♃ **6:31 pm** 3:31 pm

16 SUNDAY
☽ ⚻ ☿ **7:12 am** 4:12 am
☽ ✶ ♅ **8:58 am** 5:58 am
☉ ☌ ♇ **9:51 am** 6:51 am
☽ ⚻ ♄ **2:42 pm** 11:42 am
☽ ☍ ♀ **3:50 pm** 12:50 pm

17 MONDAY
☽ △ ♆ **5:19 am** 2:19 am
☽ ⚻ ♂ **1:24 pm** 10:24 am
♀ ⚺ ♄ **2:44 pm** 11:44 am
☽ ☍ ♇ **4:08 pm** 1:08 pm
☽ ☍ ☉ **6:48 pm** 3:48 pm

18 TUESDAY
☽ ⚻ ♃ **7:15 am** 4:15 am
☽ ☍ ☿ **3:39 pm** 12:39 pm
☽ □ ♅ **8:11 pm** 5:11 pm
☽ ⚻ ♀ 9:47 pm
☽ ☍ ♄ 11:19 pm

19 WEDNESDAY
☽ ⚻ ♀ **12:47 am**
☽ ☍ ♄ **2:19 am**
♂ ⚺ ♇ **1:30 pm** 10:30 am
☽ ⚻ ♆ **4:00 pm** 1:00 pm
☽ ⚻ ♇ 11:30 pm

20 THURSDAY
☽ ⚻ ♇ **2:30 am**
☽ △ ♂ **3:15 am** 12:15 am
☽ ⚻ ☉ **10:02 am** 7:02 am
☽ ☍ ♃ **5:58 pm** 2:58 pm
☽ ⚻ ☿ **8:55 pm** 5:55 pm

21 FRIDAY
☽ △ ♅ **5:28 am** 2:28 am
☽ △ ♀ **8:19 am** 5:19 am
☽ ⚻ ♄ **11:54 am** 8:54 am
☿ ⚺ ♃ **11:00 pm** 8:00 pm
☽ ☍ ♆ 9:43 pm

22 SATURDAY
☽ ☍ ♆ **12:43 am**
☽ △ ♇ **10:53 am** 7:53 am
☽ □ ♂ **2:46 pm** 11:46 am
☽ △ ☉ **10:43 pm** 7:43 pm
☽ △ ☿ **11:47 pm** 8:47 pm
☽ ⚻ ♃ 11:37 pm

23 SUNDAY
☽ ⚻ ♃ **2:37 am**
☉ ☌ ☿ **5:28 am** 2:28 am
☽ ⚻ ♅ **12:45 pm** 9:45 am
☽ □ ♀ **2:22 pm** 11:22 am
☽ △ ♄ **7:26 pm** 4:26 pm

24 MONDAY
☽ ⚻ ♆ **7:23 am** 4:23 am
☽ □ ♇ **5:10 pm** 2:10 pm
☽ ✶ ♂ **11:48 pm** 8:48 pm
☽ □ ☿ 9:51 pm

25 TUESDAY
☽ □ ☿ **12:51 am**
☿ ⚺ ♂ **7:46 am** 4:46 am
☽ □ ☉ **8:41 am** 5:41 am
☽ △ ♃ **9:01 am** 6:01 am
☉ ⚺ ♃ **2:32 pm** 11:32 am
☽ ☍ ♅ **5:52 pm** 2:52 pm
☽ ✶ ♀ **6:41 pm** 3:41 pm
☽ □ ♄ 9:42 pm

26 WEDNESDAY
☽ □ ♄ **12:42 am**
☽ △ ♆ **11:47 am** 8:47 am
☽ ✶ ♇ **9:10 pm** 6:10 pm
☽ ✶ ☿ 9:28 pm

27 THURSDAY
☽ ✶ ☿ **12:28 am**
☽ ⚺ ♂ **6:09 am** 3:09 am
☽ □ ♃ **1:02 pm** 10:02 am
☽ ✶ ☉ **3:47 pm** 12:47 pm
☽ ⚻ ♅ **8:43 pm** 5:43 pm
☽ ⚺ ♀ **9:08 pm** 6:08 pm

28 FRIDAY
☽ ✶ ♄ **3:39 am** 12:39 am
☽ □ ♆ **2:00 pm** 11:00 am
☽ ⚺ ♇ **11:02 pm** 8:02 pm
☽ ⚺ ☿ **11:03 pm** 8:03 pm
☿ ☌ ♇ **11:16 pm** 8:16 pm

29 SATURDAY
☽ ☌ ♂ **10:10 am** 7:10 am
☽ ✶ ♃ **3:03 pm** 12:03 pm
☽ ⚺ ☉ **8:34 pm** 5:34 pm
☽ △ ♅ **9:47 pm** 6:47 pm
☽ ☌ ♀ **10:08 pm** 7:08 pm

30 SUNDAY
☽ ⚺ ♄ **4:56 am** 1:56 am
☉ □ ♅ **2:32 pm** 11:32 am
☽ ✶ ♆ **2:48 pm** 11:48 am
☉ ⚺ ♀ **8:29 pm** 5:29 pm
☽ ☌ ☿ **9:26 pm** 6:26 pm
☽ ☌ ♇ **11:44 pm** 8:44 pm

31 MONDAY
☽ ⚺ ♂ **1:14 pm** 10:14 am
☽ ⚺ ♃ **4:22 pm** 1:22 pm
☽ □ ♅ **10:25 pm** 7:25 pm
☽ ⚺ ♀ **10:58 pm** 7:58 pm
☽ ☌ ☉ 9:46 pm

Eastern time in bold type
Pacific time in medium type

JANUARY 2022

DATE	SID.TIME	SUN	MOON	NODE	MERCURY	VENUS	MARS	JUPITER	SATURN	URANUS	NEPTUNE	PLUTO	CERES	PALLAS	JUNO	VESTA	CHIRON
1 Sa	6 42 30	10♑31 44	15♐29	1♊12R	28♑11	23♑18R	13♐06	0♒33	11♒54	10♉57R	20♓40	25♑56	28♑38R	16♓28	17♑23	24♏32	8♈30
2 Su	6 46 27	11 32 55	0♑37	1 10	29 35	22 48	13 49	0 45	12 01	10 56	20 41	25 58	28 32	16 43	17 46	25 04	8 31
3 M	6 50 23	12 34 06	15 46	1 05	0♒35	22 16	14 31	0 57	12 07	10 56	20 42	26 00	28 27	16 58	18 00	25 36	8 32
4 T	6 54 20	13 35 17	0♒47	0 59	2 16	21 43	15 14	1 08	12 14	10 55	20 43	26 02	28 22	17 13	18 13	26 08	8 33
5 W	6 58 17	14 36 28	15 31	0 51	3 32	21 09	15 57	1 20	12 20	10 54	20 45	26 04	28 18	17 29	18 33	26 40	8 34
6 Th	7 2 13	15 37 38	29 50	0 44	4 43	20 34	16 40	1 33	12 27	10 53	20 46	26 06	28 14	17 45	18 56	27 13	8 34
7 F	7 6 10	16 38 48	13♓41	0 38	5 50	19 58	17 23	1 45	12 34	10 53	20 47	26 08	28 11	18 01	19 20	27 45	8 35
8 Sa	7 10 6	17 39 58	27 03	0 34	6 52	19 21	18 05	1 57	12 41	10 52	20 48	26 10	28 08	18 17	19 43	28 17	8 36
9 Su	7 14 3	18 41 07	9♈57	0 32D	7 47	18 44	18 48	2 09	12 47	10 52	20 49	26 12	28 05	18 33	20 07	28 49	8 38
10 M	7 17 59	19 42 16	22 27	0 32	8 35	18 08	19 31	2 22	12 54	10 51	20 51	26 14	28 03	18 49	20 30	29 21	8 39
11 T	7 21 56	20 43 24	4♉39	0 32	9 15	17 31	20 14	2 34	13 01	10 51	20 52	26 16	28 01	19 06	20 54	29 53	8 40
12 W	7 25 52	21 44 32	16 38	0 34	9 46	16 55	20 57	2 47	13 08	10 50	20 53	26 18	28 00	19 23	21 18	0♐25	8 41
13 Th	7 29 49	22 45 40	28 28	0 34R	10 08	16 20	21 40	3 00	13 15	10 50	20 55	26 20	27 59	19 40	21 41	0 57	8 42
14 F	7 33 45	23 46 46	10♊14	0 34	10 19R	15 46	22 24	3 12	13 22	10 50	20 56	26 22	27 58D	19 57	22 05	1 29	8 44
15 Sa	7 37 42	24 47 53	22 01	0 31	10 19	15 13	23 07	3 25	13 28	10 49	20 58	26 24	27 58	20 14	22 28	2 01	8 45
16 Su	7 41 39	25 48 58	3♋52	0 26	10 07	14 41	23 50	3 38	13 35	10 49	20 59	26 26	27 58	20 32	22 52	2 33	8 47
17 M	7 45 35	26 50 03	15 50	0 18	9 43	14 11	24 33	3 51	13 42	10 49	21 01	26 29	27 59	20 49	23 16	3 04	8 48
18 T	7 49 32	27 51 08	27 57	0 09	9 08	13 43	25 16	4 04	13 49	10 49D	21 02	26 31	28 01	21 07	23 40	3 36	8 50
19 W	7 53 28	28 52 12	10♌12	29♉57	8 22	13 17	26 00	4 17	13 56	10 49	21 04	26 33	28 03	21 25	24 03	4 08	8 51
20 Th	7 57 25	29 53 15	22 39	29 46	7 26	12 53	26 43	4 30	14 03	10 49	21 05	26 35	28 05	21 43	24 27	4 40	8 53
21 F	8 1 21	0♒54 18	5♍16	29 34	6 22	12 31	27 26	4 44	14 11	10 49	21 07	26 37	28 08	22 01	24 51	5 12	8 54
22 Sa	8 5 18	1 55 21	18 04	29 25	5 11	12 12	28 10	4 57	14 18	10 49	21 08	26 39	28 11	22 19	25 15	5 43	8 56
23 Su	8 9 15	2 56 22	1♎04	29 18	3 56	11 55	28 53	5 10	14 25	10 50	21 10	26 41	28 14	22 38	25 38	6 15	8 58
24 M	8 13 11	3 57 24	14 17	29 12D	2 40	11 40	29 37	5 24	14 32	10 50	21 12	26 43	28 18	22 56	26 02	6 47	9 00
25 T	8 17 8	4 58 25	27 45	29 12	1 23	11 28	0♑20	5 37	14 39	10 50	21 13	26 45	28 22	23 15	26 26	7 18	9 02
26 W	8 21 4	5 59 25	11♏30	29 12R	0 09	11 19	1 04	5 51	14 46	10 51	21 15	26 47	28 27	23 34	26 50	7 50	9 04
27 Th	8 25 1	7 00 25	25 31	29 12	29♑00	11 12	1 47	6 04	14 53	10 51	21 17	26 49	28 32	23 53	27 14	8 21	9 06
28 F	8 28 57	8 01 25	9♐49	29 12	27 57	11 07	2 31	6 18	15 00	10 51	21 19	26 51	28 37	24 12	27 38	8 53	9 08
29 Sa	8 32 54	9 02 24	24 23	29 12	27 01	11 05D	3 15	6 31	15 08	10 52	21 20	26 53	28 43	24 31	28 01	9 24	9 10
30 Su	8 36 50	10 03 23	9♑09	29 05	26 13	11 05	3 58	6 45	15 15	10 52	21 22	26 55	28 49	24 50	28 25	9 55	9 12
31 M	8 40 47	11 04 20	24 00	28 57	25 34	11 05	4 42	6 59	15 22	10 53	21 24	26 57	28 55	25 10	28 49	10 27	9 14

EPHEMERIS CALCULATED FOR 12 MIDNIGHT GREENWICH MEAN TIME. ALL OTHER DATA AND FACING ASPECTARIAN PAGE IN **EASTERN TIME (BOLD)** AND PACIFIC TIME (REGULAR).

FEBRUARY 2022

☽ Last Aspect			☽ Ingress		
day	ET / hr:mn / PT	asp	sign	day	ET / hr:mn / PT
1	**6:01 am** 3:01 am	☌ ♄	♓	2	**6:00 am** 3:00 am
4	**4:41 am** 1:41 am	⚹ ♇	♈	4	**9:57 am** 6:57 am
6	**12:21 pm** 9:21 am	□ ♇	♉	6	**5:52 pm** 2:52 pm
8	**11:48 pm** 8:48 pm	△ ♇	♊	9	**5:27 am** 2:27 am
11	**3:23 am** 12:23 am	△ ☉	♋	11	**6:27 pm** 3:27 pm
14	**5:27 am** 2:27 am	☍ ☿	♌	14	**6:17 am** 3:17 am
16	**11:56 am** 8:56 am	☍ ☉	♍	16	**3:42 pm** 12:42 pm
18	**6:20 pm** 3:20 pm	△ ♇	♎	18	**10:51 pm** 7:51 pm
20	9:02 pm	□ ♇	♏	21	**4:19 am** 1:19 am
21	**12:02 am**	□ ♇	♏	21	**4:19 am** 1:19 am
23	**4:24 am** 1:24 am	⚹ ♇	♐	23	**8:29 am** 5:29 am
24	**10:24 pm** 7:24 pm	□ ♆	♑	25	**11:27 am** 8:27 am
27	**9:49 am** 6:49 am	☌ ♇	♒	27	**1:36 pm** 10:36 am
28	**9:01 pm** 6:01 pm	☌ ♄	♓	3/1	**3:53 pm** 12:53 pm

☽ Phases & Eclipses		
phase	day	ET / hr:mn / PT
New Moon	1/31	9:46 pm
New Moon	1	**12:46 am**
2nd Quarter	8	**8:50 am** 5:50 am
Full Moon	16	**11:56 am** 8:56 am
4th Quarter	23	**5:32 pm** 2:32 pm

Planet Ingress			
		day	ET / hr:mn / PT
⚵	♒	1	**6:04 pm** 3:04 pm
⚳	♊	8	**9:13 pm** 6:13 pm
♀	♈	13	9:53 pm
♀	♈	14	**12:53 am**
☿	♒	14	**4:54 pm** 1:54 pm
☉	♓	18	**11:43 am** 8:43 am

Planetary Motion			
		day	ET / hr:mn / PT
☿	D	3	**11:13 pm** 8:13 pm

1 TUESDAY
☽ ☌ ☉ **12:46 am**
☽ ☌ ♄ **6:01 am** 3:01 am
☽ ⚺ ♆ **3:46 pm** 12:46 pm
☽ ⚺ ☿ **9:05 pm** 6:05 pm
☽ ⚺ ♇ 9:57 pm

2 WEDNESDAY
☽ ⚺ ♇ **12:57 am**
☽ ⚹ ♂ **5:33 pm** 2:33 pm
☽ ☌ ♃ **6:57 pm** 3:57 pm
☽ ⚹ ♅ 9:30 pm
☽ ⚹ ♀ 10:35 pm

3 THURSDAY
☽ ⚹ ♅ **12:30 am**
☽ ⚹ ♀ **1:35 am**
☽ ⚺ ☉ **6:52 am** 3:52 am
☽ ⚺ ♄ **8:54 am** 5:54 am
☽ ☌ ♆ **6:54 pm** 3:54 pm
☽ ⚹ ☿ **11:55 pm** 8:55 pm

4 FRIDAY
☽ ⚹ ♇ **4:41 am** 1:41 am
♂ ⚹ ♃ **8:38 am** 5:38 am
☉ ☌ ♄ **2:05 pm** 11:05 am
☽ ⚺ ♃ 9:48 pm
☽ □ ♂ 10:27 pm

5 SATURDAY
☽ ⚺ ♃ **12:48 am**
☽ □ ♂ **1:27 am**
☽ ⚺ ♅ **5:53 am** 2:53 am
☽ □ ♀ **7:56 am** 4:56 am
☽ ⚹ ♄ **3:22 pm** 12:22 pm
☽ ⚹ ☉ **5:17 pm** 2:17 pm
☽ ⚺ ♆ 10:47 pm

6 SUNDAY
☽ ⚺ ♆ **1:47 am**
☽ □ ☿ **7:42 am** 4:42 am
☽ □ ♇ **12:21 pm** 9:21 am

7 MONDAY
☽ ⚹ ♃ **10:58 am** 7:58 am
☽ △ ♂ **2:12 pm** 11:12 am
☽ ☌ ♅ **3:22 pm** 12:22 pm
☽ △ ♀ **7:00 pm** 4:00 pm
☽ □ ♄ 11:01 pm

8 TUESDAY
☽ □ ♄ **2:01 am**
☽ □ ☉ **8:50 am** 5:50 am
♂ △ ♅ **9:57 am** 6:57 am
☽ ⚹ ♆ **12:40 pm** 9:40 am
☽ △ ☿ **8:48 pm** 5:48 pm
☽ △ ♇ **11:48 pm** 8:48 pm

9 WEDNESDAY
☽ □ ♃ 9:28 pm

10 THURSDAY
☽ □ ♃ **12:28 am**
☽ ⚺ ♅ **3:53 am** 12:53 am
☽ ⚻ ♂ **6:36 am** 3:36 am
☉ ⚺ ♆ **7:29 am** 4:29 am
☽ ⚻ ♀ **9:35 am** 6:35 am
☽ △ ♄ **3:20 pm** 12:20 pm
☽ □ ♆ 10:43 pm

11 FRIDAY
☽ □ ♆ **1:43 am**
☽ △ ☉ **3:23 am** 12:23 am
☿ ☌ ♇ **9:04 am** 6:04 am
☽ ⚻ ♇ **12:56 pm** 9:56 am
☽ ⚻ ☿ **1:11 pm** 10:11 am

12 SATURDAY
☽ △ ♃ **2:35 pm** 11:35 am
☽ ⚹ ♅ **4:49 pm** 1:49 pm
☽ ☍ ♂ **11:21 pm** 8:21 pm
☽ ☍ ♀ 9:45 pm

13 SUNDAY
☽ ☍ ♀ **12:45 am**
☽ ⚻ ♄ **4:33 am** 1:33 am
☽ △ ♆ **2:15 pm** 11:15 am
☽ ⚻ ☉ **9:09 pm** 6:09 pm
☽ ☍ ♇ 10:07 pm

14 MONDAY
☽ ☍ ♇ **1:07 am**
☽ ☍ ☿ **5:27 am** 2:27 am
☽ ⚻ ♃ 11:49 pm

15 TUESDAY
☽ ⚻ ♃ **2:49 am**
☽ □ ♅ **3:56 am** 12:56 am
☽ ⚻ ♂ **1:45 pm** 10:45 am
☽ ⚻ ♀ **2:02 pm** 11:02 am
☽ ☍ ♄ **3:38 pm** 12:38 pm
☉ ⚺ ♇ **10:17 pm** 7:17 pm
☽ ⚻ ♆ 9:31 pm

16 WEDNESDAY
☽ ⚻ ♆ **12:31 am**
♀ ☌ ♂ **9:29 am** 6:29 am
☽ ⚻ ♇ **10:53 am** 7:53 am
☽ ☍ ☉ **11:56 am** 8:56 am
☽ ⚻ ☿ **7:31 pm** 4:31 pm

17 THURSDAY
♂ ⚺ ♄ **3:34 am** 12:34 am
♀ ⚺ ♄ **9:09 am** 6:09 am
☽ ☍ ♃ **12:26 pm** 9:26 am
☽ △ ♅ **12:33 pm** 9:33 am
♃ ⚹ ♅ **7:13 pm** 4:13 pm
☽ ⚻ ♄ 9:11 pm
☽ △ ♀ 9:47 pm
☽ △ ♂ 10:13 pm

18 FRIDAY
☽ ⚻ ♄ **12:11 am**
☽ △ ♀ **12:47 am**
☽ △ ♂ **1:13 am**
☽ ☍ ♆ **8:22 am** 5:22 am
☽ △ ♇ **6:20 pm** 3:20 pm
☽ ⚻ ☉ **11:46 pm** 8:46 pm

19 SATURDAY
☽ △ ☿ **7:18 am** 4:18 am
☽ ⚻ ♅ **7:06 pm** 4:06 pm
☽ ⚻ ♃ **7:53 pm** 4:53 pm

20 SUNDAY
☽ △ ♄ **6:46 am** 3:46 am
☽ □ ♀ **9:33 am** 6:33 am
☽ □ ♂ **10:25 am** 7:25 am
☽ ⚻ ♆ **2:22 pm** 11:22 am
☽ □ ♇ 9:02 pm

21 MONDAY
☽ □ ♇ **12:02 am**
☽ △ ☉ **9:28 am** 6:28 am
☽ □ ☿ **5:28 pm** 2:28 pm
☽ ☍ ♅ 9:10 pm
☽ △ ♃ 10:45 pm

22 TUESDAY
☽ ☍ ♅ **12:10 am**
☽ △ ♃ **1:45 am**
☽ □ ♄ **11:53 am** 8:53 am
☽ ⚹ ♀ **4:55 pm** 1:55 pm
☽ ⚹ ♂ **5:58 pm** 2:58 pm
☽ △ ♆ **7:00 pm** 4:00 pm

23 WEDNESDAY
☽ ⚹ ♇ **4:24 am** 1:24 am
♂ ⚹ ♆ **2:12 pm** 11:12 am
☽ □ ☉ **5:32 pm** 2:32 pm
☽ ⚹ ☿ 11:17 pm

24 THURSDAY
☽ ⚹ ☿ **2:17 am**
☽ ⚻ ♅ **3:59 am** 12:59 am
☽ □ ♃ **6:19 am** 3:19 am
♀ ⚹ ♆ **11:04 am** 8:04 am
☽ ⚹ ♄ **3:45 pm** 12:45 pm
☿ □ ♅ **9:22 pm** 6:22 pm
☽ □ ♆ **10:24 pm** 7:24 pm
☽ ⚺ ♀ **11:00 pm** 8:00 pm
☽ ⚺ ♂ 9:06 pm

25 FRIDAY
☽ ⚺ ♂ **12:06 am**
☽ ⚺ ♇ **7:33 am** 4:33 am
☽ ⚹ ☉ 9:10 pm

26 SATURDAY
☽ ⚹ ☉ **12:10 am**
☽ △ ♅ **6:40 am** 3:40 am
☿ ⚺ ♃ **7:16 am** 4:16 am
☽ ⚹ ♃ **9:43 am** 6:43 am
☽ ⚺ ☿ **9:55 am** 6:55 am
☽ ⚺ ♄ **6:32 pm** 3:32 pm
☽ ⚹ ♆ 9:49 pm

27 SUNDAY
☽ ⚹ ♆ **12:49 am**
☽ ☌ ♀ **4:06 am** 1:06 am
☽ ☌ ♂ **5:06 am** 2:06 am
☽ ☌ ♇ **9:49 am** 6:49 am

28 MONDAY
☽ ⚺ ☉ **5:59 am** 2:59 am
☽ □ ♅ **8:50 am** 5:50 am
☽ ⚺ ♃ **12:37 pm** 9:37 am
☽ ☌ ☿ **5:11 pm** 2:11 pm
☽ ☌ ♄ **9:01 pm** 6:01 pm

Eastern time in bold type
Pacific time in medium type

FEBRUARY 2022

DATE	SID. TIME	SUN	MOON	NODE	MERCURY	VENUS	MARS	JUPITER	SATURN	URANUS	NEPTUNE	PLUTO	CERES	PALLAS	JUNO	VESTA	CHIRON
1 T	8 44 44	12≈05 17	8≈48	28♉47℞	25♑03℞	11♑13℞	5♑26	7♓13	15≈29	10♉54	21♓26	26♑57	28♊55	25♓29	29♐37	10♑58	9♈16
2 W	8 48 40	13 06 12	23 25	28 35	24 41	11 30	6 10	7 27	15 36	10 54	21 28	26 59	29 02	25 49	0♑02	11 29	9 18
3 Th	8 52 37	14 07 07	7♓42	28 23	24 28	11 42	6 54	7 40	15 43	10 55	21 30	27 01	29 09	26 09	0 25	12 01	9 21
4 F	8 56 33	15 08 00	21 35	28 12	24 23 D	11 56	7 37	7 54	15 51	10 56	21 32	27 03	29 17	26 29	0 49	12 32	9 23
5 Sa	9 0 30	16 08 52	5♈01	28 04	24 25	12 12	8 21	8 08	15 58	10 57	21 33	27 05	29 25	26 49	1 13	13 03	9 25
6 Su	9 4 26	17 09 42	18 00	27 58	24 35	12 30	9 05	8 22	16 05	10 58	21 35	27 07	29 33	27 09	1 37	13 34	9 28
7 M	9 8 23	18 10 31	0♉35	27 55	24 51	12 50	9 49	8 36	16 12	10 59	21 37	27 08	29 41	27 30	2 01	14 05	9 30
8 T	9 12 19	19 11 19	12 50	27 54 D	25 13	13 12	10 33	8 50	16 19	11 00	21 39	27 10	29 50	27 50	2 24	14 36	9 33
9 W	9 16 16	20 12 05	24 50	27 54℞	25 41	13 35	11 17	9 05	16 27	11 01	21 41	27 12	29 59	28 11	2 48	15 07	9 35
10 Th	9 20 13	21 12 50	6♊41	27 54	26 15	14 01	12 01	9 19	16 34	11 02	21 43	27 14	0♋09	28 31	3 12	15 38	9 38
11 F	9 24 9	22 13 33	18 28	27 52	26 53	14 28	12 45	9 33	16 41	11 03	21 45	27 16	0 18	28 52	3 36	16 09	9 40
12 Sa	9 28 6	23 14 14	0♋16	27 49	27 35	14 57	13 30	9 47	16 48	11 05	21 47	27 18	0 28	29 13	4 00	16 39	9 43
13 Su	9 32 2	24 14 54	12 11	27 42	28 21	15 27	14 14	10 01	16 55	11 06	21 49	27 19	0 39	29 34	4 24	17 10	9 45
14 M	9 35 59	25 15 33	24 15	27 31	29 11	15 59	14 58	10 16	17 02	11 07	21 52	27 21	0 49	29 55	4 48	17 41	9 48
15 T	9 39 55	26 16 10	6♌32	27 21	0≈05	16 32	15 42	10 30	17 10	11 09	21 54	27 23	1 00	0♈16	5 12	18 11	9 51
16 W	9 43 52	27 16 45	19 02	27 08	1 01	17 07	16 26	10 44	17 17	11 10	21 56	27 25	1 12	0 37	5 36	18 42	9 54
17 Th	9 47 48	28 17 19	1♍46	26 56	2 01	17 43	17 11	10 59	17 24	11 11	21 58	27 27	1 23	0 59	6 00	19 13	9 56
18 F	9 51 45	29 17 51	14 43	26 46	3 03	18 20	17 55	11 13	17 31	11 13	22 00	27 28	1 35	1 20	6 24	19 43	9 59
19 Sa	9 55 42	0♓18 22	27 52	26 29	4 07	18 59	18 39	11 27	17 38	11 15	22 02	27 30	1 47	1 42	6 47	20 13	10 02
20 Su	9 59 38	1 18 51	11≏13	26 20	5 14	19 39	19 24	11 42	17 45	11 16	22 04	27 32	2 00	2 03	7 11	20 44	10 05
21 M	10 3 35	2 19 19	24 43	26 14	6 23	20 20	20 08	11 56	17 52	11 18	22 06	27 33	2 12	2 25	7 35	21 14	10 08
22 T	10 7 31	3 19 46	8♏22	26 11	7 34	21 02	20 52	12 10	17 59	11 20	22 09	27 35	2 25	2 47	7 59	21 44	10 11
23 W	10 11 28	4 20 11	22 11	26 10	8 47	21 45	21 37	12 25	18 06	11 21	22 11	27 37	2 38	3 09	8 23	22 14	10 14
24 Th	10 15 24	5 20 35	6♐08	26 10	10 01	22 29	22 21	12 39	18 13	11 23	22 13	27 38	2 52	3 31	8 47	22 44	10 17
25 F	10 19 21	6 20 58	20 15	26 10	11 18	23 14	23 06	12 54	18 20	11 25	22 15	27 40	3 05	3 53	9 10	23 14	10 20
26 Sa	10 23 17	7 21 20	4♑30	26 08	12 35	24 00	23 51	13 08	18 27	11 27	22 17	27 42	3 19	4 15	9 34	23 44	10 23
27 Su	10 27 14	8 21 40	18 51	26 03	13 55	24 47	24 35	13 23	18 34	11 29	22 20	27 43	3 33	4 37	9 58	24 14	10 26
28 M	10 31 11	9 21 58	3≈15	25 55	15 15	25 35	25 20	13 37	18 41	11 31	22 22	27 45	3 48	5 00	10 22	24 44	10 29

EPHEMERIS CALCULATED FOR 12 MIDNIGHT GREENWICH MEAN TIME. ALL OTHER DATA AND FACING ASPECTARIAN PAGE IN **EASTERN TIME (BOLD)** AND PACIFIC TIME (REGULAR).

MARCH 2022

☽ Last Aspect day	ET / hr:mn / PT		asp	☽ Ingress sign	day	ET / hr:mn / PT	
2/28	**9:01 pm**	6:01 pm	☌ ♄	♓	1	**3:53 pm**	12:53 pm
3	**4:45 pm**	1:45 pm	⚹ ♂	♈	3	**7:52 pm**	4:52 pm
5	**11:02 pm**	8:02 pm	□ ♇	♉	6	**3:00 am**	12:00 am
8	**9:35 am**	6:35 am	△ ♇	♊	8	**1:40 pm**	10:40 am
10	**11:43 am**	8:43 am	□ ♆	♋	10		11:24 pm
10	**11:43 am**	8:43 am	□ ♆	♋	11	**2:24 am**	
13	**11:44 am**	8:44 am	☍ ♇	♌	13	**3:32 pm**	12:32 pm
15	**6:56 am**	3:56 am	☍ ♄	♍	15		9:59 pm
15	**6:56 am**	3:56 am	☍ ♄	♍	16	**12:59 am**	
18	**4:11 am**	1:11 am	△ ♇	♎	18	**7:26 am**	4:26 am
20	**8:40 am**	5:40 am	□ ♇	♏	20	**11:45 am**	8:45 am
22	**12:01 pm**	9:01 am	⚹ ♇	♐	22	**2:59 pm**	11:59 am
24	**8:59 am**	5:59 am	□ ☿	♑	24	**5:54 pm**	2:54 pm
26	**7:51 pm**	4:51 pm	⚹ ☿	♒	26	**8:55 pm**	5:55 pm
28	**10:11 am**	7:11 am	☌ ♄	♓	28		9:32 pm
28	**10:11 am**	7:11 am	☌ ♄	♓	29	**12:32 am**	
30		11:37 pm	⚹ ♇	♈	31	**5:30 am**	2:30 am
31	**2:37 am**		⚹ ♇	♈	31	**5:30 am**	2:30 am

☽ Phases & Eclipses phase	day	ET / hr:mn / PT	
New Moon	2	**12:35 pm**	9:35 am
2nd Quarter	10	**5:45 am**	2:45 am
Full Moon	18	**3:18 am**	12:18 am
4th Quarter	24		10:37 pm
4th Quarter	25	**1:37 am**	
New Moon	31		11:24 pm
New Moon	4/1	**2:24 am**	

Planet Ingress		day	ET / hr:mn / PT	
♂	♒	5		10:23 pm
♂	♒	6	**1:23 am**	
♀	♒	5		10:30 pm
♀	♒	6	**1:30 am**	
☿	♓	9	**8:32 pm**	5:32 pm
⚶	♒	10	**1:22 pm**	10:22 am
☉	♈	20	**11:33 am**	8:33 am
☿	♈	27	**3:44 am**	12:44 am

Planetary Motion	day	ET / hr:mn / PT

1 TUESDAY
☽ ⚺ ♆ **3:05 am** 12:05 am
☽ ⚺ ♀ **9:14 am** 6:14 am
☽ ⚺ ♂ **10:02 am** 7:02 am
☽ ⚺ ♇ **12:09 pm** 9:09 am
☉ ⚹ ♅ 9:05 pm

2 WEDNESDAY
☉ ⚹ ♅ **12:05 am**
☿ ☌ ♄ **11:33 am** 8:33 am
☽ ⚹ ♅ **11:43 am** 8:43 am
☽ ☌ ☉ **12:35 pm** 9:35 am
☽ ☌ ♃ **4:24 pm** 1:24 pm
☽ ⚺ ♄ 9:37 pm
☽ ⚺ ☿ 11:00 pm

3 THURSDAY
☽ ⚺ ♄ **12:37 am**
☽ ⚺ ☿ **2:00 am**
♂ ☌ ♇ **3:43 am** 12:43 am
☽ ☌ ♆ **6:37 am** 3:37 am
♀ ☌ ♇ **12:56 pm** 9:56 am
☽ ⚹ ♇ **4:03 pm** 1:03 pm
☽ ⚹ ♀ **4:15 pm** 1:15 pm
☽ ⚹ ♂ **4:45 pm** 1:45 pm

4 FRIDAY
☽ ⚺ ♅ **4:55 pm** 1:55 pm
☽ ⚺ ☉ **10:05 pm** 7:05 pm
☽ ⚺ ♃ **10:45 pm** 7:45 pm
☿ ⚺ ♆ **10:50 pm** 7:50 pm

5 SATURDAY
☽ ⚹ ♄ **6:56 am** 3:56 am
☉ ☌ ♃ **9:06 am** 6:06 am
☽ ⚺ ♆ **1:01 pm** 10:01 am
☽ ⚹ ☿ **2:49 pm** 11:49 am
☽ □ ♇ **11:02 pm** 8:02 pm
♀ ☌ ♂ 11:12 pm

6 SUNDAY
♀ ☌ ♂ **2:12 am**
☽ □ ♂ **3:06 am** 12:06 am
☽ □ ♀ **3:07 am** 12:07 am
☽ ☌ ♅ 10:38 pm

7 MONDAY
☽ ☌ ♅ **1:38 am**
☽ ⚹ ♃ **8:49 am** 5:49 am
☽ ⚹ ☉ **12:03 pm** 9:03 am
☽ □ ♄ **4:56 pm** 1:56 pm
☽ ⚹ ♆ **11:03 pm** 8:03 pm

8 TUESDAY
☽ □ ☿ **9:04 am** 6:04 am
☽ △ ♇ **9:35 am** 6:35 am
☿ ⚺ ♇ **1:05 pm** 10:05 am
☽ △ ♂ **5:40 pm** 2:40 pm
☽ △ ♀ **6:27 pm** 3:27 pm

9 WEDNESDAY
☽ ⚺ ♅ **1:35 pm** 10:35 am
☽ □ ♃ **10:07 pm** 7:07 pm

10 THURSDAY
☽ □ ☉ **5:45 am** 2:45 am
☽ △ ♄ **5:48 am** 2:48 am
☉ ⚺ ♄ **6:17 am** 3:17 am
☽ □ ♆ **11:43 am** 8:43 am
☽ ⚻ ♇ **10:23 pm** 7:23 pm

11 FRIDAY
☽ △ ☿ **7:00 am** 4:00 am
☽ ⚻ ♂ **10:34 am** 7:34 am
☽ ⚻ ♀ **12:19 pm** 9:19 am
☽ ⚹ ♅ 11:37 pm

12 SATURDAY
☽ ⚹ ♅ **2:37 am**
☽ △ ♃ **12:07 pm** 9:07 am
☽ ⚻ ♄ **6:59 pm** 3:59 pm
☽ △ ☉ **11:52 pm** 8:52 pm
☽ △ ♆ 9:25 pm

13 SUNDAY
☽ △ ♆ **12:25 am**
☿ ⚺ ♂ **5:44 am** 1:44 am
☉ ☌ ♆ **7:43 am** 4:43 am
☽ ☍ ♇ **11:44 am** 8:44 am

14 MONDAY
☽ ☍ ♂ **3:17 am** 12:17 am
☽ ⚻ ☿ **5:05 am** 2:05 am
☽ ☍ ♀ **6:00 am** 3:00 am
☽ □ ♅ **3:02 pm** 12:02 pm
☿ ⚺ ♀ **7:51 pm** 4:51 pm
☽ ⚻ ♃ 10:02 pm

15 TUESDAY
☽ ⚻ ♃ **1:02 am**
☽ ☍ ♄ **6:56 am** 3:56 am
☽ ⚻ ♆ **11:46 am** 8:46 am
☽ ⚻ ☉ **4:01 pm** 1:01 pm
☽ ⚻ ♇ **9:29 pm** 6:29 pm

16 WEDNESDAY
☽ ⚻ ♂ **3:35 pm** 12:35 pm
☽ ⚻ ♀ **7:09 pm** 4:09 pm
☽ ☍ ☿ **10:08 pm** 7:08 pm
☽ △ ♅ **11:25 pm** 8:25 pm

17 THURSDAY
☿ ⚹ ♅ **8:13 am** 5:13 am
☽ ☍ ♃ **9:44 am** 6:44 am
☽ ⚻ ♄ **2:44 pm** 11:44 am
☽ ☍ ♆ **7:02 pm** 4:02 pm

18 FRIDAY
☽ ☍ ☉ **3:18 am** 12:18 am
☽ △ ♇ **4:11 am** 1:11 am
☉ ⚹ ♇ **3:37 pm** 12:37 pm
☽ △ ♂ 9:29 pm

19 SATURDAY
☽ △ ♂ **12:29 am**
☽ △ ♀ **4:52 am** 1:52 am
☽ ⚻ ♅ **5:02 am** 2:02 am
♀ □ ♅ **7:16 am** 4:16 am
☽ ⚻ ☿ **11:20 am** 8:20 am
☽ ⚻ ♃ **3:43 pm** 12:43 pm

☽ △ ♄ **7:59 pm** 4:59 pm
☽ ⚻ ♆ **11:53 pm** 8:53 pm

20 SUNDAY
☽ □ ♇ **8:40 am** 5:40 am
☽ ⚻ ☉ **11:45 am** 8:45 am
☿ ☌ ♃ 11:06 pm

21 MONDAY
☿ ☌ ♃ **2:06 am**
☽ □ ♂ **7:17 am** 4:17 am
☽ ☍ ♅ **8:58 am** 5:58 am
☽ □ ♀ **12:34 pm** 9:34 am
☽ △ ♃ **8:09 pm** 5:09 pm
☽ △ ☿ **10:26 pm** 7:26 pm
☽ □ ♄ **11:49 pm** 8:49 pm

22 TUESDAY
☽ △ ♆ **3:26 am** 12:26 am
☿ ⚺ ♄ **9:48 am** 6:48 am
☽ ⚹ ♇ **12:01 pm** 9:01 am
♂ □ ♅ **4:44 pm** 1:44 pm
☽ △ ☉ **6:52 pm** 3:52 pm

23 WEDNESDAY
☽ ⚻ ♅ **12:10 pm** 9:10 am
☽ ⚹ ♂ **1:12 pm** 10:12 am
☿ ☌ ♆ **1:44 pm** 10:44 am
☽ ⚹ ♀ **7:29 pm** 4:29 pm
☽ □ ♃ **11:59 pm** 8:59 pm

24 THURSDAY
☽ ⚹ ♄ **3:09 am** 12:09 am
☽ □ ♆ **6:30 am** 3:30 am
☽ □ ☿ **8:59 am** 5:59 am

☽ ⚺ ♇ **3:00 pm** 12:00 pm
☽ □ ☉ 10:37 pm

25 FRIDAY
☽ □ ☉ **1:37 am**
☽ △ ♅ **3:16 pm** 12:16 pm
☽ ⚺ ♂ **6:59 pm** 3:59 pm
☽ ⚺ ♀ 11:22 pm

26 SATURDAY
☽ ⚺ ♀ **2:22 am**
☽ ⚹ ♃ **3:48 am** 12:48 am
☽ ⚺ ♄ **6:27 am** 3:27 am
☿ ⚹ ♇ **6:35 am** 3:35 am
☽ ⚹ ♆ **9:37 am** 6:37 am
☽ ☌ ♇ **6:04 pm** 3:04 pm
☽ ⚹ ☿ **7:51 pm** 4:51 pm

27 SUNDAY
♀ ⚺ ♃ **3:34 am** 12:34 am
☽ ⚹ ☉ **8:35 am** 5:35 am
☽ □ ♅ **6:38 pm** 3:38 pm
☽ ☌ ♂ 10:08 pm

28 MONDAY
☽ ☌ ♂ **1:08 am**
☽ ⚺ ♃ **8:02 am** 5:02 am
☽ ☌ ♀ **9:48 am** 6:48 am
☽ ☌ ♄ **10:11 am** 7:11 am
☽ ⚺ ♆ **1:10 pm** 10:10 am
♀ ☌ ♄ **3:27 pm** 12:27 pm
☽ ⚺ ♇ **9:40 pm** 6:40 pm

29 TUESDAY
☽ ⚺ ☿ **7:52 am** 4:52 am
☽ ⚺ ☉ **4:27 pm** 1:27 pm
☽ ⚹ ♅ **10:54 pm** 7:54 pm

30 WEDNESDAY
♀ ⚺ ♆ **8:15 am** 5:15 am
☽ ⚺ ♂ **8:27 am** 5:27 am
☽ ☌ ♃ **1:24 pm** 10:24 am
☽ ⚺ ♄ **3:04 pm** 12:04 pm
☽ ☌ ♆ **5:55 pm** 2:55 pm
☽ ⚺ ♀ **6:42 pm** 3:42 pm
☽ ⚹ ♇ 11:37 pm

31 THURSDAY
☽ ⚹ ♇ **2:37 am**
☽ ☌ ☿ **10:35 pm** 7:35 pm
☽ ☌ ☉ 11:24 pm

Eastern time in bold type
Pacific time in medium type

MARCH 2022

DATE	SID.TIME	SUN	MOON	NODE	MERCURY	VENUS	MARS	JUPITER	SATURN	URANUS	NEPTUNE	PLUTO	CERES	PALLAS	JUNO	VESTA	CHIRON
1 T	10 35 7	10♓22 15	17≈36	25♉45R	16≈08	25♑35	26♑04	13♓52	18≈48	11♉33	22♓24	27♑46	4♊02	5♈22	10≈46	25♑14	10♈32
2 W	10 39 4	11 22 31	1♓50	25 33	18 01	26 24	26 49	14 06	18 55	11 35	22 26	27 48	4 17	5 45	11 09	25 43	10 35
3 Th	10 43 0	12 22 44	15 50	25 21	19 26	27 13	27 34	14 21	19 02	11 37	22 29	27 50	4 32	6 07	11 33	26 13	10 38
4 F	10 46 57	13 22 56	29 30	25 10	20 52	28 03	28 19	14 35	19 08	11 39	22 31	27 51	4 48	6 30	11 57	26 42	10 42
5 Sa	10 50 53	14 23 06	12♈50	25 01	22 19	28 54	29 03	14 50	19 15	11 41	22 33	27 53	5 03	6 53	12 20	27 12	10 45
6 Su	10 54 50	15 23 13	25 46	24 55	23 48	29 46	29 48	15 04	19 22	11 43	22 35	27 54	5 19	7 15	12 44	27 41	10 48
7 M	10 58 46	16 23 19	8♉21	24 51	25 18	0≈38	0≈38	15 19	19 29	11 46	22 38	27 55	5 35	7 38	13 07	28 11	10 51
8 T	11 2 43	17 23 23	20 38	24 50	26 49	1 31	1 18	15 33	19 35	11 48	22 40	27 57	5 51	8 01	13 31	28 40	10 55
9 W	11 6 39	18 23 25	2♊40	24 50	28 21	2 25	2 03	15 48	19 42	11 50	22 42	27 58	6 08	8 24	13 55	29 09	10 58
10 Th	11 10 36	19 23 24	14 32	24 51R	29 54	3 19	2 47	16 02	19 49	11 53	22 44	28 00	6 24	8 48	14 18	29 38	11 01
11 F	11 14 33	20 23 22	26 21	24 51	1♓28	4 13	3 32	16 17	19 55	11 55	22 47	28 01	6 41	9 11	14 42	0≈07	11 05
12 Sa	11 18 29	21 23 17	8♋12	24 49	3 04	5 09	4 17	16 31	20 02	11 58	22 49	28 02	6 58	9 34	15 05	0 36	11 08
13 Su	11 22 26	22 23 10	20 09	24 45	4 41	6 04	5 02	16 46	20 08	12 00	22 51	28 04	7 15	9 57	15 29	1 04	11 11
14 M	11 26 22	23 23 01	2♌17	24 39	6 19	7 01	5 47	17 00	20 14	12 03	22 54	28 05	7 33	10 21	15 52	1 33	11 15
15 T	11 30 19	24 22 50	14 40	24 30	7 58	7 58	6 32	17 15	20 21	12 05	22 56	28 06	7 50	10 44	16 15	2 02	11 18
16 W	11 34 15	25 22 36	27 20	24 21	9 38	8 55	7 17	17 29	20 27	12 08	22 58	28 07	8 06	11 08	16 39	2 30	11 22
17 Th	11 38 12	26 22 20	10♍19	24 10	11 20	9 53	8 02	17 44	20 34	12 10	23 00	28 09	8 26	11 32	17 02	2 59	11 25
18 F	11 42 8	27 22 03	23 35	24 00	13 02	10 51	8 47	17 58	20 40	12 13	23 03	28 10	8 44	11 55	17 25	3 27	11 28
19 Sa	11 46 5	28 21 43	7♎07	23 51	14 46	11 49	9 32	18 13	20 46	12 16	23 05	28 11	9 02	12 19	17 48	3 55	11 32
20 Su	11 50 2	29 21 22	20 53	23 45	16 31	12 48	10 17	18 27	20 52	12 18	23 07	28 12	9 21	12 43	18 12	4 23	11 35
21 M	11 53 58	0♈20 58	4♏18	23 41	18 18	13 48	11 02	18 41	20 58	12 21	23 09	28 13	9 39	13 07	18 35	4 51	11 39
22 T	11 57 55	1 20 33	18 51	23 39D	20 05	14 48	11 47	18 56	21 04	12 24	23 12	28 14	9 58	13 31	18 58	5 19	11 42
23 W	12 1 51	2 20 06	2♐57	23 39	21 54	15 48	12 33	19 10	21 10	12 27	23 14	28 15	10 17	13 55	19 21	5 47	11 46
24 Th	12 5 48	3 19 37	17 06	23 40	23 45	16 48	13 18	19 24	21 16	12 30	23 16	28 17	10 36	14 19	19 44	6 15	11 49
25 F	12 9 44	4 19 07	1♑14	23 41R	25 36	17 49	14 03	19 39	21 22	12 33	23 18	28 18	10 56	14 43	20 07	6 43	11 53
26 Sa	12 13 41	5 18 34	15 22	23 41	27 29	18 51	14 48	19 53	21 28	12 35	23 21	28 19	11 15	15 07	20 30	7 10	11 56
27 Su	12 17 37	6 18 01	29 28	23 38	29 23	19 52	15 33	20 07	21 34	12 38	23 23	28 20	11 35	15 32	20 53	7 38	12 00
28 M	12 21 34	7 17 25	13≈29	23 34	1♈18	20 54	16 19	20 21	21 40	12 41	23 25	28 20	11 54	15 56	21 16	8 05	12 03
29 T	12 25 31	8 16 47	27 24	23 28	3 15	21 56	17 04	20 36	21 46	12 44	23 27	28 21	12 14	16 21	21 39	8 32	12 07
30 W	12 29 27	9 16 08	11♓09	23 21	5 13	22 59	17 49	20 50	21 51	12 47	23 30	28 22	12 34	16 45	22 01	8 59	12 10
31 Th	12 33 24	10 15 27	24 42	23 13	7 12	24 02	18 34	21 04	21 57	12 50	23 32	28 23	12 54	17 09	22 24	9 26	12 14

EPHEMERIS CALCULATED FOR 12 MIDNIGHT GREENWICH MEAN TIME. ALL OTHER DATA AND FACING ASPECTARIAN PAGE IN **EASTERN TIME (BOLD)** AND PACIFIC TIME (REGULAR).

APRIL 2022

☽ Last Aspect day	ET / hr:mn / PT	asp	☽ Ingress sign	day	ET / hr:mn / PT
2	**9:51 am** 6:51 am	□♇	♉	2	**12:50 pm** 9:50 am
4	**9:53 pm** 6:53 pm	□♀	♊	4	**11:04 pm** 8:04 pm
6	**11:15 pm** 8:15 pm	△♂	♋	7	**11:30 am** 8:30 am
9	**9:01 pm** 6:01 pm	☍♇	♌	9	9:00 pm
9	**9:01 pm** 6:01 pm	☍♇	♌	10	**12:00 am**
12	**6:16 am** 3:16 am	☍♂	♍	12	**10:07 am** 7:07 am
14	**2:11 pm** 11:11 am	△♇	♎	14	**4:46 pm** 1:46 pm
16	**5:57 pm** 2:57 pm	□♇	♏	16	**8:23 pm** 5:23 pm
18	**7:55 pm** 4:55 pm	⚹♇	♐	18	**10:16 pm** 7:16 pm
20	**4:56 pm** 1:56 pm	□♃	♑	20	**11:52 pm** 8:52 pm
22	**11:53 pm** 8:53 pm	☌♇	♒	22	11:17 pm
22	**11:53 pm** 8:53 pm	☌♇	♒	23	**2:17 am**
24	**8:33 pm** 5:33 pm	□☿	♓	25	**6:15 am** 3:15 am
27	**9:36 am** 6:36 am	⚹♇	♈	27	**12:10 pm** 9:10 am
29	**5:38 pm** 2:38 pm	□♇	♉	29	**8:19 pm** 5:19 pm

☽ Phases & Eclipses phase	day	ET / hr:mn / PT
New Moon	3/31	11:24 pm
New Moon	1	**2:24 am**
2nd Quarter	8	11:48 pm
2nd Quarter	9	**2:48 am**
Full Moon	16	**2:55 pm** 11:55 am
4th Quarter	23	**7:56 am** 4:56 am
New Moon	30	**4:28 pm** 1:28 pm
●	30	10° ♉ 28'

Planet Ingress	day	ET / hr:mn / PT
♀ ♓	5	**11:18 am** 8:18 am
☿ ♉	10	**10:09 pm** 7:09 pm
♂ ♓	14	**11:06 pm** 8:06 pm
☉ ♉	19	**10:24 pm** 7:24 pm
⚵ ♓	20	**11:51 am** 8:51 am
☿ ♊	29	**6:23 pm** 3:23 pm
⚴ ♉	30	**4:50 am** 1:50 am

Planetary Motion	day	ET / hr:mn / PT
♇ ℞	29	**2:38 pm** 11:38 am

1 FRIDAY
☽ ☌ ☉ **2:24 am**
☽ ⚺ ♅ **4:59 am** 1:59 am
☽ ⚹ ♂ **6:07 pm** 3:07 pm
☽ ⚺ ♃ **8:57 pm** 5:57 pm
☽ ⚹ ♄ **10:04 pm** 7:04 pm
☽ ⚺ ♆ 9:49 pm

2 SATURDAY
☽ ⚺ ♆ **12:49 am**
☽ ⚹ ♀ **6:24 am** 3:24 am
☽ □ ♇ **9:51 am** 6:51 am
☉ ⚺ ♅ **2:10 pm** 11:10 am
☿ ⚺ ♅ **4:49 pm** 1:49 pm
☉ ☌ ☿ **7:11 pm** 4:11 pm

3 SUNDAY
☽ ☌ ♅ **1:47 pm** 10:47 am
☽ ⚺ ☉ **3:43 pm** 12:43 pm
☽ ⚺ ☿ **5:50 pm** 2:50 pm
♀ ⚺ ♇ 9:16 pm

4 MONDAY
♀ ⚺ ♇ **12:16 am**
☽ □ ♂ **7:09 am** 4:09 am
☽ ⚹ ♃ **7:29 am** 4:29 am
☽ □ ♄ **7:58 am** 4:58 am
☽ ⚹ ♆ **10:36 am** 7:36 am
♂ ⚺ ♃ **2:47 pm** 11:47 am
☽ △ ♇ **8:00 pm** 5:00 pm
♂ ☌ ♄ **9:51 pm** 6:51 pm
☽ □ ♀ **9:53 pm** 6:53 pm

5 TUESDAY
♃ ⚺ ♄ **11:24 pm** 8:24 pm
☽ ⚺ ♅ 10:25 pm

6 WEDNESDAY
☽ ⚺ ♅ **1:25 am**
☽ ⚹ ☉ **8:32 am** 5:32 am
♂ ⚺ ♆ **5:34 pm** 2:34 pm
☽ ⚹ ☿ **5:57 pm** 2:57 pm
☽ △ ♄ **8:26 pm** 5:26 pm
☽ □ ♃ **8:42 pm** 5:42 pm
☽ □ ♆ **10:54 pm** 7:54 pm
☽ △ ♂ **11:15 pm** 8:15 pm

7 THURSDAY
☽ ⚻ ♇ **8:25 am** 5:25 am
☿ ⚹ ♄ **8:37 am** 5:37 am
☿ ⚺ ♃ **11:14 am** 8:14 am
☽ △ ♀ **4:20 pm** 1:20 pm
☿ ⚺ ♆ **10:33 pm** 7:33 pm

8 FRIDAY
☿ ⚹ ♂ **2:19 pm** 11:19 am
☽ ⚹ ♅ **2:28 pm** 11:28 am
☽ □ ☉ 11:48 pm

9 SATURDAY
☽ □ ☉ **2:48 am**
☽ ⚻ ♄ **9:35 am** 6:35 am
☽ △ ♃ **10:36 am** 7:36 am
☽ △ ♆ **11:46 am** 8:46 am
☽ ⚻ ♂ **4:01 pm** 1:01 pm
☽ □ ☿ **7:25 pm** 4:25 pm
☽ ☍ ♇ **9:01 pm** 6:01 pm

10 SUNDAY
☿ □ ♇ **4:45 am** 1:45 am
☽ ⚻ ♀ **10:37 am** 7:37 am
☽ □ ♅ 11:25 pm

11 MONDAY
☽ □ ♅ **2:25 am**
☽ △ ☉ **7:01 pm** 4:01 pm
☽ ☍ ♄ **8:50 pm** 5:50 pm
☽ ⚻ ♃ **10:30 pm** 7:30 pm
☽ ⚻ ♆ **10:42 pm** 7:42 pm

12 TUESDAY
☽ ☍ ♂ **6:16 am** 3:16 am
☽ ⚻ ♇ **7:21 am** 4:21 am
♃ ☌ ♆ **10:42 am** 7:42 am
☽ △ ☿ **4:55 pm** 1:55 pm
☉ ⚹ ♄ **8:14 pm** 5:14 pm
♂ ⚺ ♇ 9:30 pm
☽ ☍ ♀ 10:27 pm

13 WEDNESDAY
♂ ⚺ ♇ **12:30 am**
☽ ☍ ♀ **1:27 am**
☽ △ ♅ **11:15 am** 8:15 am
☉ ⚺ ♆ **7:48 pm** 4:48 pm

14 THURSDAY
☉ ⚺ ♃ **4:14 am** 1:14 am
☽ ⚻ ♄ **4:37 am** 1:37 am
☽ ☍ ♆ **6:11 am** 3:11 am
☽ ☍ ♃ **6:49 am** 3:49 am
☽ ⚻ ☉ **6:58 am** 3:58 am
☽ △ ♇ **2:11 pm** 11:11 am
☽ ⚻ ♂ **4:23 pm** 1:23 pm

15 FRIDAY
☽ ⚻ ☿ **8:12 am** 5:12 am
☽ ⚻ ♀ **11:48 am** 8:48 am
☽ ⚻ ♅ **4:37 pm** 1:37 pm

16 SATURDAY
☽ △ ♄ **9:06 am** 6:06 am
☽ ⚻ ♆ **10:26 am** 7:26 am
☽ ⚻ ♃ **11:45 am** 8:45 am
☽ ☍ ☉ **2:55 pm** 11:55 am
☽ □ ♇ **5:57 pm** 2:57 pm
☽ △ ♂ **10:55 pm** 7:55 pm

17 SUNDAY
☽ ☍ ☿ **6:43 pm** 3:43 pm
☽ △ ♀ **6:51 pm** 3:51 pm
☽ ☍ ♅ **7:28 pm** 4:28 pm
☿ ⚹ ♀ **9:09 pm** 6:09 pm
☿ ☌ ♅ 9:51 pm

18 MONDAY
☿ ☌ ♅ **12:51 am**
♀ ⚹ ♅ **3:15 am** 12:15 am
☉ □ ♇ **11:14 am** 8:14 am
☽ □ ♄ **11:31 am** 8:31 am
☽ △ ♆ **12:40 pm** 9:40 am
☽ △ ♃ **2:37 pm** 11:37 am
☽ ⚹ ♇ **7:55 pm** 4:55 pm
☽ ⚻ ☉ **8:32 pm** 5:32 pm

19 TUESDAY
☽ □ ♂ **3:30 am** 12:30 am
☽ ⚻ ♅ **9:15 pm** 6:15 pm
☽ □ ♀ 9:33 pm

20 WEDNESDAY
☽ □ ♀ **12:33 am**
☽ ⚻ ☿ **3:02 am** 12:02 am
☽ ⚹ ♄ **1:18 pm** 10:18 am
☽ □ ♆ **2:20 pm** 11:20 am
☽ □ ♃ **4:56 pm** 1:56 pm
☽ ⚺ ♇ **9:31 pm** 6:31 pm
☽ △ ☉ 10:43 pm

21 THURSDAY
☽ △ ☉ **1:43 am**
☽ ⚹ ♂ **7:53 am** 4:53 am
☽ △ ♅ **11:18 pm** 8:18 pm

22 FRIDAY
☽ ⚹ ♀ **6:43 am** 3:43 am
☽ △ ☿ **11:13 am** 8:13 am
☽ ⚺ ♄ **3:43 pm** 12:43 pm
☽ ⚹ ♆ **4:38 pm** 1:38 pm
☽ ⚹ ♃ **7:58 pm** 4:58 pm
☽ ☌ ♇ **11:53 pm** 8:53 pm

23 SATURDAY
☽ □ ☉ **7:56 am** 4:56 am
☽ ⚺ ♂ **1:24 pm** 10:24 am
☽ □ ♅ 11:35 pm

24 SUNDAY
☽ □ ♅ **2:35 am**
☿ □ ♄ **9:50 am** 6:50 am
☽ ⚺ ♀ **2:33 pm** 11:33 am
☿ ⚹ ♆ **6:37 pm** 3:37 pm
☽ ☌ ♄ **7:33 pm** 4:33 pm
☽ ⚺ ♆ **8:22 pm** 5:22 pm
☽ □ ☿ **8:33 pm** 5:33 pm
☽ ⚺ ♃ 9:32 pm

25 MONDAY
☽ ⚺ ♃ **12:32 am**
☽ ⚺ ♇ **3:46 am** 12:46 am
☽ ⚹ ☉ **4:09 pm** 1:09 pm
☽ ☌ ♂ **8:51 pm** 5:51 pm

26 TUESDAY
☽ ⚹ ♅ **7:39 am** 4:39 am
☽ ☌ ♀ 9:50 pm
☿ ⚹ ♃ 10:11 pm
☽ ⚺ ♄ 10:18 pm
☽ ☌ ♆ 11:02 pm

27 WEDNESDAY
☽ ☌ ♀ **12:50 am**
☿ ⚹ ♃ **1:11 am**
☽ ⚺ ♄ **1:18 am**
☽ ☌ ♆ **2:02 am**
♀ ⚺ ♄ **6:43 am** 3:43 am
☽ ☌ ♃ **7:07 am** 4:07 am
☽ ⚹ ☿ **7:35 am** 4:35 am
☽ ⚹ ♇ **9:36 am** 6:36 am
♀ ☌ ♆ **3:12 pm** 12:12 pm
☽ ⚺ ☉ 11:52 pm

28 THURSDAY
☽ ⚺ ☉ **2:52 am**
☽ ⚺ ♂ **6:45 am** 3:45 am
☿ △ ♇ **8:05 am** 5:05 am
☽ ⚺ ♅ **2:52 pm** 11:52 am

29 FRIDAY
☽ ⚹ ♄ **9:16 am** 6:16 am
☽ ⚺ ♆ **9:53 am** 6:53 am
☽ ⚺ ♀ **1:59 pm** 10:59 am
☽ ⚺ ♃ **4:01 pm** 1:01 pm
☽ □ ♇ **5:38 pm** 2:38 pm
☽ ⚺ ☿ **8:28 pm** 5:28 pm

30 SATURDAY
☽ ☌ ☉ **4:28 pm** 1:28 pm
♀ ☌ ♃ **5:14 pm** 2:14 pm
☽ ⚹ ♂ **7:23 pm** 4:23 pm
☽ ☌ ♅ 9:24 pm

Eastern time in bold type
Pacific time in medium type

APRIL 2022

DATE	SID.TIME	SUN	MOON	NODE	MERCURY	VENUS	MARS	JUPITER	SATURN	URANUS	NEPTUNE	PLUTO	CERES	PALLAS	JUNO	VESTA	CHIRON
1 F	12 37 20	11♈14 43	8♉00	23♉06℞	9♈12	25≈05	19≈26	21♓18	22≈02	12♉53	23♓34	28♑24	13♊15	17♈34	22≈47	9≈53	12♈17
2 Sa	12 41 17	12 13 58	21 02	22 57	11 13	26 08	20 10	21 32	22 08	12 56	23 36	28 25	13 35	17 59	23 09	10 20	12 21
3 Su	12 45 13	13 13 10	3♊46	22 55D	13 15	27 11	20 50	21 46	22 13	13 00	23 38	28 26	13 56	18 23	23 32	10 46	12 24
4 M	12 49 10	14 12 21	16 14	22 56	15 18	28 15	21 35	22 00	22 19	13 03	23 41	28 26	14 16	18 48	23 54	11 13	12 28
5 T	12 53 6	15 11 29	28 27	22 58	17 22	29 19	22 21	22 14	22 24	13 06	23 43	28 27	14 37	19 13	24 17	11 39	12 31
6 W	12 57 3	16 10 35	10♋28	22 58	19 27	0♓23	23 06	22 28	22 29	13 09	23 45	28 28	14 58	19 38	24 39	12 06	12 35
7 Th	13 1 0	17 09 39	22 21	23 00	21 31	1 28	23 51	22 42	22 34	13 12	23 47	28 28	15 19	20 03	25 02	12 32	12 38
8 F	13 4 56	18 08 41	4♌11	23 00	23 36	2 32	24 37	22 56	22 39	13 15	23 49	28 29	15 40	20 28	25 24	12 58	12 42
9 Sa	13 8 53	19 07 40	16 02	23 01℞	25 41	3 37	25 22	23 09	22 44	13 19	23 51	28 30	16 02	20 53	25 46	13 24	12 45
10 Su	13 12 49	20 06 37	28 00	23 00	27 45	4 42	26 07	23 23	22 49	13 22	23 53	28 30	16 23	21 18	26 08	13 49	12 49
11 M	13 16 46	21 05 32	10♍08	22 59	29 49	5 48	26 53	23 37	22 54	13 25	23 55	28 31	16 44	21 43	26 30	14 15	12 52
12 T	13 20 42	22 04 25	22 33	22 56	1♉52	6 53	27 38	23 50	22 59	13 29	23 57	28 31	17 06	22 08	26 52	14 40	12 56
13 W	13 24 39	23 03 15	5♎17	22 52	3 53	7 59	28 23	24 04	23 04	13 32	24 00	28 32	17 28	22 34	27 14	15 06	12 59
14 Th	13 28 35	24 02 03	18 22	22 47	5 53	9 04	29 09	24 18	23 08	13 35	24 02	28 32	17 50	22 59	27 36	15 31	13 03
15 F	13 32 32	25 00 49	1♏50	22 43	7 50	10 10	29 54	24 31	23 13	13 38	24 04	28 33	18 12	23 24	27 58	15 56	13 06
16 Sa	13 36 29	25 59 32	15 39	22 39	9 45	11 16	0♓40	24 45	23 18	13 42	24 06	28 33	18 34	23 50	28 20	16 21	13 10
17 Su	13 40 25	26 58 14	29 47	22 36	11 38	12 23	1 25	24 58	23 22	13 45	24 08	28 34	18 56	24 15	28 41	16 46	13 13
18 M	13 44 22	27 56 54	14♐08	22 35D	13 27	13 29	2 10	25 11	23 26	13 48	24 10	28 34	19 18	24 41	29 03	17 10	13 17
19 T	13 48 18	28 55 32	28 37	22 35	15 13	14 36	2 56	25 25	23 31	13 52	24 12	28 34	19 41	25 06	29 24	17 35	13 20
20 W	13 52 15	29 54 08	13♑10	22 37	16 56	15 43	3 41	25 38	23 35	13 55	24 13	28 35	20 03	25 32	29 46	17 59	13 23
21 Th	13 56 11	0♉52 42	27 40	22 38	18 35	16 49	4 26	25 51	23 39	13 58	24 15	28 35	20 26	25 57	0♓07	18 23	13 27
22 F	14 0 8	1 51 15	12♒04	22 38	20 09	17 57	5 12	26 04	23 43	14 02	24 17	28 35	20 48	26 23	0 29	18 47	13 30
23 Sa	14 4 4	2 49 47	26 18	22 39℞	21 40	19 04	5 57	26 17	23 47	14 05	24 19	28 35	21 11	26 49	0 50	19 11	13 34
24 Su	14 8 1	3 48 16	10♓21	22 39	23 06	20 11	6 42	26 30	23 51	14 09	24 21	28 35	21 34	27 15	1 11	19 35	13 37
25 M	14 11 58	4 46 44	24 10	22 38	24 27	21 19	7 28	26 43	23 55	14 12	24 23	28 36	21 57	27 40	1 32	19 58	13 40
26 T	14 15 54	5 45 11	7♈46	22 36	25 44	22 26	8 13	26 56	23 59	14 16	24 25	28 36	22 20	28 06	1 53	20 22	13 44
27 W	14 19 51	6 43 36	21 08	22 34	26 57	23 34	8 59	27 09	24 02	14 19	24 27	28 36	22 43	28 32	2 14	20 45	13 47
28 Th	14 23 47	7 41 59	4♉16	22 32	28 04	24 42	9 44	27 21	24 06	14 22	24 28	28 36℞	23 06	28 58	2 34	21 08	13 50
29 F	14 27 44	8 40 20	17 10	22 30	29 06	25 50	10 29	27 34	24 10	14 26	24 30	28 36	23 30	29 24	2 55	21 31	13 54
30 Sa	14 31 40	9 38 40	29 50	22 29	0♊04	26 58	11 15	27 47	24 13	14 29	24 32	28 36	23 53	29 50	3 16	21 53	13 57

EPHEMERIS CALCULATED FOR 12 MIDNIGHT GREENWICH MEAN TIME. ALL OTHER DATA AND FACING ASPECTARIAN PAGE IN **EASTERN TIME (BOLD)** AND PACIFIC TIME (REGULAR).

MAY 2022

☽ Last Aspect day	ET / hr:mn / PT		asp	☽ Ingress sign	day	ET / hr:mn / PT	
2	**6:13 am**	3:13 am	☽⚹♀	♊	2	**6:47 am**	3:47 am
4	**4:37 pm**	1:37 pm	□♃	♋	4	**7:05 pm**	4:05 pm
7	**6:26 am**	3:26 am	△♃	♌	7	**7:50 am**	4:50 am
9	**8:39 am**	5:39 am	☍♄	♍	9	**6:53 pm**	3:53 pm
11		9:00 pm	△♇	♎	11		11:34 pm
12	**12:00 am**		△♇	♎	12	**2:34 am**	
14	**4:07 am**	1:07 am	□♇	♏	14	**6:34 am**	3:34 am
16	**5:28 am**	2:28 am	⚹♇	♐	16	**7:50 am**	4:50 am
17	**11:59 pm**	8:59 pm	⚹♄	♑	18	**8:02 am**	5:02 am
20	**8:00 am**	5:00 am	△☉	♒	20	**8:53 am**	5:53 am

☽ Last Aspect day	ET / hr:mn / PT		asp	☽ Ingress sign	day	ET / hr:mn / PT	
22	**3:19 am**	12:19 am	☌♄	♓	22	**11:49 am**	8:49 am
24	**5:33 pm**	2:33 pm	☌♂	♈	24	**5:39 pm**	2:39 pm
26	**11:20 pm**	8:20 pm	□♇	♉	26		11:22 pm
26	**11:20 pm**	8:20 pm	□♇	♉	27	**2:22 am**	
29	**10:11 am**	7:11 am	△♇	♊	29	**1:23 pm**	10:23 am
31	**4:10 pm**	1:10 pm	△♄	♋	31		10:49 pm
31	**4:10 pm**	1:10 pm	△♄	♋	6/1	**1:49 am**	

☽ Phases & Eclipses phase	day	ET / hr:mn / PT	
2nd Quarter	8	**8:21 pm**	5:21 pm
Full Moon	15		9:14 pm
Full Moon	16	**12:14 am**	
●	15/16	25° ♏ 18'	
4th Quarter	22	**2:43 pm**	11:43 am
New Moon	30	**7:30 am**	4:30 am

Planet Ingress		day	ET / hr:mn / PT	
♀	♈	2	**12:10 pm**	9:10 am
♃	♈	10	**7:22 pm**	4:22 pm
⚳	♋	15	**3:11 am**	12:11 am
☉	♊	20	**9:23 pm**	6:23 pm
☿	♉	22	**9:15 pm**	6:15 pm
⚶	♓	24	**5:46 am**	2:46 am
♂	♈	24	**7:17 pm**	4:17 pm
♀	♉	28	**10:46 am**	7:46 am

Planetary Motion		day	ET / hr:mn / PT	
☿	℞	10	**7:47 am**	4:47 am

1 SUNDAY
☽ ☌ ♅ **12:24 am**
♀ ⚹ ♇ **6:37 am** 3:37 am
☽ □ ♄ **7:33 pm** 4:33 pm
☽ ⚹ ♆ **8:04 pm** 5:04 pm

2 MONDAY
☽ ⚹ ♃ **3:19 am** 12:19 am
☽ △ ♇ **4:00 am** 1:00 am
☽ ⚹ ♀ **6:13 am** 3:13 am
☽ ☌ ☿ **11:05 am** 8:05 am

3 TUESDAY
☽ ⚺ ☉ **8:54 am** 5:54 am
☽ □ ♂ **10:41 am** 7:41 am
☽ ⚺ ♅ **12:10 pm** 9:10 am
♃ ⚹ ♇ **6:33 pm** 3:33 pm

4 WEDNESDAY
☽ △ ♄ **7:51 am** 4:51 am
☽ □ ♆ **8:16 am** 5:16 am
♂ ⚹ ♅ **11:47 am** 8:47 am
☽ ⚻ ♇ **4:14 pm** 1:14 pm
☽ □ ♃ **4:37 pm** 1:37 pm
☽ □ ♀ 9:57 pm
☽ ⚺ ☿ 11:33 pm

5 THURSDAY
☽ □ ♀ **12:57 am**
☽ ⚺ ☿ **2:33 am**
☉ ☌ ♅ **3:22 am** 12:22 am
☽ ⚹ ♅ 10:13 pm
☿ ⚹ ♀ 11:01 pm

6 FRIDAY
☽ ⚹ ♅ **1:13 am**
☿ ⚹ ♀ **2:01 am**
☽ ⚹ ☉ **3:03 am** 12:03 am
☽ △ ♂ **3:34 am** 12:34 am
☽ ⚻ ♄ **8:55 pm** 5:55 pm
☽ △ ♆ **9:13 pm** 6:13 pm

7 SATURDAY
☽ ☍ ♇ **4:59 am** 1:59 am
☉ ⚹ ♂ **5:48 am** 2:48 am
☽ △ ♃ **6:26 am** 3:26 am
☽ ⚹ ☿ **4:59 pm** 1:59 pm
☽ △ ♀ **8:02 pm** 5:02 pm

8 SUNDAY
☽ □ ♅ **1:41 pm** 10:41 am
☽ ⚻ ♂ **7:38 pm** 4:38 pm
☽ □ ☉ **8:21 pm** 5:21 pm

9 MONDAY
☽ ☍ ♄ **8:39 am** 5:39 am
☽ ⚻ ♆ **8:50 am** 5:50 am
☽ ⚻ ♇ **4:09 pm** 1:09 pm
☽ ⚻ ♃ **6:30 pm** 3:30 pm

10 TUESDAY
☽ □ ☿ **4:10 am** 1:10 am
☽ ⚻ ♀ **12:19 pm** 9:19 am
☽ △ ♅ **11:27 pm** 8:27 pm

11 WEDNESDAY
☽ ☍ ♂ **8:17 am** 5:17 am
☽ △ ☉ **10:02 am** 7:02 am
☽ ⚻ ♄ **5:10 pm** 2:10 pm
☽ ☍ ♆ **5:17 pm** 2:17 pm
☽ △ ♇ 9:00 pm

12 THURSDAY
☽ △ ♇ **12:00 am**
☽ ☍ ♃ **3:02 am** 12:02 am
☽ △ ☿ **10:54 am** 7:54 am
☽ ☍ ♀ **11:49 pm** 8:49 pm

13 FRIDAY
☽ ⚻ ♅ **5:27 am** 2:27 am
☽ ⚻ ♂ **4:28 pm** 1:28 pm
☽ ⚻ ☉ **7:00 pm** 4:00 pm
☽ △ ♄ **9:54 pm** 6:54 pm
☽ ⚻ ♆ **9:57 pm** 6:57 pm

14 SATURDAY
☽ □ ♇ **4:07 am** 1:07 am
☽ ⚻ ♃ **7:42 am** 4:42 am
☽ ⚻ ☿ **1:31 pm** 10:31 am

15 SUNDAY
☽ ⚻ ♀ **6:55 am** 3:55 am
☽ ☍ ♅ **8:04 am** 5:04 am
☉ □ ♄ **2:49 pm** 11:49 am
☉ ⚹ ♆ **3:15 pm** 12:15 pm
☽ △ ♂ **9:02 pm** 6:02 pm
♀ ⚺ ♅ **10:14 pm** 7:14 pm
☽ □ ♄ **11:38 pm** 8:38 pm
☽ △ ♆ **11:40 pm** 8:40 pm
☽ ☍ ☉ 9:14 pm

16 MONDAY
☽ ☍ ☉ **12:14 am**
☽ ⚹ ♇ **5:28 am** 2:28 am
☽ △ ♃ **9:34 am** 6:34 am
☽ ☍ ☿ **1:19 pm** 10:19 am

17 TUESDAY
☽ ⚻ ♅ **8:46 am** 5:46 am
☽ △ ♀ **11:31 am** 8:31 am
♄ ⚺ ♆ **11:39 am** 8:39 am
☽ □ ♂ **11:51 pm** 8:51 pm
☽ □ ♆ **11:59 pm** 8:59 pm
☽ ⚹ ♄ **11:59 pm** 8:59 pm
♂ ☌ ♆ 11:33 pm
♂ ⚺ ♄ 11:43 pm

18 WEDNESDAY
♂ ☌ ♆ **2:33 am**
♂ ⚺ ♄ **2:43 am**
☽ ⚻ ☉ **3:48 am** 12:48 am
☽ ⚺ ♇ **5:39 am** 2:39 am
☽ □ ♃ **10:21 am** 7:21 am
☽ ⚻ ☿ **12:00 pm** 9:00 am

19 THURSDAY
☉ △ ♇ **8:11 am** 5:11 am
☽ △ ♅ **9:16 am** 6:16 am
☽ □ ♀ **4:02 pm** 1:02 pm
☿ ⚹ ♃ **9:33 pm** 6:33 pm
☽ ⚹ ♆ 9:41 pm
☽ ⚺ ♄ 9:43 pm

20 FRIDAY
☽ ⚹ ♆ **12:41 am**
☽ ⚺ ♄ **12:43 am**
☽ ⚹ ♂ **3:07 am** 12:07 am
☽ ☌ ♇ **6:24 am** 3:24 am
☽ △ ☉ **8:00 am** 5:00 am
☽ △ ☿ **11:11 am** 8:11 am
☽ ⚹ ♃ **11:54 am** 8:54 am

21 SATURDAY
☽ □ ♅ **11:16 am** 8:16 am
☉ ☌ ☿ **3:18 pm** 12:18 pm
☽ ⚹ ♀ **10:40 pm** 7:40 pm

22 SUNDAY
☽ ⚺ ♆ **3:17 am** 12:17 am
☽ ☌ ♄ **3:19 am** 12:19 am
☽ ⚺ ♂ **8:39 am** 5:39 am
☽ ⚺ ♇ **9:11 am** 6:11 am
☽ □ ☿ **12:12 pm** 9:12 am
☽ □ ☉ **2:43 pm** 11:43 am
☽ ⚺ ♃ **3:40 pm** 12:40 pm
♂ ⚹ ♇ **6:15 pm** 3:15 pm

23 MONDAY
☉ ⚹ ♃ **7:05 am** 4:05 am
☽ ⚹ ♅ **3:54 pm** 12:54 pm
☿ ⚹ ♂ **11:27 pm** 8:27 pm

24 TUESDAY
♀ ⚺ ♆ **6:30 am** 3:30 am
♀ ⚹ ♄ **7:06 am** 4:06 am
☽ ☌ ♆ **8:41 am** 5:41 am
☽ ⚺ ♄ **8:45 am** 5:45 am
☽ ⚺ ♀ **8:54 am** 5:54 am
☽ ⚹ ♇ **2:49 pm** 11:49 am
☽ ⚹ ☿ **3:50 pm** 12:50 pm
☽ ☌ ♂ **5:33 pm** 2:33 pm
☽ ☌ ♃ **10:27 pm** 7:27 pm
☽ ⚹ ☉ 10:03 pm

25 WEDNESDAY
☽ ⚹ ☉ **1:03 am**
☿ △ ♇ **5:49 pm** 2:49 pm
☽ ⚺ ♅ **11:33 pm** 8:33 pm

26 THURSDAY
☽ ⚺ ♆ **5:03 pm** 2:03 pm
☽ ⚹ ♄ **5:06 pm** 2:06 pm
☿ ⚺ ♀ **5:07 pm** 2:07 pm
☽ ⚺ ☿ **10:16 pm** 7:16 pm
☽ ☌ ♀ **11:00 pm** 8:00 pm
☽ □ ♇ **11:20 pm** 8:20 pm
♀ □ ♇ 11:29 pm

27 FRIDAY
♀ □ ♇ **2:29 am**
☽ ⚺ ♂ **5:54 am** 2:54 am
☽ ⚺ ♃ **8:12 am** 5:12 am
☽ ⚺ ☉ **2:56 pm** 11:56 am

28 SATURDAY
☽ ☌ ♅ **9:50 am** 6:50 am

29 SUNDAY
☽ ⚹ ♆ **3:49 am** 12:49 am
☽ □ ♄ **3:51 am** 12:51 am
♂ ☌ ♃ **6:31 am** 3:31 am
☽ ☌ ☿ **7:15 am** 4:15 am
☽ △ ♇ **10:11 am** 7:11 am
☽ ⚺ ♀ **4:15 pm** 1:15 pm
☽ ⚹ ♃ **8:12 pm** 5:12 pm
☽ ⚹ ♂ **8:55 pm** 5:55 pm

30 MONDAY
☽ ☌ ☉ **7:30 am** 4:30 am
☽ ⚺ ♅ **10:00 pm** 7:00 pm

31 TUESDAY
♀ ⚺ ♃ **2:34 pm** 11:34 am
☽ □ ♆ **4:10 pm** 1:10 pm
☽ △ ♄ **4:10 pm** 1:10 pm
♄ ⚺ ♆ **6:03 pm** 3:03 pm
☽ ⚺ ☿ **6:19 pm** 3:19 pm
☽ ⚻ ♇ **10:30 pm** 7:30 pm

Eastern time in bold type
Pacific time in medium type

MAY 2022

DATE	SID.TIME	SUN	MOON	NODE	MERCURY	VENUS	MARS	JUPITER	SATURN	URANUS	NEPTUNE	PLUTO	CERES	PALLAS	JUNO	VESTA	CHIRON
1 Su	14 35 37	10♉36 58	12♊18	22♉28ᴚ	0♊56	28♓06	12♓56	27♓48	24≈16	14♉33	24♓34	28♑36ᴚ	24♓16	0♉17	3♓36	22≈16	14♈00
2 M	14 39 33	11 35 14	24 33	22 28	1 43	29 14	13 30	28 12	24 20	14 36	24 35	28 36	24 40	0 43	3 57	22 38	14 03
3 T	14 43 30	12 33 29	6♋38	22 28	2 25	0♈22	13 30	28 24	24 23	14 40	24 37	28 36	25 04	1 09	4 17	23 00	14 06
4 W	14 47 27	13 31 42	18 36	22 29	3 02	1 31	14 16	28 36	24 26	14 43	24 39	28 36	25 27	1 35	4 37	23 22	14 10
5 Th	14 51 23	14 29 52	0♌27	22 29	3 33	2 39	15 01	28 49	24 29	14 47	24 40	28 36	25 51	2 01	4 57	23 43	14 13
6 F	14 55 20	15 28 01	12 16	22 30	3 59	3 48	15 46	29 01	24 32	14 50	24 42	28 35	26 15	2 28	5 17	24 05	14 16
7 Sa	14 59 16	16 26 09	24 08	22 31	4 20	4 57	16 31	29 13	24 35	14 54	24 45	28 35	26 39	2 54	5 37	24 26	14 19
8 Su	15 3 13	17 24 14	6♍05	22 31	4 36	6 05	17 17	29 25	24 37	14 57	24 45	28 35	27 03	3 21	5 57	24 47	14 22
9 M	15 7 9	18 22 17	18 12	22 32ᴚ	4 46	7 14	18 02	29 37	24 40	15 01	24 47	28 35	27 27	3 47	6 16	25 08	14 25
10 T	15 11 6	19 20 18	0♎35	22 32	4 51ᴚ	8 23	18 47	29 49	24 42	15 04	24 48	28 34	27 51	4 14	6 36	25 29	14 28
11 W	15 15 2	20 18 17	13 17	22 32	4 51	9 32	19 32	0♈00	24 45	15 07	24 50	28 34	28 15	4 40	6 55	25 49	14 31
12 Th	15 18 59	21 16 15	26 21	22 31	4 46	10 41	20 17	0 12	24 47	15 11	24 51	28 34	28 40	5 07	7 14	26 09	14 34
13 F	15 22 56	22 14 11	9♏50	22 31D	4 36	11 51	21 02	0 24	24 49	15 14	24 52	28 33	29 04	5 33	7 33	26 29	14 37
14 Sa	15 26 52	23 12 04	23 45	22 31	4 22	13 00	21 47	0 35	24 52	15 18	24 54	28 33	29 28	6 00	7 52	26 49	14 40
15 Su	15 30 49	24 09 57	8♏,05	22 31ᴚ	4 04	14 09	22 32	0 46	24 54	15 21	24 55	28 33	29 53	6 27	8 11	27 08	14 43
16 M	15 34 45	25 07 47	22 41	22 31	3 42	15 19	23 17	0 58	24 56	15 25	24 57	28 32	0♈57ᴚ	6 53	8 30	27 28	14 46
17 T	15 38 42	26 05 37	7♐33	22 31	3 16	16 28	24 02	1 09	24 58	15 28	24 58	28 32	0 42	7 20	8 49	27 48	14 49
18 W	15 42 38	27 03 25	22 30	22 31	2 48	17 38	24 47	1 20	24 59	15 31	24 59	28 31	1 06	7 47	9 07	28 06	14 51
19 Th	15 46 35	28 01 12	7♑26	22 30	2 17	18 47	25 32	1 31	25 01	15 35	25 01	28 31	1 31	8 14	9 25	28 24	14 54
20 F	15 50 31	28 58 57	22 11	22 30	1 45	19 57	26 17	1 42	25 02	15 38	25 02	28 30	1 56	8 41	9 44	28 42	14 57
21 Sa	15 54 28	29 56 41	6≈41	22 29	1 11	21 07	27 02	1 53	25 04	15 42	25 03	28 30	2 21	9 08	10 02	29 00	15 00
22 Su	15 58 25	0♊54 25	20 51	22 29D	0 36	22 16	27 47	2 03	25 06	15 45	25 04	28 29	2 45	9 35	10 20	29 18	15 02
23 M	16 2 21	1 52 07	4♓40	22 29	0 02	23 26	28 32	2 14	25 07	15 48	25 05	28 29	3 10	10 02	10 37	29 36	15 05
24 T	16 6 18	2 49 48	18 08	22 29	29♉28	24 36	29 17	2 24	25 08	15 52	25 06	28 28	3 35	10 29	10 55	29 53	15 08
25 W	16 10 14	3 47 28	1♈16	22 30	28 55	25 46	0♈01	2 35	25 09	15 55	25 08	28 27	4 00	10 56	11 13	0♓10	15 10
26 Th	16 14 11	4 45 07	14 07	22 31	28 24	26 56	0 46	2 45	25 10	15 58	25 09	28 26	4 25	11 23	11 30	0 27	15 13
27 F	16 18 7	5 42 45	26 42	22 32	27 55	28 07	1 31	2 55	25 11	16 02	25 10	28 26	4 51	11 50	11 47	0 43	15 15
28 Sa	16 22 4	6 40 22	9♉04	22 33	27 28	29 17	2 16	3 05	25 12	16 05	25 11	28 25	5 16	12 18	12 04	0 59	15 18
29 Su	16 26 0	7 37 58	21 16	22 33ᴚ	27 05	0♉27	3 00	3 15	25 13	16 08	25 12	28 24	5 41	12 45	12 21	1 15	15 20
30 M	16 29 57	8 35 33	3♊19	22 33	26 45	1 37	3 45	3 25	25 13	16 12	25 13	28 23	6 06	13 12	12 37	1 31	15 23
31 T	16 33 54	9 33 07	15 16	22 32	26 29	2 48	4 29	3 35	25 14	16 15	25 14	28 23	6 32	13 39	12 54	1 46	15 25

EPHEMERIS CALCULATED FOR 12 MIDNIGHT GREENWICH MEAN TIME. ALL OTHER DATA AND FACING ASPECTARIAN PAGE IN **EASTERN TIME (BOLD)** AND PACIFIC TIME (REGULAR).

JUNE 2022

☽ Last Aspect day	ET / hr:mn / PT	asp	☽ Ingress sign	day	ET / hr:mn / PT
3	**11:15 am** 8:15 am	☍♇	♌	3	**2:38 pm** 11:38 am
5	**7:12 pm** 4:12 pm	☐☿	♍	5	11:22 pm
5	**7:12 pm** 4:12 pm	☐☿	♍	6	**2:22 am**
8	**8:09 am** 5:09 am	△♇	♎	8	**11:23 am** 8:23 am
10	**1:36 pm** 10:36 am	☐♇	♏	10	**4:41 pm** 1:41 pm
12	**5:40 pm** 2:40 pm	☍☿	♐	12	**6:31 pm** 3:31 pm
14	**10:58 am** 7:58 am	☐♆	♑	14	**6:14 pm** 3:14 pm
16	**2:41 pm** 11:41 am	☌♇	♒	16	**5:44 pm** 2:44 pm
18	**2:50 pm** 11:50 am	△☉	♓	18	**7:01 pm** 4:01 pm
20	**11:11 pm** 8:11 pm	☐☉	♈	20	**11:37 pm** 8:37 pm
23	**4:02 am** 1:02 am	☐♇	♉	23	**7:58 am** 4:58 am
25	**3:02 pm** 12:02 pm	△♇	♊	25	**7:13 pm** 4:13 pm
27	**10:38 pm** 7:38 pm	☐♆	♋	28	**7:53 am** 4:53 am
30	**4:14 pm** 1:14 pm	☍♇	♌	30	**8:40 pm** 5:40 pm

☽ Phases & Eclipses phase	day	ET / hr:mn / PT
2nd Quarter	7	**10:48 am** 7:48 am
Full Moon	14	**7:52 am** 4:52 am
4th Quarter	20	**11:11 pm** 8:11 pm
New Moon	28	**10:52 pm** 7:52 pm

Planet Ingress	day	ET / hr:mn / PT
☿ ♊	13	**11:27 am** 8:27 am
☉ ♋	21	**5:14 am** 2:14 am
♀ ♊	22	**8:34 pm** 5:34 pm

Planetary Motion	day	ET / hr:mn / PT
☿ D	3	**4:00 am** 1:00 am
♄ ℞	4	**5:47 pm** 2:47 pm
♆ ℞	28	**3:55 am** 12:55 am

1 WEDNESDAY
☽☐♃ **9:35 am** 6:35 am
☽✶♀ **11:24 am** 8:24 am
☽☐♂ **1:31 pm** 10:31 am
☽⚺☉ 10:33 pm

2 THURSDAY
☽⚺☉ **1:33 am**
☽✶♅ **11:05 am** 8:05 am

3 FRIDAY
☽⚻♄ **5:02 am** 2:02 am
☽△♆ **5:05 am** 2:05 am
☽✶☿ **6:44 am** 3:44 am
☽☍♇ **11:15 am** 8:15 am
♀⚺♂ **5:18 pm** 2:18 pm
☽△♃ **11:09 pm** 8:09 pm

4 SATURDAY
☽△♂ **6:15 am** 3:15 am
☽☐♀ **6:47 am** 3:47 am
☽✶☉ **7:23 pm** 4:23 pm
☽☐♅ **11:47 pm** 8:47 pm

5 SUNDAY
☽☍♄ **5:03 pm** 2:03 pm
☽⚻♆ **5:10 pm** 2:10 pm
☽☐☿ **7:12 pm** 4:12 pm
☽⚻♇ **11:01 pm** 8:01 pm

6 MONDAY
☽⚻♃ **11:19 am** 8:19 am
☽⚻♂ **9:09 pm** 6:09 pm
☽△♀ 9:05 pm

7 TUESDAY
☽△♀ **12:05 am**
☉⚺♅ **5:36 am** 2:36 am
☽△♅ **10:26 am** 7:26 am
☽☐☉ **10:48 am** 7:48 am
☽⚻♄ 11:34 pm
☽☍♆ 11:44 pm

8 WEDNESDAY
☽⚻♄ **2:34 am**
☽☍♆ **2:44 am**
☽△☿ **5:56 am** 2:56 am
☽△♇ **8:09 am** 5:09 am
☽☍♃ **8:26 pm** 5:26 pm

9 THURSDAY
☽☍♂ **8:16 am** 5:16 am
☽⚻♀ **1:08 pm** 10:08 am
☽⚻♅ **5:39 pm** 2:39 pm
☽△☉ **9:57 pm** 6:57 pm

10 FRIDAY
☽△♄ **8:27 am** 5:27 am
☽⚻♆ **8:41 am** 5:41 am
☽⚻☿ **1:27 pm** 10:27 am
☽☐♇ **1:36 pm** 10:36 am
☿△♇ **5:21 pm** 2:21 pm
☽⚻♃ 10:38 pm

11 SATURDAY
☽⚻♃ **1:38 am**
☽⚻♂ **2:55 pm** 11:55 am
♀☌♅ **6:58 pm** 3:58 pm
☽☍♅ **9:05 pm** 6:05 pm
☽☍♀ **9:16 pm** 6:16 pm

12 SUNDAY
☽⚻☉ **4:29 am** 1:29 am
☽☐♄ **10:45 am** 7:45 am
☽△♆ **11:01 am** 8:01 am
☽✶♇ **3:34 pm** 12:34 pm
☽☍☿ **5:40 pm** 2:40 pm

13 MONDAY
☽△♃ **3:26 am** 12:26 am
☽△♂ **6:05 pm** 3:05 pm
☽⚻♅ **9:40 pm** 6:40 pm
☽⚻♀ 10:47 pm

14 TUESDAY
☽⚻♀ **1:47 am**
☽☍☉ **7:52 am** 4:52 am
☽✶♄ **10:38 am** 7:38 am
☽☐♆ **10:58 am** 7:58 am
☽⚺♇ **3:18 pm** 12:18 pm
☽⚻☿ **7:55 pm** 4:55 pm

15 WEDNESDAY
☽☐♃ **3:21 am** 12:21 am
☽☐♂ **7:50 pm** 4:50 pm
☽△♅ **9:10 pm** 6:10 pm

16 THURSDAY
☉△♄ **3:13 am** 12:13 am
☽△♀ **5:09 am** 2:09 am
☉☐♆ **9:41 am** 6:41 am
☽⚺♄ **9:58 am** 6:58 am
☽✶♆ **10:23 am** 7:23 am
☽⚻☉ **10:26 am** 7:26 am
☽☌♇ **2:41 pm** 11:41 am
☽△☿ **10:30 pm** 7:30 pm
♂⚺♅ 10:37 pm

17 FRIDAY
♂⚺♅ **1:37 am**
☽✶♃ **3:28 am** 12:28 am
☽☐♅ **9:37 pm** 6:37 pm
☽✶♂ **10:35 pm** 7:35 pm

18 SATURDAY
☽☐♀ **10:10 am** 7:10 am
☽☌♄ **10:47 am** 7:47 am
☽⚺♆ **11:19 am** 8:19 am
☽△☉ **2:50 pm** 11:50 am
☽⚺♇ **3:45 pm** 12:45 pm
♀☐♄ **5:32 pm** 2:32 pm
♀✶♆ 9:06 pm

19 SUNDAY
♀✶♆ **12:06 am**
☽☐☿ **4:01 am** 1:01 am
☉⚻♇ **4:10 am** 1:10 am
☽⚺♃ **5:45 am** 2:45 am
☽✶♅ 9:50 pm

20 MONDAY
☽✶♅ **12:50 am**
☿✶♃ **3:44 am** 12:44 am
☽⚺♂ **4:35 am** 1:35 am
☽⚺♄ **2:41 pm** 11:41 am
☽☌♆ **3:21 pm** 12:21 pm
☽✶♀ **7:11 pm** 4:11 pm
☽✶♇ **8:01 pm** 5:01 pm
☽☐☉ **11:11 pm** 8:11 pm

21 TUESDAY
♀△♇ **4:23 am** 1:23 am
☽☌♃ **11:37 am** 8:37 am
☽✶☿ **2:34 pm** 11:34 am

22 WEDNESDAY
☽⚺♅ **7:50 am** 4:50 am
☽☌♂ **2:58 pm** 11:58 am
☽✶♄ **10:19 pm** 7:19 pm
☽⚺♆ **11:10 pm** 8:10 pm

23 THURSDAY
☽☐♇ **4:02 am** 1:02 am
☽⚺♀ **9:10 am** 6:10 am
☽✶☉ **12:12 pm** 9:12 am
☽⚺♃ **9:13 pm** 6:13 pm

24 FRIDAY
☽⚺☿ **6:48 am** 3:48 am
☽☌♅ **6:15 pm** 3:15 pm

25 SATURDAY
☽⚺♂ **5:14 am** 2:14 am
☽☐♄ **9:02 am** 6:02 am
☽✶♆ **10:05 am** 7:05 am
☽△♇ **3:02 pm** 12:02 pm

26 SUNDAY
☽☌♀ **3:03 am** 12:03 am
☽⚺☉ **4:47 am** 1:47 am
☽✶♃ **9:27 am** 6:27 am

27 MONDAY
☽☌☿ **3:22 am** 12:22 am
☽⚺♅ **6:44 am** 3:44 am
♂✶♄ **6:29 pm** 3:29 pm
☽△♄ **9:23 pm** 6:23 pm
☽✶♂ **9:35 pm** 6:35 pm
☽☐♆ **10:38 pm** 7:38 pm

28 TUESDAY
☽⚻♇ **3:33 am** 12:33 am
☿⚺♅ **5:02 am** 2:02 am
♂⚺♆ **3:08 pm** 12:08 pm
☉☐♃ **8:59 pm** 5:59 pm
☽⚺♀ **10:37 pm** 7:37 pm
☽☐♃ **10:44 pm** 7:44 pm
☽☌☉ **10:52 pm** 7:52 pm
♀✶♃ **11:52 pm** 8:52 pm

29 WEDNESDAY
☉⚺♀ **10:09 am** 7:09 am
☽✶♅ **7:48 pm** 4:48 pm
☽⚺☿ 11:00 pm

30 THURSDAY
☽⚺☿ **2:00 am**
☽⚻♄ **10:01 am** 7:01 am
☽△♆ **11:28 am** 8:28 am
☽☐♂ **2:17 pm** 11:17 am
☽☍♇ **4:14 pm** 1:14 pm

Eastern time in bold type
Pacific time in medium type

JUNE 2022

DATE	SID.TIME	SUN	MOON	NODE	MERCURY	VENUS	MARS	JUPITER	SATURN	URANUS	NEPTUNE	PLUTO	CERES	PALLAS	JUNO	VESTA	CHIRON
1 W	16 37 50	10♊30 40	27♊08	22♉30R	26♉17R	3♉58	5♈14	3♈44	25≈14	16♉18	25♓15	28♑21R	6♋57	14♉07	13♓10	2♈10	15♈27
2 Th	16 41 47	11 28 12	8♋58	22 27	26 09	5 09	5 58	3 54	25 15	16 21	25 15	28 20	7 22	14 34	13 26	2 16	15 30
3 F	16 45 43	12 25 43	20 47	22 24	26 05D	6 19	6 42	4 03	25 15	16 25	25 16	28 20	7 48	15 02	13 42	2 30	15 32
4 Sa	16 49 40	13 23 12	2♌40	22 20	26 06	7 30	7 27	4 12	25 16R	16 28	25 17	28 19	8 13	15 29	13 58	2 44	15 34
5 Su	16 53 36	14 20 40	14 38	22 18	26 11	8 40	8 11	4 21	25 15	16 31	25 18	28 18	8 39	15 57	14 13	2 58	15 36
6 M	16 57 33	15 18 07	26 45	22 15	26 21	9 51	8 55	4 30	25 15	16 34	25 18	28 17	9 04	16 24	14 29	3 11	15 38
7 T	17 1 29	16 15 33	9♍06	22 14D	26 35	11 01	9 39	4 39	25 15	16 37	25 19	28 16	9 30	16 52	14 44	3 24	15 40
8 W	17 5 26	17 12 58	21 44	22 14	26 54	12 12	10 23	4 48	25 15	16 40	25 19	28 15	9 56	17 19	14 59	3 37	15 42
9 Th	17 9 23	18 10 21	4≏43	22 15	27 17	13 23	11 07	4 57	25 14	16 43	25 20	28 14	10 21	17 47	15 14	3 49	15 44
10 F	17 13 19	19 07 43	18 06	22 16	27 44	14 34	11 51	5 05	25 14	16 47	25 20	28 13	10 47	18 15	15 28	4 01	15 46
11 Sa	17 17 16	20 05 04	1♏56	22 18	28 16	15 45	12 35	5 13	25 13	16 50	25 21	28 12	11 13	18 42	15 42	4 12	15 48
12 Su	17 21 12	21 02 25	16 13	22 19R	28 52	16 56	13 19	5 21	25 13	16 53	25 22	28 11	11 39	19 10	15 56	4 24	15 50
13 M	17 25 9	21 59 44	0♐55	22 19	29 32	18 06	14 03	5 29	25 12	16 56	25 22	28 10	12 05	19 38	16 10	4 35	15 52
14 T	17 29 5	22 57 03	15 55	22 17	0♊16	19 17	14 47	5 37	25 11	16 59	25 22	28 09	12 30	20 06	16 24	4 45	15 54
15 W	17 33 2	23 54 21	1♑07	22 14	1 04	20 28	15 31	5 45	25 10	17 01	25 23	28 08	12 56	20 33	16 37	4 55	15 55
16 Th	17 36 59	24 51 38	16 20	22 10	1 56	21 40	16 14	5 53	25 09	17 04	25 23	28 07	13 22	21 01	16 51	5 05	15 57
17 F	17 40 55	25 48 55	1≈25	22 05	2 52	22 51	16 58	6 00	25 08	17 07	25 24	28 06	13 48	21 29	17 04	5 14	15 59
18 Sa	17 44 52	26 46 12	16 12	22 01	3 52	24 02	17 41	6 08	25 07	17 10	25 24	28 05	14 14	21 57	17 16	5 24	16 00
19 Su	17 48 48	27 43 28	0♓35	21 57	4 55	25 13	18 25	6 15	25 06	17 13	25 25	28 03	14 40	22 25	17 29	5 32	16 02
20 M	17 52 45	28 40 43	14 31	21 55	6 02	26 24	19 08	6 22	25 04	17 16	25 25	28 02	15 06	22 53	17 41	5 40	16 04
21 T	17 56 41	29 37 59	28 00	21 54	7 12	27 36	19 51	6 29	25 03	17 19	25 25	28 00	15 33	23 21	17 53	5 48	16 05
22 W	18 0 38	0♋35 14	11♈04	21 54	8 26	28 47	20 35	6 35	25 01	17 21	25 26	28 00	15 59	23 49	18 05	5 56	16 06
23 Th	18 4 34	1 32 29	23 47	21 56	9 44	29 58	21 18	6 42	24 59	17 24	25 26	27 58	16 25	24 17	18 16	6 03	16 08
24 F	18 8 31	2 29 44	6♉11	21 57	11 05	1♊10	22 01	6 48	24 58	17 27	25 26	27 57	16 51	24 45	18 27	6 09	16 09
25 Sa	18 12 28	3 26 59	18 22	21 58R	12 28	2 21	22 44	6 55	24 56	17 29	25 26	27 56	17 17	25 13	18 38	6 15	16 10
26 Su	18 16 24	4 24 14	0♊23	21 58	13 56	3 33	23 27	7 01	24 54	17 32	25 26	27 55	17 44	25 42	18 49	6 21	16 12
27 M	18 20 21	5 21 29	12 18	21 56	15 27	4 44	24 10	7 07	24 52	17 35	25 27R	27 53	18 10	26 10	18 59	6 26	16 13
28 T	18 24 17	6 18 43	24 09	21 52	17 02	5 56	24 53	7 12	24 50	17 37	25 27	27 51	18 36	26 38	19 09	6 31	16 14
29 W	18 28 14	7 15 58	5♋58	21 45	18 39	7 07	25 35	7 18	24 47	17 40	25 27	27 51	19 03	27 06	19 19	6 35	16 15
30 Th	18 32 10	8 13 12	17 48	21 38	20 20	8 19	26 18	7 24	24 45	17 42	25 27	27 49	19 29	27 34	19 28	6 39	16 16

EPHEMERIS CALCULATED FOR 12 MIDNIGHT GREENWICH MEAN TIME. ALL OTHER DATA AND FACING ASPECTARIAN PAGE IN **EASTERN TIME (BOLD)** AND PACIFIC TIME (REGULAR).

JULY 2022

☽ Last Aspect day	ET / hr:mn	PT	asp	☽ Ingress sign	day	ET / hr:mn	PT
3	**5:59 am**	2:59 am	△♂	♍	3	**8:31 am**	5:31 am
5	**2:04 pm**	11:04 am	△♇	♎	5	**6:25 pm**	3:25 pm
7	**9:04 pm**	6:04 pm	□♇	♏	7		10:15 pm
7	**9:04 pm**	6:04 pm	□♇	♏	8	**1:15 am**	
9		9:34 pm	⚹♇	♐	10	**4:34 am**	1:34 am
10	**12:34 am**		⚹♇	♐	10	**4:34 am**	1:34 am
11	**9:42 pm**	6:42 pm	□♆	♑	12	**5:01 am**	2:01 am
13		9:17 pm	☌♇	♒	14	**4:13 am**	1:13 am
14	**12:17 am**		☌♇	♒	14	**4:13 am**	1:13 am
15		9:36 pm	△♀	♓	16	**4:18 am**	1:18 am
16	**12:36 am**		△♀	♓	16	**4:18 am**	1:18 am
17		11:43 pm	⚹♇	♈	18	**7:17 am**	4:17 am
18	**2:43 am**		⚹♇	♈	18	**7:17 am**	4:17 am
20	**10:19 am**	7:19 am	□☉	♉	20	**2:23 pm**	11:23 am
22	**7:45 pm**	4:45 pm	△♇	♊	22		10:11 pm
22	**7:45 pm**	4:45 pm	△♇	♊	23	**1:11 am**	
25	**4:14 am**	1:14 am	□♆	♋	25	**1:54 pm**	10:54 am
27	**8:54 pm**	5:54 pm	☍♇	♌	27		11:36 pm
27	**8:54 pm**	5:54 pm	☍♇	♌	28	**2:36 am**	
29		9:29 pm	☍♄	♍	30	**2:11 pm**	11:11 am
30	**12:29 am**		☍♄	♍	30	**2:11 pm**	11:11 am

☽ Phases & Eclipses phase	day	ET / hr:mn	PT
2nd Quarter	6	**10:14 pm**	7:14 pm
Full Moon	13	**2:38 pm**	11:38 am
4th Quarter	20	**10:19 am**	7:19 am
New Moon	28	**1:55 pm**	10:55 am

Planet Ingress		day	ET / hr:mn	PT
♀	♊	4	**11:16 pm**	8:16 pm
♂	♉	4		11:04 pm
♂	♉	5	**2:04 am**	
☿	♋	4		11:25 pm
☿	♋	5	**2:25 am**	
♀	♋	17	**9:32 pm**	6:32 pm
☿	♌	19	**8:35 am**	5:35 am
☉	♌	22	**4:07 pm**	1:07 pm
⚳	♌	23	**1:29 pm**	10:29 am

Planetary Motion		day	ET / hr:mn	PT
⚴	℞	7	**5:30 pm**	2:30 pm
⚷	℞	19	**11:21 am**	8:21 am
⚵	℞	24		11:48 pm
⚵	℞	25	**2:48 am**	
♃	℞	28	**4:37 pm**	1:37 pm

1 FRIDAY
☽ △ ♃ **11:49 am** 8:49 am
☽ ⚺ ☉ **4:46 pm** 1:46 pm
☽ ⚹ ♀ **5:59 pm** 2:59 pm
♂ □ ♇ **10:14 pm** 7:14 pm

2 SATURDAY
☿ △ ♄ **6:39 am** 3:39 am
☽ □ ♅ **8:22 am** 5:22 am
☿ □ ♆ **4:53 pm** 1:53 pm
☽ ☍ ♄ **9:55 pm** 6:55 pm
☽ ⚻ ♆ **11:31 pm** 8:31 pm
☽ ⚹ ☿ 9:43 pm

3 SUNDAY
☽ ⚹ ☿ **12:43 am**
☽ ⚻ ♇ **4:05 am** 1:05 am
☽ △ ♂ **5:59 am** 2:59 am
☿ ⚻ ♇ **10:13 pm** 7:13 pm
☽ ⚻ ♃ **11:41 pm** 8:41 pm

4 MONDAY
☽ ⚹ ☉ **9:03 am** 6:03 am
☽ □ ♀ **11:38 am** 8:38 am
☽ △ ♅ **7:23 pm** 4:23 pm
☿ ⚹ ♂ 11:37 pm

5 TUESDAY
☿ ⚹ ♂ **2:37 am**
☽ ⚻ ♄ **8:02 am** 5:02 am
☽ ☍ ♆ **9:46 am** 6:46 am
☽ △ ♇ **2:04 pm** 11:04 am
☽ ⚻ ♂ **7:22 pm** 4:22 pm
☽ □ ☿ **9:20 pm** 6:20 pm

6 WEDNESDAY
☽ ☍ ♃ **9:13 am** 6:13 am
☽ □ ☉ **10:14 pm** 7:14 pm
☽ △ ♀ 10:54 pm

7 THURSDAY
☽ △ ♀ **1:54 am**
☽ ⚻ ♅ **3:43 am** 12:43 am
☽ △ ♄ **3:18 pm** 12:18 pm
☽ ⚻ ♆ **5:06 pm** 2:06 pm
☽ □ ♇ **9:04 pm** 6:04 pm
♀ ⚺ ♅ **10:27 pm** 7:27 pm

8 FRIDAY
☽ ☍ ♂ **5:06 am** 2:06 am
☽ △ ☿ **1:31 pm** 10:31 am
☽ ⚻ ♃ **3:23 pm** 12:23 pm
☿ □ ♃ 11:14 pm

9 SATURDAY
☿ □ ♃ **2:14 am**
☽ △ ☉ **7:10 am** 4:10 am
☽ ☍ ♅ **8:34 am** 5:34 am
☽ ⚻ ♀ **11:38 am** 8:38 am
☽ □ ♄ **7:04 pm** 4:04 pm
☽ △ ♆ **8:56 pm** 5:56 pm
☽ ⚹ ♇ 9:34 pm

10 SUNDAY
☽ ⚹ ♇ **12:34 am**
☉ ⚹ ♅ **4:39 am** 1:39 am
☽ ⚻ ♂ **10:44 am** 7:44 am
☽ △ ♃ **6:02 pm** 3:02 pm
☽ ⚻ ☿ 9:29 pm

11 MONDAY
☽ ⚻ ☿ **12:29 am**
☽ ⚻ ♅ **10:07 am** 7:07 am
☽ ⚻ ☉ **12:03 pm** 9:03 am
☽ ☍ ♀ **5:12 pm** 2:12 pm
☽ ⚹ ♄ **7:48 pm** 4:48 pm
☽ □ ♆ **9:42 pm** 6:42 pm
☽ ⚺ ♇ 10:07 pm

12 TUESDAY
☽ ⚺ ♇ **1:07 am**
☽ △ ♂ **1:12 pm** 10:12 am
☽ □ ♃ **6:07 pm** 3:07 pm
♀ △ ♄ 9:28 pm

13 WEDNESDAY
♀ △ ♄ **12:28 am**
☽ ☍ ☿ **7:59 am** 4:59 am
☽ △ ♅ **9:41 am** 6:41 am
☽ ☍ ☉ **2:38 pm** 11:38 am
☽ ⚺ ♄ **6:55 pm** 3:55 pm
☿ ⚹ ♅ **8:17 pm** 5:17 pm
☽ ⚻ ♀ **8:34 pm** 5:34 pm
☽ ⚹ ♆ **8:57 pm** 5:57 pm
☽ ☌ ♇ 9:17 pm
♀ □ ♆ 10:24 pm

14 THURSDAY
☽ ☌ ♇ **12:17 am**
♀ □ ♆ **1:24 am**
☽ □ ♂ **2:39 pm** 11:39 am
☽ ⚹ ♃ **5:30 pm** 2:30 pm

15 FRIDAY
☽ □ ♅ **9:16 am** 6:16 am
☽ ⚻ ☿ **3:25 pm** 12:25 pm
☽ ⚻ ☉ **5:30 pm** 2:30 pm
☽ ☌ ♄ **6:27 pm** 3:27 pm
♀ ⚻ ♇ **6:51 pm** 3:51 pm
☽ ⚺ ♆ **8:43 pm** 5:43 pm
☽ ⚺ ♇ 9:08 pm
☽ △ ♀ 9:36 pm

16 SATURDAY
☽ ⚺ ♇ **12:08 am**
☽ △ ♀ **12:36 am**
☉ ⚻ ♄ **7:34 am** 4:34 am
☿ ⚻ ♄ **11:55 am** 8:55 am
☉ ☌ ☿ **3:38 pm** 12:38 pm
☽ ⚹ ♂ **5:37 pm** 2:37 pm
☽ ⚺ ♃ **6:21 pm** 3:21 pm

17 SUNDAY
☿ △ ♆ **3:52 am** 12:52 am
♂ ⚺ ♃ **9:58 am** 6:58 am
☽ ⚹ ♅ **11:01 am** 8:01 am
☉ △ ♆ **6:55 pm** 3:55 pm
☽ ⚺ ♄ **8:31 pm** 5:31 pm
☽ ☌ ♆ **11:07 pm** 8:07 pm
☽ △ ☉ **11:26 pm** 8:26 pm
☽ △ ☿ 11:40 pm
☽ ⚹ ♇ 11:43 pm

18 MONDAY
☽ △ ☿ **2:40 am**
☽ ⚹ ♇ **2:43 am**
☿ ☍ ♇ **3:01 am** 12:01 am
☽ □ ♀ **8:15 am** 5:15 am
☽ ☌ ♃ **10:35 pm** 7:35 pm
☽ ⚺ ♂ 9:27 pm

19 TUESDAY
☽ ⚺ ♂ **12:27 am**
☽ ⚺ ♅ **4:35 pm** 1:35 pm
☉ ☍ ♇ **9:39 pm** 6:39 pm
☽ ⚹ ♄ 11:28 pm

20 WEDNESDAY
☽ ⚹ ♄ **2:28 am**
☽ ⚺ ♆ **5:30 am** 2:30 am
☽ □ ♇ **9:20 am** 6:20 am
☽ □ ☉ **10:19 am** 7:19 am
☽ □ ☿ **8:19 pm** 5:19 pm
☽ ⚹ ♀ **9:17 pm** 6:17 pm

21 THURSDAY
☽ ⚺ ♃ **6:58 am** 3:58 am
☿ ⚺ ♀ **9:02 am** 6:02 am
☽ ☌ ♂ **12:06 pm** 9:06 am
☽ ☌ ♅ 11:14 pm

22 FRIDAY
☽ ☌ ♅ **2:14 am**
☽ □ ♄ **12:18 pm** 9:18 am
☽ ⚹ ♆ **3:45 pm** 12:45 pm
☽ △ ♇ **7:45 pm** 4:45 pm
☽ ⚹ ☉ 10:58 pm

23 SATURDAY
☽ ⚹ ☉ **1:58 am**
☿ △ ♃ **1:52 pm** 10:52 am
☽ ⚺ ♀ **3:06 pm** 12:06 pm
☽ ⚹ ♃ **6:38 pm** 3:38 pm
☽ ⚹ ☿ **7:36 pm** 4:36 pm

24 SUNDAY
☽ ⚺ ♂ **3:26 am** 12:26 am
☽ ⚺ ♅ **2:36 pm** 11:36 am
☽ △ ♄ 9:27 pm
♀ □ ♃ 11:13 pm

25 MONDAY
☽ △ ♄ **12:27 am**
♀ □ ♃ **2:13 am**
☽ □ ♆ **4:14 am** 1:14 am
☽ ⚻ ♇ **8:15 am** 5:15 am
☽ ⚺ ☉ **8:02 pm** 5:02 pm

26 TUESDAY
☽ □ ♃ **7:35 am** 4:35 am
☽ ☌ ♀ **10:54 am** 7:54 am
☿ □ ♂ **3:13 pm** 12:13 pm
☽ ⚹ ♂ **7:57 pm** 4:57 pm
☽ ⚺ ☿ **8:33 pm** 5:33 pm

27 WEDNESDAY
☽ ⚹ ♅ **3:36 am** 12:36 am
☽ ⚻ ♄ **12:56 pm** 9:56 am
☽ △ ♆ **4:58 pm** 1:58 pm
☽ ☍ ♇ **8:54 pm** 5:54 pm

28 THURSDAY
☽ ☌ ☉ **1:55 pm** 10:55 am
☿ □ ♅ **5:16 pm** 2:16 pm
☽ △ ♃ **8:03 pm** 5:03 pm

29 FRIDAY
☽ ⚺ ♀ **6:04 am** 3:04 am
☽ □ ♂ **11:38 am** 8:38 am
☽ □ ♅ **3:48 pm** 12:48 pm
☽ ☌ ☿ **7:49 pm** 4:49 pm
☽ ☍ ♄ 9:29 pm

30 SATURDAY
☽ ☍ ♄ **12:29 am**
☽ ⚻ ♆ **4:42 am** 1:42 am
☽ ⚻ ♇ **8:30 am** 5:30 am
☿ ☍ ♄ 11:05 pm

31 SUNDAY
☿ ☍ ♄ **2:05 am**
☽ ⚺ ☉ **6:12 am** 3:12 am
☽ ⚻ ♃ **7:11 am** 4:11 am
☉ △ ♃ **6:36 pm** 3:36 pm
☽ ⚹ ♀ **11:19 pm** 8:19 pm
☽ △ ♂ 10:35 pm
☽ △ ♅ 11:30 pm

Eastern time in bold type
Pacific time in medium type

JULY 2022

DATE	SID.TIME	SUN	MOON	NODE	MERCURY	VENUS	MARS	JUPITER	SATURN	URANUS	NEPTUNE	PLUTO	CERES	PALLAS	JUNO	VESTA	CHIRON
1 F	18 36 7	9♋10 26	29♋40	21♉29R.	22♊14	9♊31	27♈00	7♈29	24≈43R.	17♉45	25♓26R.	27♑48R.	19♋55	28♋03	19♊37	6♓43	16♈17
2 Sa	18 40 3	10 07 39	11♌37	21 20	23 51	10 43	27 43	7 34	24 40	17 47	25 26	27 47	20 22	28 31	19 46	6 46	16 18
3 Su	18 44 0	11 04 53	23♌40	21 12	25 41	11 54	28 25	7 39	24 38	17 49	25 26	27 45	20 48	28 59	19 54	6 48	16 19
4 M	18 47 57	12 02 06	5♍57	21 05	27 33	13 06	29 07	7 44	24 35	17 52	25 26	27 43	21 15	29 28	20 03	6 50	16 20
5 T	18 51 53	12 59 19	18♍14	21 00	29 29	14 18	29 49	7 48	24 32	17 54	25 26	27 41	21 41	29 56	20 10	6 52	16 20
6 W	18 55 50	13 56 31	0♎51	20 57	1♋27	15 30	0♉31	7 53	24 30	17 56	25 26	27 40	22 08	0♌25	20 18	6 53	16 21
7 Th	18 59 46	14 53 44	13♎46	20 56D	3 27	16 42	1 13	7 57	24 27	17 59	25 25	27 39	22 34	0 53	20 25	6 54R.	16 21
8 F	19 3 43	15 50 56	27♎03	20 56	5 29	17 54	1 55	8 01	24 24	18 01	25 25	27 37	23 01	1 21	20 32	6 54	16 22
9 Sa	19 7 39	16 48 07	10♏44	20 57R.	7 33	19 06	2 37	8 05	24 21	18 03	25 25	27 37	23 27	1 50	20 38	6 54	16 23
10 Su	19 11 36	17 45 19	24♏51	20 57	9 39	20 18	3 18	8 08	24 18	18 05	25 24	27 36	23 54	2 18	20 44	6 53	16 24
11 M	19 15 32	18 42 31	9♐24	20 56	11 46	21 30	4 00	8 12	24 15	18 07	25 24	27 34	24 20	2 47	20 50	6 52	16 24
12 T	19 19 29	19 39 43	24♐19	20 53	13 54	22 42	4 41	8 15	24 11	18 09	25 24	27 33	24 47	3 15	20 56	6 50	16 24
13 W	19 23 26	20 36 54	9♑58	20 47	16 03	23 54	5 23	8 18	24 08	18 11	25 23	27 31	25 14	3 44	21 01	6 48	16 25
14 Th	19 27 22	21 34 06	24♑47	20 39	18 12	25 06	6 04	8 21	24 05	18 13	25 23	27 30	25 40	4 12	21 05	6 45	16 25
15 F	19 31 19	22 31 19	9≈58	20 30	20 21	26 18	6 45	8 24	24 01	18 15	25 22	27 29	26 07	4 41	21 10	6 42	16 25
16 Sa	19 35 15	23 28 31	24≈55	20 21	22 30	27 31	7 26	8 27	23 58	18 17	25 22	27 27	26 33	5 10	21 14	6 38	16 26
17 Su	19 39 12	24 25 44	9♓28	20 13	24 39	28 43	8 07	8 29	23 54	18 19	25 21	27 26	27 00	5 38	21 17	6 34	16 26
18 M	19 43 8	25 22 58	23♓33	20 07	26 47	29 55	8 48	8 31	23 51	18 21	25 20	27 24	27 27	6 07	21 20	6 30	16 26
19 T	19 47 5	26 20 12	7♈08	20 04	28 54	1♋08	9 28	8 33	23 47	18 23	25 20	27 23	27 54	6 36	21 23	6 25	16 26R.
20 W	19 51 1	27 17 27	20♈15	20 02D	1♌00	2 20	10 09	8 35	23 43	18 24	25 19	27 21	28 20	7 04	21 26	6 19	16 26
21 Th	19 54 58	28 14 43	2♉56	20 02	3 05	3 32	10 49	8 37	23 39	18 26	25 18	27 20	28 47	7 33	21 28	6 13	16 26
22 F	19 58 55	29 11 59	15♉18	20 02R.	5 08	4 45	11 29	8 38	23 36	18 28	25 18	27 19	29 14	8 02	21 29	6 07	16 26
23 Sa	20 2 51	0♌09 16	27♉25	20 02	7 10	5 58	12 09	8 40	23 32	18 29	25 17	27 17	29 40	8 30	21 30	6 00	16 26
24 Su	20 6 48	1 06 35	9♊21	20 01	9 11	7 10	12 49	8 41	23 28	18 31	25 16	27 16	0♌07	8 59	21 31	5 52	16 26
25 M	20 10 44	2 03 53	21♊12	19 57	11 10	8 23	13 29	8 42	23 24	18 32	25 15	27 14	0 34	9 28	21 31R.	5 44	16 25
26 T	20 14 41	3 01 13	3♋00	19 50	13 08	9 36	14 09	8 42	23 20	18 34	25 14	27 13	1 01	9 56	21 31	5 36	16 25
27 W	20 18 37	3 58 34	14♋50	19 41	15 04	10 48	14 49	8 43	23 16	18 35	25 13	27 11	1 28	10 25	21 30	5 28	16 24
28 Th	20 22 34	4 55 55	26♋43	19 29	16 58	12 01	15 28	8 43R.	23 12	18 36	25 13	27 10	1 54	10 54	21 29	5 18	16 24
29 F	20 26 30	5 53 17	8♌41	19 16	18 50	13 14	16 07	8 43	23 07	18 38	25 12	27 09	2 21	11 23	21 29	5 09	16 24
30 Sa	20 30 27	6 50 40	20♌46	19 03	20 41	14 27	16 46	8 43	23 03	18 39	25 11	27 07	2 48	11 51	21 27	4 59	16 23
31 Su	20 34 24	7 48 03	2♍58	18 50	22 30	15 40	17 25	8 43	22 59	18 40	25 10	27 06	3 15	12 20	21 24	4 49	16 23

EPHEMERIS CALCULATED FOR 12 MIDNIGHT GREENWICH MEAN TIME. ALL OTHER DATA AND FACING ASPECTARIAN PAGE IN **EASTERN TIME (BOLD)** AND PACIFIC TIME (REGULAR).

AUGUST 2022

☽ Last Aspect day	ET / hr:mn / PT	asp	☽ Ingress sign	day	ET / hr:mn / PT
1	**6:29 pm** 3:29 pm	△♇	♎	1	9:06 pm
1	**6:29 pm** 3:29 pm	△♇	♎	2	**12:06 am**
3	11:20 pm	□♇	♏	4	**7:47 am** 4:47 am
4	**2:20 am**	□♇	♏	4	**7:47 am** 4:47 am
6	**7:24 am** 4:24 am	⚹♇	♐	6	**12:39 pm** 9:39 am
8	**6:30 am** 3:30 am	□♆	♑	8	**2:39 pm** 11:39 am
10	**12:39 pm** 9:39 am	☍♀	♒	10	**2:45 pm** 11:45 am
12	**7:07 am** 4:07 am	□♂	♓	12	**2:44 pm** 11:44 am
14	**11:11 am** 8:11 am	⚹♇	♈	14	**4:43 pm** 1:43 pm
16	**4:18 pm** 1:18 pm	□♇	♉	16	**10:22 pm** 7:22 pm

☽ Last Aspect day	ET / hr:mn / PT	asp	☽ Ingress sign	day	ET / hr:mn / PT
19	**7:06 am** 4:06 am	☌♂	♊	19	**8:06 am** 5:06 am
21	**6:06 pm** 3:06 pm	⚹☉	♋	21	**8:29 pm** 5:29 pm
24	**5:40 am** 2:40 am	⚹☿	♌	24	**9:09 am** 6:09 am
25	11:55 pm	☍♄	♍	26	**8:25 pm** 5:25 pm
26	**2:55 am**	☍♄	♍	26	**8:25 pm** 5:25 pm
28	**11:08 pm** 8:08 pm	△♇	♎	29	**5:45 am** 2:45 am
31	**6:43 am** 3:43 am	□♇	♏	31	**1:11 pm** 10:11 am

☽ Phases & Eclipses phase	day	ET / hr:mn / PT
2nd Quarter	5	**7:07 am** 4:07 am
Full Moon	11	**9:36 pm** 6:36 pm
4th Quarter	18	9:36 pm
4th Quarter	19	**12:36 am**
New Moon	27	**4:17 am** 1:17 am

Planet Ingress		day	ET / hr:mn / PT
☿	♍	3	11:58 pm
☿	♍	4	**2:58 am**
♀	♌	11	**2:30 pm** 11:30 am
♂	♊	20	**3:56 am** 12:56 am
⚶	♒	21	**6:33 am** 3:33 am
☉	♍	22	**11:16 pm** 8:16 pm
☿	♎	25	**9:03 pm** 6:03 pm

Planetary Motion		day	ET / hr:mn / PT
♅	℞	24	**9:54 am** 6:54 am

1 MONDAY
☽ △ ♂ **1:35 am**
☽ △ ♅ **2:30 am**
☿ ⚻ ♆ **7:23 am** 4:23 am
☽ ⚻ ♄ **10:30 am** 7:30 am
☽ ☍ ♆ **2:50 pm** 11:50 am
☽ ⚺ ☿ **4:03 pm** 1:03 pm
☽ △ ♇ **6:29 pm** 3:29 pm
♂ ☌ ♅ **7:53 pm** 4:53 pm

2 TUESDAY
♀ ⚹ ♅ **8:25 am** 5:25 am
☿ ⚻ ♇ **9:24 am** 6:24 am
☽ ☍ ♃ **4:27 pm** 1:27 pm
☽ ⚹ ☉ **8:12 pm** 5:12 pm
♀ ⚹ ♂ **10:00 pm** 7:00 pm

3 WEDNESDAY
☽ ⚻ ♅ **11:11 am** 8:11 am
☽ ⚻ ♂ **1:10 pm** 10:10 am
☽ □ ♀ **1:54 pm** 10:54 am
☽ △ ♄ **6:28 pm** 3:28 pm
☽ ⚻ ♆ **10:51 pm** 7:51 pm
☽ □ ♇ 11:20 pm

4 THURSDAY
☽ □ ♇ **2:20 am**
☽ ⚹ ☿ **8:29 am** 5:29 am
☽ ⚻ ♃ **11:18 pm** 8:18 pm

5 FRIDAY
☽ □ ☉ **7:07 am** 4:07 am
♀ ⚻ ♄ **12:23 pm** 9:23 am
☽ ☍ ♅ **5:13 pm** 2:13 pm
☽ ☍ ♂ **9:38 pm** 6:38 pm
☽ □ ♄ **11:46 pm** 8:46 pm
☽ △ ♀ 9:56 pm

6 SATURDAY
☽ △ ♀ **12:56 am**
☽ △ ♆ **4:08 am** 1:08 am
☽ ⚹ ♇ **7:24 am** 4:24 am
☽ □ ☿ **8:18 pm** 5:18 pm

7 SUNDAY
☽ △ ♃ **3:12 am** 12:12 am
♀ △ ♆ **12:43 pm** 9:43 am
☽ △ ☉ **2:21 pm** 11:21 am
♂ □ ♄ **3:57 pm** 12:57 pm
☽ ⚻ ♅ **8:17 pm** 5:17 pm
☽ ⚹ ♄ 11:11 pm
☽ ⚻ ♂ 11:42 pm

8 MONDAY
☽ ⚹ ♄ **2:11 am**
☽ ⚻ ♂ **2:42 am**
☽ □ ♆ **6:30 am** 3:30 am
☽ ⚻ ♀ **8:08 am** 5:08 am
☽ ⚺ ♇ **9:35 am** 6:35 am
♀ ☍ ♇ 10:18 pm

9 TUESDAY
♀ ☍ ♇ **1:18 am**
☽ △ ☿ **3:51 am** 12:51 am
☽ □ ♃ **4:24 am** 1:24 am
☿ ⚻ ♃ **9:06 am** 6:06 am
☽ ⚻ ☉ **6:33 pm** 3:33 pm
☽ △ ♅ **8:58 pm** 5:58 pm
☽ ⚺ ♄ 11:23 pm

10 WEDNESDAY
☽ ⚺ ♄ **2:23 am**
☽ △ ♂ **5:12 am** 2:12 am
☽ ⚹ ♆ **6:45 am** 3:45 am
☽ ☌ ♇ **9:45 am** 6:45 am
☽ ☍ ♀ **12:39 pm** 9:39 am

11 THURSDAY
☽ ⚹ ♃ **4:08 am** 1:08 am
☉ □ ♅ **8:53 am** 5:53 am
☽ ⚻ ☿ **9:05 am** 6:05 am
♂ ⚹ ♆ **5:44 pm** 2:44 pm
☽ □ ♅ **8:47 pm** 5:47 pm
☽ ☍ ☉ **9:36 pm** 6:36 pm
☽ ☌ ♄ 10:58 pm

12 FRIDAY
☽ ☌ ♄ **1:58 am**
☽ ⚺ ♆ **6:33 am** 3:33 am
☽ □ ♂ **7:07 am** 4:07 am
☽ ⚺ ♇ **9:35 am** 6:35 am
☽ ⚻ ♀ **4:55 pm** 1:55 pm

13 SATURDAY
☽ ⚺ ♃ **4:19 am** 1:19 am
☽ ☍ ☿ **3:02 pm** 12:02 pm

☽ ⚹ ♅ **9:49 pm** 6:49 pm
☽ ⚻ ☉ 11:10 pm
☽ ⚺ ♄ 11:58 pm

14 SUNDAY
☽ ⚻ ☉ **2:10 am**
☽ ⚺ ♄ **2:58 am**
☽ ☌ ♆ **7:58 am** 4:58 am
☽ ⚹ ♂ **10:53 am** 7:53 am
☽ ⚹ ♇ **11:11 am** 8:11 am
☉ ☍ ♄ **1:11 pm** 10:11 am
♂ △ ♇ **5:28 pm** 2:28 pm
☽ △ ♀ **11:53 pm** 8:53 pm

15 MONDAY
☽ ☌ ♃ **6:59 am** 3:59 am
☽ ⚻ ☿ 9:41 pm
☽ ⚺ ♅ 11:01 pm

16 TUESDAY
☽ ⚻ ☿ **12:41 am**
☽ ⚺ ♅ **2:01 am**
☽ ⚹ ♄ **7:14 am** 4:14 am
☽ △ ☉ **10:48 am** 7:48 am
☽ ⚺ ♆ **12:50 pm** 9:50 am
☿ △ ♅ **1:46 pm** 10:46 am
☽ □ ♇ **4:18 pm** 1:18 pm
☽ ⚺ ♂ **6:39 pm** 3:39 pm

17 WEDNESDAY
☽ □ ♀ **11:54 am** 8:54 am
☽ ⚺ ♃ **1:32 pm** 10:32 am
☉ ⚻ ♆ **1:57 pm** 10:57 am

18 THURSDAY
♀ △ ♃ **4:03 am** 1:03 am
☽ ☌ ♅ **10:20 am** 7:20 am
☿ ⚻ ♄ **3:06 pm** 12:06 pm
☽ □ ♄ **3:34 pm** 12:34 pm
☽ △ ☿ **3:37 pm** 12:37 pm
☽ ⚹ ♆ **9:49 pm** 6:49 pm
☽ □ ☉ 9:36 pm
☽ △ ♇ 10:32 pm

19 FRIDAY
☽ □ ☉ **12:36 am**
☽ △ ♇ **1:32 am**
☽ ☌ ♂ **7:06 am** 4:06 am
☉ ⚻ ♇ **12:10 pm** 9:10 am
☽ ⚹ ♃ **11:52 pm** 8:52 pm

20 SATURDAY
☽ ⚹ ♀ **5:09 am** 2:09 am
☽ ⚺ ♅ **10:01 pm** 7:01 pm

21 SUNDAY
☽ △ ♄ **3:04 am** 12:04 am
☿ ☍ ♆ **3:40 am** 12:40 am
☽ □ ♆ **9:47 am** 6:47 am
☽ □ ☿ **10:29 am** 7:29 am
☽ ⚻ ♇ **1:38 pm** 10:38 am
☽ ⚹ ☉ **6:06 pm** 3:06 pm
☽ ⚺ ♂ **10:35 pm** 7:35 pm

22 MONDAY
☽ □ ♃ **12:10 pm** 9:10 am
☿ △ ♇ **5:59 pm** 2:59 pm
☽ ⚺ ♀ 9:55 pm

23 TUESDAY
☽ ⚺ ♀ **12:55 am**
☽ ⚹ ♅ **10:51 am** 7:51 am
☽ ⚻ ♄ **3:30 pm** 12:30 pm

☽ △ ♆ **10:26 pm** 7:26 pm
☽ ☍ ♇ 11:17 pm

24 WEDNESDAY
☽ ☍ ♇ **2:17 am**
☽ ⚹ ☿ **5:40 am** 2:40 am
☽ ⚺ ☉ **12:07 pm** 9:07 am
☽ ⚹ ♂ **2:16 pm** 11:16 am
☽ △ ♃ 9:10 pm

25 THURSDAY
☽ △ ♃ **12:10 am**
☽ ☌ ♀ **7:50 pm** 4:50 pm
☽ □ ♅ **10:45 pm** 7:45 pm
☽ ☍ ♄ 11:55 pm

26 FRIDAY
☽ ☍ ♄ **2:55 am**
☽ ⚻ ♆ **9:53 am** 6:53 am
☽ ⚻ ♇ **1:39 pm** 10:39 am
☽ ⚺ ☿ **10:28 pm** 7:28 pm
♀ □ ♅ 9:34 pm
☉ □ ♂ 10:27 pm

27 SATURDAY
♀ □ ♅ **12:34 am**
☉ □ ♂ **1:27 am**
☽ □ ♂ **4:11 am** 1:11 am
☽ ☌ ☉ **4:17 am** 1:17 am
☽ ⚻ ♃ **10:33 am** 7:33 am

28 SUNDAY
☽ △ ♅ **8:47 am** 5:47 am
☽ ⚺ ♀ **12:17 pm** 9:17 am
☽ ⚻ ♄ **12:30 pm** 9:30 am
♀ ☍ ♄ **2:27 pm** 11:27 am
☽ ☍ ♆ **7:27 pm** 4:27 pm
☽ △ ♇ **11:08 pm** 8:08 pm

29 MONDAY
☽ ☌ ☿ **12:10 pm** 9:10 am
☽ △ ♂ **3:50 pm** 12:50 pm
☽ ⚺ ☉ **6:00 pm** 3:00 pm
☽ ☍ ♃ **7:00 pm** 4:00 pm

30 TUESDAY
☉ ⚻ ♃ **6:09 am** 3:09 am
☽ ⚻ ♅ **4:54 pm** 1:54 pm
☽ △ ♄ **8:13 pm** 5:13 pm
☽ ⚹ ♀ 11:07 pm

31 WEDNESDAY
☽ ⚹ ♀ **2:07 am**
☽ ⚻ ♆ **3:08 am** 12:08 am
☽ □ ♇ **6:43 am** 3:43 am
♀ ⚻ ♆ **12:37 pm** 9:37 am
☽ ⚺ ☿ **10:54 pm** 7:54 pm
☽ ⚻ ♂ 10:16 pm
☽ ⚻ ♃ 10:35 pm

Eastern time in bold type
Pacific time in medium type

AUGUST 2022

DATE	SID.TIME	SUN	MOON	NODE	MERCURY	VENUS	MARS	JUPITER	SATURN	URANUS	NEPTUNE	PLUTO	CERES	PALLAS	JUNO	VESTA	CHIRON
1 M	20 38 20	8♌45 27	15♍20	18♉40R	24♌18	16♋52	18♉04	8♈42R	22≈55R	18♉41	25♓09R	27♑04R	3♌42	12♊49	21♊22R	4♋38R	16♈22R
2 T	20 42 17	9 42 52	27 51	18 31	26 04	18 05	18 43	8 41	22 50	18 43	25 08	27 03	4 09	13 18	21 19	4 27	16 21
3 W	20 46 13	10 40 18	10≏34	18 28	27 48	19 18	19 21	8 40	22 46	18 44	25 08	27 02	4 35	13 48	21 15	4 15	16 20
4 Th	20 50 10	11 37 44	23 32	18 23	29 31	20 31	20 00	8 39	22 42	18 45	25 06	27 00	5 02	14 15	21 11	4 04	16 20
5 F	20 54 6	12 35 10	6♏47	18 22	1♍09	21 44	20 38	8 38	22 37	18 46	25 05	26 59	5 29	14 44	21 07	3 51	16 19
6 Sa	20 58 3	13 32 38	20 22	18 22	2 51	22 58	21 16	8 36	22 33	18 47	25 04	26 57	5 56	15 13	21 02	3 39	16 18
7 Su	21 1 59	14 30 06	4✗19	18 22	4 28	24 11	21 54	8 35	22 29	18 48	25 02	26 56	6 23	15 41	20 57	3 26	16 17
8 M	21 5 56	15 27 35	18 38	18 20	6 04	25 24	22 31	8 33	22 24	18 48	25 01	26 55	6 50	16 10	20 51	3 13	16 16
9 T	21 9 53	16 25 05	3♑18	18 15	7 39	26 37	23 09	8 31	22 20	18 49	25 00	26 53	7 17	16 39	20 45	3 00	16 15
10 W	21 13 49	17 22 35	18 14	18 08	9 12	27 50	23 46	8 29	22 15	18 50	24 59	26 52	7 43	17 08	20 38	2 46	16 14
11 Th	21 17 46	18 20 07	3≈18	17 59	10 43	29 03	24 23	8 26	22 11	18 51	24 58	26 51	8 10	17 36	20 31	2 33	16 13
12 F	21 21 42	19 17 39	18 22	17 48	12 12	0♌17	25 00	8 23	22 06	18 51	24 56	26 50	8 37	18 05	20 24	2 19	16 12
13 Sa	21 25 39	20 15 13	3♓14	17 37	13 40	1 30	25 37	8 21	22 02	18 52	24 55	26 48	9 04	18 34	20 16	2 05	16 11
14 Su	21 29 35	21 12 47	17 47	17 27	15 06	2 44	26 13	8 17	21 57	18 52	24 54	26 47	9 31	19 02	20 08	1 50	16 10
15 M	21 33 32	22 10 23	1♈54	17 14	16 31	3 57	26 50	8 14	21 53	18 53	24 52	26 46	9 58	19 31	19 59	1 36	16 08
16 T	21 37 28	23 08 01	15 33	17 14	17 54	5 10	27 26	8 11	21 48	18 53	24 51	26 44	10 24	20 00	19 50	1 21	16 07
17 W	21 41 25	24 05 40	28 43	17 10D	19 15	6 24	28 02	8 07	21 44	18 54	24 50	26 43	10 51	20 28	19 41	1 06	16 06
18 Th	21 45 22	25 03 20	11♉28	17 10R	20 34	7 37	28 37	8 03	21 39	18 54	24 48	26 42	11 18	20 57	19 31	0 52	16 04
19 F	21 49 18	26 01 02	23 52	17 10	21 51	8 51	29 13	7 59	21 35	18 54	24 47	26 41	11 45	21 26	19 21	0 37	16 03
20 Sa	21 53 15	26 58 46	5♊59	17 10	23 07	10 05	29 48	7 55	21 30	18 55	24 46	26 40	12 12	21 54	19 11	0 22	16 01
21 Su	21 57 11	27 56 32	17 55	17 05	24 21	11 18	0♊23	7 51	21 26	18 55	24 44	26 38	12 38	22 23	19 00	0 07	16 00
22 M	22 1 8	28 54 19	29 46	17 05	25 32	12 32	0 58	7 46	21 21	18 55	24 43	26 37	13 05	22 51	18 49	29≈52	15 58
23 T	22 5 4	29 52 07	11♋35	16 58	26 42	13 46	1 33	7 42	21 17	18 55	24 41	26 36	13 32	23 20	18 37	29 37	15 56
24 W	22 9 1	0♍49 58	23 27	16 48	27 49	15 00	2 07	7 37	21 13	18 55R	24 40	26 35	13 59	23 48	18 25	29 22	15 55
25 Th	22 12 57	1 47 50	5♌25	16 38	28 55	16 13	2 42	7 32	21 08	18 55	24 38	26 34	14 26	24 17	18 13	29 07	15 53
26 F	22 16 54	2 45 43	17 32	16 26	29 57	17 27	3 16	7 27	21 04	18 55	24 37	26 33	14 52	24 45	18 00	28 52	15 51
27 Sa	22 20 51	3 43 38	29 47	16 13	0≏58	18 41	3 49	7 21	20 59	18 55	24 35	26 32	15 19	25 13	17 48	28 37	15 49
28 Su	22 24 47	4 41 35	12♍13	16 01	1 55	19 55	4 23	7 16	20 55	18 55	24 34	26 31	15 46	25 42	17 35	28 22	15 47
29 M	22 28 44	5 39 33	24 50	15 50	2 50	21 09	4 56	7 10	20 51	18 55	24 32	26 29	16 13	26 10	17 21	28 08	15 46
30 T	22 32 40	6 37 32	7≏35	15 37	3 42	22 23	5 29	7 05	20 47	18 55	24 31	26 28	16 39	26 38	17 07	27 53	15 44
31 W	22 36 37	7 35 33	20 35	15 37	4 31	23 37	6 01	6 59	20 42	18 54	24 29	26 27	17 06	27 06	16 54	27 39	15 42

EPHEMERIS CALCULATED FOR 12 MIDNIGHT GREENWICH MEAN TIME. ALL OTHER DATA AND FACING ASPECTARIAN PAGE IN **EASTERN TIME (BOLD)** AND PACIFIC TIME (REGULAR).

SEPTEMBER 2022

☽ Last Aspect day	ET / hr:mn / PT		asp	☽ Ingress sign	day	ET / hr:mn / PT	
2	**1:22 pm**	10:22 am	□♀	♐	2	**6:39 pm**	3:39 pm
4	**9:51 pm**	6:51 pm	△♀	♑	4	**10:03 pm**	7:03 pm
6	**5:43 pm**	2:43 pm	☌♇	♒	6	**11:41 pm**	8:41 pm
8	**8:34 am**	5:34 am	☌♄	♓	8		9:42 pm
8	**8:34 am**	5:34 am	☌♄	♓	9	**12:42 am**	
10	**8:29 pm**	5:29 pm	✶♇	♈	10		11:47 pm
10	**8:29 pm**	5:29 pm	✶♇	♈	11	**2:47 am**	
12		9:53 pm	□♇	♉	13	**7:39 am**	4:39 am
13	**12:53 am**		□♇	♉	13	**7:39 am**	4:39 am
15	**8:59 am**	5:59 am	△♇	♊	15	**4:16 pm**	1:16 pm
17	**5:52 pm**	2:52 pm	□☉	♋	18	**3:59 am**	12:59 am
20	**11:57 am**	8:57 am	✶☉	♌	20	**4:38 pm**	1:38 pm
22	**7:07 am**	4:07 am	☍♄	♍	23	**3:53 am**	12:53 am
25	**8:49 am**	5:49 am	☌☿	♎	25	**12:43 pm**	9:43 am
27	**12:21 pm**	9:21 am	□♇	♏	27	**7:15 pm**	4:15 pm
29	**5:20 pm**	2:20 pm	✶♇	♐	29		9:03 pm
29	**5:20 pm**	2:20 pm	✶♇	♐	30	**12:03 am**	

☽ Phases & Eclipses phase	day	ET / hr:mn / PT	
2nd Quarter	3	**2:08 pm**	11:08 am
Full Moon	10	**5:59 am**	2:59 am
4th Quarter	17	**5:52 pm**	2:52 pm
New Moon	25	**5:55 pm**	2:55 pm

Planet Ingress	day	ET / hr:mn / PT	
♀ ♍	4		9:05 pm
♀ ♍	5	**12:05 am**	
☿ ♋	5		10:04 pm
☿ ♋	6	**1:04 am**	
☉ ♎	22	**9:04 pm**	6:04 pm
☿ ♍	23	**8:04 am**	5:04 am
♀ ♎	29	**3:49 am**	12:49 am
⚳ ♍	29	**4:59 am**	1:59 am

Planetary Motion	day	ET / hr:mn / PT	
☿ ℞	9	**11:38 pm**	8:38 pm

1 THURSDAY

☽ ⚻ ♂	**1:16 am**	
☽ ⚻ ♃	**1:35 am**	
☽ ✶ ☉	**5:20 am**	2:20 am
♂ ✶ ♃	**7:52 am**	4:52 am
☽ ☍ ♅	**11:06 pm**	8:06 pm
☽ □ ♄		11:02 pm
♀ ⚻ ♇		11:33 pm

2 FRIDAY

☽ □ ♄	**2:02 am**	
♀ ⚻ ♇	**2:33 am**	
☽ △ ♆	**8:52 am**	5:52 am
☽ ✶ ♇	**12:23 pm**	9:23 am
☽ □ ♀	**1:22 pm**	10:22 am
☿ ☍ ♃	**9:49 pm**	6:49 pm

3 SATURDAY

☽ △ ♃	**6:10 am**	3:10 am
☽ ✶ ☿	**6:37 am**	3:37 am
☽ ☍ ♂	**8:23 am**	5:23 am
☽ □ ☉	**2:08 pm**	11:08 am

4 SUNDAY

☽ ⚻ ♅	**3:13 am**	12:13 am
☽ ✶ ♄	**5:50 am**	2:50 am
☽ □ ♆	**12:32 pm**	9:32 am
☽ ⚺ ♇	**3:57 pm**	12:57 pm
☽ △ ♀	**9:51 pm**	6:51 pm

5 MONDAY

☽ □ ♃	**8:44 am**	5:44 am
☽ □ ☿	**11:21 am**	8:21 am
☽ ⚻ ♂	**1:09 pm**	10:09 am
☽ △ ☉	**8:25 pm**	5:25 pm

6 TUESDAY

☽ △ ♅	**5:23 am**	2:23 am
☽ ⚺ ♄	**7:43 am**	4:43 am
☽ ✶ ♆	**2:21 pm**	11:21 am
☽ ☌ ♇	**5:43 pm**	2:43 pm

7 WEDNESDAY

☽ ⚻ ♀	**4:04 am**	1:04 am
☽ ✶ ♃	**9:45 am**	6:45 am
☽ △ ☿	**1:48 pm**	10:48 am
☽ △ ♂	**4:13 pm**	1:13 pm
☽ ⚻ ☉		10:04 pm

8 THURSDAY

☽ ⚻ ☉	**1:04 am**	
☽ □ ♅	**6:26 am**	3:26 am
☽ ☌ ♄	**8:34 am**	5:34 am
☽ ⚺ ♆	**3:17 pm**	12:17 pm
☽ ⚺ ♇	**6:41 pm**	3:41 pm

9 FRIDAY

☽ ☍ ♀	**9:39 am**	6:39 am
☽ ⚺ ♃	**10:26 am**	7:26 am
☽ ⚻ ☿	**3:24 pm**	12:24 pm
♀ ⚻ ♃	**6:06 pm**	3:06 pm
☽ □ ♂	**7:08 pm**	4:08 pm

10 SATURDAY

☽ ☍ ☉	**5:59 am**	2:59 am
☽ ✶ ♅	**7:51 am**	4:51 am
☽ ⚺ ♄	**9:52 am**	6:52 am
☽ ☌ ♆	**4:56 pm**	1:56 pm
☽ ✶ ♇	**8:29 pm**	5:29 pm

11 SUNDAY

☉ △ ♅	**9:09 am**	6:09 am
☽ ☌ ♃	**12:31 pm**	9:31 am
☽ ⚻ ♀	**5:05 pm**	2:05 pm
☽ ☍ ☿	**5:52 pm**	2:52 pm
☽ ✶ ♂	**11:56 pm**	8:56 pm
☿ ⚺ ♀		9:49 pm

12 MONDAY

☿ ⚺ ♀	**12:49 am**	
☽ ⚺ ♅	**11:27 am**	8:27 am
☉ ⚻ ♄	**12:09 pm**	9:09 am
☽ ✶ ♄	**1:25 pm**	10:25 am
☽ ⚻ ☉	**1:31 pm**	10:31 am
☽ ⚺ ♆	**9:02 pm**	6:02 pm
☽ □ ♇		9:53 pm

13 TUESDAY

☽ □ ♇	**12:53 am**	
☽ ⚺ ♃	**5:33 pm**	2:33 pm
☽ ⚻ ☿	**10:32 pm**	7:32 pm

14 WEDNESDAY

☽ △ ♀	**4:41 am**	1:41 am
☽ ⚺ ♂	**8:23 am**	5:23 am
☽ ☌ ♅	**6:34 pm**	3:34 pm
☽ □ ♄	**8:30 pm**	5:30 pm
☽ △ ☉		10:31 pm

15 THURSDAY

☽ △ ☉	**1:31 am**	
☽ ✶ ♆	**4:47 am**	1:47 am
☽ △ ♇	**8:59 am**	5:59 am
☽ ✶ ♃		11:14 pm

16 FRIDAY

☽ ✶ ♃	**2:14 am**	
☽ △ ☿	**5:36 am**	2:36 am
♀ □ ♂	**2:49 pm**	11:49 am
☉ ☍ ♆	**6:21 pm**	3:21 pm
☽ ☌ ♂	**8:52 pm**	5:52 pm
☽ □ ♀	**9:18 pm**	6:18 pm

17 SATURDAY

☽ ⚺ ♅	**5:13 am**	2:13 am
☽ △ ♄	**7:04 am**	4:04 am
☽ □ ♆	**3:54 pm**	12:54 pm
☽ □ ☉	**5:52 pm**	2:52 pm
☽ ⚻ ♇	**8:21 pm**	5:21 pm

18 SUNDAY

☽ □ ♃	**1:38 pm**	10:38 am
☽ □ ☿	**1:56 pm**	10:56 am
☿ ☍ ♃	**6:34 pm**	3:34 pm
☉ △ ♇	**11:58 pm**	8:58 pm

19 MONDAY

☽ ⚺ ♂	**11:41 am**	8:41 am
☽ ✶ ♀	**4:53 pm**	1:53 pm
☽ ✶ ♅	**5:43 pm**	2:43 pm
☽ ⚻ ♄	**7:25 pm**	4:25 pm
♀ △ ♅		9:44 pm

20 TUESDAY

♀ △ ♅	**12:44 am**	
☽ △ ♆	**4:25 am**	1:25 am
☽ ☍ ♇	**8:58 am**	5:58 am
☽ ✶ ☉	**11:57 am**	8:57 am
♀ ⚻ ♄	**4:12 pm**	1:12 pm
☽ ✶ ☿	**9:52 pm**	6:52 pm
☽ △ ♃		10:32 pm

21 WEDNESDAY

☽ △ ♃	**1:32 am**	
☽ ✶ ♂		11:00 pm

22 THURSDAY

☽ ✶ ♂	**2:00 am**	
☽ □ ♅	**5:36 am**	2:36 am
☽ ☍ ♄	**7:07 am**	4:07 am
☽ ⚺ ♀	**11:42 am**	8:42 am
☽ ⚻ ♆	**3:57 pm**	12:57 pm
☽ ⚻ ♇	**8:28 pm**	5:28 pm
☉ ☌ ☿		11:50 pm

23 FRIDAY

☉ ☌ ☿	**2:50 am**	
☽ ⚺ ☿	**4:13 am**	1:13 am
☽ ⚺ ☉	**4:28 am**	1:28 am
☽ ⚻ ♃	**11:50 am**	8:50 am

24 SATURDAY

♀ ☍ ♆	**4:51 am**	1:51 am
☽ □ ♂	**1:51 pm**	10:51 am
☽ △ ♅	**3:17 pm**	12:17 pm
☽ ⚻ ♄	**4:38 pm**	1:38 pm
☽ ☍ ♆		10:10 pm

25 SUNDAY

☽ ☍ ♆	**1:10 am**	
☽ ☌ ♀	**3:24 am**	12:24 am
☽ △ ♇	**5:35 am**	2:35 am
☽ ☌ ☿	**8:49 am**	5:49 am
☽ ☌ ☉	**5:55 pm**	2:55 pm
☽ ☍ ♃	**7:45 pm**	4:45 pm
♀ △ ♇		10:46 pm

26 MONDAY

♀ △ ♇	**1:46 am**	
♂ ⚺ ♅	**10:14 am**	7:14 am
☿ ☌ ♀	**1:59 pm**	10:59 am
☉ ☍ ♃	**3:33 pm**	12:33 pm
☽ ⚻ ♅	**10:31 pm**	7:31 pm
☽ △ ♂	**10:54 pm**	7:54 pm
☽ △ ♄	**11:44 pm**	8:44 pm

27 TUESDAY

☽ ⚻ ♆	**8:01 am**	5:01 am
☿ △ ♇	**8:56 am**	5:56 am
☽ ⚺ ☿	**12:10 pm**	9:10 am
☽ □ ♇	**12:21 pm**	9:21 am
☽ ⚺ ♀	**3:54 pm**	12:54 pm
☽ ⚻ ♃		10:29 pm
♂ △ ♄		10:49 pm

28 WEDNESDAY

☽ ⚻ ♃	**1:29 am**	
♂ △ ♄	**1:49 am**	
☽ ⚺ ☉	**4:31 am**	1:31 am

29 THURSDAY

☽ ☍ ♅	**3:49 am**	12:49 am
☽ □ ♄	**4:57 am**	1:57 am
☽ ⚻ ♂	**5:46 am**	2:46 am
☽ △ ♆	**1:03 pm**	10:03 am
☽ ✶ ☿	**2:58 pm**	11:58 am
☽ ✶ ♇	**5:20 pm**	2:20 pm
☽ ✶ ♀		11:04 pm

30 FRIDAY

☽ ✶ ♀	**2:04 am**	
☽ △ ♃	**5:38 am**	2:38 am
☽ ✶ ☉	**1:05 pm**	10:05 am

Eastern time in bold type
Pacific time in medium type

SEPTEMBER 2022

DATE	SID.TIME	SUN	MOON	NODE	MERCURY	VENUS	MARS	JUPITER	SATURN	URANUS	NEPTUNE	PLUTO	CERES	PALLAS	JUNO	VESTA	CHIRON
1 Th	22 40 33	8♍33 35	3♏46	15♉35 D	5♎17	24♌51	6♊34	6♈53R	20♒38R	18♉54R	24♓26R	26♑25R	17♌33	27♊34	16♉40R	27♒25R	15♈40R
2 F	22 44 30	9 31 39	17♏09	15 34	5 59	26 05	7 06	6 46	20 34	18 53	24 26	26 24	17 59	28 02	16 26	27 11	15 38
3 Sa	22 48 26	10 29 44	0♐46	15♉35 R	6 37	27 19	7 37	6 40	20 30	18 53	24 24	26 24	18 26	28 30	16 12	26 58	15 36
4 Su	22 52 23	11 27 51	13♐10	15 35	7 11	28 33	8 09	6 33	20 26	18 52	24 23	26 23	18 53	28 58	15 57	26 44	15 33
5 M	22 56 20	12 25 59	28♐47	15 34	7 41	29 47	8 40	6 27	20 22	18 51	24 21	26 22	19 19	29 26	15 43	26 31	15 31
6 T	23 0 16	13 24 08	13♑10	15 31	8 06	1♍09	9 11	6 20	20 18	18 51	24 20	26 21	19 46	29 54	15 28	26 18	15 29
7 W	23 4 13	14 22 19	27♑45	15 25	8 27	2 16	9 42	6 13	20 14	18 50	24 18	26 20	20 12	0♋22	15 13	26 06	15 27
8 Th	23 8 9	15 20 32	12♒26	15 17	8 42	3 30	10 12	6 06	20 10	18 49	24 16	26 19	20 39	0 50	14 59	25 54	15 25
9 F	23 12 6	16 18 45	27♒08	15 09	8 51	4 44	10 42	5 59	20 06	18 49	24 15	26 18	21 06	1 17	14 44	25 42	15 22
10 Sa	23 16 2	17 17 01	11♓42	14 59	8 55♎R	5 59	11 11	5 52	20 03	18 48	24 13	26 17	21 32	1 45	14 29	25 30	15 20
11 Su	23 19 59	18 15 18	26♓01	14 51	8 53	7 13	11 41	5 45	19 59	18 47	24 11	26 16	21 59	2 12	14 14	25 19	15 18
12 M	23 23 55	19 13 37	9♈59	14 45	8 45	8 27	12 10	5 38	19 55	18 46	24 10	26 15	22 25	2 40	13 59	25 08	15 15
13 T	23 27 52	20 11 58	23♈34	14 40	8 30	9 42	12 38	5 30	19 51	18 45	24 08	26 14	22 51	3 07	13 44	24 58	15 13
14 W	23 31 49	21 10 21	6♉43	14 38 D	8 08	10 56	13 07	5 23	19 48	18 44	24 07	26 14	23 18	3 34	13 30	24 48	15 11
15 Th	23 35 45	22 08 46	19♉29	14 38	7 39	12 11	13 35	5 15	19 45	18 43	24 05	26 13	23 44	4 01	13 15	24 38	15 08
16 F	23 39 42	23 07 13	1♊55	14 39	7 04	13 25	14 02	5 07	19 41	18 42	24 03	26 12	24 11	4 28	13 00	24 29	15 06
17 Sa	23 43 38	24 05 42	14♊04	14♉40 R	6 22	14 40	14 29	5 00	19 38	18 41	24 02	26 12	24 37	4 55	12 46	24 20	15 03
18 Su	23 47 35	25 04 14	26♊03	14 41	5 34	15 54	14 56	4 52	19 35	18 39	24 00	26 11	25 03	5 22	12 32	24 12	15 01
19 M	23 51 31	26 02 48	7♋55	14 40	4 41	17 09	15 22	4 44	19 32	18 38	23 58	26 10	25 29	5 49	12 17	24 04	14 58
20 T	23 55 28	27 01 24	19♋46	14 37	3 43	18 23	15 48	4 36	19 29	18 37	23 57	26 09	25 56	6 16	12 03	23 56	14 56
21 W	23 59 24	28 00 02	1♌41	14 32	2 42	19 38	16 14	4 28	19 26	18 36	23 55	26 09	26 22	6 42	11 50	23 49	14 53
22 Th	0 3 21	28 58 42	13♌43	14 26	1 38	20 52	16 39	4 20	19 23	18 34	23 53	26 08	26 48	7 09	11 36	23 43	14 51
23 F	0 7 18	29 57 24	25♌56	14 18	0 33	22 07	17 04	4 12	19 20	18 33	23 52	26 08	27 14	7 35	11 23	23 36	14 48
24 Sa	0 11 14	0♎56 09	8♍22	14 10	29♍28	23 22	17 28	4 04	19 17	18 31	23 50	26 07	27 40	8 01	11 10	23 31	14 45
25 Su	0 15 11	1 54 55	21♍02	14 02	28 28	24 37	17 52	3 56	19 14	18 30	23 48	26 07	28 06	8 27	10 57	23 25	14 43
26 M	0 19 7	2 53 43	3♎57	13 56	27 28	25 51	18 15	3 48	19 12	18 28	23 47	26 06	28 32	8 53	10 44	23 21	14 40
27 T	0 23 4	3 52 34	17♎05	13 51	26 35	27 06	18 38	3 40	19 09	18 27	23 45	26 06	28 58	9 19	10 32	23 16	14 37
28 W	0 27 0	4 51 26	0♏25	13 49	25 48	28 21	19 01	3 32	19 07	18 25	23 43	26 05	29 24	9 44	10 20	23 12	14 35
29 Th	0 30 57	5 50 20	13♏58	13 48	25 10	29 36	19 23	3 24	19 04	18 24	23 42	26 05	29 50	10 10	10 08	23 09	14 32
30 F	0 34 53	6 49 17	27♏40	13 48	24 41	0♎50	19 44	3 16	19 02	18 24	23 40	26 06	0♍16	10 35	9 57	23 06	14 29

EPHEMERIS CALCULATED FOR 12 MIDNIGHT GREENWICH MEAN TIME. ALL OTHER DATA AND FACING ASPECTARIAN PAGE IN **EASTERN TIME (BOLD)** AND PACIFIC TIME (REGULAR).

OCTOBER 2022

☽ Last Aspect day	ET / hr:mn / PT	asp	☽ Ingress sign	day	ET / hr:mn / PT
1	**5:46 pm** 2:46 pm	□ ☿	♑	2	**3:38 am** 12:38 am
3	**11:49 pm** 8:49 pm	☌ ♇	♒	4	**6:20 am** 3:20 am
5	**6:46 pm** 3:46 pm	△ ♂	♓	6	**8:47 am** 5:47 am
8	**7:10 am** 4:10 am	☍ ☿	♈	8	**11:57 am** 8:57 am
10	**10:02 am** 7:02 am	□ ♇	♉	10	**5:04 pm** 2:04 pm
12	**5:42 pm** 2:42 pm	△ ♇	♊	12	10:08 pm
12	**5:42 pm** 2:42 pm	△ ♇	♊	13	**1:08 am**
14	9:11 pm	☌ ♂	♋	15	**12:11 pm** 9:11 am
15	**12:11 am**	☌ ♂	♋	15	**12:11 pm** 9:11 am
17	**4:56 pm** 1:56 pm	☍ ♇	♌	17	9:45 pm
17	**4:56 pm** 1:56 pm	☍ ♇	♌	18	**12:45 am**
20	**6:35 am** 3:35 am	✶ ☉	♍	20	**12:25 pm** 9:25 am
22	**2:17 pm** 11:17 am	△ ♇	♎	22	**9:24 pm** 6:24 pm
24	**8:36 pm** 5:36 pm	□ ♇	♏	25	**3:18 am** 12:18 am
26	9:27 pm	✶ ♇	♐	27	**6:55 am** 3:55 am
27	**12:27 am**	✶ ♇	♐	27	**6:55 am** 3:55 am
29	**9:10 am** 6:10 am	□ ♃	♑	29	**9:21 am** 6:21 am
31	**11:14 am** 8:14 am	✶ ♃	♒	31	**11:43 am** 8:43 am

☽ Phases & Eclipses phase	day	ET / hr:mn / PT
2nd Quarter	2	**8:14 pm** 5:14 pm
Full Moon	9	**4:55 pm** 1:55 pm
4th Quarter	17	**1:15 pm** 10:15 am
New Moon	25	**6:49 am** 3:49 am
●	25	2° ♏ 00'
2nd Quarter	31	11:37 pm
2nd Quarter	11/1	**2:37 am**

Planet Ingress	day	ET / hr:mn / PT
☿ ♎	10	**7:51 pm** 4:51 pm
♀ ♏	23	**3:52 am** 12:52 am
☉ ♏	23	**6:36 am** 3:36 am
♃ ♓	27	10:10 pm
♃ ♓	28	**1:10 am**
☿ ♏	29	**3:22 pm** 12:22 pm

Planetary Motion	day	ET / hr:mn / PT
☿ D	2	**5:07 am** 2:07 am
⚳ D	5	**2:10 pm** 11:10 am
♇ D	8	**5:56 pm** 2:56 pm
♄ D	22	9:07 pm
♄ D	23	**12:07 am**
⚵ D	23	**9:05 am** 6:05 pm
♂ ℞	30	**9:26 am** 6:26 am

1 SATURDAY
☽ ⚻ ♅ **7:43 am** 4:43 am
☽ ✶ ♄ **8:48 am** 5:48 am
☽ ☍ ♂ **11:03 am** 8:03 am
♀ ☍ ♃ **2:12 pm** 11:12 am
☽ □ ♆ **4:45 pm** 1:45 pm
☽ □ ☿ **5:46 pm** 2:46 pm
☽ ⚺ ♇ **9:02 pm** 6:02 pm

2 SUNDAY
☽ □ ♃ **8:37 am** 5:37 am
☽ □ ♀ **10:35 am** 7:35 am
☽ □ ☉ **8:14 pm** 5:14 pm

3 MONDAY
☽ △ ♅ **10:37 am** 7:37 am
☽ ⚺ ♄ **11:39 am** 8:39 am
☽ ⚻ ♂ **3:12 pm** 12:12 pm
☽ ✶ ♆ **7:31 pm** 4:31 pm
☽ △ ☿ **8:59 pm** 5:59 pm
☽ ☌ ♇ **11:49 pm** 8:49 pm

4 TUESDAY
☽ ✶ ♃ **10:48 am** 7:48 am
☽ △ ♀ **6:04 pm** 3:04 pm
☽ △ ☉ 11:31 pm

5 WEDNESDAY
☽ △ ☉ **2:31 am**
☽ □ ♅ **12:58 pm** 9:58 am
☽ ☌ ♄ **2:00 pm** 11:00 am
☽ △ ♂ **6:46 pm** 3:46 pm
☽ ⚺ ♆ **9:51 pm** 6:51 pm
☽ ⚻ ☿ 10:06 pm
☽ ⚺ ♇ 11:14 pm

6 THURSDAY
☽ ⚻ ☿ **1:06 am**
☽ ⚺ ♇ **2:14 am**
☽ ⚺ ♃ **12:49 pm** 9:49 am
☿ △ ♇ **11:56 pm** 8:56 pm
☽ ⚻ ♀ 10:28 pm

7 FRIDAY
☽ ⚻ ♀ **1:28 am**
☽ ⚻ ☉ **8:54 am** 5:54 am
☽ ✶ ♅ **3:35 pm** 12:35 pm
☽ ⚺ ♄ **4:39 pm** 1:39 pm
☽ □ ♂ **10:40 pm** 7:40 pm
☽ ☌ ♆ 9:40 pm

8 SATURDAY
☽ ☌ ♆ **12:40 am**
☽ ✶ ♇ **5:14 am** 2:14 am
☽ ☍ ☿ **7:10 am** 4:10 am
☽ ☌ ♃ **3:37 pm** 12:37 pm

9 SUNDAY
☽ ☍ ♀ **10:20 am** 7:20 am
☽ ☍ ☉ **4:55 pm** 1:55 pm
☽ ⚺ ♅ **7:39 pm** 4:39 pm
☽ ✶ ♄ **8:48 pm** 5:48 pm

10 MONDAY
☽ ✶ ♂ **4:14 am** 1:14 am
☽ ⚺ ♆ **5:09 am** 2:09 am
☽ □ ♇ **10:02 am** 7:02 am
☽ ⚻ ☿ **4:47 pm** 1:47 pm
☽ ⚺ ♃ **8:25 pm** 5:25 pm

11 TUESDAY
☉ ⚻ ♅ **5:13 am** 2:13 am
☉ △ ♄ **9:07 pm** 6:07 pm
☽ ⚻ ♀ **10:29 pm** 7:29 pm
♂ □ ♆ 10:46 pm
☽ ☌ ♅ 11:20 pm

12 WEDNESDAY
♂ □ ♆ **1:46 am**
☽ ☌ ♅ **2:20 am**
☿ ☍ ♃ **3:24 am** 12:24 am
☽ □ ♄ **3:37 am** 12:37 am
☽ ⚻ ☉ **4:10 am** 1:10 am
☽ ✶ ♆ **12:25 pm** 9:25 am
☽ ⚺ ♂ **12:38 pm** 9:38 am
☽ △ ♇ **5:42 pm** 2:42 pm

13 THURSDAY
☽ ✶ ♃ **4:08 am** 1:08 am
☽ △ ☿ **7:29 am** 4:29 am
♀ ⚻ ♅ **12:57 pm** 9:57 am
♀ △ ♄ 11:21 pm

14 FRIDAY
♀ △ ♄ **2:21 am**
☽ ⚺ ♅ **12:07 pm** 9:07 am
☽ △ ♄ **1:33 pm** 10:33 am
☽ △ ♀ **2:51 pm** 11:51 am
☽ △ ☉ **7:23 pm** 4:23 pm
☽ □ ♆ **10:46 pm** 7:46 pm
☽ ☌ ♂ 9:11 pm

15 SATURDAY
☽ ☌ ♂ **12:11 am**
☽ ⚻ ♇ **4:26 am** 1:26 am
☽ □ ♃ **2:44 pm** 11:44 am

16 SUNDAY
☽ □ ☿ **3:19 am** 12:19 am
☉ ⚻ ♆ **11:39 am** 8:39 am
☽ ✶ ♅ 9:09 pm
☽ ⚻ ♄ 10:44 pm

17 MONDAY
☽ ✶ ♅ **12:09 am**
☽ ⚻ ♄ **1:44 am**
☽ □ ♀ **10:14 am** 7:14 am
☽ △ ♆ **11:04 am** 8:04 am
☽ □ ☉ **1:15 pm** 10:15 am
☽ ⚺ ♂ **1:35 pm** 10:35 am
☽ ☍ ♇ **4:56 pm** 1:56 pm
♀ ⚻ ♆ **6:00 pm** 3:00 pm
☉ △ ♂ **6:05 pm** 3:05 pm
☽ △ ♃ 11:44 pm

18 TUESDAY
☽ △ ♃ **2:44 am**
♀ △ ♂ **10:20 pm** 7:20 pm
☽ ✶ ☿ 10:16 pm

19 WEDNESDAY
☽ ✶ ☿ **1:16 am**
☉ □ ♇ **9:33 am** 6:33 am
☽ □ ♅ **12:17 pm** 9:17 am
☽ ☍ ♄ **1:59 pm** 10:59 am
☽ ⚻ ♆ **11:02 pm** 8:02 pm
♀ □ ♇ 11:03 pm
☽ ✶ ♂ 11:23 pm

20 THURSDAY
♀ □ ♇ **2:03 am**
☽ ✶ ♂ **2:23 am**
☽ ⚻ ♇ **4:53 am** 1:53 am
☽ ✶ ♀ **5:13 am** 2:13 am
☽ ✶ ☉ **6:35 am** 3:35 am
☽ ⚻ ♃ **1:50 pm** 10:50 am

21 FRIDAY
☽ ⚺ ☿ **8:54 pm** 5:54 pm
☽ △ ♅ **10:19 pm** 7:19 pm
☽ ⚻ ♄ 9:06 pm

22 SATURDAY
☽ ⚻ ♄ **12:06 am**
☿ ⚻ ♅ **7:24 am** 4:24 am
☽ ☍ ♆ **8:37 am** 5:37 am
☽ □ ♂ **12:27 pm** 9:27 am
☽ △ ♇ **2:17 pm** 11:17 am
☉ ☌ ♀ **5:17 pm** 2:17 pm
☽ ⚺ ☉ **8:38 pm** 5:38 pm
☽ ⚺ ♀ **8:43 pm** 5:43 pm
☿ △ ♄ **9:00 pm** 6:00 pm
☽ ☍ ♃ **10:17 pm** 7:17 pm

23 SUNDAY
♀ ⚻ ♃ **11:58 am** 8:58 am
☉ ⚻ ♃ **4:21 pm** 1:21 pm

24 MONDAY
☽ ⚻ ♅ **5:18 am** 2:18 am
☽ △ ♄ **7:08 am** 4:08 am
☽ ☌ ☿ **12:01 pm** 9:01 am
☽ ⚻ ♆ **3:07 pm** 12:07 pm
☽ △ ♂ **7:12 pm** 4:12 pm
☽ □ ♇ **8:36 pm** 5:36 pm

25 TUESDAY
☽ ⚻ ♃ **3:46 am** 12:46 am
☽ ☌ ☉ **6:49 am** 3:49 am
☽ ☌ ♀ **8:04 am** 5:04 am
☿ ⚻ ♆ **12:30 pm** 9:30 am

26 WEDNESDAY
☽ ☍ ♅ **9:34 am** 6:34 am
☽ □ ♄ **11:30 am** 8:30 am
☽ △ ♆ **7:04 pm** 4:04 pm
☽ ⚺ ☿ **11:17 pm** 8:17 pm
☽ ⚻ ♂ **11:19 pm** 8:19 pm
☿ △ ♂ **11:37 pm** 8:37 pm
☽ ✶ ♇ 9:27 pm

27 THURSDAY
☽ ✶ ♇ **12:27 am**
☽ △ ♃ **7:01 am** 4:01 am
☿ □ ♇ **9:09 am** 6:09 am
☽ ⚺ ☉ **2:11 pm** 11:11 am
☽ ⚺ ♀ **4:30 pm** 1:30 pm

28 FRIDAY
☽ ⚻ ♅ **12:13 pm** 9:13 am
☽ ✶ ♄ **2:17 pm** 11:17 am
☽ □ ♆ **9:37 pm** 6:37 pm
☽ ☍ ♂ 10:59 pm

29 SATURDAY
☽ ☍ ♂ **1:59 am**
☽ ⚺ ♇ **3:01 am** 12:01 am
☽ ✶ ☿ **8:34 am** 5:34 am
☽ □ ♃ **9:10 am** 6:10 am
☿ ⚻ ♃ **1:32 pm** 10:32 am
☽ ✶ ☉ **8:20 pm** 5:20 pm
☽ ✶ ♀ **11:41 pm** 8:41 pm

30 SUNDAY
☽ △ ♅ **2:21 pm** 11:21 am
☽ ⚺ ♄ **4:36 pm** 1:36 pm
☽ ✶ ♆ **11:51 pm** 8:51 pm

31 MONDAY
☽ ⚻ ♂ **4:19 am** 1:19 am
☽ ☌ ♇ **5:23 am** 2:23 am
☽ ✶ ♃ **11:14 am** 8:14 am
☽ □ ☿ **5:37 pm** 2:37 pm
☽ □ ☉ 11:37 pm

Eastern time in bold type
Pacific time in medium type

OCTOBER 2022

DATE	SID.TIME	SUN	MOON	NODE	MERCURY	VENUS	MARS	JUPITER	SATURN	URANUS	NEPTUNE	PLUTO	CERES	PALLAS	JUNO	VESTA	CHIRON
1 Sa	0 38 50	7♎48 14	11♐32	13♉50	24♍22R	2♎05	20♊05	3♈08R	18♒58R	18♉22R	23♓39R	26♑08R	0♉42	11♋00	9♓46R	23♒03R	14♈27R
2 Su	0 42 47	8 47 14	25 32	13 51	24 13D	3 20	20 25	3 00	18 56	18 20	23 37	26 07	1 08	11 25	9 36	23 00	14 24
3 M	0 46 43	9 46 16	9♑39	13 52R	24 14	4 35	20 45	2 52	18 54	18 18	23 35	26 07	1 34	11 50	9 26	23 00	14 21
4 T	0 50 40	10 45 19	23 51	13 51	24 26	5 50	21 04	2 44	18 52	18 17	23 34	26 07	1 59	12 15	9 16	22 58D	14 19
5 W	0 54 36	11 44 24	8♒08	13 49	24 47	7 05	21 23	2 36	18 50	18 15	23 32	26 07	2 25	12 39	9 07	22 58	14 16
6 Th	0 58 33	12 43 31	22 25	13 45	25 19	8 20	21 41	2 29	18 48	18 13	23 31	26 07	2 50	13 03	8 58	22 59	14 13
7 F	1 2 29	13 42 39	6♓38	13 41	25 59	9 35	21 59	2 21	18 47	18 11	23 29	26 07	3 16	13 27	8 50	23 00	14 11
8 Sa	1 6 26	14 41 49	20 44	13 37	26 49	10 50	22 16	2 13	18 45	18 09	23 28	26 07D	3 41	13 51	8 42	23 01	14 08
9 Su	1 10 22	15 41 01	4♈38	13 33	27 46	12 04	22 32	2 06	18 44	18 07	23 26	26 07	4 07	14 15	8 35	23 04	14 05
10 M	1 14 19	16 40 15	18 17	13 30	28 50	13 19	22 48	1 58	18 43	18 05	23 25	26 07	4 32	14 38	8 28	23 06	14 02
11 T	1 18 15	17 39 31	1♉37	13 28D	0♎00	14 34	23 03	1 51	18 42	18 03	23 23	26 07	4 57	15 02	8 21	23 09	14 00
12 W	1 22 12	18 38 49	14 38	13 27	1 17	15 49	23 18	1 43	18 41	18 01	23 22	26 07	5 23	15 25	8 15	23 12	13 57
13 Th	1 26 9	19 38 10	27 19	13 28	2 37	17 04	23 32	1 36	18 40	17 59	23 20	26 07	5 48	15 47	8 10	23 16	13 54
14 F	1 30 5	20 37 32	9♊44	13 29	4 03	18 19	23 45	1 29	18 39	17 57	23 19	26 08	6 13	16 10	8 05	23 20	13 52
15 Sa	1 34 2	21 36 57	21 54	13 31	5 31	19 35	23 58	1 22	18 38	17 55	23 18	26 08	6 38	16 32	8 00	23 25	13 49
16 Su	1 37 58	22 36 24	3♋54	13 32	7 03	20 50	24 10	1 15	18 37	17 53	23 16	26 08	7 03	16 54	7 56	23 30	13 46
17 M	1 41 55	23 35 54	15 47	13 33R	8 37	22 05	24 21	1 08	18 37	17 50	23 15	26 08	7 28	17 16	7 52	23 35	13 44
18 T	1 45 51	24 35 26	27 39	13 33	10 13	23 20	24 31	1 01	18 36	17 48	23 13	26 08	7 53	17 38	7 49	23 41	13 41
19 W	1 49 48	25 35 00	9♌35	13 33	11 51	24 35	24 41	0 55	18 36	17 46	23 12	26 09	8 18	17 59	7 47	23 47	13 38
20 Th	1 53 45	26 34 36	21 38	13 31	13 30	25 50	24 50	0 48	18 35	17 44	23 11	26 09	8 43	18 20	7 45	23 53	13 36
21 F	1 57 41	27 34 14	3♍54	13 29	15 09	27 05	24 59	0 42	18 35	17 41	23 09	26 09	9 07	18 41	7 43	24 00	13 33
22 Sa	2 1 38	28 33 55	16 25	13 27	16 50	28 20	25 06	0 35	18 35	17 39	23 08	26 10	9 32	19 01	7 42	24 07	13 30
23 Su	2 5 34	29 33 38	29 15	13 25	18 31	29 35	25 13	0 29	18 35D	17 37	23 07	26 10	9 56	19 21	7 42D	24 14	13 28
24 M	2 9 31	0♏33 23	12♎23	13 23	20 12	0♏51	25 19	0 23	18 35	17 34	23 06	26 11	10 21	19 41	7 42	24 22	13 25
25 T	2 13 27	1 33 10	25 51	13 22D	21 54	2 06	25 24	0 18	18 35	17 32	23 04	26 11	10 45	20 01	7 42	24 30	13 23
26 W	2 17 24	2 32 59	9♏35	13 22	23 35	3 21	25 28	0 12	18 36	17 30	23 03	26 11	11 10	20 19	7 43	24 38	13 20
27 Th	2 21 20	3 32 50	23 35	13 22	25 17	4 36	25 31	0 06	18 36	17 27	23 01	26 12	11 34	20 38	7 45	24 46	13 18
28 F	2 25 17	4 32 43	7♐45	13 23	26 58	5 51	25 34	0 01	18 37	17 25	23 01	26 12	11 58	20 56	7 47	24 53	13 15
29 Sa	2 29 13	5 32 37	22 02	13 23	28 39	7 06	25 36	29♓56	18 37	17 23	23 00	26 13	12 22	21 14	7 49	24 58	13 13
30 Su	2 33 10	6 32 34	6♑21	13 24	0♏19	8 22	25 37R	29 51	18 38	17 20	22 59	26 14	12 46	21 32	7 52	25 08	13 10
31 M	2 37 7	7 32 32	20 47	13 24	2 00	9 37	25 37	29 46	18 38	17 18	22 58	26 14	13 10	21 49	7 56	25 18	13 08

EPHEMERIS CALCULATED FOR 12 MIDNIGHT GREENWICH MEAN TIME. ALL OTHER DATA AND FACING ASPECTARIAN PAGE IN EASTERN TIME (BOLD) AND PACIFIC TIME (REGULAR).

NOVEMBER 2022

☽ Last Aspect day	ET / hr:mn / PT		asp	☽ Ingress sign	day	ET / hr:mn / PT	
2	7:08 am	4:08 am	△♂	♓	2	2:46 pm	11:46 am
4	6:05 pm	3:05 pm	☌♃	♈	4	7:07 pm	4:07 pm
6	5:30 pm	2:30 pm	□♇	♉	6		9:15 pm
6	5:30 pm	2:30 pm	□♇	♉	7	12:15 am	
9	7:00 am	4:00 am	⚹♃	♊	9	8:37 am	5:37 am
11	5:28 pm	2:28 pm	□♃	♋	11	7:22 pm	4:22 pm
14	5:41 am	2:41 am	△♃	♌	14	7:48 am	4:48 am
16	6:55 pm	3:55 pm	□☿	♍	16	8:04 pm	5:04 pm
19	3:47 am	12:47 am	☍♃	♎	19	5:58 am	2:58 am
21	6:14 am	3:14 am	□♇	♏	21	12:16 pm	9:16 am
23	1:16 pm	10:16 am	△♃	♐	23	3:16 pm	12:16 pm
25	2:22 pm	11:22 am	□♃	♑	25	4:18 pm	1:18 pm
27	3:11 pm	12:11 pm	⚹♃	♒	27	5:07 pm	2:07 pm
28		10:53 pm	☌♄	♓	29	7:15 pm	4:15 pm
29	1:53 am		☌♄	♓	29	7:15 pm	4:15 pm

☽ Phases & Eclipses phase	day	ET / hr:mn / PT	
2nd Quarter	10/31		11:37 pm
2nd Quarter	1	2:37 am	
Full Moon	8	6:02 am	3:02 am
(lunar eclipse)	8	16° ♉ 01'	
4th Quarter	16	8:27 am	5:27 am
New Moon	23	5:57 pm	2:57 pm
2nd Quarter	30	9:37 am	6:37 am

Planet Ingress		day	ET / hr:mn / PT	
♀	♐	15		10:09 pm
♀	♐	16	1:09 am	
☿	♐	17	3:42 am	12:42 am
⚵	♓	20	4:25 pm	1:25 pm
☉	♐	22	3:20 am	12:20 am

Planetary Motion		day	ET / hr:mn / PT	
♃	D	23	6:02 pm	3:02 pm
♀	℞	30	3:33 am	12:33 am

1 TUESDAY
☽□☉	2:37 am	
☽□♀	7:05 am	4:05 am
☽□♅	4:54 pm	1:54 pm
☽☌♄	7:22 pm	4:22 pm
☽⚺♆		11:38 pm

2 WEDNESDAY
☽⚺♆	2:38 am	
☽△♂	7:08 am	4:08 am
☽⚺♇	8:21 am	5:21 am
☽⚺♃	2:01 pm	11:01 am

3 THURSDAY
☽△☿	3:43 am	12:43 am
☽△☉	10:01 am	7:01 am
☽△♀	3:43 pm	12:43 pm
☽⚹♅	8:28 pm	5:28 pm
☽⚺♄	11:14 pm	8:14 pm

4 FRIDAY
☽☌♆	6:34 am	3:34 am
☽□♂	11:02 am	8:02 am
☽⚹♇	12:34 pm	9:34 am
☽☌♃	6:05 pm	3:05 pm

5 SATURDAY
☽⚻☿	3:49 pm	12:49 pm
♀☍♅	6:22 pm	3:22 pm
☽⚻☉	7:15 pm	4:15 pm
☽⚺♅		10:37 pm
☽⚻♀		11:23 pm

6 SUNDAY
☽⚺♅	1:37 am	
☽⚻♀	1:23 am	
☽⚹♄	3:44 am	1:44 am
☽⚺♆	11:10 am	8:10 am
☽⚹♂	3:30 pm	12:30 pm
☽□♇	5:30 pm	2:30 pm
☽⚺♃	10:56 pm	7:56 pm
♀□♄		11:34 pm

7 MONDAY
♀□♄	2:34 am	

8 TUESDAY
☽☍☿	5:44 am	2:44 am
☽☍☉	6:02 am	3:02 am
☽☌♅	7:47 am	4:47 am
☽□♄	11:20 am	8:20 am
☉☌☿	11:42 am	8:42 am
☽☍♀	2:51 pm	11:51 am
☽⚹♆	6:54 pm	3:54 pm
☿☍♅	9:40 pm	6:40 pm
☽⚺♂	10:57 pm	7:57 pm
☽△♇		10:38 pm

9 WEDNESDAY
☽△♇	1:38 am	
☉☍♅	3:26 am	12:26 am
☽⚹♃	7:00 am	4:00 am
☿□♄		11:52 pm

10 THURSDAY
☿□♄	2:52 am	
♀△♆	7:22 am	4:22 am
☽⚺♅	5:20 pm	2:20 pm
☽⚻☉	8:52 pm	5:52 pm
☽△♄	9:22 pm	6:22 pm
☽⚻☿		9:06 pm

11 FRIDAY
☽⚻☿	12:06 am	
☉□♄	3:04 am	12:04 am
☽□♆	5:03 am	2:03 am
☽⚻♀	7:34 am	4:34 am
☽☌♂	8:34 am	5:34 am
☽⚻♇	12:12 pm	9:12 am
♀⚻♂	4:07 pm	1:07 pm
☽□♃	5:28 pm	2:28 pm

12 SATURDAY
☿△♆	1:36 pm	10:36 am

13 SUNDAY
♀⚹♇	4:41 am	1:41 am
☽⚹♅	4:59 am	1:59 am
☽⚻♄	9:30 am	6:30 am
☿⚻♂	10:47 am	7:47 am
☽△☉	2:22 pm	11:22 am
☽△♆	5:08 pm	2:08 pm
☽⚺♂	7:50 pm	4:50 pm
☽△☿	9:25 pm	6:25 pm
☽☍♇		9:35 pm
☽△♀		11:54 pm

14 MONDAY
☽☍♇	12:35 am	
☽△♀	2:54 am	
☽△♃	5:41 am	2:41 am
☿⚹♇	9:27 pm	6:27 pm
☉△♆	10:43 pm	7:43 pm

15 TUESDAY
♀△♃	4:36 am	1:36 am
☽□♅	5:23 pm	2:23 pm
☉⚻♂	8:07 pm	5:07 pm
☽☍♄	10:17 pm	7:17 pm

16 WEDNESDAY
☽⚻♆	5:36 am	2:36 am
☽⚹♂	7:12 am	4:12 am
☽□☉	8:27 am	5:27 am
☿△♃	10:43 am	7:43 am
☽⚻♇	1:04 pm	10:04 am
☽⚻♃	5:51 pm	2:51 pm
☽□☿	6:55 pm	3:55 pm
☽□♀	10:14 pm	7:14 pm

18 FRIDAY
☽△♅	4:23 am	1:23 am
☽⚻♄	9:28 am	6:28 am
☽☍♆	4:12 pm	1:12 pm
☽□♂	4:35 pm	1:35 pm
☉⚹♇	4:38 pm	1:38 pm
☽△♇	11:26 pm	8:26 pm
☽⚹☉		9:00 pm

19 SATURDAY
☽⚹☉	12:00 am	
☽☍♃	3:47 am	12:47 am
♂□♆	10:43 am	7:43 am
☽⚹☿	12:54 pm	9:54 am
☽⚹♀	2:15 pm	11:15 am

20 SUNDAY
☽⚻♅	12:11 pm	9:11 am
☽△♄	5:18 pm	2:18 pm
☽△♂	10:37 pm	7:37 pm
☉△♃	11:07 pm	8:07 pm
☽⚻♆	11:22 pm	8:22 pm

21 MONDAY
☽□♇	6:14 am	3:14 am
☽⚻♃	10:10 am	7:10 am
☽⚺☉	11:04 am	8:04 am
☿☌♀	5:55 pm	2:55 pm
☽⚺♀		10:21 pm
☽⚺☿		10:32 pm

22 TUESDAY
☽⚺♀	1:21 am	
☽⚺☿	1:32 am	
☽☍♅	4:24 pm	1:24 pm
☽□♄	9:33 pm	6:33 pm
☽⚻♂		10:16 pm

23 WEDNESDAY
☽⚻♂	1:16 am	
☽△♆	3:03 am	12:03 am
☽⚹♇	9:38 am	6:38 am
☽△♃	1:16 pm	10:16 am
☽☌☉	5:57 pm	2:57 pm

24 THURSDAY
☽☌♀	8:26 am	5:26 am
☽☌☿	9:49 am	6:49 am
☽⚻♅	6:00 pm	3:00 pm
☽⚹♄	11:16 pm	8:16 pm
☽☍♂		10:36 pm

25 FRIDAY
☽☍♂	1:36 am	
☽□♆	4:24 am	1:24 am
☽⚺♇	10:53 am	7:53 am
☽□♃	2:22 pm	11:22 am
☽⚺☉	10:32 pm	7:32 pm

26 SATURDAY
☽⚺♀	1:43 pm	10:43 am
☽⚺☿	4:14 pm	1:14 pm
☽△♅	6:35 pm	3:35 pm
☽⚺♄		9:09 pm
☽⚻♂		10:11 pm

27 SUNDAY
☽⚺♄	12:09 am	
☽⚻♂	1:11 am	
☽⚹♆	5:06 am	2:06 am
☽☌♇	11:43 am	8:43 am
☿⚻♅	2:16 pm	11:16 am
☽⚹♃	3:11 pm	12:11 pm

28 MONDAY
☽⚹☉	3:06 am	12:06 am
♂△♄	12:56 pm	9:56 am
☽⚹♀	7:40 pm	4:40 pm
☽□♅	7:48 pm	4:48 pm
♀⚻♅	9:19 pm	6:19 pm
☽⚹☿	11:26 pm	8:26 pm
☽△♂		10:31 pm
☽☌♄		10:53 pm

29 TUESDAY
☽△♂	1:31 am	
☽☌♄	1:53 am	
☽⚺♆	6:47 am	3:47 am
☽⚺♇	1:44 pm	10:44 am
☿☍♂	3:30 pm	12:30 pm
☽⚺♃	5:19 pm	2:19 pm
☿⚹♄	11:18 pm	8:18 pm

30 WEDNESDAY
☽□☉	9:37 am	6:37 am
☽⚹♅	10:58 pm	7:58 pm
♀☍♂		9:28 pm

Eastern time in bold type
Pacific time in medium type

NOVEMBER 2022

DATE	SID.TIME	SUN	MOON	NODE	MERCURY	VENUS	MARS	JUPITER	SATURN	URANUS	NEPTUNE	PLUTO	CERES	PALLAS	JUNO	VESTA	CHIRON
1 T	2 41 3	8♏32 32	4≈54	13♉24℞	3♏40	10♏52	25♊36℞	29♈42℞	18≈39	17♉15℞	22♓57℞	26♑15℞	13♍34	22♋06	8♓06	25≈26	13♈05℞
2 W	2 45 0	9 32 33	19 02	13 24	5 19	12 07	25 34	29 37	18 40	17 13	22 56	26 15	13 57	22 22	8 04	25 37	13 03
3 Th	2 48 56	10 32 36	3♓02	13 24	6 58	13 23	25 32	29 33	18 41	17 10	22 55	26 16	14 21	22 38	8 09	25 48	13 01
4 F	2 52 53	11 32 40	16 52	13 24D	8 37	14 38	25 28	29 29	18 43	17 08	22 53	26 17	14 44	22 54	8 15	25 59	12 58
5 Sa	2 56 49	12 32 45	0♈30	13 24	10 15	15 53	25 24	29 25	18 44	17 05	22 52	26 18	15 08	23 09	8 21	26 11	12 56
6 Su	3 0 46	13 32 53	13 56	13 24	11 53	17 08	25 19	29 21	18 45	17 03	22 52	26 19	15 31	23 24	8 27	26 24	12 54
7 M	3 4 42	14 33 02	27 09	13 24	13 31	18 23	25 13	29 18	18 47	17 00	22 51	26 19	15 54	23 38	8 34	26 36	12 52
8 T	3 8 39	15 33 13	10♉07	13 24℞	15 08	19 39	25 06	29 14	18 48	16 58	22 50	26 20	16 17	23 52	8 41	26 49	12 49
9 W	3 12 36	16 33 25	22 52	13 24	16 44	20 54	24 58	29 11	18 50	16 55	22 49	26 21	16 40	24 06	8 49	27 02	12 47
10 Th	3 16 32	17 33 39	5♊23	13 24	18 21	22 09	24 49	29 08	18 52	16 53	22 48	26 22	17 03	24 18	8 58	27 16	12 45
11 F	3 20 29	18 33 56	17 42	13 23	19 57	23 24	24 40	29 05	18 54	16 51	22 48	26 23	17 26	24 30	9 06	27 29	12 43
12 Sa	3 24 25	19 34 14	29 49	13 22	21 32	24 40	24 29	29 03	18 56	16 49	22 47	26 24	17 49	24 42	9 16	27 43	12 41
13 Su	3 28 22	20 34 34	11♋47	13 21	23 08	25 55	24 18	29 00	18 58	16 46	22 46	26 25	18 11	24 53	9 25	27 58	12 39
14 M	3 32 18	21 34 56	23 41	13 20	24 43	27 10	24 06	28 58	19 00	16 43	22 45	26 26	18 33	25 04	9 35	28 12	12 37
15 T	3 36 15	22 35 19	5♌32	13 19D	26 17	28 25	23 53	28 56	19 02	16 41	22 45	26 27	18 56	25 14	9 46	28 27	12 35
16 W	3 40 12	23 35 45	17 26	13 19	27 52	29 41	23 39	28 55	19 04	16 38	22 44	26 28	19 18	25 23	9 57	28 42	12 33
17 Th	3 44 8	24 36 12	29 28	13 19	29 26	0✗56	23 25	28 53	19 07	16 36	22 44	26 29	19 40	25 33	10 08	28 58	12 31
18 F	3 48 5	25 36 41	11♍41	13 19	1✗00	2 11	23 09	28 52	19 09	16 33	22 43	26 30	20 02	25 41	10 20	29 13	12 29
19 Sa	3 52 1	26 37 12	24 11	13 20	2 34	3 27	22 53	28 50	19 12	16 31	22 43	26 31	20 24	25 49	10 32	29 29	12 28
20 Su	3 55 58	27 37 45	7♎01	13 22	4 07	4 42	22 36	28 50	19 15	16 28	22 42	26 33	20 45	25 56	10 45	29 45	12 26
21 M	3 59 54	28 38 20	20 14	13 23	5 40	5 57	22 19	28 49	19 18	16 26	22 42	26 34	21 07	26 03	10 58	0♓02	12 24
22 T	4 3 51	29 38 56	3♏52	13 24℞	7 13	7 12	22 01	28 48D	19 21	16 24	22 41	26 35	21 28	26 09	11 11	0 18	12 23
23 W	4 7 47	0✗39 34	17 53	13 24	8 46	8 28	21 42	28 48	19 24	16 21	22 41	26 36	21 49	26 14	11 25	0 35	12 21
24 Th	4 11 44	1 40 13	2✗16	13 23	10 19	9 43	21 22	28 48	19 27	16 19	22 40	26 37	22 10	26 19	11 39	0 52	12 19
25 F	4 15 40	2 40 54	16 53	13 21	11 51	10 58	21 02	28 48	19 30	16 16	22 40	26 39	22 31	26 23	11 54	1 10	12 18
26 Sa	4 19 37	3 41 36	1♑40	13 19	13 24	12 14	20 42	28 48	19 33	16 14	22 40	26 40	22 52	26 26	12 09	1 27	12 16
27 Su	4 23 34	4 42 20	16 27	13 16	14 56	13 29	20 21	28 49	19 37	16 12	22 40	26 41	23 13	26 29	12 24	1 45	12 15
28 M	4 27 30	5 43 04	1≈09	13 13	16 28	14 44	19 59	28 50	19 40	16 09	22 39	26 43	23 33	26 31	12 40	2 03	12 14
29 T	4 31 27	6 43 50	15 38	13 11	18 00	16 00	19 37	28 51	19 44	16 07	22 39	26 44	23 53	26 33℞	12 56	2 22	12 12
30 W	4 35 23	7 44 36	29 51	13 09D	19 32	17 15	19 15	28 52	19 47	16 05	22 39	26 46	24 14	26 33	13 12	2 40	12 11

EPHEMERIS CALCULATED FOR 12 MIDNIGHT GREENWICH MEAN TIME. ALL OTHER DATA AND FACING ASPECTARIAN PAGE IN **EASTERN TIME (BOLD)** AND PACIFIC TIME (REGULAR).

DECEMBER 2022

D Last Aspect
day	ET / hr:mn / PT	asp
1	9:44 am 6:44 pm	♂
	9:46 am	♂
4	12:46 am	♂
6	2:02 pm 11:02 am	♂
	10:13 am	
8	1:13 am	
11	1:49 pm 10:49 am	★
13	10:52 pm 7:52 am	□
16	2:13 pm 11:13 am	★
18	5:35 pm 2:35 pm	□
20	9:45 am 6:45 pm	★

D Ingress
sign	day	ET / hr:mn / PT
♈	1	11:41 pm 8:41 pm
♉	4	6:38 am 3:38 am
♊	6	6:38 am 3:38 am
♋	8	3:49 pm 12:49 pm
		11:49 pm
♌	9	2:49 am
♍	11	3:09 pm 12:09 pm
♎	13	3:45 am 12:45 am
♏	16	2:49 am 11:49 pm
♐	18	10:31 pm 7:31 pm
♑	20	

D Last Aspect
day	ET / hr:mn / PT	asp
20	9:45 am 6:45 pm	★
22	3:16 pm 12:16 pm	□
22	3:16 pm 12:16 pm	□
24	10:11 am 7:11 am	♂
24	10:11 am 7:11 am	♂
26	1:19 pm 10:19 am	★
26	1:19 pm 10:19 am	★
28		
29	1:21 am	
31	7:44 am 4:44 am	

D Ingress
sign	day	ET / hr:mn / PT
★	21	2:12 am
		11:49 pm
♑	23	2:49 am
♒	24	11:14 am
♓	25	11:34 am
♈	27	2:34 am
♉	29	5:36 am 2:36 am
♊	31	12:08 am 9:08 am

Planet Ingress
	day	ET / hr:mn / PT
☿ ♐	6	5:00 pm 2:08 pm
♀ ♐	9	10:54 pm 7:54 pm
♀ ♑	18	6:34 pm 3:34 pm
☿ ♑	20	9:32 pm 6:32 pm
☉ ♑	21	4:48 pm 1:48 pm

Planetary Motion
	day	ET / hr:mn / PT
Ψ D	3	7:15 am 4:15 pm
♇ D	23	4:31 am 1:31 am
♃ R	29	4:32 am 1:32 am

D Phases & Eclipses
phase	day	ET / hr:mn / PT
Full Moon	7	11:08 pm 8:08 pm
4th Quarter	16	3:56 am 12:56 am
New Moon	23	5:17 am 2:17 am
2nd Quarter	29	8:21 pm 5:21 pm

---

1 THURSDAY
7:10 am 4:10 am
7:50 am 4:50 am

2 FRIDAY

3 SATURDAY

4 SUNDAY

5 MONDAY

6 TUESDAY

7 WEDNESDAY

8 THURSDAY

9 FRIDAY

10 SATURDAY

11 SUNDAY

12 MONDAY

13 TUESDAY

14 WEDNESDAY

15 THURSDAY

16 FRIDAY

17 SATURDAY

18 SUNDAY

19 MONDAY

20 TUESDAY

21 WEDNESDAY

22 THURSDAY

23 FRIDAY

24 SATURDAY

25 SUNDAY

26 MONDAY

27 TUESDAY

28 WEDNESDAY

29 THURSDAY

30 FRIDAY

31 SATURDAY

Eastern time in bold type
Pacific time in medium type

DECEMBER 2022

DATE	SID.TIME	SUN	MOON	NODE	MERCURY	VENUS	MARS	JUPITER	SATURN	URANUS	NEPTUNE	PLUTO	CERES	PALLAS	JUNO	VESTA	CHIRON
1 Th	4 39 20	8♐45 24	13♓46	13♉09	21♐03	18♐30	18Ⅱ53℞	28♓53	19♒51	16♉03℞	22♓39℞	26♑47	24♐34	26♋33℞	13♋29	2♓59	12♈10℞
2 F	4 43 16	9 46 12	27 23	13 10	22 34	19 46	18 30	28 55	19 55	16 00	22 39	26 48	24 53	26 32	13 46	3 18	12 09
3 Sa	4 47 13	10 47 01	10♈42	13 12	24 06	21 01	18 07	28 56	19 59	15 58	22 39	26 50	25 13	26 30	14 03	3 37	12 08
4 Su	4 51 10	11 47 51	23 45	13 13	25 36	22 16	17 44	28 58	20 03	15 56	22 39D	26 51	25 32	26 28	14 21	3 56	12 06
5 M	4 55 6	12 48 41	6♉35	13 15℞	27 07	23 31	17 21	29 01	20 07	15 54	22 39	26 53	25 52	26 25	14 39	4 16	12 05
6 T	4 59 3	13 49 33	19 12	13 13	28 37	24 47	16 58	29 03	20 11	15 52	22 39	26 54	26 11	26 22	14 57	4 35	12 04
7 W	5 2 59	14 50 26	1♊39	13 10	0♑07	26 02	16 34	29 06	20 15	15 50	22 39	26 56	26 30	26 17	15 16	4 55	12 04
8 Th	5 6 56	15 51 20	13 56	13 05	1 36	27 17	16 11	29 08	20 20	15 48	22 39	26 57	26 48	26 12	15 35	5 15	12 03
9 F	5 10 52	16 52 15	26 04	13 03	3 05	28 32	15 48	29 11	20 24	15 46	22 39	26 59	27 07	26 06	15 55	5 35	12 02
10 Sa	5 14 49	17 53 10	8♋06	12 59	4 33	29 48	15 25	29 14	20 29	15 44	22 39	27 01	27 25	25 59	16 14	5 56	12 01
11 Su	5 18 45	18 54 07	20 02	12 52	6 01	1♑03	15 03	29 18	20 33	15 42	22 40	27 02	27 43	25 52	16 34	6 16	12 00
12 M	5 22 42	19 55 05	1♌54	12 45	7 27	2 18	14 40	29 21	20 38	15 40	22 40	27 04	28 01	25 44	16 54	6 37	12 00
13 T	5 26 39	20 56 04	13 45	12 38	8 53	3 34	14 18	29 25	20 42	15 38	22 40	27 05	28 19	25 35	17 15	6 58	11 59
14 W	5 30 35	21 57 03	25 39	12 33	10 17	4 49	13 57	29 29	20 47	15 36	22 40	27 07	28 36	25 26	17 36	7 19	11 59
15 Th	5 34 32	22 58 04	7♍38	12 30	11 40	6 04	13 35	29 33	20 52	15 34	22 40	27 09	28 54	25 15	17 57	7 40	11 58
16 F	5 38 28	23 59 06	19 47	12 29D	13 01	7 19	13 14	29 38	20 57	15 32	22 41	27 11	29 11	25 04	18 18	8 01	11 58
17 Sa	5 42 25	25 00 09	2♎11	12 29	14 20	8 35	12 54	29 42	21 02	15 30	22 41	27 12	29 29	24 53	18 40	8 23	11 57
18 Su	5 46 21	26 01 12	14 55	12 30	15 36	9 50	12 34	29 47	21 07	15 29	22 42	27 14	29 44	24 41	19 02	8 44	11 57
19 M	5 50 18	27 02 17	28 03	12 31	16 50	11 05	12 14	29 52	21 12	15 27	22 42	27 16	0♑00	24 28	19 24	9 06	11 57
20 T	5 54 14	28 03 22	11♏38	12 32℞	18 01	12 20	11 55	29 57	21 18	15 25	22 43	27 17	0 16	24 14	19 46	9 28	11 56
21 W	5 58 11	29 04 29	25 41	12 31	19 08	13 36	11 37	0♈02	21 23	15 24	22 43	27 19	0 32	24 00	20 09	9 50	11 56
22 Th	6 2 8	0♑05 36	10♐12	12 28	20 10	14 51	11 20	0 08	21 28	15 22	22 44	27 21	0 48	23 45	20 32	10 12	11 56
23 F	6 6 4	1 06 44	25 05	12 23	21 08	16 06	11 03	0 13	21 34	15 21	22 44	27 23	1 03	23 30	20 55	10 35	11 56
24 Sa	6 10 1	2 07 52	10♑13	12 16	21 59	17 21	10 46	0 19	21 39	15 19	22 45	27 25	1 18	23 14	21 18	10 57	11 56
25 Su	6 13 57	3 09 01	25 26	12 08	22 44	18 37	10 31	0 25	21 45	15 18	22 46	27 26	1 33	22 57	21 42	11 20	11 56
26 M	6 17 54	4 10 09	10♒32	11 59	23 22	19 52	10 16	0 31	21 50	15 16	22 47	27 28	1 48	22 40	22 06	11 42	11 56D
27 T	6 21 50	5 11 18	25 18	11 53	23 51	21 07	10 02	0 37	21 56	15 15	22 48	27 30	2 02	22 23	22 30	12 05	11 56
28 W	6 25 47	6 12 27	9♓52	11 48	24 11	22 22	9 49	0 44	22 02	15 14	22 49	27 32	2 16	22 05	22 54	12 28	11 56
29 Th	6 29 44	7 13 36	23 56	11 45	24 21℞	23 37	9 36	0 51	22 07	15 12	22 50	27 34	2 30	21 46	23 19	12 51	11 57
30 F	6 33 40	8 14 45	7♈33	11 44	24 19	24 53	9 25	0 57	22 13	15 11	22 50	27 36	2 43	21 28	23 44	13 14	11 57
31 Sa	6 37 37	9 15 54	20 46	11 44	24 07	26 08	9 14	1 04	22 19	15 10	22 51	27 38	2 56	21 09	24 09	13 38	11 58

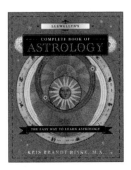

Notes